P9-CEY-093

The Theory of Choice

[B]

The Theory of Choice
A Critical Guide

Shaun Hargreaves Heap
Martin Hollis
Bruce Lyons
Robert Sugden
Albert Weale

BLACKWELL
Oxford UK & Cambridge USA

First published 1992

Blackwell Publishers
108 Cowley Road
Oxford OX4 1JF
UK

Three Cambridge Center
Cambridge, Massachusetts 02142
USA

British Library Cataloguing in Publication Data
A CIP catalogue record for this book is available from the British Library

Library of Congress Cataloging in Publication Data
The Theory of Choice : A Critical Guide / Shaun Hargreaves Heap . . . [et al.].
p. cm.
Includes bibliographical references and index.
ISBN 0–631–17174–6 (hardback) — ISBN 0–631–18322–1 (pbk.)
1. Social choice. 2. Consumers' preferences. 3. Game theory.
4. Choice (Psychology) I. Heap, Shaun Hargreaves, 1951–.
HB846.8.T44   1992
330.1–dc20   91–25052   CIP

Typeset in 10 on 12 pt Sabon
by Colset Private Ltd., Singapore

Printed and bound in Great Britain by Marston Lindsay Ross International Ltd. Oxfordshire

Contents

Introduction   vii

Part I   Individual Choice   1

1   **Rationality**   3

2   Consumer Theory   26

3   How People Choose   36

4   Risk, Ignorance and Imagination   51

5   *Homo economicus, Homo sociologicus*   62

6   **Autonomy**   73

Part II   Interactive Choice   91

7   **Game Theory**   93

8   Bargaining   130

9   Game Theory Applied   144

10   Organizations   155

11   Cultural Exchange   170

12   **Anarchic Order**   179

vi *Contents*

Part III   Collective Choice   197

13 Social Choice   199
14 Democracy   217
15 Power   228
16 Planning   238
17 Agendas   249
18 Social Justice   259

            Keywords   287

Bibliography   375
Index   391

Introduction

Apples or pears? Guns or butter? Liberty or death? We experience life as a series of choices, large and small. What makes a choice rational? A common answer is that all depends on what we want, how much we want it and how likely we are to get it. Each option has costs and consequences. Where consequences are certain and costs are equal, a rational agent chooses by the measure of what outcome he or she most prefers. Where they are not, the agent chooses among options by calculating the probable net benefits of each. Rationality is thus a matter of means, not of ends. It is a relation of consistency between preferences, information and action.

This simple but powerful idea lies at the root of economics. Economics starts from the idea of rational choice for a single agent, traditionally Robinson Crusoe, alone in a natural environment and deciding, for instance, whether the trouble of making a fishing net would be repaid by the pleasures of eating more fish. A rational choice is one which selects the most effective means to satisfy the agent's preferences, where those preferences are consistent with one another and 'complete' in the sense that all possible courses of action can be ranked as more, equally or less preferred. When the notion of rational individual choice has been defined, it is time for the arrival of a second rational agent, Man Friday. As Crusoe and Friday each learn to allocate scarce resources with an eye to what the other will choose, a theory of cooperation and competition emerges step by step. As simple logic yields to complex mathematics, the island microcosm takes on more twentieth-century form, and economics starts to show its power as a technical discipline. But the underlying logic remains neat, clear and capable of study at some depth without the technicalities.

Although the ability of economists to disagree with one another is proverbial, they have shown remarkable unanimity in accepting Lionel Robbins' famous definition of economics as 'the science which studies the allocation of scarce resources which have alternative uses'. Notice that this definition says nothing that might restrict economics to the study of those features of the social world that are usually thought of as 'economic'; money, prices, employment, production, exchange rates, taxes, and so on. According to this definition, economics applies to all human action. As the Chicago economist Gary Becker puts it, in a book aptly entitled *The Economic Approach to Human Behavior* (1976, p. 8):

> Indeed, I have come to the position that the economic approach is a comprehensive one that is applicable to all human behavior, be it behavior involving money prices or imputed shadow prices, repeated or infrequent decisions, emotional or mechanical ends, rich or poor persons, men or women, adults or children, brilliant or stupid persons, patients or therapists, businessmen or politicians, teachers or students.

The 'economic approach' is thus both a precise, often technical study of the allocation of scarce resources and, potentially, a sweeping vision of human life. If the latter seems wildly ambitious, reflect that time, energy and emotion are scarce resources with alternative uses. We invest them so as to obtain the best return by the test of what matters to us. If all our choices have a broadly cost–benefit structure, then all human behaviour might yield its secrets to an 'economic' analysis.

Few people are quite as confident as Becker in the universality of the theory of rational choice. But the idea that this theory can fruitfully be applied outside the traditional realm of economics is very widely held, and not only by economists with imperialistic ambitions for the expansion of their discipline. It also has a long history: rational choice theory is neither the exclusive invention nor the exclusive preserve of economists.

One of the earliest, and still most illuminating, applications of the idea of rational choice to social phenomena is Thomas Hobbes's *Leviathan*. Hobbes analyses the institution of government as if it had been established by agreement between rational individuals as a means of securing their lives against the dangers of a 'war of all against all'. The 'social contract' tradition of political theory, which extends from Hobbes in the seventeenth century to the modern work of John Rawls, parallels rather than is derived from the development of economics. What now constitutes the received theory of rational choice owes more to Jeremy Bentham, who developed the theory of utilitarianism at the end of the eighteenth century and applied it to issues of criminal justice, than it does to Adam Smith. Public choice theory, which analyses the workings of the political process in terms of the rational choices of individual agents, was pioneered in the eighteenth century by the mathematician Jean-Charles de Borda and the polymath the Marquis de Condorcet.

In its modern form, rational choice theory is the result of three intellectual achievements which occurred in the period from roughly 1930 to 1955. The first of these was the development, by Frank Ramsey, Paul Samuelson, John von Neumann, Oskar Morgenstern and Leonard Savage, of a formal, 'axiomatic' theory of rational individual choice which rests on axioms of consistency rather than on the traditional psychological assumptions of utilitarianism. The second, also due to von Neumann and Morgenstern, was the invention, virtually from scratch, of game theory. The essential idea of game theory is to analyse human interactions as 'games' between rational agents, each of whom is aware that he or she is playing against opponents who are rational. The third development was the rediscovery, by Kenneth Arrow and Duncan Black, of the long-dormant theory of public choice. These three strands of rational choice theory correlate with the three subdivisions of this *Guide*: Individual Choice, Interactive Choice and Collective Choice.

Since these theoretical developments were primarily made by economists and mathematicians, it is not surprising that their first impact was on economics. Most economic theorizing is now based on the axiomatic theory of rational choice, and a great deal of it is game-theoretic in approach. But rational choice theory has also had a considerable influence on the other social sciences and on philosophy. Much current work in political science follows on from the work of Arrow and Black, analysing the workings of the political process in terms of voters who make rational choices between political parties, and politicians who make rational choices between policies with the object of attracting votes. Much current political philosophy is written in the social contract tradition, and draws on the concepts of game theory to analyse the emergence of a civil society from a pre-social 'state of nature' or 'original position'. A different kind of political theory can be found in the growing literature of 'analytical' or 'rational choice' marxism, in which the theory of rational choice is used to develop marxist themes. In moral philosophy, there are some distinguished recent attempts at analysing moral principles as solutions to the problems that would be caused by the unconstrained interaction of rational, self-interested individuals. Whether human behaviour can be understood in terms of rationality and whether social institutions can be explained as the product of rational individual action are matters of vigorous debate in the philosophy of action and in social theory. Political scientists, social theorists and philosophers are also using and analysing the technicalities of rational choice theory, and an understanding of the theory is fast becoming a necessary tool of the trade.

This *Guide* is designed to provide an introduction to the fundamental principles of rational choice theory. We have deliberately called it a *critical* guide. The theory of rational choice contains many puzzles and paradoxes. Individually rational choices can sum to collectively irrational outcomes, as when everyone in a sports stadium stands up to get a better view. There are patterns that can be found in most people's choices which appear perfectly sensible, but which the received theory of individual choice deems to be irrational. Game theorists have developed an immensely sophisticated analysis of 'equilibrium' strategies in games, but precisely why (and indeed if) it is rational for players to choose these strategies remains a matter of dispute. These puzzles and paradoxes are the stuff of current discussion and are an immensely fertile source of theoretical progress. But they may also be, as some commentators maintain, signs of fundamental weaknesses in the whole structure of rational choice theory. We do not try to sweep these difficulties under the carpet, but rather draw attention to them.

Some proponents of rational choice theory, such as Becker, maintain that all human behaviour can be brought within its scope, since anything that people could conceivably want or value can be included within the 'preferences' that motivate them. Critics of the theory reply that there are forms of motivation – moral, norm-based, expressive and creative – which, although rational in the sense that they provide coherent reasons for choice, cannot be fitted into the logic of the conventional theory of rational choice. Without taking up any collective position on these unresolved questions, we present some of these alternative accounts of rationality alongside the received theory.

We believe that progress in the social sciences depends on refining a suitable notion of rationality and on establishing its scope and limits. This is a project on which many people, across a wide range of disciplines, are currently working. We cannot forecast where this project will lead. (Individually, we each have our hunches; but we do not agree.) This *Critical Guide* is intended to introduce the reader not only to an established body of knowledge, but also to a set of open questions.

The Plan of the Book

The table of contents gives a natural order of topics, but does not convey the two-dimensional scheme underlying the book. This is done in the nearby table, with its three columns and three rows. The first column, headed 'Individual Choice', concentrates on a single rational agent. The second, 'Interactive choice', explores 'non-cooperative games'. These are games in which the players choose their strategies independently or, if they do reach agreements, are not bound by them. The third column, 'Collective Choice',

	Individual Choice	*Interactive Choice*	*Collective Choice*
Analytical	1 **Rationality**	7 **Game Theory**	13 Social choice
Applied	2 Consumer Theory	8 Bargaining	14 Democracy
	3 How People Choose	9 Game Theory Applied	15 Power
	4 Risk, Ignorance and Imagination	10 Organizations	16 Planning
	5 *Homo economicus, Homo sociologicus*	11 Cultural Exchange	17 Agendas
Evaluative	6 **Autonomy**	12 **Anarchic Order**	18 Social Justice

examines decision-making by groups within a context of norms and institutions, ensuring that agreements are carried out. Since the typical and in many ways the most important group-actor is the state, this column focuses mainly on political choices.

The relation of the second column to the third raises a deep and disputed question. Provisionally, 'Interactive Choice' deals with non-cooperative games and 'Collective Choice' with cooperative games, the difference being that players comply with norms and agreements in the former only when they find it individually rational to do so, whereas they always comply and can count on others to comply in the latter. But this distinction is only provisional for two reasons. First, it is inexact, because some processes of collective choice, such as democratic voting, are non-cooperative and some of what is usually considered under interactive choice, such as parts of the theory of bargaining, is cooperative. Second and more profoundly, the distinction is sensitive to the view taken on the scope of the economic approach to human behaviour. Can norms and institutions be analysed as the outcome of non-cooperative games? If so, there is no break between the columns and no finally separate theory of cooperative games. If not, then the economic approach, as standardly conceived, cannot sweep the board and may, indeed, need to provide a separate place for norms and institutions even on its straightforwardly economic home ground. The issue is pursued in the chapter on ANARCHIC ORDER (12).

Meanwhile the *Guide* will be easier to follow if note is taken of its three rows. The 'Analytical' row offers a trio of basic, firmly theoretical, longer chapters. RATIONALITY (1) opens by setting out the standard model of instrumentally rational individual choice that has been sketched above. It then explores the treatment of risk and uncertainty, leading on to ideas of 'procedural' and 'bounded' rationality. Subversive thoughts about 'expressive rationality' follow, thus challenging the proposition that preferences can be deemed irrational only if they are incomplete or inconsistent. GAME THEORY (7) builds a theory of social action in which individuals must make choices which both influence and are influenced by those of others. The theory assumes highly sophisticated decision-makers, an assumption challenged at the end of the chapter. SOCIAL CHOICE (13) explains the problem of collective action and asks what happens to our idea of social welfare if there turns out to be no uniquely and universally rational way to aggregate individual preferences within the limits of conventional rational choice assumptions. The 'Analytical' row thus sets out the bones of an anatomy of choice, raising some strenuous doubts and critical queries in the process.

The 'Applied' entries form three groups of four shorter chapters which explore the scope and limits of the basic analysis. The first quartet opens piously with CONSUMER THEORY (2), illustrating a standard rational choice approach to consumer demand. But it is far from obvious that this is truly HOW PEOPLE CHOOSE (3), since there seems to be plenty of evidence that they regularly violate the axioms of choice and choose differently in what the theory deems to be similar situations. RISK, IGNORANCE AND IMAGINATION (4) explores the scope for hunch and creativity in what has so far been an apparently mechanical or computational account of choice even in the face of uncertainty. Is the future best characterized as neoclassical risk, Austrian ignorance or creative imagination? HOMO ECONOMICUS, HOMO SOCIO-LOGICUS (5) contrasts the utility-maximizing, bargain-hunting rational agent of economics with other accounts which take more account of the importance of the social construction of meaning in the life-world of individuals.

The 'interactive' quartet starts by extending game theory to BARGAINING (8). This chapter deals with rational negotiation, conflict and the influence of social context on the strategies pursued. GAME THEORY APPLIED (9) enlists the Mafia, lame-duck American presidents and second-hand car dealers as real-world players of games such as the Prisoner's Dilemma and the Chain Store game. The next chapter asks why the interaction of individuals tends to throw up ORGANIZATIONS (10). Is it for the sake of efficiency or of power? More subversively, it may be that organizations generate a culture of their own, which consequently modifies behaviour and even preferences. CULTURAL EXCHANGE (11) extends the enquiry to non-market societies, to see whether obligations can be represented as rational elements in a process of exchange. If not, a similar doubt can also be raised about the social cement of market societies.

The third quartet opens up political aspects of collective choice. DEMOCRACY (14) discusses voting, electoral systems and coalitions. Where voters must choose between more than two parties, each with a position on more than one set of issues, theories of collective choice become radically indeterminate. That makes POWER (15) an urgent topic, not least because an 'economic' approach has trouble in explaining its sources and distribution. PLANNING (16) examines some common styles and grounds of government intervention in markets prone to market failure. Intervention is argued to be an indispensable form of social choice. The chapter on AGENDAS (17) pursues the idea that politics is the art of the possible. No procedure for collective decisions can be ideally neutral in theory or immune to manoeuvre in practice: but decision-makers can at least be held to public account.

The 'evaluative' row takes critical stock in three longer chapters. AUTONOMY (6) pursues the matter of whether there is more to individual freedom than the ability to satisfy complete and consistent preferences. Is a consistently happy slave a free agent? Presumably he lacks what liberals term 'individuality'. This requires a scope for criticising preferences which extends the inquiry into ethics. ANARCHIC ORDER (12) considers the idea that social order can emerge spontaneously in a world without institutions and agencies of enforcement. If it can, then there is no analytical break between 'interactive choice' (anarchic) and 'collective choice' (presupposing institutions). Even if it cannot, however, we should be slow to assume that we can improve on the spontaneous order of the market by deliberate planning. SOCIAL JUSTICE (18) examines some notions of a just society on the assumption that the moral judgement of a rational person should derive from a set of coherent principles. This proves a hard assumption to maintain, because conflicting ideas of justice are deeply embedded in Western cultures. Is social justice a matter of the general level of human welfare? Or is justice to be judged in terms of mutual individual advantage and so, in a sense, not social at all?

If the 'Evaluative' chapters seem to raise more overtly contentious issues than the rest, it is partly because moral questions surface there explicitly. But they are at least implicit in all the topics of the book, and the task of 'evaluation' is only to bring them out. We have tried throughout to identify morally charged issues rather than settle them, and to do so without tendentiousness. This is no doubt easier said than done, but we have been helped by differing in our own views of the scope, limits and ethical or political tendency of theories of choice.

Meanwhile, another kind of evaluation is demanded by the common complaint that the standard theories presented in the 'Analytical' chapters are hopelessly 'unrealistic'. Does the idealized notion of rational choice fit actual economic behaviour, let alone all political and social behaviour? Defenders have three principal lines of response. One is to reply that exceptions are only apparent, since the behaviour will be found to be 'rational' after all when allowance is made for the agents' subjective understanding of what they were doing. Another is that the behaviour is 'as if' rational, in the sense that it could not persist unless it happened to conform to what was rationally required. The third is that, since the theory is as much normative as descriptive, it pinpoints ways in which actual agents who deviate from it could do better. These responses are all contentious and open up disagreements about method and epistemology where, as with the moral and political issues, we are not united. However, the chapters are all signed, and readers can be left to spot the divergences.

The 18 main articles are followed by a section of Keywords. This contains notes on concepts, technicalities and thinkers, to supplement references to them. Keywords are signalled in the text by a 'key' symbol (🔑) and are printed in bold type. They range from a substantial entry of 1000 words on, for instance, 'Expectations' and 'The Core', through shorter entries on 'Public Goods', 'Externalities', 'Ethical Preferences' and 'Paternalism' to brief definitions of terms such as 'Feasible set'. Each Keyword bears the initials of its author.

Another symbol needing explanation is the small square or 'box' (□) sometimes followed by a page number. It refers the reader to a revealing crux or quotation, for example to a presentation of the Prisoner's Dilemma (□ p. 99) or to Schopenhauer's delightful remark about porcupines (□ p. 163). Where the □ symbol occurs without a page number, it refers the reader to the neighbouring box.

Each chapter ends with a brief guide to. further reading. Bibliographical references are given in full detail at the end of the book.

As an exercise in collaboration, this book mixes anarchic order with collective choice. The chapters are single-authored, but the drafts have been worked over by all of us. We differ in our intellectual origins, Shaun Hargreaves Heap, Bruce Lyons and Robert Sugden being economists, Martin Hollis a philosopher and Albert Weale a political scientist; but we share a belief that choice is a federal topic. In addition, we all belong to the School of Economic and Social Studies at the University of East Anglia, where collaboration is something of a way of life and problems of collective action can (usually) be solved by walking down the corridor. Joint teaching on the School's cross-disciplinary programmes, especially that in Philosophy, Politics and Economics, has helped to develop a shared understanding of conceptual and theoretical problems, even if we still disagree about their solutions. We have published work together before in various combinations and three of us (Shaun Hargreaves Heap, Martin Hollis and Robert Sugden) have gained particularly from working together on the research project on the Foundations of Rational Choice Theory, which is supported by the Economic and Social Research Council. Our contributions to this book have been written as part of that project.

We have tried to make this *Guide* authoritative where the ground is firm, and critical where there is a crux. Although the theory of choice is not short of firm ground, it is also rich in surprises and paradoxes which are proving a vital source of theoretical progress throughout the social sciences. Many and deep questions remain open. Guidance comes with an invitation to take part in a fertile debate.

Shaun Hargreaves Heap
Martin Hollis
Bruce Lyons
Robert Sugden
Albert Weale

Part I
Individual Choice

1

Rationality

The purpose of this chapter is to introduce the different senses of individual rationality that are used in the social sciences, and to present an overview of how they contribute to the understanding and explanation of individual choice.

The most developed model of individual rational choice identifies the individual with a set of objectives, and treats an action as rational because it is the one most likely to satisfy those objectives. This is an instrumental sense of rationality, which has flourished in economics and is increasingly used by other social sciences. It is sometimes referred to as the 'rational choice' model of action, and most of this chapter will be devoted to it. However, it is not the only sense of individual rational action.

Other senses of rationality complicate the relation between action and objectives. In these alternative accounts, action is as often concerned with deciding on, creating or exploring the ends pursued, as with the choice of the most efficient means with which to achieve some given set of ends.

The picture of individuals which corresponds to these alternative senses of rationality is more open-ended than the instrumental one. People are less certain about their objectives and the environment in which they operate, less autonomous but more active and enquiring, one might say, than the people who are fully described by a set of well defined objectives. This more elusive idea of the individual has, unsurprisingly, proved to be much less mathematically tractable than the instrumental ('rational choice') version. Consequently, there are fewer theorems and elegant proofs associated with these alternative senses of rationality.

Nevertheless, it is possible to distinguish two types of rational action in

Consequentialist &
Non-Consequentialist. 2°

this mould, the procedural (or role or rule-bound) and the expressive (or existential or autonomous – the precise choice of terms varying between different disciplines and debates). The procedural puts distance between action and objectives by allowing actions to be guided by procedures or rules of thumb. People sometimes use rules of thumb to avoid the costs of acquiring the information which would enable the calculation of the optimal course of action. In these circumstances, procedural rationality is just an ersatz form of instrumental rationality ('satisficing' to take account of costly information acquisition rather than optimizing). However, on other occasions, the use of rules constitutes a significant shift away from the instrumental model. In particular, when these rules are shared, as in norms, they can become a source of reasons for action in their own right, and it is common to find reference to such irreducible norms or roles in the explanation of behaviour in sociology and political science (see HOMO ECONOMICUS, HOMO SOCIOLOGICUS (5)).

By contrast, the expressive complicates the relation between action and objectives by making people self-reflexive. They become capable of deliberating and choosing the ends they wish to pursue, and this concept of rationality is an important ingredient of discussions in political theory, as well as in the more explicitly evaluative aspects of particular social sciences, such as welfare economics.

The next section demonstrates how instrumentally rational actions can be represented as those of individuals taking actions which maximize utility or expected utility. Some of the limitations of this account of action are then discussed, and the subsequent sections introduce the alternative senses of rationality.

Instrumental Rationality: Utility and Expected Utility Maximization

Instrumental rationality is defined as the choice of actions which best satisfy a person's objectives. These objectives are treated as desires which motivate the individual. Reason can assess only their consistency not their content, since it is cast solely as the 'slave of the passions,' in Hume's (1740) words, in the work of deciding which action will best further them.

Put in this way, it presumes that an individual with a variety of objectives is capable of comparing the satisfaction of these various objectives so as to come to some overall assessment. Suppose, for instance, that you must choose between purchasing a basket of food and a theatre ticket. The one, you assume, contributes only to a natural objective of avoiding hunger, while the other contributes only to another of your objectives, a desire for entertainment. Unless you have some way of comparing the satisfaction of one desire with the other, you will be unable to say which of these actions best satisfies your objectives. The notion of the instrumentally rational action will be ill-defined.

It has traditionally been assumed that desires can be ordered on a single scale by comparing the pleasures of satisfying them. The name given to this measure is 'utility'. Thus the individual can compare the utility generated by each action, and the instrumentally rational person acts so as to maximize his or her utility.

This picture of individuals as utility machines, glowing more or less brightly with the level of utility generated, may seem quaint or, indeed, implausible. Furthermore, it has a controversial history in the social sciences, where it is intertwined with the philosophy of **utilitarianism** (▣) (for instance, see Bentham, 1789; Mill, 1863; Pigou, 1920). Consequently, it is important to appreciate that the idea of instrumental rationality can be expressed in a slightly different way, which appeals more to modern tastes by avoiding – in some degree – these controversial associations. It will be assumed that individuals have preferences and that the integration of these preferences is revealed in a **preference ordering** (▣) which determines action. Instrumentally rational action is now defined through placing certain restrictions on this preference ordering.

To illustrate this alternative way of conceptualizing instrumental rationality, consider the case of an individual choosing between different consumption bundles, where each bundle contains different combinations of goods and services. One can assume that individuals have any imaginable, complicated set of desires that they would like to satisfy through the purchase of such bundles. The desires can be 'good', 'bad', 'selfish', 'altruistic' – anything you like. The only proviso is that those desires generate a preference ordering; that is, the person can always say whether he or she prefers one bundle to another or is indifferent between them, and that the ordering satisfies the following conditions. An intuitive sketch of the conditions is provided here, as they are formally defined in the adjacent box (□).

Reflexivity (1) demands that any bundle is always as good as itself. This sounds like common sense, and indeed it is: it is included as a purely formal requirement. *Completeness* (2) means that any two bundles can always be compared and ranked. The condition of *transitivity* (3) entails that when A is preferred to B, and B to C, then A should be preferred to C. It precludes the following type of inconsistency. Suppose that an individual preferred C to A, while preferring A to B and B to C. The individual could then be traded into poverty. For instance, such a person starting, say, with bundle B would pay someone to trade A for his or her B, since A is preferred to B. This same person would also pay someone to trade C for the A which he or she has just obtained, since C is preferred to A. Finally, since B is also preferred to C, this person would pay to trade a B for his or her recently acquired C. Thus the person would return to a position of holding B, having paid someone

AXIOMS OF INSTRUMENTALLY RATIONAL CHOICE UNDER CERTAINTY

Suppose that an individual is choosing between different consumption bundles, x_1, x_2, x_3, and so on, where each bundle contains different combinations of goods and services. Consider the following conditions which might be placed on the preferences of the individual, where $A \geqslant B$ means that the individual 'prefers A to B or is indifferent between A and B': $A \rangle B$ means she or he 'strictly prefers A to B'; and $A \sim B$ means that he or she 'is indifferent between A and B':

1   *Reflexivity*. For any bundle x_i, $x_i \geqslant x_i$.
2   *Completeness*. For any two bundles, x_i and x_j, either $x_i \geqslant x_j$ or $x_j \geqslant x_i$.
3   *Transitivity*. If $x_i \geqslant x_j$ and $x_j \geqslant x_k$, then $x_i \geqslant x_k$.
4   *Continuity*. For any bundle x_i, define $A(x_i)$ as the 'at least as good as x_i' set of bundles, and $B(x_i)$ as the 'no better than x_i' set: then $A(x_i)$ and $B(x_i)$ are closed sets (which means that they are sets which include all their boundary points). It follows that if x_j is strictly preferred to x_i and x_k is a bundle close enough to x_j, then x_k must be strictly preferred to x_i.

When (1)–(3) hold, the individual has a preference ordering, and when (1)–(4) hold the preference ordering can be represented by a utility function which is unique up to a positive monotonic transformation. This means that if a function $U(x)$ represents this preference ordering, the function $V(x)$ will also represent the ordering when $V(x) = T[U(x)]$, where T is any transformation which satisfies the condition of V increasing when U increases. Thus, an individual, when acting in accordance with this preference ordering, can be represented as maximizing his or her utility.

at each of the three facilitating trades, and would – with the same set of preferences – be willing to pay again for the same cycle of trades, and so on into poverty.

Finally, *continuity* (4) implies that, given any two goods in a bundle, it will always be possible – by reducing the amount of one fractionally and increasing the amount of the other fractionally – to define another bundle which is indifferent to the first. This means that there is no good in a bundle which is absolutely necessary in some amount and which cannot be traded-off at the margin for another good – and it rules out **lexicographic** (☞) orderings. but what about complements?

Conditions (1)–(3) define a preference ordering, and when (1)–(4) hold the ordering can be represented by a **utility function** (☞) which is unique up to a positive monotonic transformation. That means that a function $U(x)$ exists which assigns numbers to each possible bundle x, such that for any pair of bundles, x_i and x_j, when x_i is preferred to x_j, then the number associated with x_i is greater than the number associated with x_j [i.e. $U(x_i) > U(x_j)$]; and when there is indifference between x_i and x_j, the numbers assigned by the function are the same [i.e. $U(x_i) = U(x_j)$]. Incidentally, it is the mapping of these latter points that yields the 'indifference curve' depiction of these utility functions, which feature so prominently on the first few pages of most microeconomic texts (see CONSUMER THEORY (2)).

Thus, it is 'as if' the individual acting on the preference ordering had a utility function and judged different bundles according to the utility which they generated, preferring the one with higher utility to the one with less. In other words, the individual, when acting in accordance with these preferences, can be represented as maximizing his or her utility.

However, it is important to note that this is only an ordinal utility function. Unlike traditional utilitarianism, it does not measure or denote some absolute quantity of sensation, pleasure or desire satisfaction which can be compared across individuals. Instead, it is just a device which expresses an ordering, and there are any number of such utility functions which could represent that ordering. So, if x_i is preferred to x_j, which is preferred to x_k, then the utilities associated with this triplet (x_i, x_j, x_k) could be any of the following; $(3, 2, 1)$ or $(6, 4, 2)$ or $(4, 3, 2)$ or $(9, 3, 2)$ or any number of other combinations. It is not the absolute value of utility assigned by the utility function to each option that matters here. What matters is the assignment of utility in relation to what other options receive, so that the ordering is preserved under each function (this is what is meant by the earlier statement that the utility function is unique up to a positive monotonic transformation (see □ p. 6).

To recap, (1)–(4) permit the representation of preferences by a utility function, where utility has been purged of any of the traditional connotations of absolute pleasure or desire satisfaction which would enable direct interpersonal comparisons of utility (☞). Since, it seems, there is nothing notably restrictive in these conditions, as they amount to no more than a demand that an individual can compare bundles and that the comparisons are internally consistent, the depiction of individual instrumental rationality as utility (suitably understood) maximization looks promisingly general.

Of course, the choice situation for which this representation has been developed is rather special, because there is no uncertainty governing the relation between actions and outcomes, and it is easy to imagine settings where there is such uncertainty. For instance, the individual who is choosing between consumption bundles is constrained by a budget and he or she may not have the full information governing the prices of different commodities, including those which could be sold to generate an income as well as those which enter directly in consumption. Equally, the utility associated with the purchase of an umbrella is not known with certainty since it depends on the weather, and so on. However, in some such conditions of uncertainty, it is possible to generalize the result: the instrumentally rational individual acts so as to maximize *expected* utility.

This generalization is one of the remarkable results of modern economics. To provide a sketch of it, some further definitions must be introduced, and additional restrictions placed on an individual's preference ordering. In so doing, we follow the original approach of von Neumann and Morgenstern (1947); Savage (1954) provides an alternative method. First, let us assume that the uncertainty surrounding decision-making can be captured by a **probability distribution** (▯) over the events (or states of the world) which determine the relation between actions and outcomes. This depiction of uncertainty is sometimes referred to as one of 'risk' (see **risk and uncertainty** (▯)) and we will follow this convention, reserving the term 'uncertainty' hereafter for situations in which there are no good reasons for believing that one probability distribution is more likely than many others.

Now, let us define a prospect vector associated with each action as the pairing of the range of possible outcomes (the x's of the previous analysis) following from this action with the probability of their occurrence. To keep matters simple, we might think of the outcomes as income, so that the prospect y consists of a vector of $\$x$, where each element ($\$x_i$) is coupled with a probability p_i, which is the probability of the state of the world occurring in which the action yields $\$x$. Therefore an action is like the purchase of a lottery ticket: if 'such and such' happens then you obtain 'this', but if 'so and so' happens then you obtain 'that'. The prospect combines the 'this' and 'that' with respective probabilities of 'such and such' and 'so and so'. Notationally, the purchase of a lottery ticket for $1, where there is a probability of $1/100$ of winning $50, is given by the prospect ($-\$1$, $\$49$; $99/100$, $1/100$).

We shall assume that the earlier axioms hold with respect to the preferences over the outcomes x, and that a further five axioms hold. These are formally defined in the adjacent box (▯) and, as before, an intuitive sketch of them follows.

The first (5) is an application of the earlier axioms to the prospects y. The preference increasing with probability (6) means that if the probability of a preferred outcome within a prospect increases while the probability of the inferior outcome falls, then the prospect improves. Therefore, suppose that one prospect is ($\$10$, $\$5$; $1/3$, $2/3$): then another prospect ($\$10$, $\$5$; $2/3$, $1/3$) will be preferred to the original one.

The new continuity (7) embodies a different sense of continuity to (4) above, and relates to the possibility, for any three prospects, of combining the 'best' and the 'worst' in some probability mix, to produce a prospect which is regarded as indifferent to the 'middle' one. The condition states that it is always possible to find such a probability mix. Thus, in the simple case

AXIOMS OF INSTRUMENTALLY RATIONAL CHOICE UNDER UNCERTAINTY

A prospect, y, is defined as the pairing of outcomes associated with an action with the probabilities of these outcomes occurring when the action is undertaken. Consider the following conditions which might be placed on an individual's preferences with respect to prospects:

5 *Preference ordering over prospects.* (1)–(3) defined in the previous box hold for all prospects y.
6 *Preference increasing with probability.* If $y_i > y_j$ and $y_1 = (y_i, y_j; p_1, 1 - p_1)$ and $y_2 = (y_i, y_j; p_2, 1 - p_2)$, then $y_1 > y_2$ if and only if $p_1 > p_2$.
7 *Continuity (ii).* If $y_i \geqslant y_j \geqslant y_k$, then there exists some probability p such that $(y_i, y_k; p, 1 - p) \sim y_j$. Let us develop an implication of this. Granted that there is a best outcome x^B and a worst outcome x^W, then a corollary of this condition is that, for any outcome x_i, there will always be some probability combination of x^B and x^W with which the individual is indifferent. For x_i define u_i such that $x_i \sim (x^B, x^W; u_i, 1 - u_i)$: u_i is known as the von Neumann–Morgenstern utility index of x_i.
8 *Strong independence.* If $y = (x_i, x_j; p, 1 - p)$ and $x_i \sim y_i$, then $y \sim (y_i, x_j; p, 1 - p)$. Following the implication in (7), we have $x_i \sim (x^B, x^W; u_i, 1 - u_i)$, and so a corollary of (8) is that $y \sim [(x^B, x^W; u_i, 1 - u_i), x_j; p, 1 - p]$.
9 *Usual rules for combining probabilities.* Consider $y = (x_i, x_j; p, 1 - p)$, from the discussion in (7) and (8). We have $y \sim [(x^B, x^W; u_i, 1 - u_i), (x^B, x^W: u_j, 1 - u_j); p, 1 - p]$. A corollary of (9) is that the probability of obtaining x^B in the prospect given by [. . .] is p times u_i plus $1 - p$ times u_j, and the probability of x^W is p times $1 - u_i$ plus $1 - p$ times $1 - u_j$, so this can be rewritten as

$$y \sim [x^B, x^W; pu_i + (1-p)u_j, p(1 - u_i) + (1 - p)(1 - u_j)]$$

Now consider $y' = (x_k, x_l; p', (1 - p'))$. By applying the same reasoning, we obtain

$$y' \sim [x^B, x^W; p'u_k + (1 - p')u_l, p'(1 - u_k) + (1 - p')(1 - u_l)]$$

Recall (6): from this we obtain

$$y \geqslant y' \quad \text{when} \quad pu_i + (1 - p)u_j \geqslant p'u_k + (1 - p')u_l$$

Finally, remember the definition of u as the utility index of x, and hence the possible interpretation that y is preferred to y' when the expected utility of y exceeds that of y'.

In short, an individual who acts on a preference ordering which satisfies these conditions can be represented as acting so as to maximize expected utility. Naturally, this interpretation relies on the definition of u as 'utility'. Furthermore, the 'utility function' representation of preferences here is arbitrary in the sense that by changing the upper or lower reference x (x^B, x^W), the utility values associated with any x will change. Through inspection of the inequality which must be satisfied when $y \geqslant y^1$, it can be seen that any linear transformation of u (i.e. $v = a + bu$) will preserve this inequality and is thus capable of representing the preference ordering.

in which prospects contain certain outcomes, for instance the triplet ($\$5; 1$), ($\$7; 1$) and ($\$10; 1$), there is some probability p such that there is indifference between the mix of best and worst, ($\$5$, $\$10; p$, $1 - p$), and the middle option, ($\$7, 1$). This may seem innocuous, but it is worth noting one implication. Consider the three prospects: I, receiving one dollar with no risk to life; II, receiving nothing with no risk to life; and III, receiving one dollar with a small risk to life. As Arrow (1970) reminds us, clearly I is preferred to II, but continuity would demand that III should be preferred to II if the probability of death is sufficiently small – and this may strike some as surprising. However, on reflection, it is perhaps not so unusual, since there are many examples in which actions involve only a small gain and yet expose us to some risk to life (for instance, when we cross the road to purchase a soft drink).

Strong independence (8) means that, in any prospect, any component object or prospect can be replaced by an object or prospect indifferent to it, and there will be indifference between the resulting prospect and the original one. Again, this may seem innocuous, but it is worth reflecting on one implication. Suppose that you are indifferent between $\$100$ for certain and a 50–50 chance of receiving $\$250$. Furthermore, suppose that there are two prospects (I and II) which are identical except for one component: in I there is $\$100$ with probability $1/5$ and in II there is a 50–50 chance of $\$250$ with probability $1/5$. Strong independence implies that you will be indifferent between I and II, since they differ only with respect to this component and you are indifferent between the two options for this component. It is sometimes felt that this is an unreasonable inference, since the $\$100$ is no longer certain in the comparison between I and II. Yet, is it really reasonable to have this indifference upset by the mere presence of other prizes? Strong independence answers 'no'.

The last condition (9) is simply an application of the rules of probability.

When these conditions hold, there exists an utility function $U(x)$, which is unique up to a linear transformation, such that given any two prospects $y = (x_i, x_j; p_1, 1 - p_1)$ and $y' = (x_k, x_l; p_2, 1 - p_2)$, then y is preferred to y' or there is indifference between them if and only if

$$p_1 U(x_i) + (1 - p_1)U(x_j) \geqslant p_2 U(x_k) + (1 - p_2)U(x_l)$$

In short, we have the remarkable result that an individual who acts on a preference ordering which satisfies these conditions can be represented as acting so as to maximize expected utility.

Much might be said about this result, but I shall restrict myself to a single observation. The utility function which represents these preference orderings is cardinal. Unlike ordinal functions, which need only preserve the ordering between objects, a cardinal function must also preserve the ratios of differences between the utilities of objects. Technically, the transformation T, referred to above, is now restricted to the class of linear transformations. This gives the concept of 'utility' more content than previously, but it still does not correspond to the traditional sense of utility as some absolute measure of pleasure. We can think of outcomes yielding utility, but the personal measurement of that utility remains arbitrary up to a linear transformation and it still cannot serve as the vehicle for **interpersonal comparisons of utility** (🕮) because there is no common unit of account.

This completes the formal description of what is implied by instrumentally rational action. I now wish to convey, in a couple of ways, the range and centrality of this rationality assumption in social science. One involves a quantitative indicator, a reference to its use in a variety of contexts; and the other is more qualitative. The references are very brief, since the essays on applications can be consulted for more detailed discussion. The obvious illustration, taken from economics, is that of consumer theory. In effect, modern economics has added to the insights concerning human motivation of the earlier utilitarian tradition in this field, while avoiding some of the more tendentious claims of that tradition with respect to the ability to measure and compare utility of different individuals (see CONSUMER THEORY (2) for further details).

A simple extension of the same consumer model is also found in political science with the 'economics of democracy' literature (see Further Reading and DEMOCRACY (14)). At its most explicit, commodities translate as policies, parties offer voters bundles of policies, and voters cast their votes so as to maximize their expected utility, now defined over prospective government policies. Likewise, at the interface of philosophy, politics and economics, the agenda of modern discussions of public choice has been set by the Arrow (1963a) impossibility result using this model of individuals (see SOCIAL CHOICE (13)). There are also particular analyses of behaviour that work within this tradition, and which become distinctive by placing further restrictions on individual preferences. For instance, **Maslow's hierarchy of human needs** (🕮) (1970) conjectures that some needs become progressively more important as wealth increases. In political theories stemming from the work of **Hobbes** (🕮), with preferences which are self-interested, individuals gain utility from an action only in so far as it satisfies their own desires and not some other person's desires. By contrast, two particular applications which build in interdependence between individuals are Fishbein and Ajzen's (1975) model of behaviour in psychology and Runciman's (1966) model of relative deprivation in sociology (see □). The former makes the social valuation of an act an important source of utility for the individual undertaking the action, while the latter makes failure relative to others a source of disutility.

While these references give some indication of the ubiquity of this rationality assumption in the social sciences, they do not suggest the full range of behaviours, in a qualitative sense, which can be driven by this sort of rationality. Indeed, quite the reverse is probably the case, since 'I did it because that is what I wanted' is likely to seem a rather transparently simple sort of behaviour. However, this can be a misleading impression because instrumental rationality can produce complex types of behaviour. Some indication of this can be provided here through a couple of examples (CONSUMER THEORY (2) and GAME THEORY APPLIED (9) offer more detailed illustrations).

One relates to a situation in which the individual interacts knowingly with another individual. Such situations are referred to as games, and are discussed in GAME THEORY (7) and GAME THEORY APPLIED (9). For now, it suffices to notice that in such settings individuals may act in a manner which seems contrary to their manifest or immediate self-interest, in order to engineer a change in other people's beliefs about them. The person acts in this manner because the change in belief aids utility maximization in future interactions. For instance, consider the teacher faced by a late assignment. It could be that to grade the assignment and return it without penalty is the simplest course of action and the one that maximizes teacher utility at that moment. However, despite the hassle of dealing with excuses and complaints, by penalizing the student a reputation for 'toughness' may result, which may maximize utility *over time* because students keep to the deadlines of teachers who have such a reputation.

The other example comes from Greek literature, and has a different temporal twist (see **time inconsistency and subgame perfection** (⚅)). Ulysses instructed his men to tie him to the mast. This was uncomfortable at the time, but it enabled him later to listen to the enchanting voices of the Sirens without succumbing to their sweet suggestion to guide the ship towards the rocks. Such a strategy is now referred to as 'self-command', and is well known to anyone who has attempted to stop smoking, lose weight, or modify behaviour in the short run so as to accrue benefit in the long term.

To conclude this section, instrumental rationality has been rigorously defined and widely used in the social sciences to explain individual choice in both certain and risky situations. It gives rise both to simple sorts of

RELATIVE FRUSTRATION

Boudon (1986) reminds us of a paradoxical relation between material progress and satisfaction which has often been observed in the social sciences. For instance, quoting de Tocqueville, he notes that 'the parts of France which must be the principal focus for this revolution are the very ones in which progress is most apparent . . . it could be fairly said that the French found their position increasingly unbearable as it became better' (p. 173). Likewise, he draws attention to the conclusions of Stouffer's study on The American Soldier: 'Military policemen who belong to a group in which the system of promotion is rare, declare themselves satisfied with the system of promotion that governs their lives. Pilots, on the other hand, though belonging to a group in which promotion is frequent, declare themselves to be unsatisfied with the system of promotion' (p. 174).

His explanation of this paradox (as well as several others) turns on Runciman's concept of relative deprivation. This exists when a person does not have a good, when there is another person who is similarly placed who does have it. To illustrate how the dissatisfaction associated with relative deprivation can rise as the opportunities for material advance improve, consider the following case.

There are N individuals each facing an option of 'winning' B in a competition which costs C to enter, and where the chances of winning diminish with the number of entrants because there are fixed number of winners, n. The individuals are identical in all the relevant respects and they are risk-neutral.

Each individual faces the choice of whether to enter the competition, and we assume that individuals will switch from non-participation to participation whenever the expected returns from participation exceed those of non-participation, and vice versa. Thus, in equilibrium we know there will be a number of participants, x, such that the expected returns from the two courses of action are equalized: this condition is given by

$$Bn/x - C = 0 \tag{1}$$

Let us take the numbers who participate and who fail to win, as a proportion of the population, to be an index of the degree of relative frustration in this society. This is given by

$$RF = (x - n)/N \tag{2}$$

Substituting (1) into (2) yields

$$RF = n(B/C - 1)/N \tag{3}$$

Inspection of this expression reveals that relative deprivation rises with the number of prizes or winners, n. Thus, it is perhaps not so surprising that dissatisfaction grows as the opportunities for material advance improve.

behaviour which transparently fit the mould of 'I did it because that is what I wanted', and to the more subtle types of behaviour associated with reputation-building and self-command. /

The Limits of Instrumental Rationality

The economists' model of instrumental rationality seems commendably general because it makes so few assumptions about the preferences of individuals. However, there are some problems with this account, and the more specific extensions of it found in other disciplines. This section singles out two which pave the way for the later discussion of the alternative senses of rationality: one is empirical and the other is theoretical.

The empirical complaint comes in two forms, one of which is quite precise. Expected utility maximization yields a variety of predictions that have been tested in experimental settings and which have been consistently falsified. (See HOW PEOPLE CHOOSE (3) for some of the experimental results, and for alternative explanations of how people choose.)

A more general empirical doubt surfaces because many human projects seem not to fit the instrumental framework. Indeed, so far are they from this model, that any attempt to fit them into this rubric would make a nonsense of the whole enterprise. For example, imagine trying to satisfy the objective of 'going to sleep' or 'being spontaneous'. As any insomniac will tell you, to attempt to 'go to sleep' is a recipe for failure. Sleep has to creep up – it cannot be willed – and no amount of deviousness will avoid this problem. You cannot do something else as an exercise in self-command in order to allow sleep to creep up on you: as any insomniac will again attest, the moment you realise that the only reason you are taking this course of action is as a device for going to sleep, the strategy collapses.

Elster (1983) has referred to such states as ones which are essentially by-products. Their pursuit involves some kind of conceptual impossibility, and so they cannot be represented as a well-behaved preference ordering. John Donne provides an early reminder that some quite central human projects might fall within this category in his poem *The Prohibition* (see □).

The difficulty with representing objectives by a well-behaved preference ordering stretches beyond objectives which are essentially by-products. For instance, there are reasons for doubting whether ethical objectives can be represented as a preference ordering (see Sen, 1970; Hollis, 1988). Some of the doubts are philosophical, while some are more practical, relating to the difficulty any ethical system may have in satisfying an axiom such as transitivity (see **ethical preferences** (🔁)). Likewise, even when they are well-ordered at a moment in time, preferences change notoriously over time, and this presents a problem for the individual as to which preferences are to be

CONTRADICTORY DESIRES

Take heed of loving me
At least remember, I forbade it thee, . . .

Take heed of hating me,
Or too much triumph in the victory
Not that I shall be mine own officer,
And hate with hate again retaliate;
But thou wilt lose the style of conqueror,
If I, thy conquest, perish by thy hate.
Then lest my being nothing lessens thee,
If thou hate me, take heed of hating me . . .

(John Donne, from 'The Prohibition')

satisfied when plans extend beyond the immediate period (see □; also Elster, 1986; Hargreaves Heap, 1989). Indeed, taken together, this apparent wholesale capacity of humans to form projects of one kind or another that cannot be represented in any obvious way as a set of well-ordered preferences is one of the factors which informs the more dynamic and evolving sense of expressive rationality, to be discussed in a later section.

The theoretical difficulty arises over the informational structure of these decisions. What does instrumental rationality require of the beliefs which service instrumental calculation? In other words, in this context, what constitutes rational beliefs?

Bayesian theory yields instructions on how to use new information to update beliefs 'rationally' in certain circumstances (see **Bayes's Rule** (⚲)). But how do individuals come by this new information? The problem may not be obvious at first, because it is tempting to think that the investment in acquiring information can be subjected to a similar instrumental calculation (see **search theory** (⚲)). In particular, what could be simpler than following the rule of investing in information up to the point at which the marginal benefit in terms of additional utility exactly matches the marginal cost in terms of utility forgone in other activities which might have been undertaken instead?

However, this formulation begs the question. How is the individual to know what the marginal benefits of further information acquisition are without knowledge of the full information set? After all, from a point just below the summit of the foothills, there may seem little advantage in climbing to the top. Yet an aerial photograph would reveal that the tops of the

MULTIPLE SELVES

To be in 'two minds' seems to be a recognizably human predicament, but it sits uneasily with the instrumental conception of rationality because it appears to deny the existence of well-ordered preference. Indeed, it often seems that more than two selves struggle within a single person. As Steedman and Krause (1986) note in their discussion of multiple selves, Bismark observed:

> Faust complained that he had two souls in his breast. I have a whole squabbling crowd. It goes on as in a Republic.

In fact, in some circumstances multiple selves at a moment in time can be reduced to an underlaying meta-self and so dissolve the tension with the instrumental account (see Steedman and Krause, 1986). In a similar fashion, Becker and Stigler (1977) have argued that many of the behaviours that seem to imply preference changes, and which give the appearance of different selves over time, can be reconciled with a stable set of preferences.

For instance, advertising does not induce a change in preferences: it provides additional information which leads individuals to change the way they satisfy given preferences. Likewise, changes in fashion can be traced back to a constant preference for 'style', and the music addict has stable preferences for music appreciation. With the latter, what changes over time as a result of listening to music is the productivity of time spent listening to music in the production of music appreciation. As Becker and Stigler put it:

> On this interpretation, the relative consumption of music appreciation rises with exposure not because tastes shift in favor of music, but because its shadow price falls as skill and experience in appreciation of music are acquired with exposure.' (p. 79)

These are ingenius explanations, but it is not obvious that Becker and Stigler have really captured the essence of being in two minds. Their individuals do not experience any inner conflict over what to do. Their music addict was always a music lover. He or she does not experience the symptomatic difficulty, for instance, of how to weigh the pleasure of another drink now with the regret which will follow it in the morning! Yet this sense of difficulty seems to be what engages us when we are in two minds.

mountains which lie beyond the foothills afford unimaginably better views than those from the foothills.

Of course, it is always possible to reply that the individual has subjective beliefs about these benefits. But this introduces an arbitrary element into the description of action, unless those subjective beliefs can themselves be justified as rational. And to reply that these beliefs are rational because the agent has acquired information on these beliefs, up to the point at which marginal benefits equal marginal costs, merely begs the question again at one stage higher in the structure of beliefs. At each stage there will be a question about the rationality of belief, which can be answered in instrumentally rational fashion only through begging a question about the rationality of the beliefs about beliefs.

In economics, it had been hoped that the so-called rational expectations (🕮) hypothesis would provide an answer. The rough argument went like this. No individual will knowingly use an expectations-generating procedure (an information-processing device) which leads to systematic errors. Individuals, being maximizers, will latch on to the mechanism generating systematic errors because they will profit from the removal of such errors. Accordingly, we can define the expectations which we expect instrumentally rational individuals to hold as ones which suffer only from random white noise errors; that is, the errors have a zero expected mean, constant variance and are serially independent. Unfortunately, this line of argument is not without its problems. For instance, in many settings there is a variety of expectations which, when held widely, could satisfy the condition of generating only white noise errors. Thus, instrumental rationality in the guise of rational expectations is not sufficient to determine the choice of which expectation to entertain. Again, something extra must be added to the account of individual decision-making if a full account of choice is to be given (see expectations (🕮) for further discussion). A similar problem arises with respect to rational belief in situations of interactive choice, when there are multiple Nash equilibria. A full discussion of this matter can be found in GAME THEORY (7).

Procedural Rationality: Bounded Rationality and Norms

These information difficulties have been well-recognized in the social sciences, and they occasion another model of individual rational action. The key to this alternative, procedural theory of rationality is that individuals use rules of thumb – simple procedures – to guide their actions.

In the world of economics, Simon (1978) treats the use of such procedures as short-cut devices for decision-making. They economize on a scarce resource, the brain's limited computational capacity. Thus for instance, an individual may use adaptive expectations, a simple extrapolation of the past into the future, rather than collect all the information which might allow the formation of a rational expectation. Equally, an individual who is deciding on which investment projects to undertake may use a simple rule of thumb such as 'undertake any project with a payback period of less than three years' rather than perform in the strictly optimal fashion by ranking projects according to the present discounted value of their expected profits.

In Simon's hands, procedural rationality is really an ersatz form of instrumental rationality. Individuals are still motivated by a desire to satisfy their objectives; it is simply that their rationality has become 'bounded' because they are not fully informed – in these circumstances, people settle for 'satisficing' rather than optimizing.

However, it is misleading to think of procedural rationality solely in this way. It is not just some imperfect version of the instrumental case, producing results which only deviate from what would otherwise be expected because there is a 'bit of grit in the system'. In economics it is now recognized that the results of procedural behaviour can be qualitatively different from those which obtain when agents are instrumentally rational (see Radner, 1980). In the wider social sciences, rule following can denote something more significant (see Giddens, 1979). It marks the irreducible social and historical location of individual action because these rules, when shared, form the building blocks of a society's culture. From this perspective, to understand individual action one must understand social context as something more than the sum of interacting instrumentally rational individuals. The vision is one of *Homo sociologicus*, and it suggests a contrast with the instrumental rationality of *Homo economicus*. For now, a few comments on this distinction will suffice, as the theme is developed more fully in HOMO SOCIOLOGICUS, HOMO ECONOMICUS (5).

One aspect of the distinction relates to the irreducible nature of these shared rules. Consider the rule which says 'give way to traffic coming from the right' at a road intersection. When this rule is shared by all road users it will coordinate the traffic at intersections perfectly. This is the sort of explicit rule which, when widely followed, helps to generate the information about other people's behaviour that is crucial for instrumental calculations to proceed. However, the rule does not operate along Simon's lines. The rule is not a second best device which substitutes for scarce computing capacity. No amount of computational power will enable you to anticipate what other people will do when their behaviour depends on what they expect of you: the circle of expectations merely becomes wider the more you calculate, as you anticipate that they will anticipate that you anticipate, and so on. In this form, the situation is characterized by uncertainty as opposed to risk ([?]), and what transforms it into one where expectations can be formed is the existence of the shared rule.

This departure from Simon's formulation of rule following subtly transforms the relationship between the use of rules and an instrumental motivation. To be sure, the use of the rule aids instrumental calculation. But the use of a particular rule cannot typically be explained by reference to instrumental considerations alone (see ANARCHIC ORDER (12)). Why 'give way to traffic coming from the left' rather than 'give way to the old'? Either of these, or any of a number of imaginable rules – once shared – would coordinate the traffic just as well. Yet the choice of convention is not a matter of insignificance. Coordination at crossroads may seem prosaic, but there are many cases of social interaction which embody aspects of a coordination game, and the distribution of the benefits from coordination at the 'crossroads of life' are likely to vary considerably with the choice of rule. Is it women who always give way to men, the old to the young, workers to capitalists, or is it tall people who have the free run in such coordination games?

These are important questions, and so the gap left by instrumental rationality appears significant. Furthermore, we are reminded by the sociology of Goffman (1975) and Garfinkel (1967) that the use of rules at crossroads and the like are only special cases of the more general use of rules in society as communication devices. All social encounters rely on a web of shared beliefs (derived from rules) which enable actions to be remarkably economical and powerful in sending non-verbal messages. There are implicit rules in our society about eye contact, physical proximity, dress and so on which enable us to interpret actions as anything from threatening to loving. They are all-pervasive, affecting the economy as deeply as our social life. For example, much of advertising is a testament to the importance of these background shared beliefs in basic economic transactions. Consider for a moment how difficult it would be, without a shared set of beliefs, to make sense of a cigarette packet which appears in an advertisement as a pyramid or an electric plug. Alternatively, how might you begin to make sense of the difference between 'Levi 501s' and any other pair of heavy blue cotton trousers without a knowledge of a society's culture in the form of its web of shared beliefs?

Anthropologists are quick to remind us that these shared beliefs are, to some degree, arbitrary when they act as a system for communication, as is the choice of words in any language system. Thus, just as there is a variety of rules which might be used at the 'crossroads of life', so it seems there are a variety of cultures. The instrumental need for expectation formation and communication only takes us so far; it cannot explain the choice of the particular rules of communication which aid instrumental calculation. Yet, in this instance, as in the 'crossroads of life', the choice of particular rules is not insignificant, as any clash of cultures demonstrates.

The appeal to procedural rationality can fill this gap, and so signals the irreducibility of shared rules which arises because individual choices cannot always be understood solely in terms of individuals acting to satisfy desires. This is an observation which has been made in various forms in the social sciences (see also GAME THEORY (7), where the underdetermination of action by reference to interacting instrumentally rational individuals surfaces in the form of multiple Nash equilibria). For instance, since we are borne into a society where there are often clear pre-existing rules which govern behaviour, this additional procedural element can be thought of as 'historical', 'institutional' or 'structural' (see structuralism (⊞)); and the idea is well illustrated by **Marx's** (⚐) (1852) famous comment that 'Men make their own history, but they do not make it just as they please; they do not make it under circumstances chosen by themselves' (p. 103).

Put in this way, the shared rules of procedural rationality provide an irreducible social and historical context within which instrumentally rational actions can be undertaken. Procedural rationality marks the limits of instrumental rationality. However, in phrasing matters in this way, it is important not to leave the impression that procedural rationality has turned the individual, in part, into some cultural dope or a simple bearer of society's roles. There can be much more to procedural rationality than this.

For instance, it is quite wrong to think of rule-following always as a mechanical activity. This may often be the case, but all rules provide more or less space for creative interpretation, because no set of rules is fully exhaustive in defining what action is appropriate in the circumstances. To make the point consider, for instance, the case of rules of conduct which are formalized in law on the statute book. However prescient the framers of a particular law might have been, there will always be circumstances that were not foreseen, and where the precise application of the law is opaque. Judges are called upon to interpret the law creatively (see Dworkin, 1986, for a lively and controversial discussion of these acts of interpretetion). Hence rule-following need not spell the demise of the individual, nor need it turn the individual into an automaton. Rather, it can draw attention to the possibility of a different sort of creative decision-making by the individual (see RISK, IGNORANCE AND IMAGINATION (4)).

I conclude this section by observing that procedural rationality may, controversially, constitute a further departure from the model of instrumentally rational action. It is not just that something is going on behind the back of the individual, so as to speak, which opens up a possibility for creative decision-making. In addition, the following of rules may generate reasons for action which cannot be sensibly assimilated to some prior set of objectives. Thus, for instance, in the game of chess the movement of a knight cannot be interpreted as an action which satisfies some idiosyncratic desire for moving wood around a chequered board. Equally, it would be misleading to treat it as simply serving some general desire for entertainment or winning, in the same way that it is misleading to think of a general desire such as warmth generating the purchase of 'Levi 501s'. Instead, it is the very rules of chess which provide the reason for moving a knight in a particular way. Although there is no need to take this any further, it will be obvious that, in so far as rule-following creates its own objectives for action, then this provides an additional reason for shifting away from the simple means–ends framework of instrumental rationality. For now, it is sufficient to draw the implication from procedural rationality that to understand individual action one must often understand social context, and social context cannot always be reduced to interacting instrumentally rational individuals.

Expressive Rationality: Making Sense of the Self Through Creative Choice

Rationality has often been thought to apply to action in a more fundamental and complicated manner than is implied by the instrumental account (see □). From **Kant** (▢), through **Marx** (▢), for instance, to Weber's (1922) '*Wertrationalität*', Habermas's (1985–6) 'communicative action' and Elster's (1983) 'broad notion of rationality', we have gained an idea that rationality is as much concerned with establishing the value of ends pursued; and that

---

REASON AND ACTION

Now in a being which has reason and a will, if the proper object of nature were its conservation, its welfare, in a word, its happiness, then nature would have hit upon a very bad arrangement in selecting the reason of the creature to carry out this purpose. . . . For reason is not competent to guide the will with certainty in regard to its objects and the satisfaction of all our wants (which to some extent it even multiplies), this being an end which an implanted instinct would have led with much greater certainty; and since, nevertheless, reason is imparted to us as a practical faculty . . ., its true destination must be to produce a will, not merely good as a means to something else, but good in itself, for which reason was absolutely necessary.

(Kant, 1788, pp. 11–12)

Social action, like all action, may be oriented in four ways. It may be:
1) Instrumentally rational [*zweckrational*], that is, determined by expectations as to the behaviour of objects in the environment and of other human beings; these expectations are used as 'conditions' or 'means' for the attainment of the actor's own rationally pursued and calculated ends;
2) Value-rational [*wertrational*], that is, determined by a conscious belief in the value for its own sake of some ethical, aesthetic, religious, or other form of behaviour, independently of its prospects of success;
3) affectual (especially emotional), that is, determined by the actor's specific affects and feeling states;
4) traditional, that is, determined by ingrained habituation.

(Weber, 1922, pp. 24–5)

> The model of purposive rational action takes as its point of departure the view that the actor is primarily oriented to attaining an end . . . that he selects the means that seem to him appropriate. . . . By contrast I shall speak of communicative action whenever the actions of the agents involved are coordinated not through egocentric calculations of success but through acts of reaching understanding. . . .
>
> Reaching understanding [*verstandigung*] is considered to be a process of reaching agreement [*einigung*] among speaking and acting subjects. . . . Agreement rests on common convictions . . .
>
> (Habermas, 1985–6, pp. 285–7)
>
> I suggest that between the thin theory of the rational and the full theory of the true and the good there is room and need for a broad theory of the rational. To say that truth is necessary for rational action is to require too much; to say that consistency is sufficient, to demand too little. Similarly, although more controversially, for rational desires: the requirement of consistency is too weak, that of ethical goodness too strong.
>
> My suggestion is that we should evaluate the broad rationality of beliefs and desires by looking at the way in which they are shaped.
>
> (Elster, 1983, p. 15)

action is as much an expression of those beliefs regarding value as it is the execution of a plan to satisfy given objectives. In this section, I shall cast this idea as expressive rationality, and treat it as a development of the theme that individuals often choose in a creative manner.

This concern with the rationality of ends pursued can be understood as a desire for self-respect. People are inclined to reflect on and find value in themselves. However, put in this way, it may be tempting to think that the account of instrumental rationality can be preserved through a suitable redefinition of the objectives which the individual pursues. All that seems to be required is to endow the individual with an objective of 'making sense of the self', and action can still be regarded as instrumental in the sense that it is designed to satisfy best this objective as well as others.

Tempting as this may be, I wish to head-off the idea. 'Making sense of the self' cannot be shoehorned into the means–end instrumental framework because it is not an objective which fits the instrumental model. It is more akin to a project which undermines the very notion of fixed 'ends' which are necessary for instrumental calculation. The objective actually reflects a central source of doubt and uncertainty within the individual. People are not sure about what they should value in themselves. Indeed, without this doubt there would be no project of 'making sense of the self'. The self would be understood and the ends of the individual could be specified. Instead, it is precisely because they cannot be specified that we have an objective of 'making sense of the self'. In short, this is the type of open-ended objective which defies the means–end framework of instrumental rationality.

The danger of eliding the expressive with the instrumental is perhaps the least of our worries here, since it is difficult to discuss expressive rationality without opening a can of philosophical and analytical worms. Major philosophical issues arise because the existential concern with making sense of the self, with finding a purpose for one's life, is an example – in what are often called 'modern' societies – of a more general human preoccupation with making sense of the world. Anthropologists remind us that all peoples seem to need a cosmology which renders their world intelligible, but it is only in modern societies that the individual has moved to the centre of these cosmologies. This centrality would be quite alien in religious and 'traditional' societies, and it means that the philosophical doubts about the world in general have been especially focused on the individual in modern societies. Accordingly, it is the individual whom we celebrate, but it is an individual who has been cut free from the supports of God or the groups or other traditional sources of authority which might otherwise give meaning and value to the individual's projects.

Plainly, this is an opening to philosophical argument, and these philosophical issues have been prominent in political theory and in the more straightforwardly evaluative branches of the other social sciences (such as welfare economics). They are side-stepped here, but receive further discussion in AUTONOMY (6). Instead, I wish to draw attention here to the way in which expressive rationality has been associated with a characteristically different sort of decision-making process.

'Judgement' is one way of drawing the contrast with instrumental calculation (see Bernstein, 1983; Hollis, 1988). It is a gesture to the idea that we do not know with any kind of certainty what makes a life worthy, and so the instrumental, calculating process cannot go to work alone. We have moral difficulties over what constitutes worthiness, and we have epistemic problems trying to weigh the contribution of considerations which, at root, seem to be incommensurable. Yet this does not mean that we are paralysed; nor does it mean that we ignore these existential concerns. Rather, action in these circumstances is an act of creativity using another capacity, that of 'judgement'. But what does judgement really amount to here?

At a general level, judgement is a stab at representing what we regard as worthy, and given the difficulties with establishing ultimate worth this somewhat heroic quest is often reduced to a messy and arbitrary kind of 'muddling through'. It is part of a continuing process, an interim and imperfect statement, like all acts of creativity, rather than the last word; and, as such, actions which flow from this concern are often regarded as ends in themselves rather than means towards some end (hence the term 'expressive').

Of course, this really serves just to embellish what has already been said. Nevertheless, it helps to draw the distinction between instrumental and expressive rationality in a manner that throws a better light on the kind of preference structures, such as those mentioned in an earlier section, which appear anomalous from an instrumental perspective. Inconsistent objectives need not be taken as evidence of irrationality. Rather, they might be regarded as marking our expressive rationality, although care is required here not to overstate the case, lest any kind of preference structure is thereby admitted!

To answer the question of what 'judgement' amounts to more specifically, in the social sciences there are a number of detailed analyses of behaviour that are not driven by instrumental calculation. 'Judgement' is not the term that is always used to describe these decision processes, but terminology is not the point. What distinguishes these processes, however described, and makes them relevant to the discussion here, is that they revolve around the internal conflicts that are so symptomatic of the type of existential uncertainty that can be associated with expressive rationality.

Typically, these analyses are to be found in psychology, where they range from the rather mechanical theories of conflict resolution such as that of **cognitive dissonance** (⬚) (see Festinger, 1957), to the Kelly (1955) model of 'man the scientist', and to the more complex mediation of conflict between different sources of value which is found in Freud (1916–17). However, they are also to be found in management science literature where, for instance, the bestselling management pot-boiler by Peters and Waterman (1982) reworks the theme that people are at their most creative when they feel good about themselves, by making this sense of self-respect depend on the mediation of the conflict which people have between wishing both to belong to groups and yet be separate from them. Finally, even economists have produced models of creative choice in the presence of this sort of uncertainty: Shackle (1955, 1958) (☐ p. 57) is a landmark development on Keynes (1921, 1936) (☐ p. 60), while Earl (1986) provides a latter-day example.

Conclusion

Three types of individual rationality have been distinguished in this chapter. They should not be regarded as competitors: rather, they provide complementary insights into human motivation which can be called on in different measures, according to the setting, to explain and understand individual choice.

There will be circumstances in which individuals have well-defined objectives and in which action can be fully described as an attempt to satisfy these objectives. However, on other occasions it will be the impact of the social context which needs to be understood, and on yet other occasions we will be concerned with action when preferences are not well-defined. And it is in these circumstances that the senses of procedural and expressive rationality give us a much needed vocabulary for discussing what are often creative rather than calculating individual choices.

Shaun Hargreaves Heap

Further Reading

The formal analysis of instrumentally rational behaviour can be found in most introductory texts in economics. Green (1971) and Deaton and Muellbauer (1980) offer extended discussions with a variety of applications. The seminal contributions to decision-making under uncertainty come from von Neumann and Morgenstern (1947) and Savage (1954), while Hey (1979) provides a contemporary survey of the theory with applications. This model is famously used in politics by Downs (1957): it was further developed by Buchanan and Tullock (1962), and Riker (1982) gives a good summary of the fruits of this approach. It has been at the centre of the Elster (1985) and Roemer (1982, 1988) reinterpretation of Marx, otherwise known as 'rational choice marxism'; and its extension to most aspects of social life has been the project of Becker (1976). Elster (1983) gives critical reflections on this sense of rationality and contrasts it with a 'broader' (expressive) notion of rationality. The particular difficulties with information are discussed further in **expectations** ($\boxed{?}$), and the empirical evidence is considered in more detail in HOW PEOPLE CHOOSE (3). Hollis (1988) is more philosophical in his critical appreciation: he develops the idea that we are creative role players (a concept bridging the procedural and the expressive) and not just instrumental maximizers. On the other hand, Hargreaves Heap (1989) focuses on the inadequacies of the instrumental model in economics and the discipline's – often implicit – reliance on the other senses of rationality. Simon (1978) is a good starting point for the claims of procedural rationality in economics, and RISK, IGNORANCE AND IMAGINATION (4) can be consulted for further references from economics on creative (expressive) decision-making. Further references, which develop these additional senses of rationality within the wider social sciences, can be found in HOMO ECONOMICUS, HOMO SOCIOLOGICUS (5) and AUTONOMY (6).

2

Consumer Theory

Consumer theory is the branch of economics that explains the demand for goods, and in particular, how demands are influenced by changes in prices and income. Traditionally, it has been the principal area of application for the theory of rational individual choice.

The starting point for consumer theory is an agent with well-defined preferences over all conceivable 'bundles' of a given set of goods. Let these goods be $1, \ldots, n$; a bundle is a list or vector $(q_1, \ldots, q_n)$ of quantities, where q_i is the quantity consumed of good i. The agent's preferences are assumed to satisfy the assumptions of completeness and transitivity, so that they constitute an ordering, and to be continuous, so that this ordering can be represented by a utility function. These are the standard assumptions of the economic theory of rational choice (see RATIONALITY (1)).

This brings us immediately to a difficulty: for most consumer goods, the spending unit is the household, and households may contain several individuals. Are we entitled to attribute rationality to the choices of such households? Consumer theory generally sweeps this problem under the carpet by treating 'household', 'individual' and 'consumer' as interchangeable terms. Many applications of consumer theory require a further and still more questionable form of aggregation. Economists typically are interested, not in the demands of any one household, but in *market* demand – the sum of the demands of many households. A common practice, particularly in econometric work, is to assume that market demands have the same properties as the demands of individual consumers. This is essentially the same as assuming that market demands are generated by a set of identical 'representative' households.

When this kind of aggregating assumption is being used, it is hard to claim that consumer theory is working out the implications of a well-grounded theory of rational individual choice. It is perhaps more appropriate to interpret the concept of a rational representative household as an 'as if' assumption which is not intended to be taken literally. Suppose that an econometric study were to show that market demands did *not* have the properties that we would expect to find in the demands of a single rational consumer. (This, in fact, is a common finding in econometric work: see Deaton and Muellbauer (1980, chapter 3).) Such a result would not necessarily refute the theory of rational choice, since it might well be the aggregating assumption that was at fault. From now on, however, we shall side-step these issues by considering the behaviour of a single household which contains only a single consumer.

Two further assumptions are typically made about preferences. The first is that more of any good is always preferred to less. The second is that preferences are *convex*. The meaning of these two assumptions can be seen most clearly for the case in which there are just two goods. In figure 2.1, the horizontal axis measures q_1, the quantity consumed of good 1, and the vertical axis measures q_2, the quantity consumed of good 2. Each point in the positive quadrant of this diagram represents a different bundle of the two goods. Each of the *indifference curves* I_1, I_2 and I_3 represents a set of bundles between which the consumer is indifferent: these may be regarded as utility contours. Since more of either good is preferred to less, indifference curves must be downward-sloping, and curves that are further away from the origin must correspond to more preferred bundles (or higher levels of

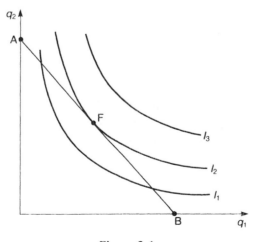

Figure 2.1.

utility). The assumption of convexity implies that indifference curves must be convex to the origin, as in the diagram.

Suppose that the consumer has an income of y, all of which is to be spent on buying goods. Each good i has a price p_i. Then the consumer's problem is to find the bundle that she most prefers, subject to the constraint that she may spend no more than y. Given her preferences, the nature of this bundle will be determined by her income and by the prices she faces. The case in which there are only two goods is illustrated in figure 2.1. Given the consumer's income and the two prices, we may construct a *budget line* AB which defines the outer limit of the set of bundles that the consumer can afford to buy. Of these affordable bundles, the most preferred is F.

For the case of many goods, this idea can be expressed mathematically by writing a *demand function* for each good i, with the form:

$$q_i = q_i\,(p_1, \ldots, p_n, y).$$

Notice that the amount the consumer buys of one good may be influenced by the prices of other goods. (If the price of rice rises, more pasta is bought.) The main task of consumer theory is to investigate the properties of such demand functions.

One such property can be derived straight away. Suppose that every price changes in the same proportion, say α, and that income also increases in the same proportion. Then there should be no change in the quantity consumed of any good: that is,

$$q_i\,(p_1, \ldots, p_n) = q_i(\alpha p_1, \ldots, \alpha p_n, \alpha y)$$

This is the property of *homogeneity*. It is easy to see why this property must hold. Initially the consumer has an income of y and faces the prices $p_1, \ldots, p_n$. Suppose that she can then just afford to buy some particular bundle. Then if all prices change in the proportion α, the cost of this bundle must change the same proportion. So if her income also changes in this proportion, she must still just be able to afford the bundle. More generally: if income and all prices increase in the same proportion, the set of affordable bundles does not change. Since the chosen bundle is simply the most preferred affordable bundle, this does not change either.

Now consider how the quantity of some good, say good i, changes with changes in its own price, p_i, if income and all other prices are held constant. For the purposes of this problem, we may treat 'all goods except good i' as a single good, and measure quantities of this 'composite commodity' in money units. In other words, consumption of the composite commodity can be defined as 'expenditure on all goods other than good i'.

Now look at figure 2.2. The horizontal axis measures consumption of good i, and the vertical axis measures consumption of the composite commodity. The consumer's income, y (and hence the maximum affordable

Figure 2.2.

amount of the composite commodity), is equal to OA. The maximum affordable amount of good i is y/p_i, where p_i is the initial price of good i. Thus the budget line, AB, has a slope whose absolute value is equal to p_i. The most preferred bundle on this budget line is F.

Now suppose that the price of good i falls to p'_i, income and all other prices remaining unchanged. The budget line shifts out to AC (the line through A whose slope has an absolute value of p'_i). The consumer now buys bundle G. The diagram has been drawn so that G lies to the right of F. This implies that consumption of good i increases as the price of good i falls, which sounds right. But is this *necessarily* the case? No, it is not. It would have been possible to draw the indifference curves so that the most preferred point on AC lay to the left of F, in which case consumption of good i would have *fallen* as the price fell.

Somewhat surprisingly, then, we cannot use the standard theory of rational choice to show that the consumption of a good rises as its price falls – that 'demand curves slope downwards'. What *can* be shown is a somewhat weaker conclusion, the *law of demand*. This can be stated as follows: if the quantity demanded of good i increases as income increases, then it must also increase as the price of good i falls. This result is proved in figure 2.2.

Suppose that, at the same time as the price of good i falls, the consumer's income were to be reduced in such a way that she could just attain her original level of utility. This is represented by the budget line DE. This is parallel to AC, signifying that the price of good i is the 'new' or 'final' price p'_i. AD is the amount that has been subtracted from the consumer's income.

The most preferred bundle on this budget line is H, which lies on the same indifference curve as F (the bundle originally bought). Notice that AD may be interpreted as the maximum amount of income the consumer would be prepared to give up in order to get the price of good i to fall from p_i to p_i', and in this sense is a money measure of the amount the consumer gains from the price change. This is called the *compensating variation* for the price change.

This device allows us to separate the effect of the fall in the price of good i into two components. The difference between H and G is the *income effect* of the price change. This is a change in consumption that can be attributed to the consumer's being better-off after the price change. The difference between F and H is the *substitution effect*. It is easy to see from the diagram that H must lie to the right of F. In other words, if the price of good i falls, the substitution effect must be in the direction of greater consumption of that good. What is not clear is the direction of the income effect. It is possible that the income effect could work in the opposite direction to the substitution effect (this is the case of an 'inferior good', one for which consumption falls as income increases). And in principle, the income effect could be so great as to outweigh the substitution effect (the case of a 'Giffen good'). But if we know that the consumption of the good increases with income, we know that G must lie to the right of H, and so consumption of good i must rise as the price falls.

The theory of rational choice has a third implication for demand functions, which is more esoteric but also more surprising. This is the property of *symmetry*. Let s_{ij} be the 'cross-substitution effect' between good i and good j. This is the amount by which consumption of good i changes, per unit change in the price of good j, after abstracting income effects. Symmetry is the property that $s_{ij} = s_{ji}$. For example, suppose that the price of cheese (good j) rises by £0.01 per kilogram and, net of income effects, this causes some consumer's weekly purchases of wine (good i) to fall by 0.02 litre. This implies that $s_{ij} = -2\text{kg litre}/£$. From this we can predict something that is not at all obvious: that if the price of wine increases by £0.01 per litre then, net of income effects, the consumer's weekly purchases of cheese will fall by 0.02 kilogram. The proof of this result can be found in most advanced microeconomics textbooks.

The assumptions of the theory, then, imply the law of demand, and that demand functions have the properties of homogeneity and symmetry. And that is just about all. One possible response to this rather disappointing conclusion is to wonder whether all the initial assumptions about the rational consumer were really necessary. One version of this response is given by Becker (1962), who shows that if each household's spending decisions are made randomly, their aggregate responses will satisfy the law of demand. Some people may draw a similar moral from the finding that under experi-

CONSUMER THEORY FOR RATS

Are rats capable of rational choice? John Kagel and three collaborators posed this question in a famous paper (Kagel *et al.*, 1981), which begins with the striking claim that 'the principles of economic behavior would be virtually unique among behavioral principles if they did not apply, with some variation of course, to the behavior of nonhumans'. Thus, if consumer theory allows us to make correct predictions about the behaviour of human consumers, we should expect it to have similar success in predicting the behaviour of other animals.

Here is one example of the kind of experiment that Kagel *et al.* carried out. A male rat was made to live for many days in a cage in which there were two levers. Above each lever was a pair of lights, which were lit each morning. Each time the rat pressed one lever, a fixed amount of food was dispensed; each time he pressed the other lever, a fixed amount of water was dispensed. After a fixed total number of lever-presses had been made in a day, the lights went out and no more food or water was dispensed for that day. This mechanism provided the rat's only source of food and water. The rat's choice problem can be interpreted as one of choosing a consumption bundle (a mix of food and water) when prices (the quantities of food and water dispensed per lever-press) and income (the total number of presses allowed per day) are fixed. The rat had to learn the nature of his budget constraint by experience. This normally took about three days, after which he settled down to a stable daily consumption pattern. The experimenters varied prices and income at intervals, allowed the rat time to learn his new budget constraint, and observed the effects of these changes on his pattern of consumption.

The main finding was that the behaviour of the rats was in accordance with the law of demand – their demand curves sloped downwards. (Purists may like to know that Kagel *et al.* used Slutsky's method of removing income effects.) Changes in the relative prices of food and water led to marked changes in the ratio of food to water consumed. It seems that rats' responses to simple problems of consumer choice are similar to those of humans. If we are to claim that our choices are the product of our rationality, then we should be prepared to admit that rats are rational too.

mental conditions, individual rats behave in accordance with the law of demand (see □), although it might be more appropriate to conclude that, in this respect, rats are capable of rational choice.

The most famous statement of the claim that consumer theory does not need all the apparatus of rational-choice theory is made by Samuelson (1947, pp. 90–113) in his *revealed preference theory*. Samuelson's theory makes no explicit assumptions about utility or preferences: the primitive concept in the theory is choice. Consider any two bundles $\mathbf{q} = (q_1, \ldots, q_n)$ and

$\mathbf{q}' = (q'_1, \ldots, q'_n)$. Suppose that the prices of the goods and the consumer's income are such that she could afford to buy either of these two bundles, and that she chooses to buy $\mathbf{q}$. Then $\mathbf{q}$ is defined to be *revealed preferred to* $\mathbf{q}'$. (Note that this is a *definition* of 'preference' and not an assumption about preference.) Samuelson's theory uses just one assumption, the *weak axiom of revealed preference*, or WARP, which may be stated as follows: for any two bundles $\mathbf{q}$ and $\mathbf{q}'$, if $\mathbf{q}$ is revealed preferred to $\mathbf{q}'$, then it is not the case that $\mathbf{q}'$ is revealed preferred to $\mathbf{q}$. In other words, if $\mathbf{q}$ is ever bought when $\mathbf{q}'$ is affordable, then $\mathbf{q}'$ is never bought when $\mathbf{q}$ is affordable.

Samuelson shows that WARP implies both the homogeneity property and the law of demand (although not the symmetry property). Perhaps, Samuelson is suggesting, economists need neither the concept of utility nor the concept of preference. Neither of these concepts denotes something directly observable; we can merely make assumptions about utility or preference and then test their implications for behaviour. So why not start with the simpler assumption of WARP, which can be given a direct interpretation in terms of consumer behaviour?

Interestingly, WARP provides no interpretation for the concept of indifference: whenever a consumer chooses one bundle and rejects another, she is defined to prefer the bundle she chose. How has Samuelson managed to exclude indifference from his theory? The answer is that Samuelson considers only a very special kind of choice problem, one in which a consumer has to spend a given budget on a set of continuously divisible goods, each of which has a given price. Under the standard assumptions of consumer theory, this particular problem has a uniquely optimal solution (essentially, the point of tangency of an indifference curve and a budget line). Thus, according to standard theory, the chosen bundle *is* strictly preferred to all the other bundles that the consumer could have afforded. Similarly, there is nothing in WARP which corresponds with the idea of transitivity. Revealed preferences, as defined by WARP, may turn out to have the property that bundle $\mathbf{q}$ is preferred to bundle $\mathbf{q}'$, $\mathbf{q}'$ is preferred to $\mathbf{q}''$, and $\mathbf{q}''$ is preferred to $\mathbf{q}$. (This is not easy to prove: it requires us to consider bundles containing at least three goods, and so intuitions based on two-dimensional diagrams are inadequate.) The implication is that the concept of transitivity, like that of indifference, is not necessary – *if* the object is to derive the law of demand and the homogeneity property. However, this is not to say that indifference and transitivity can be dispensed with in other areas in which we might want to use a theory of rational choice.

One of the main applications of consumer theory is in cost–benefit analysis (see PLANNING (16)). Cost–benefit analysts often need to evaluate the effects on consumers of changes in the prices of particular goods. The principle behind such evaluation exercises is that of the *compensation test* (see **Pareto optimality** (🔢)). Suppose that the price of good i falls from p_i to p'_i.

Consider a typical consumer, who benefits from this change. The extent of this benefit is measured by the compensating variation; that is, by the maximum amount of money the consumer would be willing to pay in return for the fall in the price. It is one thing to show the compensating variation in a diagram (recall that it is AD in figure 2.2) and another to measure it using practically observable data. Consumer theory shows how such compensating variations can be measured.

Price and quantity combinations for good i are shown in figure 2.3. Suppose that the consumer starts with an income of y and buys the quantity q at the price p. (To simplify the notation, the i subscripts are omitted from now on.) The price then falls to p', the consumer's income and all other prices remaining constant. The consumer buys the quantity q'. A and B represent the initial and final price/quantity combinations, and thus A and B lie on a *Marshallian demand curve*, which has been plotted on the assumption that income is constant at the level y.

We know that the consumer has benefited from this price change by an amount equal to the compensating variation, which we may denote by v. Now suppose that we were to require the consumer to pay v in return for the fall in the price. Let q'' be the quantity that would be bought at price p' in this case; that is, q'' is the quantity that would be bought at price p' if income were $y - v$. If the good is 'normal' (that is, if consumption increases as income increases), then q'' will be less than q', as in the diagram. (The difference between q'' and q' is the income effect of the price fall.) Notice that A and C represent price/quantity combinations at which the consumer's level of utility is the same. (This follows from the definition of the compensating variation as the amount of money that must be taken from the

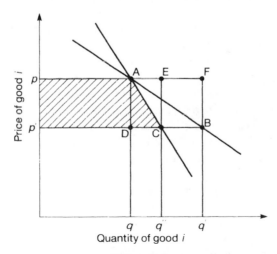

Figure 2.3.

consumer so as to maintain her utility at its initial level.) A and C lie on a *Hicksian demand curve*, a demand curve that has been plotted on the assumption that the consumer's utility is held constant at its initial level.

Now imagine that the consumer is compelled to buy the quantity q at all prices. Then when the price falls from p to p', the only effect is that the consumer saves the amount of money $(p - p')q$; that is, the area $pADp'$. In this case, the maximum amount she would be willing to pay for the price fall would be exactly equal to this area. We know, however, that although she chooses to buy q at price p, she chooses to buy more than q at price p', even though the option of buying q is still open to her. Thus we may conclude that the compensating variation is greater than the area $pADp'$. (That area shows how much she would be willing to pay in return for the price fall, if she were prevented from changing her level of consumption: she would be willing to pay more for the additional privilege of being free to choose how much to consume at the final price.)

A similar argument can be used to set an upper limit to the value of the compensating variation. Imagine that the consumer is compelled to buy the quantity q'' at all prices. Starting from point C, imagine that the price rises from p' to p. Then the consumer loses the amount of money $(p - p')q''$; that is, the area $pECp'$. This is the amount that would have to be added to her income to compensate her for the price rise, given the constraint that she must buy q''. We know, however, that if she is fully compensated and is free to choose her own level of consumption, she will consume q (that is, she will choose to be at point A). Thus a sum of money less than the area $pECp'$ will be sufficient to compensate her for a move from C to A. Inverting this result, this implies that she will not be willing to pay as much as $pECp'$ to move from A to C. In other words, the compensating variation for the price fall is less than $pECp'$.

Now suppose that we were to treat the change in price from p to p' as a succession of very small steps. At each step we reduce the consumer's income by the corresponding compensating variation. Then the compensating variation for the change from p to p' would be the sum of the compensating variations for the many small price changes. By this device, we can reduce the gap between the upper and lower limits of our measure of compensating variation. As the number of steps is increased, the upper and lower estimates both converge on the area that is shaded in figure 2.3. Hence the compensating variation for a price change can be measured by the area of a strip to the left of the Hicksian demand curve.

In most practical cost–benefit analysis, approximations are used. The demand data that are most readily available relate total consumption of a good (that is, consumption by all consumers taken together) to the price of that good, the prices of other goods and the average income of consumers. Holding average income and the prices of all other goods constant, we may plot a market demand curve. Using the assumption of a representative consumer, this curve may be interpreted as the horizontal sum of the Marshallian demand curves of all consumers. For a given price change, the usual practice is to use the area of a strip to the left of the market demand curve as a measure of the sum of all consumers' compensating variations. This amounts to using areas to the left of Marshallian demand curves as approximate measures of areas to the left of Hicksian demand curves. This approximation is reasonably accurate provided that each consumer's compensating variation is fairly small in relation to her income. (This conclusion is derived formally in Willig (1976).) Where this condition is not met, better estimates can be arrived at by making use of information about the income elasticity of demand (that is, the relationship between quantity consumed and average income).

As this brief survey has probably suggested, consumer theory is something of a closed world. Much effort is devoted to working out the implications of a given set of assumptions, which are typically justified on *a priori* grounds, as representing the idea of individual rationality. This work provides the framework within which most economists think about demand in real markets, and within which the data generated by these markets are interpreted. It is well to remember, however, that the idea of the rational consumer, with her well-defined system of preferences, is ultimately no more than an invention of economists – a building block in an edifice of theory. The theory has been immensely useful in allowing economists to impose some sort of order on their observations of market behaviour, but we should not be fooled into thinking that the rational consumers of the theory are really to be found out there in the real world, consulting their indifference maps as they push their trolleys round supermarkets.

Robert Sugden

Further Reading

Consumer theory is covered in almost all microeconomic textbooks. If you really want to study the theory in detail, and are not afraid of mathematics, you should read Deaton and Muellbauer (1980). The concept of consumer's surplus is covered in detail in Boadway and Bruce (1984).

3

How People Choose

The standard theory of the choices of a rational individual, as developed by economists and decision theorists, is expected utility theory (see RATIONALITY (1) and CONSUMER THEORY (2)). This theory is compact, elegant and tractable. It is intended to serve both as a normative model of how a fully rational agent would choose, and as a foundation for theories which predict how real people choose in economic, political and social contexts.

The theory has been constructed by *a priori* reasoning from premises about rationality, rather than by observing choice behaviour and then building a theory to fit those observations: the approach has been deductive rather than inductive. Increasingly, however, the theory is being challenged as a result of observations of people's choices, particularly in experimental situations. Some of the first challenges came from informal 'mental experiments': a commentator would present a specific set of imaginary choice problems and invite his readers to tackle them, predicting that they would find themselves contravening the theory of rational choice in particular ways. More recently, investigators have started to carry out 'laboratory' experiments in which large numbers of individuals are presented with real choice problems (problems in which they stand to win real money) in carefully controlled settings. Such experiments are revealing many types of choice problem in which people tend to behave contrary to the standard theory. In this chapter three particularly well-known types of problem will be examined, but there are many more.

THE ALLAIS PARADOX

Imagine that you face Problem 1, shown below. The pay-offs are in money: their absolute values do not matter – you may interpret them in any currency of your choice.

Problem 1: Choose between

A: 2500 with probability 0.33,   B: 2400 with certainty.
     2400 with probability 0.66,
        0 with probability 0.01;

Now imagine that you face this problem instead:

Problem 2: Choose between

C: 2500 with probability 0.33,   D: 2400 with probability 0.34,
        0 with probability 0.67;   0 with probability 0.66.

In experiments which use pairs of problems of this kind, many people choose B in Problem 1 and C in Problem 2. (The particular example given here is taken from an experiment carried out by Kahneman and Tversky (1979), with pay-offs in Israeli pounds. In this experiment, each of the two problems was presented to 72 people. In Problem 1, 82 per cent of the sample chose B; in Problem 2, 83 per cent chose C.) According to expected utility theory, this pattern of choice is irrational: any rational person who chooses B in Problem 1 must choose D in Problem 2, and vice versa.

Problems and Paradoxes

In the early 1950s, expected utility theory was just beginning to gain acceptance among economists. Allais (1953) formulated a pair of choice problems as part of a challenge to this theory. This has come to be known as the *Allais Paradox* (see □).

Allais conjectured that many people would choose B in Problem 1 and C in Problem 2, while relatively few people would choose A and then D. In Problem 1, A is riskier than B; if you choose A, there is a small chance that you will receive nothing. The idea of taking this risk, just for the chance of increasing your pay-off from 2400 to 2500, seems unattractive. In Problem 2, C seems only slightly riskier than D, and the extra risk may seem worth taking for the chance of the larger pay-off.

The interesting thing about these problems is that someone whose preferences satisfy the axioms of expected utility theory and who chooses B in Problem 1 *must* choose D in Problem 2. Similarly, someone who chooses A in Problem 1 *must* choose C in Problem 2. Why this is so can be seen by rewriting the two problems as follows:

Problem 1*: Choose between

A*:	2400 with probability 0.66,	B*:	2400 with probability 0.66,
	0 with probability 0.01,		2400 with probability 0.34.
	2500 with probability 0.33;		

Problem 2*: Choose between

C*:	0 with probability 0.66,	D*:	0 with probability 0.66,
	0 with probability 0.01,		2400 with probability 0.34.
	2500 with probability 0.33;		

Note that $A*$ and $B*$ both contain the component '2400 with probability 0.66'. According to the independence axiom of expected utility theory, any preference between $A*$ and $B*$ should not be influenced by the nature of such a common component. In other words, we may substitute any other consequence for 2400 in the first rows of the descriptions of $A*$ and $B*$, and preference should remain unchanged. Suppose that we substitute 0 for 2400 in this way. Then $A*$ is translated into $C*$ and $B*$ is translated into $D*$. Thus if $A*$ is preferred to $B*$, then $C*$ must be preferred to $D*$; conversely, if $B*$ is preferred to $A*$, then $D*$ must be preferred to $C*$.

Repeated experiments have shown that, just as Allais conjectured, people do tend to choose contrary to expected utility theory in problems of this kind. This seems to be an instance of a more general pattern in people's attitudes to gambles. People seem to be unduly attracted (unduly, that is, in terms of expected utility theory) by small chances of good outcomes and unduly repelled by small chances of bad ones. Thus in Problem 1 of the Allais Paradox, people are repelled by the 0.01 chance of winning nothing if A is chosen. (Winning nothing would be a very bad outcome for someone who had turned down the certainty of 2400, and who had had a 0.99 chance of winning at least 2400.) In Problem 2, in contrast, both options offer relatively small chances of winning. In this context, risk-taking seems to have more appeal, and people are inclined to go for the smaller chance of the larger prize.

This pattern occurs in a number of different experimental observations. It is also found in the gambling market. It seems to be a universal feature of race course betting that the average returns from betting on favourites are significantly greater than those from betting on outsiders (see Thaler and Ziemba (1988) for a survey of this evidence). The most plausible explanation for this observation is that punters are disproportionately attracted by gambles which offer relatively large prizes with relatively low probability (that is, bets on outsiders); gambles offering relatively small prizes with relatively high probability (bets on favourites) are found less attractive. With a *pari mutuel* betting system, such a pattern of betting will automatically lead to greater average returns for bets on favourites. (The *pari mutuel* or totalisator system is one in which all stakes are pooled, and the pool, less some deduction to cover administrative costs, is divided among those people who bet on the winning horse, in proportion to the amounts they bet.)

The above description of the 'general pattern' behind the Allais Paradox has been made deliberately imprecise. There is as yet no single, generally accepted explanation of the paradox. Instead, there are a number of competing explanations: each sees the paradox as an instance of a different overall pattern of behaviour.

One view, particularly associated with Kahneman and Tversky (1979), is that the paradox arises out of the way in which people process information when making decisions. Information about probabilities tends to become distorted as it is processed: people tend to 'over-weight' small probabilities and 'under-weight' large ones, while recognizing certainties and impossibilities (that is, probabilities of 1 and 0) at their true values. The effect of this is to make the difference between 0.99 (the chance of winning at least 2400 on option A) and certainty seem greater than the difference between 0.33 (the chance of winning on option C) and 0.34 (the chance of winning on option D). In Kahneman and Tversky's *prospect theory*, this effect is modelled by introducing a 'weighting function' which translates probabilities into 'decision weights'. Individuals are then assumed to behave as though maximizing expected utility, but with decision weights substituted for probabilities.

This kind of explanation connects with the more general idea of *bounded rationality.* Departures from the theory of rational choice occur because of the limitations of human mental processes. Thus if we are to explain how people actually choose, we must investigate those processes: *a priori* reasoning about rational choice is not enough. We might expect to find people using many different processes when tackling complex decision-making problems, and if these processes involve simplifications and rules of thumb, we might then find many different kinds of violation of the theory of rational choice. This is the line taken by Kahneman and Tversky: their prospect theory incorporates a range of different 'information-processing' or bounded-rationality effects, of which the distortion of probabilities is only one.

This kind of approach can account for *framing effects*, in which people's responses to a choice problem depend on the way in which the problem is presented to them. An example of a framing effect is given in the adjacent box (□). Here there can be no question that the two groups of people are being presented with the same choice problem and are being given exactly the same information. But people respond differently according to whether they are led to think in terms of survival rates or mortality rates. The dangers of surgery seem greater if you compare '10 die' with 'none die' than if you compare '90 live' with '100 live'. In Kahneman and Tversky's terms, although the difference between a probability of 0.0 and a probability of 0.1 is equal to the difference between a probability of 0.9 and a probability of

[handwritten margin notes: But how does weighting take care of the qualitative aspect of prioritizing?]

SURGERY OR RADIATION?

McNeil *et al.* (1982) presented people with a hypothetical choice between two treatments for lung cancer: surgery and radiation. The following statistical information was given, in exactly this form:

> Surgery: Of 100 people having surgery 90 live through the post-operative period, 68 are alive at the end of the first year and 34 are alive at the end of five years.
> Radiation Therapy: Of 100 people having radiation therapy all live through the treatment, 77 are alive at the end of one year and 22 are alive at the end of five years.

Only 18 per cent of 247 respondents preferred radiation therapy. In contrast, 44 per cent of 336 repondents preferred radiation therapy when exactly the same information was presented in the following way:

> Surgery: Of 100 people having surgery 10 die during surgery or the post-operative period, 32 die by the end of the first year and 66 die by the end of five years.
> Radiation Therapy: Of 100 people having radiation therapy, none die during treatment, 23 die by the end of one year and 78 die by the end of five years.

Thus the advantages of surgery are perceived to be less significant when the information is presented in terms of mortality rates than when it is presented in terms of survival rates. Perhaps rather worryingly, this 'framing effect' was found to be just as marked when the problem was presented to a group of experienced physisicans as when it was presented to clinic patients.

1.0, the differences between the corresponding decision weights need not be equal.

The bounded-rationality approach does not challenge the *normative* status of the standard theory of rational choice. If the Allais Paradox results from the limited information-processing capacities of the human mind, then this pattern of behaviour might still be called irrational: it might still be one that a self-conscious person would wish to avoid. (Indeed, one important reason for studying the mental processes of human decision-making is to show us how to correct in-built biases.) However, some commentators have seen the Allais Paradox as revealing limitations in the theory of rational choice rather than in ordinary people's decision-making. On this view, people who choose option *B* and then option *C* may be acting perfectly rationally.

Allais (1979) himself takes this line. He argues that any gamble must be appraised *as a whole*: the value of one component of a gamble cannot necessarily be defined independently of the other components. To say this is to reject the independence axiom as a principle of rationality. Consider Allais's two problems when written in the form of Problems 1* and 2*. Notice that options *A** and *C** each contain a component '0 with probability 0.01'. The independence axiom requires, in effect, that this component should have the same subjective value in the two options. But why should we require this? Consider an analogy. The subjective value (or utility) of one component of a consumption bundle may depend on the nature of the rest of the bundle. (The utility of a washing machine may depend on the availability of electricity: the utility of a holiday in Scotland this year may depend on whether last year's holiday was spent in Scotland or Spain.) Such effects are taken into account in consumer theory. Why not in the theory of choice under uncertainty?

The usual answer is that the component parts of a consumption bundle are consumed *together*, whereas the component parts of a gamble are *mutually exclusive*. But this reply is not entirely convincing. The psychic significance of '0 with probability 0.01' may be very different as between gambles *A** and *C**. Someone who takes option *A** starts out with a 0.99 chance of winning 2400 or more. In this context, the possibility of winning nothing may be a source of unease or fear until the gamble is played out; if this possibility occurs, there may be intense disappointment. In contrast, someone who takes option *C** will start out with lower expectations, and so the possibility of winning nothing will tend to generate less fear and less potential for disappointment. More generally, the emotions of hope and fear, elation and disappointment can be understood as psychic relationships among the components of a gamble. The independence axiom excludes all such considerations from the domain of rational choice. Critics such as Allais argue that this is an arbitrary exclusion. *Are emotions rational?*

The implication of this critique of expected utility theory is that we should drop the independence axiom. If we keep the transitivity axiom, we shall still have a theory in which preference orderings can be defined over gambles. We may be able to give such a theory more predictive power by imposing additional restrictions which, unlike the independence axiom, are consistent with experimental observations. A number of theories of this kind have been proposed. Among the best-known are Quiggin's (1982) *anticipated utility theory*, Machina's (1982) *generalized expected utility theory* and Chew's (1983) *weighted utility theory*.

Yet another explanation of the Allais Paradox makes use of the concept of *regret*. Formal theories of the influence of regret on decision-making have been presented by Bell (1982) and by Loomes and Sugden (1982). Think again about the difference between winning nothing on Option *A* and winning nothing on option *C*. Suppose you choose option *A* in Problem 1, thus rejecting the certainty of 2400. And suppose you are unlucky and win

nothing. You will then know that, had you chosen differently, you would
have won 2400. This comparison between 'what is' and 'what might have
been' may give rise to the pain of regret. In contrast, suppose you choose
option C in Problem 2, and again suppose you win nothing. Then if the
random processes governing the gambles in C and D are independent of one
another, there is only a 0.34 chance that there is anything to regret: had you
chosen D, you would only have had a 0.34 chance of winning anything.
Thus the potential for regret is diluted in the second case. Because of considerations of this kind, someone who is averse to regret may choose B in
Problem 1 and C in Problem 2.

Notice that regret, like fear and disappointment, is a psychic relationship
between mutually exclusive outcomes. The difference is that regret is a relationship between the outcomes of *different* gambles (the gamble chosen and
the gamble rejected), whereas fear and disappointment are relationships
between different outcomes of the *same* gambles. Because regret is defined
across gambles, the subjective value of one gamble cannot be defined in isolation from other gambles: the value of what is chosen may depend on what
was rejected. This means that preferences that are influenced by regret need
not be transitive.

For example, imagine that a ball is to be drawn at random from an urn
containing equal numbers of blue, white and green balls. X, Y and Z are
three possible gambles, with the following pay-offs (in the currency of your
choice):

	Blue	White	Green
X	0	50	100
Y	100	0	50
Z	50	100	0

Suppose you are offered a choice between X and Y; Z is not on offer. X and
Y both offer the same probability distribution of pay-offs (that is, a 1/3
probability of winning 100, a 1/3 probability of winning 50, and a 1/3
probability of winning nothing). However, the potential for regret is different as between the two gambles. If you choose X, you have a 1/3 chance of
the intense regret of winning nothing when you might have won 100; if you
choose Y, you have a 2/3 chance of experiencing regret, but the regret will
be less intense. If you wish to avoid intense regret, you might prefer Y. But
now suppose that, instead, you are offered a choice between Y and Z, X not
being on offer. By exactly the same argument, an aversion to intense regret
may lead you to prefer Z. Finally, suppose that you are offered a choice
between Z and X. The same aversion to intense regret may lead you to prefer
X. Thus you might quite consistently choose Y in a straight choice between

X and *Y*, *Z* in a straight choice between *Y* and *Z*, and *X* in a straight choice between *Z* and *X*. *I'm utterly confused!*

Cycles of pairwise choices have in fact been observed in experiments. The phenomenon of *preference reversal* (see □) may be interpreted as an example. Preference reversals were first reported by Lichtenstein and Slovic (1971) and by Lindman (1971); they have since been found by many investigators.

According to the conventional theory of rational choice, anyone who confronts these problems should have some preference as between the two gambles: either you prefer *Q*, or you prefer *R*, or you are indifferent. If you prefer *Q*, then you should pick *Q* in the straight choice between the gambles; but you should also put a higher money value on *Q* than on *R*. Similarly, if

PREFERENCE REVERSAL

Consider these two gambles:

Gamble *Q*: 7/36 chance of winning 9.00, 29/36 chance of losing 0.50
Gamble *R*: 29/36 chance of winning 2.00, 7/36 chance of losing 1.00

As in the case of the Allais Paradox, pay-offs are to be understood as amounts of money, in whatever currency you wish to choose. *Q* and *R* are gambles on the number of a ball, to be drawn at random from a bingo cage. The balls in the cage are numbered 1–36, with prizes paid on the higher-numbered balls. Thus, for example, gamble *Q* produces a win of 9.00 win on balls 8–36 and a loss of 0.50 on balls 1–7.

Your first problem is to say which of the two gambles you would prefer to play, if given a choice between the two. Your next problem (which, in an experiment, would be given to you after some interval of time) is to say how much gamble *Q* is worth to you. Imagine that you have the right to play gamble *Q*, and then state the smallest sum of money which you would be willing to accept in exchange for the gamble. Your final problem is to say how much gamble *R* is worth to you.

In experiments of this kind, many people choose *R* in the straight choice, but put a higher money value on *Q*. The straight choices of such people appear to reveal a preference for *R* over *Q*, while their valuations appear to reveal the opposite preference – hence the term 'preference reversal'. (The example given here is taken from an experiment carried out by Grether and Plott (1979), with pay-offs in US dollars. There were 46 people in the experiment, each of whom was presented with six pairs of bets on the model of *Q* and *R*. This gave 276 observations. In 91 cases out of 276, the preferences revealed in straight choices were in the opposite direction to those revealed in valuations. Of these 91 preference reversals, 69 took the form in which *R* was chosen in the straight choice, but *Q* was given the higher valuation.)

you prefer *R* you should pick *R* in the straight choice and put a higher value on *R* than on *Q*. In fact, however, the preference that is revealed in the straight choice is often in the opposite direction to that revealed in the money valuations. More importantly, these reversals are predominantly in one direction. There is a tendency for people to pick *R* (the gamble for which the probability of winning is higher) in the straight choice, but to put the higher money value on *Q* (the gamble which offers the larger prize).

This may be thought of as a tendency for pairwise choices to cycle. Suppose, for example, that someone chooses *R* in the straight choice, values *Q* at 1.40 and values *R* at 1.10 – a typical case of preference reversal. If we take this person's replies at face value, we must infer that he is indifferent between gamble *R* and 1.10. If more money is preferred to less, he must prefer the certainty of, say 1.25 to gamble *R*. And since he is indifferent between gamble *Q* and 1.40, he must prefer gamble *Q* to the certainty of 1.25. But he also prefers gamble *R* to gamble *Q*, which completes the cycle. Cycles of this kind can be explained by regret theory (see Loomes, Starmer and Sugden, 1989).

Slovic and Lichtenstein (1983) offer an alternative explanation of preference reversal in terms of bounded rationality. They suggest that the mental processes that people bring to bear on choice problems are different from those that are used for valuation problems. When asked to *choose* between two gambles which (like *Q* and *R*) have similar expected money values, people tend to focus on the relative probabilities of winning, and to choose the gamble for which this probability is higher. In contrast, when asked to put a *money value* on a gamble people tend to use an 'anchor and adjustment' process: they first 'anchor' on the money value of the best outcome and then adjust this value downwards to allow for the probability of not winning. This way of processing information tends to generate high valuations for gambles which offer large prizes, even if the probability of winning is low. For this reason, gamble *Q* tends to be valued more highly than gamble *R*.

The Ellsberg Paradox (see □), first presented in Ellsberg (1961), is perhaps easier to explain than either the Allais Paradox or preference reversal. But the explanation challenges a fundamental principle of the standard theory of rational choice: that probabilities can be defined subjectively. Ellsberg conjectured that many people would choose option I in the first problem and option IV in the second. In the first problem, you know you have 30 chances out of 90 of winning if you choose option I, while with option II you do not know what the chance of winning is. Thus it may seem safer to go for option I. Similarly, you know that option IV gives you 60 chances out of 90 of winning, while with option III you do not know what the chance of winning is; so it may seem safer to go for option IV.

But look again at the choice between options I and II. You are being asked to choose between winning 100 in the event 'red' and winning 100 in the

THE ELLSBERG PARADOX

Suppose that you are shown an urn which contains 90 balls. Of these, 30 are red. The remaining 60 balls are some mixture of black and yellow, but you do not know what the mixture is. One ball is to be drawn at random from the urn. You are asked to choose one of two options: option I will give you 100 if a red ball is drawn, while option II will give you 100 if a black ball is drawn. (Once again, pay-offs are in money – the currency does not matter). This choice may be written as follows:

	Red	Black	Yellow
Option I	100	0	0
Option II	0	100	0

Which would you choose?

Now suppose, instead, that you are offered a different choice of options, defined in terms of the same draw of a ball from the same urn. You must choose one of Options III and IV:

	Red	Black	Yellow
Option III	100	0	100
Option IV	0	100	100

Which would you choose now?

If you chose options I and IV, ask yourself the following question: Which do you regard as more probable, that a red ball will be drawn or that a black ball will be drawn? If your answer is 'red', why did you choose option IV? If your answer is 'black', why did you choose option I? But you need not feel embarrassed about having made this pair of choices, because you are in good company. Ellsberg presented this pair of problems to a number of leading economists and decision theorists. Many of his respondents reported that they were inclined to choose options I and IV. Among these respondents was Leonard Savage, the author of what is perhaps the most elegant derivation of expected utility theory. Savage was well aware that this pattern of choice contravened one of the fundamental axioms of his own theory. With exemplary frankness, he reported that, even after careful reconsideration of the problem in the light of his theory, he would still want to choose I and IV (Ellsberg, 1961, p. 656).

event 'black'. It seems natural to say that your choice should be determined by your judgement as to which of the two events is more likely to occur. Theories of subjective probability – most notably, that of Savage (1954) – typically *define* probability so that it is revealed in choices of this kind (compare Samuelson's concept of revealed preference: see CONSUMER THEORY (2)). Thus if someone prefers option I to option II, she is deemed to attach a higher subjective probability to 'red' than to 'black'. However, by exactly the same argument, someone who prefers option IV to option III is deemed to attach a higher subjective probability to 'black or yellow' than to 'red or yellow', which implies that 'black' has a higher probability than 'red'. Thus the choice of I and IV generates a contradiction.

The standard theory of rational choice is based on a 'Bayesian' view of probability, in which the probability of an event, as judged by any given individual, is a statement of that person's degree of belief in the occurrence of that event. It is crucial for the standard theory that an individual can attach a subjective probability to any event, and that every belief about an event that is relevant for decision-making can be captured in the single dimension of 'probability'. (In some versions of expected utility theory, the existence of such probabilities is presupposed. In other versions, such as Savage's, it is implied by certain axioms concerning preferences.) The message of the Ellsberg Paradox is that beliefs about uncertainty *cannot* be reduced to a single dimension.

The person who prefers to bet on 'red' rather than on 'black' does not necessarily believe 'red' to be more probable. In one sense, she may attach a probability of 1/3 to each event; but she has more *confidence* in her belief that there is a 1/3 chance of drawing a red ball than in her corresponding belief about a black ball: or, as Ellsberg puts it, there is more *ambiguity* about the probability of drawing a black ball. It seems that many people are averse to ambiguity as well as to risk, and it is hard to argue that ambiguity aversion is any more irrational than risk aversion.

Newcomb's Problem (⌘) is yet another problem in which many people say they are inclined to choose contrary to the standard theory of rational choice. Newcomb's problem is an intriguing one, and raises some deep questions about rationality. However, the scenario (which includes a superintelligent being with the ability to predict people's choices with almost perfect accuracy) is too fantastic for the problem to be considered as a case of 'how people choose'.

The Status of Expected Utility Theory

How far do these experimental observations call expected utility theory into question? That depends on how the theory is interpreted. So far, it has been viewed as uncontroversial that expected utility theory has empirical content: that is, I have assumed that the theory excludes certain patterns of potentially observable behaviour. (Among the patterns excluded are those found in the Allais Paradox, preference reversal and the Ellsberg Paradox.) On the descriptive interpretation of expected utility theory, such behaviour, if observed, would count as evidence against the theory. On the normative interpretation, it would count as evidence of the irrationality of the person making the choices.

However, some people argue that the theory has no such empirical content. According to this view, the theory of rational choice is a set of formal principles concerning the relationship between propositions about preference or choice. The status of these principles is seen as being similar to that of the principles of mathematics or of formal logic: they are seen as *necessary* truths or tautologies, whose validity need not be, and cannot be, verified by observation. For example, the transitivity axiom might be interpreted as stating a logical property of the relation 'is more preferred than'. It is intrinsic to the concept of preference, it might be said, that the conjunction of '*A* is preferred to *B*' and '*B* is preferred to *C*' entails '*A* is preferred to *C*'.

What, then, are we to make of a case like that discussed on p. 42, where there are three gambles, *X*, *Y* and *Z*, and where (because of an aversion to intense regret) a person would choose *X* if faced with a straight choice between *X* and *Y*, *Y* if faced with a choice between *Y* and *Z*, and *Z* if faced with a choice between *Z* and *X*? The answer must be that, despite these choices, the person does not really *prefer* *X* to *Y*, *Y* to *Z*, and *Z* to *X*. One way of supporting this claim is to argue that '*X*', '*Y*' and '*Z*' are merely shorthand descriptions for complex options, and that, say, the *X* that is chosen in the choice between *X* and *Y* is not the same as the *X* that is rejected in the choice between *Z* and *X*. If, for example, the person has been influenced by thoughts of regret, then we might say that the choice that in shorthand is called a choice between *X* and *Y* is really between 'having *X*, knowing that *Y* (and only *Y*) has been rejected' and 'having *Y*, knowing that *X* (and only *X*) has been rejected'. Let us write the first of these two options as (*X*, *Y*) and the second as (*Y*, *X*). Then someone who prefers (*X*, *Y*) to (*Y*, *X*) and who prefers (*Y*, *Z*) to (*Z*, *Y*) is *not* committed by the transitivity axiom to preferring (*X*, *Z*) to (*Z*, *X*).

It is questionable, however, whether this kind of approach is compatible with the standard axioms of expected utility theory. As presented by Savage, for example, these axioms use the concept of a 'consequence' (or 'outcome') as a primitive. It is crucial for Savage's derivation of expected utility theory that a person has a preference over *every* pair of consequences. Thus if 'having *X*, knowing that *Y* (and only *Y*) has been rejected' and 'having *Z*, knowing that *Y* (and only *Y*) has been rejected' are to count as consequences, we must be able to attach a meaning to a preference between these two things. But such a preference cannot be interpreted as any kind of disposition to choose, since a choice between these two things is logically impossible. (To say that a person has the option of 'having X, knowing that Y (and only Y) has been rejected' is to say that he faces a pairwise choice between X and Y; if this is the choice he faces, then 'having Z, knowing that Y (and only Y) has been rejected' cannot be an option for him.) So if we are to say that the axioms of expected utility theory are necessary truths, we need to find an interpretation of 'preference' which divorces preference from choice.

One obvious possibility, of course, would be to go back to the traditional utilitarian approach of thinking in terms of pyschological sensations of pleasure. Then we might read 'X is preferred to Y' as 'X gives more pleasure than Y'. However, in the eyes of its founders, one of the main objects of the axiomatic theory of rational choice was to avoid the philosophical and psychological difficulties of utilitarianism; and so we must accept that experimental observations such as the Allais Paradox, preference reversal and the Ellsberg Paradox constitute violations of expected utility theory, as that theory is normally understood.

Nevertheless, some choice theorists profess not to be greatly concerned about these observations. Three lines of argument are commonly used to defend expected utility theory against the challenge from experimental investigations.

One line is to argue that expected utility theory is a normative theory. Then, clearly, observations of actual choices cannot constitute a direct challenge: the object of a normative theory is to tell people how they *ought* to choose (if they are to act rationally), and there need be no presumption that ordinary people always act in a fully rational way. But this response is appropriate only if the observed contraventions of the theory can be explained satisfactorily in terms of bounded rationality.

This is where mental experiments have a role. Take the Allais Paradox. Suppose that you are shown the two Allais problems and your immediate response is that you would choose B and C. You are then shown that these choices contravene the independence axiom. The nature of this axiom, and the reasons for thinking of it as a principle of rationality, are also explained to you. If this convinces you that your original choices were mistaken, then there is no challenge to the normative status of the independence axiom. But suppose, instead, that you still want to stick to your original choices, and you feel that you are able to give adequate reasons for them. Then perhaps it is the axiom and not your choices that are at fault. Perhaps the argument that it is irrational to contravene the axiom has overlooked some factor, present in the Allais Paradox, that really is relevant to the deliberations of a rational chooser. Thus experimental observations may present an indirect challenge to expected utility theory, even if that theory is interpreted normatively.

A second line of defence is to argue that the theory of rational choice is intended only as a building block for theories which predict the behaviour of people *in the aggregate*. In such theories the assumption of the perfectly rational individual has a status similar to that of frictionless surfaces in mechanics, or of a flat Earth in the surveying of small areas; it is not supposed to be literally true, but it allows us to make predictions which are good enough for our purposes. This would be an adequate response if the deviations from expected utility theory found in experiments were very minor (such as the errors resulting from assuming a flat Earth when surveying the plot for a building), or if they were random (so that they could be expected to cancel out in aggregate behaviour). But large and systematic deviations, such as those found in investigations of the Allais Paradox, cannot be talked away so easily. If individual choices deviate from the theory in such a way, there must be a presumption that aggregate behaviour will also deviate. *Cartwright.*

A final line of defence, common among economists, is to deny the relevance of experimental observations because they have not been gathered from 'real' choices. But in what sense are these choices not real? Some critics claim that the monetary pay-offs offered in experiments are too small to motivate people. But it is now quite common for experimental subjects to have the chance of winning sums of around £20 (US$ 40). It is true that this is small relative to the sums involved in buying a house or a car; but an enormous volume of consumer spending is on individual items which cost much less than £20, and consumer theory has always been supposed to apply to such spending. And, of course, the claim that people would not be prone to, say, the Allais Paradox when very large sums of real money were at stake is no more than a hypothesis: there is no evidence to support it. If (as Allais did) we ask people how they think they would behave when the stakes were large, they tend to report that they think they would contravene expected utility theory. It is pure faith to believe that if the stakes really were large, people would behave according to the theory. Other critics point to the one-off nature of most experimental decisions, and suggest (another article of faith) that when people face the same decision repeatedly, they will learn to behave more rationally. But, again, much consumer spending has a one-off character, and this has not usually been thought to make consumer theory inapplicable.

It is easy to affect unsurprise after the event. Many of the findings of experimental investigations have come as a great surprise to economists, and it is only with the benefit of hindsight that they have set about drawing frontiers between the domain of experiments and that of 'real' economic behaviour. We should always be suspicious of attempts to isolate theories from evidence that might refute them.

Robert Sugden

Further Reading

Schoemaker (1982), Sugden (1986a), Appleby and Starmer (1987), Machina (1987) and Weber and Camerer (1987) provide accessible surveys of the experimental evidence on choice under uncertainty, and of the attempts that have been made to develop theories to explain this evidence. For a more wide-ranging survey of experimental work in economics, see Roth (1988). The methodological discussion towards the end of the present chapter is developed more fully in Sugden (1991).

4

Risk, Ignorance and Imagination

This chapter is about how people represent the future when formulating their choices. Is uncertainty about the future the same as calculable risk and mathematical probability? Is it ignorance of the facts? Or is it a matter for our imagination? The agenda is set with characteristic elegance by George Shackle who asks 'whether it is better to treat life as though it were an examination paper in arithmetic, where the problems have right answers if only we can work them out, or whether life is better looked on as the artist's canvas whereon, with such pigments as he possesses, he may freely attempt whatever picture he can imagine' (Shackle, 1955, p. 38). The answer determines how we view the act of mediation between present and future, which is how I define entrepreneurship. It also has profound implications for the role of government. In passing, I shall also touch on the deeper issue of whether we are driven by a single logic that leads us down an immutable path determined by Mother Nature herself, or whether we have the power to create our own future.

I begin with the 'arithmetic' view, which is dominant in the social sciences. It is a view which has become known as 'neoclassical' in economics, and that is the term I shall use here. The key ideas have already been developed (see RATIONALITY (1) and CONSUMER THEORY (2)) and so I can be selective in outlining them. The neoclassical view endows individuals with three sets of information which, together, are sufficient fully to describe the future. First, people are supposed to know with certainty all the conceivable, potential consequences of their actions. For instance, contemplating the purchase of a ticket for a football match, you know all the possible results (your team might win, lose or draw), all the possible scores (from nil upwards for each team), and anything else that might affect your pleasure at the game (the match might be dull or cut-and-thrust, different types of person might sit next to you, and so on). Combinations of these possibilities are called states of nature. Second, people must also know how every possible state of nature (for example, your team loses 6–0, it is pouring with rain and the man next to you has halitosis) would affect their utility given each possible action they might choose (for example, go to the match or stay at home). The third set of information consists of a **probability distribution** (⯑), or set of likelihood weights, attached to each of the states of nature. For example, you assess that there is a 1 per cent chance that your team will win 4–1 in glorious sunshine, and that you will sit next to a quiet old lady.

Given all this information, we can proceed to argue over how rational people will process it (see HOW PEOPLE CHOOSE (3)). But where does this knowledge come from? Do we have it intuitively, is it given to us, do we search for it, do we stumble across it, or do we make it up ourselves? Consider the second set of information, relating to the utilities attached to potential states of nature in the light of alternative actions. In the neoclassical view, individuals have their own tastes which can be summarized as indifference curves (see CONSUMER THEORY (2)), and there is no need to specify where they came from. It may be genetic, cultural or random – the source of private tastes is not central (but see the discussion of advertising below). Individuals are the best judges of their own utility, and so individuals are allowed the freedom to imagine the consequences of their actions in any state of nature. But they are not free to imagine what future events might unfurl. All possible states of nature are determined by Mother Nature and there is no room to imagine anything else. The world is as it is or, more precisely, as it will be, and our imagination can do nothing to change it. Of course, there may be potential states of nature that we have failed to perceive, but since we have failed to perceive them, they do not, in the neoclassical view, affect our decision-making. We make no allowance for events that are beyond our knowledge.

Next, consider the source of the probabilities which we attach to the potential states of nature. For some straightforward, clearly specified problems, which are faced repeatedly, we are able to attach objective actuarial probabilities (that is, they are determined by Mother Nature). Although the roll of an unbiased die is not precisely predictable, we do know that there is a one in six chance that any specified number will come up. For simple problems of actuarial risk, we may have such objective information readily available to us. More often, though, the best we can start with is an initial guess, sometimes called a 'prior'. This guess forms the basis for subjective probabilities which can be used to map out the expected future in much the same way as objective probabilities. Beyond this suggestion, there is less agreement within the broad neoclassical view. To some, prior probability assessments are, like tastes, part of individual personality, and social scientists can have little to say about where they come from. They are simply a personal appraisal of the likelihood of various events. To others, if two rational people are given exactly the same information (for example, about how the history of similar problems evolved in the past), then they must logically come up with exactly the same objective priors: there can be no discretion left to personal tastes when it comes to contemplating what the independently minded Mother Nature will do in the future.

There is also disagreement about how people revise their priors in the light of new information. For instance, a range of estimating techniques might be used. However, there is a powerful school of thought which holds the view that there is only one rational way of updating initial guesses, this being to use **Bayes's rule** (⬚). Combining Bayesian learning with objectively based priors effectively eliminates the subjectivity, or personality, from subjective probability. This particularly mechanistic view of the world is known as the Harsanyi Doctrine, and although it has its attractions as a theory of rationality, it can hardly be said to represent the way most people actually picture the future. The general neoclassical claim, then, is that people act as though they attach subjective probabilities to potential events. Although this seems quite plausible, the evidence on systematic biases in the way most people – even trained statisticians in their unguarded moments – assess and revise probabilities is too strong to place too much emphasis on objectivity and formal statistical theory (Tversky and Kahneman, 1974). For example, direct observation of a motor accident will have a much greater impact on our assessment of the dangers of driving than would reading a graphic account in the newspaper. For further discussion of the difference between objective and subjective risk, see **risk and uncertainty** (⬚).

Given this neoclassical vision of how we represent the future, what is the role of the entrepreneur, the mediator between present and future? The word 'entrepreneur' is taken from the French verb *entreprendre*, to undertake, and the word 'undertaker' was used until the mid-eighteenth century to mean anyone who undertook a business venture. Around that time, the figurative meaning was eased out of common usage by the graphic funereal job description with which the English word is now indelibly associated. Nevertheless, the entrepreneur as the undertaker of a project remains a reasonable description of his neoclassical role. In neoclassical economics, he is a factor of production, and his purpose is to take optimizing decisions. Perhaps he has a talent for implicitly solving complex mathematical problems, or even for having more accurate probability estimates. But he is a rather dull fellow, who needs no imagination because his decision-making is unaffected by unconceived possibilities. In fact, his decision-making is qualitatively identical to that of the shopper choosing between apples and oranges, although the magnitude of the consequences of his actions may be greater. In politics, the neoclassical entrepreneur might organise a political party or pressure group, he might carefully choose the order of AGENDAS (17) so as to maximize the chances of his policy being adopted, but he would not creatively introduce new issues into the agenda, issues that others had not previously perceived as possibilities.

All this might suggest a very static view of the future, but that would be misleading. The neoclassical vision is flexible enough to accommodate change from at least three sources. First, the act of saving and accumulation increases wealth over time, and this opens up new opportunities for exploitation. Second, it is possible to invest in search behaviour to seek out more information from Mother Nature's book of blueprints (see **search theory** (🔲)). Third, new opportunities might arrive like manna from Heaven. These three can be illustrated by the entrepreneurship exercised by Robinson Crusoe, fishing alone on his desert island. Initially he catches fish by hand, but what vision of the future is it that enables him to use a fishing rod by the end of next week? Did he always know that the rod technology existed, but it took time to implement because other necessary tasks took up much of his day? Did he always perceive a range of possibilities (such as throwing rocks, throwing a spear, making a net, and so on), attach probabilities to their likely success and engage in research and development activity to find the most efficient? Or did the idea come to him in a dream one night? The first two sit very neatly in the neoclassical framework and are central to modern theories of economic growth and technological progress. The third is something of a *deus ex machina* in the neoclassical world, designed to explain anything that does not fit into the view that one can envisage the full set of possible states of nature. However, this uncomfortable source of new knowledge for the neoclassical view is central to the Austrian vision.

The Austrian school, including von Mises, Hayek and Kirzner, has emphasized the importance of what we do not know, our ignorance, rather than what we do know, our knowledge. It is beyond the comprehension of any one person to have complete knowledge about all possible forms that the future might take. Individuals can only discover pieces of knowledge and reduce their ignorance. The word 'knowledge' is used in place of information to emphasize that facts, not probabilities, are being discovered. When someone becomes sufficiently convinced that she has pieced together enough of Nature's jigsaw to establish that an opportunity exists, then she will act to exploit that opportunity. This is the Austrian role of entrepreneurship, and it is something that everyone does to a greater or lesser extent. It does not consist of calculation, but of being alert to new knowledge and acting on it. A shopper is being entrepreneurial when she finds a cheap source of oranges on a particular market stall. Similarly, an entrepreneur observes that apples are selling for £1 in Norwich and £2 in London, so she buys in Norwich to sell at a profit in London. Notice that there is no probabilistic calculation involved. Either she knows that this is a good idea or she does not. It all depends on how alert she has been in putting together different bits of knowledge (see □).

There is no reason why these ideas cannot be applied to politics. A politician might become convinced that the leader of his party has become unpopular and that the time is right to bid for the leadership. He is aware that this might meet resistance, because other people do not have his exact knowledge of the general mood; but that is why he is prepared to bid now, and they are not. He is ready to act entrepreneurially. Compare this with the neoclassical view that leadership candidates weigh up the chances of victory and differ in their conclusions only to the extent that they have different subjective probabilities attached to success. To the Austrian school, other potential candidates may not even have thought of the prospect of a change of leader – they may remain ignorant of the possibilities.

One important fact that the Austrian school emphasizes that we do know is that something we had never thought of might happen. When assessing the future, then, we have to make an allowance for the fact that we are ignorant of many possible states of the world, and not just of their probabilities of occurring. We, therefore, have to make decisions on this basis, and remain alert to the discovery of knowledge. The Austrian entrepreneur is much more centrally dynamic than her neoclassical cousin. Her function is to bring about change. For instance, her actions change the knowledge of others, not

ENTREPRENEURSHIP

The perfect business is one in which the entrepreneur, with minimal overheads, stands in the middle and rakes in money from both sides.

It was achieved by a *louche* acquaintance of mine in the 1960s who provided prestigious hotels with book-matches at a reasonable price, and received rather more than this from the companies which paid him to distribute these matches (with their messages) to people of taste and distinction.

Similar, though short-term, success was achieved recently by an East Anglian milkman who charged some American airmen £10 to effect introductions to nice girls at an adjacent college for young ladies – and then persuaded the girls to pay £2 each to receive their letters of assignation.

The judiciary took a less enlightened view of his enterprise, though I think that the school, in failing to acquaint its pupils of their market value, cannot be allowed to emerge without blame.

(Clement Freud, *The Sunday Times*, 3 September 1989)

by inducing them to revise their prior probabilities, but by extending the range of possibilities that they are aware of. A nice example of this contrast is in understanding the motivation behind advertising. The neoclassical view of advertising is that consumers are being informed about the product. It is not a question of changing tastes, but of giving information that will modify a potential consumer's beliefs about the characteristics of the product (that is, the state of nature). In general, this information may be true or false, but its function is to revise prior beliefs. To the Austrian, however, advertising is a way of 'relieving the consumer of the necessity to be his own entrepreneur' (Kirzner, 1973, p. 136). It is a way of alerting people to their own tastes. For this purpose, brash, apparently meaningless advertisements can often be more effective than could clinical, informative advertisements. Amongst all the distractions of life, consumers need to be alerted to unsuspected opportunities.

Both the neoclassical and Austrian views share a common thought that Mother Nature has determined the way the future looks, and our problem is to either estimate or discover her secrets. Austrian lay much greater stress on the importance of the discovery process than do neoclassicals on estimation. For Austrians, alertness is crucial to the dynamics of the economy, and this makes economic events particularly sensitive to current choices. Nevertheless, it is not for us to create the future, but to seek it out. George Shackle disagrees, arguing that the future is indeterminate. Real decision 'is creative and is able to be so through the freedom which uncertainty gives for the creation of *unpredictable hypotheses*' (Shackle, 1961, p. 6). It is our own inspiration, not Mother Nature, that determines the important possibilities that might unfold in the future (see 'Reason and Imagination' □). Shackle is fierce in his critique of the use of probability. Important decisions relate to isolated events for which probability provides no useful guide – either something will happen or something else will. We will either have chosen rightly or wrongly, but it is nonsense to attach a mathematical weighting to the alternatives, because only one can ever be true (see **expected value** (🗊)). Even when events are repeated, the use of probability is misguided because the act of repetition changes the experience and significance of events: 'Part of the satisfaction we get by imagination of any contemplated act is the thrill of its success, if that should come. But this thrill cannot be the same on any later occasion as it was the first time' (Shackle, 1955, p. 6). The box on 'Probability and Uncertainty' (□ p. 58) illustrates the point.

So how do people choose in this world where the future is waiting to be created by our own imagination? Surely we can imagine what we like? Although this is true, Shackle argues that not all images will have the same power to stimulate the decision-maker's mind. In particular, there are two important constraints. First is the capacity of ideas to arouse interest and release mental energies. Thus, we may reject certain dull or unfashionable

REASON AND IMAGINATION

Economics has been defined as the logic of choice. Amongst what, then, are men free to choose? Not amongst situations or events which exist or occur in some objective reality, for when something is actual the time is too late for choosing something else. Not amongst perfectly specified situations or events whose occurrence in some future is somehow guaranteed, for there is no such perfect knowledge and no such guarantee. Men choose amongst their own imaginations of what rival available policies will bring them. Each conceived policy or course of action will in general provide a basis, more or less firm, for many different imagined outcomes. Who knows whether, in seeking to list such outcomes, a man is wholly constrained by his experience and his present circumstances, so that these thoughts are determinate and, if we knew enough, wholly explicable by reference to the past? If they are not capable of being thus wholly explained away, there is room, in this process of listing rival imagined outcomes of a policy, for both *freedom* and *reason*: freedom in creating the objects amongst which there is choice, viz. the bundles of rival outcomes, one bundle for each available policy; and *reason* in choosing amongst these bundles and thus amongst these policies.

Economists have said that their subject is about reason, and some of them have developed it by reason alone from a brief and simple list of axioms taken for granted or even declared to be self-evidently true. But almost none of them have said that their subject is concerned with imagination.

(Shackle, 1966, p. ix)

thoughts and promote those that are more exciting or fearful (see **cognitive dissonance'** (🔑)). Second is the potential surprise attached to the imagined outcome actually arising. Shackle emphasizes that surprise is quite different from probability. If you were to roll two dice and add up the dots, you might score any number between two and twelve. Any such number would be equally unsurprising, but a total of seven is six times more probable than a total of two. Certain imagined outcomes gain ascendency in our thoughts because they blend an impressive combination of high interest and low potential surprise. Shackle goes on to argue that since the mind can picture only one such scenario at a time, we begin to whittle away at our imagination until only the two most stimulating remain, one good and one bad, as we switch between our more optimistic and pessimistic thoughts. We create these dual pictures for each action we could take, and choose the action that creates the most attractive combination of images.

PROBABILITY AND UNCERTAINTY

In his novel *The Widows of the Magistrate*, Keith West tells how certain Chinese officials once plotted rebellion against their Emperor. The brief passage that I am going to reproduce describes the thoughts of a certain sentry, who had to decide whether to obey his immediate superior, the treacherous Captain of the Guard, or to stand alone against the rebels in loyal defence of the Emperor's representative, the Lady Hibiscus:

> In the room above, where the great drum stood, the sentry named Kwong Hui was testing the stacked bows of mulberry wood and setting the arrows in order.
>
> 'I am a man who seizes opportunity', he told the admiring women and the sleeping children.
>
> 'If I obey the Captain of the Guard, two things may happen. Either the rebellion succeeds, and I remain a soldier in the guard, or the rebellion fails, when I lose my head. Whereas if I obey the Lady Hibiscus, two things may happen. Either the rebellion succeeds, and I lose my head, or the rebellion fails, when I shall receive rewards quite beyond my imagination to conceive. Now of these four possibilities, the last only attracts me. So I shall strive to hold this tower unentered, as long as is possible, until the arrival of help from elsewhere. That is the course of wisdom, as well as the course of courage, and I am deficient in neither wisdom nor courage.'

This eminently wise and sensible decision, reached with such incisive logic, might not have been so readily attained had the sentry been acquainted with the theory of probability. For then he might have argued thus: 'I find in the record of history a thousand cases similar to my own, wherein the person concerned decided upon treachery, and in only four hundred of these cases the rebellion failed and he was beheaded. On balance, therefore, the advantage seems to lie with treachery, provided one does it often enough.'

Having one's head cut off is, for the person concerned, rather final. Had the sentry decided to support the rebellion, he might have had time, just before the axe fell, to reflect that he would never, in fact, be able to repeat his experiment a thousand times, and that thus the guidance given him by actuarial considerations had proved illusory.

(Shackle, 1949, p. 161)

On this radical subjectivist view, we create our own futures by choosing between imaginations and then acting accordingly. Consequently, the role of the entrepreneur is to provide the imagination for the important decisions. And the role of advertising is to create tastes by stimulating the consumer's own imagination (Littlechild, 1986). Thus, a Coca Cola advertisement does not inform about the thirst-quenching value of the drink, nor does it alert people to its existence; but it creates an image that people can savour every bit as much as the taste. Without advertising, people's appreciation of 'a Coke' would be quite different.

At this point, you might accept that there is some truth in each view of how people represent the future when formulating their choices. Few would disagree with this limited statement. But passions are aroused when it comes to assessing the relative importance of each. Since it is not immediately obvious why these apparently esoteric arguments are so fundamentally important, I conclude this short chapter with a sketch of some implications of each view for the general principle of government intervention in individual decision-making.

If economic decisions are formulated preponderantly in the neoclassical way, then it is possible to argue, following Kenneth Arrow and Gerard Debreu, that provided that there exists a complete set of competitive markets, then unfettered free competition is in a precise sense an economic system which maximizes efficiency. The precise sense is that it satisfies **Pareto optimality** (🖳). The general argument is set out in more detail in ANARCHIC ORDER (12), but one detail is worth elaborating here. A complete set of markets does not simply mean that apples and oranges must be available at a competitive price. The optimality theorems require much more. There must also be contingency markets in which, for example, people who are worried about the future apple crop can buy future apples from those willing to take the risk. Such markets may be superfluous for most consumers, but farmers might have strong reasons to want them. In fact, many contingency markets do exist in capitalist systems, in the form of insurance and stock markets. For example, the apple farmer can pay a small premium in return for a larger sum of money that is payable only if certain states of the world occur (such as a late frost or a drought). This is equivalent to the farmer buying future apples with delivery conditional on certain adverse states being chosen by Mother Nature. Alternatively, he could sell shares in his farm and pay dividends only if there is a reasonable crop. This is equivalent to selling future apples with delivery conditional on favourable states of the world. Where such contigency markets exist and are competitive, they ensure efficient risk-spreading. But very often they fail to exist or are non-competitive. This may, for example, be because insurance companies worry that farmers will not properly irrigate their crops once they are insured against drought. This problem, known as moral hazard, and the institutional response to it, are explored more fully in ORGANIZATIONS (10). Thus, the neoclassical representation of the future provides a remarkably deep insight into the institutions of capitalism, and their limitations. This, in turn, provides a firm foundation for a policy of carefully targeted intervention in markets which are either not competitive or which would otherwise fail to exist (see PLANNING (16)).

Even such a cautious statement is vehemently challenged by those who believe that the Austrian view is what drives all important decision-making. If different people have discovered different pieces of knowledge, then there is no way that any single person or group of civil servants could act omnipotently to improve the allocation of resources. If an entrepreneur in pursuit of personal profit has not discovered a valuable market opportunity, why should a salaried employee do any better? And if the market already exists but is generating monopoly profits, then government intervention could only be harmful, because profits are crucial as a signal for entrepreneurs to be alert to an opportunity. The function of profits is not so much to reward past effort as to attract future enterprise. In an Austrian school world, the suppression of profits by government intervention inevitably results in stagnation and, in Hayek's graphic words, leads us down the road to serfdom.

What if the world is in the hands of Shackle's radical subjectivist decision-makers? The box on 'Animal Spirits' (□) gives Keynes's view. We are vulner-

ANIMAL SPIRITS

Even apart from the instability due to speculation, there is the instability due to the characteristic of human nature that a large proportion of our positive activities depend on spontaneous optimism rather than on a mathematical expectation, whether moral or hedonistic or economic. Most, probably, of our decisions to do something positive, the full consequences of which will be drawn out over many days to come, can only be taken as a result of animal spirits – of a spontaneous urge to action rather than inaction, and not as the outcome of a weighted average of quantitative benefits multiplied by quantitative probabilities. Enterprise only pretends to itself to be mainly actuated by the statements in its own prospectus, however candid and sincere. Only a little more than an expedition to the South Pole, is it based on an exact calculation of benefits to come. Thus if the animal spirits are dimmed and the spontaneous optimism falters, leaving us to depend on nothing but a mathematical expectation, enterprise will fade and die; – though fears of loss may have a basis no more reasonable than hopes of profit had before.

. . . human decisions affecting the future, whether personal or political or economic, cannot depend on strict mathematical expectation, since the basis for making such calculations does not exist; and . . . it is our innate urge to activity which makes the wheels go round, our rational selves choosing between the alternatives as best we are able, calculating where we can, but often falling back for our motive on whim or sentiment or chance.

(Keynes, 1936, Book 4, ch. 12)

able to fleeting changes of mood that might make entrepreneurs stop in their tracks simply because they imagined something different, or because just one entrepreneur became more pessimistic and his actions influenced the imaginations of the others. The economy is like a kaleidoscope, holding its ephemeral pattern for a short while before collapsing to emerge again in a new shape. The government's role in this kaleidoscopic world must be to stabilize confidence, avoid swings of mood and nurture creativity.

You are free to choose whether the future is best characterized as neo-classical risk, Austrian ignorance or Shackelian imagination. But you can be sure that your choice has important political as well as economic implications.

Bruce Lyons

Further Reading

Further implications of the three views developed in this chapter are clearly and concisely set out in Littlechild (1986). The neoclassical view is predominant throughout the economics literature and Arrow (1963b) is a classic application to government policy on health insurance. The foundations of subjective probability theory are only available in journals and very advanced texts, but the ambitious reader could try Kreps (1990). The Austrian views on entrepreneurship and advertising are elaborated in Kirzner (1973), and the wider economic and political issues are developed in Hayek (1944, 1978). The characterization of Austrian views in this chapter is largely based on the work of Kirzner, and many who would claim to be Austrians would veer towards Shackle on many issues. Shackle has written numerous books about imagination and choice, and the reader could dip into any of those mentioned in this chapter.

5

Homo economicus, Homo sociologicus

The terms *Homo economicus* and *Homo sociologicus* refer to two ways of conceiving human action, and hence two modes of explanation for social, economic and political behaviour. *Homo economicus* is an instrumentally rational and calculating seeker of preference satisfaction. He is the figure who typically appears in neoclassical economic theory as a maximizer of utility (see RATIONALITY (1)). The sources of this utility need not be selfish, in the sense that *Homo economicus* is always seeking his own advantage. On the contrary, he may be altruistic in the sense that the utility of others enters his utility calculation, but it must always be true that *Homo economicus* acts on his own preferences. As Marx sarcastically, but accurately, pointed out the paradigmatic figure for *Homo economicus* is Robinson Crusoe. Marx noted that Crusoe's situation, at least before the arrival of Man Friday, is indisputably an individualist one, and since necessity compels him to apportion his time between different kinds of work, Crusoe needs to calculate the relative effort he devotes to different ends and, having rescued a watch, ledger, pen and ink from the wreck begins to keep a set of books 'like a good Englishman' (Marx, 1867, p. 170). Instrumental, calculating behaviour in relation to the attainment of one's own ends is the essence of *Homo economicus* (and Marx implies the appropriate mind-set for members of the nation that first achieved capitalist industrialization).

In theories that use the model of *Homo economicus* extensively, most obviously neoclassical economics and rational choice accounts of politics, the emphasis is upon the way in which individual agents work out the consequences of their preferences over alternative outcomes in a context in which other individuals have different and conflicting preferences over those outcomes. The elaborated theories of markets and collective choice (see ANARCHIC ORDER (12) and SOCIAL CHOICE (13)) take individual preferences as given, and consider how preferences are aggregated within specified institutional arrangements. No attention is paid to the source of these preferences, or the extent to which they may be modified in the light of reflection and argument. Moreover, the assumption of maximizing is treated axiomatically: individuals are assumed to wish to achieve as high a point as they can on their scale of preference within the circumstances in which they find themselves. Given this account of motivation, it is hardly surprising that the main activity of *Homo economicus* is to calculate preference satisfaction within the available freedom of manoeuvre.

One way in which to introduce the figure of *Homo sociologicus* is to investigate how this freedom of manoeuvre might be bounded by the existence of others in society. Within the formulation of *Homo economicus*, the bounds are usually constituted by the prevailing technology in any economy and by the preferences of others. The conjoining of these two sets of conditions prescribes what it is possible for *Homo economicus* to achieve as a feasible outcome. Yet there is another constraint on human action, namely norms, and the associated sociological concept of a role. Roles are constituted by the expectations that others in a society have of an individual's behaviour in a given situation, so that a role may be defined as 'a typified response to a typified expectation' (Berger, 1966, p. 112; Emmet, 1966, pp. 138–66). In other words, roles encode norms and conformity to norms becomes a motive of behaviour.

In one version of *Homo sociologicus*, therefore, the appropriate motto of action is, to use Bradley's (1927, p. 163) quaint but accurate phrase, 'my station and its duties'. *Homo sociologicus* lives according to rules, roles and relations. As *Homo sociologicus* grows up, he must undergo rites of passage in the transition from boyhood to manhood, having been socialized into the appropriate norms of behaviour. At work he will need to adjust to the division of labour, and when he falls ill he does not simply suffer physical malfunctioning but also adopts the sick role. Politically he adopts the attitudes appropriate to someone with his education, occupation, social status and place of abode. Should *Homo sociologicus* turn out to be a woman (a relatively late but important twist to the intellectual story), she will find that her education and socialization will have inducted her into roles and relationships that systematically construct the feminine role she is to play. *haha!*

An understanding of human action as behaviour in accordance with norms involving the performance of roles has a number of consequences. The first of these is that individual preferences become of diminishing importance in understanding the behaviour of persons in society, and even the limited freedom of manoeuvre of *Homo economicus* disappears. In Mead's (1934, pp. 135–226) theory, for example, the genesis of the self is interpreted as the discovery of society and the self is construed as being socially constituted. One significant implication of this way of thinking is that those who are victims of prejudice tend to internalize the identity given to them by their oppressors, unless there are other sources of communal support available to sustain counter-identities. Activities of 'consciousness-raising' groups among women, gays and members of ethnic minorities provide an example of a response to such identity-forming prejudice. Their task is to provide the alternative sources of social support for creating and sustaining identities that a wider society denies to some groups.

One natural development of this approach is to stress that interpretation is always involved in acting in accordance with norms. On this account individuals are players of roles with socially constituted understandings of themselves, but their role performance is mediated through their understanding of the norms and conventions that govern their society. In this approach individuals are seen not simply as the bearers of socially determined processes but, instead, as involved actively in the reproduction of their social life through their appropriation of meaning. How much creativity is allowed in this process of reproducing social life through a reinterpretation of meanings is a matter for dispute within this tradition. Some, such as Schutz (1973, pp. 7–10), stress the taken-for-granted quality of the meanings embodied in social life; while others, such as Goffman (1968, 1969) bring out the possibility of individual manipulation and reworking of these meanings by individuals who are able to distance themselves from their roles.

A second possible theoretical development implicit in the role model of human action is the construction of a theory in which the basic units of account are collective entities rather than individual motives. If individuals are conceived as players of roles in which their personal identities are constituted by the roles they occupy, then the focus of theoretical attention can be on the set of roles contained in society rather than the individuals occupying those roles. Roles may therefore be seen as part of a social system, whose elements are assigned certain functions in the maintenance of the whole. From this holist perspective, the functionality of roles becomes the key to understanding patterns of behaviour (Emmet, 1958, pp. 12–105). Even conflict can be assigned a social function, and group disputes can be seen as playing a part by integrating persons in a social system (Coser, 1956).

Despite these differences between functionalist and interpretative accounts of *Homo sociologicus*, both may be said to be distinguished from *Homo economicus* by a stress on the social notion of norms rather than the individualistic concept of preferences. The contrast between norms and preferences simplifies and exaggerates for the purposes of exposition, but not extravagantly. In sphere after sphere of social life, interesting phenomena attract putative explanations based on these two models: crime is seen as deviance or as the rational calculation of opportunity costs; voting is seen as a function of social position or as a rational choice of candidates; educational drop-outs are seen as conforming to a culture of poverty, or making a rational calculation about the relevance of further qualifications to their future career prospects; and strikes are viewed as a consequence of poor industrial relations or as a response to the tax-benefit opportunities available to strikers.

There is one other contrast between *Homo economicus* and *Homo sociologicus* which I mention, largely so that it can be dismissed. This is a supposed historical contrast between different types of society, captured well in Maine's (1880, p. 170) remark that the development of modern society represents the movement from status to contract. On this account precapitalist societies represent the realm of ascribed status in which social mobility is low and conformity to collective norms is high. By contrast, capitalist societies represent the triumph of individualism, with persons bound to one another by the free choice of contract rather than the ascribed position of role. This distinction between pre-capitalist and capitalist societies is widely canvassed and underlies attempts (such as that of Macpherson, 1962) to interpret the contractarian political thought of Hobbes and Locke as instances of a rising ideology of 'possessive individualism'. Its main problem, as Macfarlane (1978) has pointed out, is that in England many of the relevant marks of capitalist modernity date back to at least the twelfth century: land was in individual, not family, ownership; there was an extensive market in land and agricultural commodities; rates of social and geographical mobility were high; and there is evidence of contractual elements suffusing the relationship between parents and children. Rather than seeing status and contract as modes of social relationship distinguishing successive societies, we should see them instead as permanently possible forms of social organization. This, as we shall see, makes it especially difficult to know when it is appropriate to use the model of *Homo economicus* as distinct from the model of *Homo sociologicus*.

Economic Models and Social Interests

It would be fair to say that in recent years the economic model of human action has been given a pretty good run for its money outside the sphere of market exchange where it most naturally has a place. Consider some of the following examples. Halsey, Heath and Ridge (1980) seek to explain the inverse relationship between social class and length of schooling as a rational response by working-class children to limited career opportunities. In a similar vein, Pateman (1988) cites the lower professional qualifications of women as a rational response to gender discrimination and patriarchy in the economy. In moral philosophy, Gauthier (1986) has sought to establish a theory of social justice on an account of rational bargaining between individuals. Becker notoriously attempted to extend strict economic logic into personal relationship with a treatise on the family, whose purpose was 'to analyze marriage, births, divorce, division of labour in households, prestige, and other non material behaviour with the tools and frameworks developed for material behaviour' (Becker, 1976, p. ix). Finally, in political science, the discipline that in terms of its subject-matter is closest to economics, the adoption of economic logic has been most complete, as any copy of the *American Political Science Review* of the past decade will testify. Behind this flourishing of the economic paradigm for the new normal science of politics, there stand the pathbreaking works of Downs (1957), Riker (1962), Riker and Ordeshook (1973), Olson (1965) and Hirschman (1970). Whatever else he may have done in the past few years, *Homo economicus* has come out of the closet.

The use of the economic model resembles the process that Kuhn (1970) describes as 'normal science'. Normal science is characterized, on Kuhn's account, by the dominance of a particular theoretical paradigm. Paradigms order and structure knowledge, providing a series of tests about what counts as valid or invalid. However, since theory and observation never entirely coincide, there will always be anomalies within any theoretical scheme. On the Kuhnian account of normal science, intellectual effort is devoted to eliminating these anomalies by seeking to reinterpret evidence within the framework of the dominant theoretical paradigm. An implication of this view is that if we wish to understand the strains and conflicts between paradigms, we should examine the points of anomaly. In the case of *Homo economicus*, these anomalies are most clearly revealed in the case of the motivation that individuals have to contribute towards collective goods, and it is by examining the logic of this motivation that we can best highlight the issues in the contrast between *Homo economicus* and *Homo sociologicus*.

Consider the commonsense reaction to the question of why individuals should make contributions to a collective good. When asked 'Why vote?' or 'Why pick up your litter from the beach?' the obvious commonsense reply is something along the lines of 'Because it is what is expected of me' or 'Because it is the done thing'. In other words, the commonsense reply relies upon an appeal to a prevalent social norm as a reason for action. As is well known, the appeal to this norm finds it difficult to withstand the test of instrumental rationality. If individuals are asked how *their* act of voting or *their* picking up of their litter contributes to the achievement of a collective benefit, they are hard pressed to reply, since generally enough other voters of one's own party turn out to make individual contributions redundant to securing any party's victory, and one piece of litter here or there is unlikely to make any significant difference to environmental amenity. Yet, as is equally well known, if all individuals reason in this instrumental way, their collective inaction fails to supply the collective benefit, or at least fails to supply optimal levels of the collective benefit (see GAME THEORY (7)).

Here is the source of the anomaly within rational choice theory. The level of individual contributions to collective goods predicted by the theory often tends to fall below the level that is actually observed. Individuals therefore cannot be following the logic stated in the theory. One response to this anomaly retains the framework of rational choice theory, but ascribes to *Homo economicus* false beliefs about the efficacy of individual collective action. Thus, Hardin (1982, p. 115) argues that individuals support environmental campaigning organizations because they overestimate the value of their individual contributions. Another, and more radical, response is to drop the logic of the efficacy of individual action, and ascribe the motive to contribute to collective goods in terms of norms. Thus, Riker and Ordeshook (1973, p. 63) say that the decision to vote stems from the satisfaction of complying with the ethic of voting. However, the difficulty with this move should be obvious. Once such a motive has been introduced, *Homo economicus* has been replaced by *Homo sociologicus*, since a straightforward desire to act on social norms is what identifies *Homo sociologicus* in either the functionalist or reflexive varieties.

In order to see how the two logics diverge, it is useful to consider the case of penalties for non-compliance with collectively imposed norms. Suppose, for example, that we have an electoral system in which voting is compulsory, as it is in Australia. Part of the compulsion consists of a penalty levied on those who fail to vote. How does the existence of such a penalty affect the motivation of individual votes? On the rational choice account it functions as a tax, so that the act of not voting comes to resemble drinking or smoking; namely, an activity for which one has to pay a tax specifically imposed on the commodity. Simply because activities are taxed, there is no reason to feel guilty or ashamed in indulging in them, and there need be no sense that one has violated a norm. After all, there may be all sorts of non-moral reasons for imposing such a tax; for example, inelasticity of demand or ease of administration. By contrast, on a sociological account, such a penalty is supposed to be more than a tax. It is supposed to express a social norm, and by doing so acquires an extra motivational force other than that implied by the economic value of the fine. It is assumed that people will feel guilty or ashamed about breaking norms, and these moral sentiments are expected to provide some motivation to action. At some level it is an empirical question as to how far and in what ways this added motivational force of norms operates among people in any particular society at any particular time. However, it does seem clear that this additional motivational aspect of social norms is logically distinct from the incentives and penalites provided by an actor's cost–benefit calculus of alternative courses of action.

If the logical distinction between the motivational force of norms and the incentive effects of costs and benefits is accepted, then it might seem as though the choice of model between that of *Homo economicus* and *Homo sociologicus* is partly one of empirical relevance (perhaps there are more character types corresponding to *Homo economicus* in North America than in Europe, say) and partly one of pragmatic purpose (perhaps the assumption of economic rationality is most suited to an interest in consumer spending, whereas that of a normative orientation is more suited to understanding religious observance). However, writers in the tradition of rational choice theory have sought to go one stage beyond this, by asserting that there is a deeper instrumental rationality to the acceptance of norms, and that the attitudes and assumptions of *Homo sociologicus* are really to be accounted for as rational adaptations to problems inherent in the long-term pursuit of self-interest. From this point of view, inside every *Homo sociologicus* there is, so to speak, an *Homunculus economicus* at work.

To see the logic of this position it is worth recalling that the economic system of market transactions and contractual bargaining is located within a broader set of institutions, and that successful economic performance often depends upon being able to draw upon the resources of those institutions. Thus, any sophisticated economy will provide opportunities in which some parties to a contract will be in a position to cheat or otherwise take advantage of others. Yet taking these opportunities in the short term may turn out to be counterproductive in the long term. A reputation for cheating or exploiting temporary shortages by rising prices to extortionate levels may drive away customers or lead them to seek out alternative suppliers. Conversely, a reputation for reliability and trustworthiness may be one of the most valuable economic assets a firm possesses.

A willingness to abide by norms of trustworthiness and reliability is a disposition, not merely a sum of acts, and it is at least a plausible psychological conjecture that the acquisition of this disposition depends upon a genuine internalization of the relevant social norms, and not simply a sharp-eyed calculation as to when seeming virtuous will turn out to be profitable. If this is true, then long-term rationality would lead individuals to acquire the dispositions that made them most admired in terms of social norms. They would appear to be orientated to norms because they had genuinely internalized the claims of social obligation, but a rational reconstruction of those dispositions would reveal this as the chosen outcome of rational deliberation. It is just such an account of the rational basis for morality that Gauthier (1986) offers, and it is significant that the content of that morality refers to what Hume called the social, as distinct from the monkish, virtues (see □). If such a project could be successfully accomplished, it would indeed show that inside every *Homo sociologicus* there was an *Homunculus economicus* calculating over the choice of dispositions and character.

There are likely to be many arguments against making instrumental

THE SOCIAL AND MONKISH VIRTUES

And as every quality, which is useful or agreeable to ourselves or others, is, in common life, allowed to be a part of personal merit; so no other will ever be received, where men judge of things by their natural, unprejudiced reason, without the delusive glosses of superstition and false religion. Celibacy, fasting, penance, mortification, self-denial, humility, silence, solitude, and the whole train of monkish virtues; for what reason are they every where rejected by men of sense, but because they serve to no manner of purpose; neither advance a man's fortune in the world, nor render him a more valuable member of society; neither qualify him for the entertainment of company, nor increase his power of self-enjoyment? We observe, on the contrary, that they cross all these desirable ends; stupify the understanding and harden the heart, obscure the fancy and sour the temper.

Hume (1751, p. 270)

rationality the deep structure of character in this way, but perhaps the most important relies upon questioning the notion that an individual defined in terms of abstract rationality can choose his or her character. There seems to be no point of view from which individuals can choose to adopt one character rather than another. The choice of character, within the framework of a maximizing account of rationality, will presumably depend upon a judgement about how well off the individual will be in adopting one character rather than another. You do not have to believe, with Mead, that society goes all the way down to hold that there is something incoherent about this type of radical choice. Judgements about how well one's life goes are made within the confines of character, not outside of them. There simply is no conception of the good possessed by abstract rational individuals providing the criteria of choice that would enable them to make a rational choice of character and the norms by which their actions were to be orientated. *Homo sociologicus* cannot be derived from *Homunculus economicus*. The two types inevitably stand in an adversarial relationship one to another.

Sociological Models and Economic Interests

So far, we have seen that it is by no means straightforward to extend rational choice models of behaviour into the social world. Economics is unlikely to be able to annex the disciplines of sociology and political science. In order to test the limits of tolerance for different types of model, it is worth asking the question of what happens if we turn our assumptions on their head. Up to this point we have assumed that rational choice is fine for the economy as the sphere in which contract is paramount, and the relevant question is how far modes of thought suitable for economic analysis can be extended to society and politics. Suppose that we overturn that assumption, and ask whether rational choice analysis is appropriate even for the economy. Might sociological models be more apposite in understanding the processes of production and exchange than economic ones? Could *Homo sociologicus* come to occupy a prominent place in our understanding of the economy?

Consider the role of economic incentives. Clearly, economic incentives are important in motivation, but the point at issue between sociological and economic models is not whether they are important but how they are important. In conventional economics money incentives are important because they provide the means to increased consumption, which is assumed to be the primary motivating force of all economic activity. By contrast, in sociological models economic incentives are important because they provide a visible symbol of one's status and place within an organization; although it was an economist, Walter Bagehot, who drew attention to the independent role of status, in his discussion of the recruitment of civil servants. Comparing the reward structure of British and German civil servants in the nineteenth century, he noted that British governments 'could not buy with the cheap currency of pure honour' the services of their civil servants in the same way that German governments could (see □). Had his sociology been even sharper at this point (often it was very good, as when he wrote on the popular appeal of the royal family), he would have noticed that high material rewards play an important role in symbolizing status, and that economic incentives and social prestige were typically positively, not negatively, correlated.

Issues of consumption within the economy are also relevant at this point. Suppose that we accept that all productive effort is intended solely to obtain the means of consumption. What would follow from this observation?

THE CURRENCY OF HONOUR

Abroad a man under Government is a superior being: he is higher than the rest of the world; he is envied by almost all of it. This gives the Government the easy pick of the *elite* of the nation. . . . Our Government cannot buy for minor clerks the best ability of the nation in the cheap currency of pure honour, and no Government is rich enough to buy very much of it in money.

(Bagehot, 1867, p. 206)

Unless we can exclude sociological elements from our account of consumption, our economics will still rest upon sociological assumptions. Here we need to be reminded that 'the world of goods' (Douglas and Isherwood, 1979) is also a symbolic world in which consumption conveys meanings as well as satisfies wants. Consumption of food, for example, is not simply a way of maintaining bodily functioning, but also provides a means of forming and maintaining social relationships, and these social aspects of the process may develop a much greater importance than the satisfaction of the physical needs which underlie these activities. It is this insight which informs Townsend's (1979, pp. 913–16) work on relative deprivation, in which poverty is seen not merely as the absence of the material conditions of subsistence but also as exclusion from participation in the normal activities of social life. (The equivocation on 'normal' here is significant, since it is implicit in Townsend's work that the prevalent is also the socially desired.) In other words, if we take the sociological perspective seriously, our understanding of consumption should not be focused exclusively on goods as means to preference satisfaction. We should also take into account the social world within which individual consumption is located, and which provides the norms and standards of adequate and acceptable consumption.

Conclusion

Homo economicus and *Homo sociologicus* reflect two aspects of the social world. Just as there is rational strategic calculation in politics and social practices more generally, so there are rule-governed and normative aspects to the economy. We have no theoretical paradigm that adequately integrates the two – nor are we likely to have one. The conceptual stock on which each draws and the presuppositions about character formation contained in each are so radically distinct that is difficult to see how the two might be confused. Neither *Homo economicus* nor *Homo sociologicus* is liable to displace the other in our reasoning about individuals in society for the foreseeable future.

Albert Weale

Further Reading

There are many traditions of sociological approaches to human action, and a useful introduction is provided by Giddens (1989). Although somewhat dated, Berger (1966) provides an elegant introductory discussion of the relationship between individuals and the roles they occupy. The collected papers of Alfred Schutz (1973) offer a sophisticated account of the phenomenology of social life, in which the problems of meaning and interpretation are addressed. Barry (1978) compares economic and sociological approaches to democracy, rather to the detriment of the latter, but his discussion provides a good introduction to some of the key points at issue. Since the problem of collective action is so much of a testing ground for theories of motivation, Scott's (1990) discussion of ideology and social movements provides extensive evidence of how little of collective action can be explained by rational action models. Gauthier (1986) contains an attempted derivation of normative dispositions from a hypothetical rational calculation, an approach that may be contrasted with Walzer's (1983) contextualist understanding of social relationships, in which meaning plays an important role. Douglas and Isherwood (1979) show how even ordinary commercial transactions go beyond the instrumentally calculating.

6
Autonomy

Standard microtheories of rational behaviour posit a 'rational individual' far removed from human flesh and blood. This *Homo economicus* is a mere embodiment of ordered preferences, organized information and accurate calculation. He has no essential relationship with others, no social or historical location and, unless one counts the maximizing of utility, no particular goals which mark him as human. He is defined through his rationality, not through his humanity. Therefore, an economist might not see a need to say much about autonomy, beyond remarking that it is presumably a species of consistency. Philosophers and political theorists, on the other hand, have a great deal to say, especially if they are interested in the liberal tradition, to which much orthodox economics belongs. This chapter will suggest, among other things, that there is more to autonomy than consistency.

'Negative' Freedom

'Autonomy' has a general dictionary meaning of being subject to one's own rules, from the Greek *auto* (self) and *nomos* (a rule or norm). An autonomous agent is a free agent, being self-directed in that he both knows what he wants and is not obstructed in the pursuit of it. This gives enough of a definition to work with for purposes of exploring the relation of autonomy to rationality. I shall start with the idea that the theory of rational choice goes hand-in-hand with a 'negative' notion of freedom, non-committal about ends but strong enough to underpin liberal notions of autonomy. Then I shall raise a series of difficulties, which will require that an autonomous agent be *reflectively* consistent. Finally, having suggested that interdependence is as crucial as independence for autonomy, I shall sketch out a case for a 'positive' notion of freedom.

The distinction between 'negative' and 'positive' here is a matter of whether a free agent must have any particular moral character or goals, such as, for instance, the living of a full or good life (the 'positive' line), or whether any goal will serve as well as any other (the 'negative'). John Stuart Mill declared stoutly in the opening chapter of *On Liberty* (1859) that 'the only freedom which deserves the name is that of pursuing our own good in our own way'. This book is often taken to contain a classic statement of the 'negative' view that 'our own good' is as each person decides it to be for himself, and that questions of autonomy are solely to do with whether there are obstacles to his pursuing it in his own way (with due regard for the liberties of others). So let us start with this morally neutral and thoroughly open-ended interpretation of what it means to be autonomous, since it is so conveniently close to the economist's idea of consumer sovereignty. A sovereign consumer can demand whatever he fancies without being told that he cannot or should not have it. A free market is one in which nothing obstructs the interplay of supply and demand. The accent is on rational choice and the rational customer is always right.

It is worth noting that consumer sovereignty involves resources as well as opportunities. The most 'negative' account of freedom says nothing about resources and demands merely an absence of coercion and legal prohibitions. By this test a pauper is free to buy a Rolls Royce, or a slum-dweller is free to become President of the United States of America. Other exponents of 'negative' liberty insist that a free agent must be able to satisfy his desires in some more realistic sense involving a social power as well as a legal right, and hence resources. In what follows I shall bypass this dispute, by focusing on what all 'negative' accounts have in common, their insistence that what matters is not which desires one has, but whether there are obstacles external to oneself to prevent one from satisfying them. The question is thus whether there is more to autonomy than the ability to make rational choices which are effective in satisfying one's preferences.

Consistent Preferences and Complete Information

In the ideal-type case, with which the chapter on RATIONALITY (1) began, the agent has fully ordered preferences and complete information. Preferences are given, in the manner of tastes: *de gustibus non est disputandum*. Information covers the likely consequences and costs of trying to satisfy them. A choice is rational if it maximizes the agent's expected utility. So an irrational choice is presumably one marked by a disorder in the agent's preferences or information. But both kinds of disorder set problems for rational choice theory.

Consider an addicted gambler who stakes more than he can afford to lose, given that he plans an expensive holiday next week or loves the family whose welfare he is risking. Is he acting irrationally? Not necessarily, one could argue. If his fever is great enough, then his *present* preferences may be consistently ordered, even if he knows that he will regret having acted on them. Tomorrow's utilities will be different but that is only information now, and today's desire to provide for them is weaker than today's desire to gamble. To choose is to choose *now* in the light of what one wants *now* and believes *now*.

This line of thought poses an awkward question. We readily speak of tastes varying over time, of the desire for something being stronger today than yesterday or tomorrow, of preferences which we do not have now but foresee that we will have or would have if we chose a particular course of action. Are 'fully ordered preferences' consistent at one time, presumably now, or over a period, perhaps a lifetime? Either answer soon sounds distinctly peculiar, as a suitable version of Aesop's fable of the ant and the grasshopper shows (see □). But to make rational choice a matter of the mere strength of present desires is especially awkward, as it threatens to render irrational all investment of time and resources in desires foreseen but not yet felt. It also threatens to fragment the self into a series of momentary selves, each needing to be found a reason to be concerned for later ones – as will become clear. Therefore it sounds more promising to call for preferences to be consistent over a period.

In that case distant utilities can still be discounted because they are less certain to be achieved, but not merely because they are distant. The agent is, in effect, to be credited with preferences which extend through time and let him choose now in accordance with rational choice theory but without being insanely short-sighted. Yet this is easier said than done. Psychologically, we usually experience our desires of the moment as stronger than our future desires, and are being asked to act as if we had preferences which differ from those we report by introspection. Philosophically, we are being asked to subscribe to present desires to act on future desires, so as to be able to act now in the absence of those future desires. The model is rapidly becoming more speculative than it seemed to be when preferences were simply given.

The extent of the shift is concealed, if one thinks, as economists are inclined to do, in terms of a constant desire to maximize utility. That sounds like a continuous, underlying, dispositional preference which can be used to convert what, from the point of view of one moment, is information about preferences at other moments into fully ordered preferences for every moment. Thus the gambler is rational in having a periodic flutter which can

THE ANT AND THE GRASSHOPPER

All summer long the Grasshopper consumed and the Ant invested. 'You are acting very irrationally', the Ant warned, 'and you will be sorry when winter comes.' 'I shall be very sorry', replied the Grasshopper with a chirrup, 'but I am not acting irrationally. To be rational is to do what one most values at the time, and I value present delight above its cost in future sorrow. Surely you too would rather sit in the sun and sing?' 'Much rather', said the Ant, 'but to be rational is to do what best promotes one's interests over a lifetime. Future grief has constant weight (where there is no uncertainty about it). So, being rational, I must keep busy investing against winter.'

Winter came and the Grasshopper was hungry. He appealed to the Ant for help. 'I wish I could', said the Ant; 'there is nothing I would like better. But, being rational, I cannot prefer your interests to mine, and you have nothing to offer in return. Are you not sorry you sang all summer?' 'Very sorry', the Grasshopper sighed, 'just as I knew I would be. But now is now – I acted rationally then. It is you who are irrational, in resisting your present desire to help me.'

The Ant reconsidered but found that he had only just enough in store to last him until it was time to start investing again. 'Now is every time', he explained, 'but I can help in one way. Do you know the leaves of the Epicurus plant over there? They are nourishing and delicious. I would eat them myself (and save the trouble of making my own granary), but it makes insects very ill after a time and, being rational, I cannot abuse my lifetime's interests. For you, however, the present ecstasy would outweigh the consequences, silly fellow.'

So the Grasshopper sampled an Epicurus leaf and found it excellent, but was soon in agony. 'Is it worth it?' asked the Ant. 'No it *isn't*', the Grasshopper groaned, 'but it *was*.' 'Then I have bad news for you – there is an antidote.' 'Quick, quick', begged the Grasshopper. 'It is no use to you' the Ant lamented, 'since taking it makes your present distress far worse, even though it works rapidly thereafter.' 'Bad news indeed! I *cannot* invest. Farewell!'

The Grasshopper expired, and the Ant lived on into grey old age without ever once doing anything which caused him a moment's overall regret. 'It is hard never to be able to do what one most wants to do', he mused arthritically, 'but then the life of a rational being is a hard life.'

Moral: *It is hard to be wise, but there are many ways to be foolish.*

Hollis (1988, pp. 95–6)

be accommodated in his overall reckoning of his concerns, but irrational if he overvalues his present fever. Notice, however, that his considered preferences no longer change at all between today and next week. They are both constant and specific. This becomes increasingly implausible as the timespan lengthens. As life advances from mewling infant to slippered pantaloon, preferences surely seem to change, partly as tastes and character develop, partly because of change of circumstance and partly because earlier choices have effects on the chooser. Even during the course of one year, most of us revise our enthusiasms and make choices which we would have rejected before. If preferences are to be regarded as constant, they cannot be specifically for, say, apples rather than pears, or tennis rather than shuffleboard, or one friendship rather than another. Yet they cannot all reduce to a single unspecific desire to maximize utility. The question becomes whether to think in terms of fairly specific preferences which reflect constant dispositions or whether to show how rational choices can be made despite a change in preferences.

Before answering, let us complicate the part played in rational choice by information. Initially, a rational agent knows his preferences but needs information about the means with which to satisfy them. Ignorance reduces autonomy. Yet information can also affect what the agent wants. Recall the old advertising slogan 'Top People Take *The Times*'. It did not just give lesser people the useful information that *The Times* was a high-level source of news, as evidenced by its high-level purchasers. It also informed them that in buying the newspaper they were acting like Top People, and it hinted that they might thus become Top People too. Alternatively, consider the successful marketing of some unremarkable mint chocolates by showing vignettes of elegant, candle-lit dinners, crowned with mints and the best coffee. So engaging is the image that the mints have truly found their way into candle-lit dinners. Here, as in the matter of how ideologies work, for which the examples are a small allegory, it is unclear where information stops and persuasion begins. We could suppose that people who are persuaded to buy *The Times* or the mints must have had an underlying desire for, say, status which is now better informed. Or we could think of preferences as malleable and caught up in the process which, initially, they served to explain. Either way, it will not be simple to keep preferences and information apart.

Now turn to a large-scale example, in which the idea of constant dispositional preferences, immune to reshaping by information, is plainly hard to maintain. In figure 6.1 are outlined the possible lives, which Adam, now aged 30, might lead, by setting out possible formative choices as nodes in a set of forking paths. The paths are of varying length and, to focus some puzzles, I have added notional utility numbers for the stretches between nodes. Thus, in the long top path he picks a quiet life, makes a quiet marriage, fathers quiet children and lives quietly to a demure three score

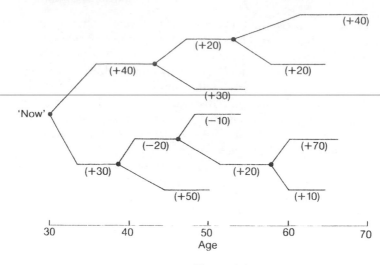

Figure 6.1.

years and ten. On the short bottom path his days are brief but merry or, if he so chooses at 40, less brief and, until the last decade, less merry; and so forth.

In real life, of course, Adam would not have so clear a set of options. But he would still have moments of major decision which shape his life in ways he can roughly foresee and, in so far as uncertainty is a function merely of ignorance, I have filtered it out for an autonomous agent with complete information. Thus I have supposed that the effects and utilities of choosing a steady job, or a place in a church-going community, are foreseeable, including delayed effects – as when he comes to value church attendance, but only after he has turned 50. How, rationally speaking, shall he pursue his own good in his own way? It is difficult to see how the theory of rational choice can merely refuse the question. An autonomous agent is not one who makes small choices while paralysed by major ones. Once armed with enough information, he should be in a position to rank the life opportunities that are open to him. But at this degree of magnification even fairly broad dispositions, such as status-seeking or pleasure in female company, lose their fixed character as given measures and sources of utility. There are possible paths where he eschews both (for instance, by taking up a religious and celibate life) and he therefore needs scales on which they are merely a weight, not an overall measure.

The apparent answer is that he can assign utilities to each path, as in figure 6.1. But then what is he to do? Is he to pick the path with the greatest total (the long humdrum life) or the highest average (the short and merry one) or, for that matter, the one with the least unpleasantness (maximin) or highest high point (maximax)? Any case for one of these alternatives presupposes something permanent in his character, thus begging the question. Meanwhile there is a related – if deeper – difficulty about assigning utilities to stretches of the path. Presumably they are prospective, in that they are governed by the dispositions present at the previous node. But some nodes involve a change of dispositions, thus changing the value of what went before as well as of what would come after, were he to remain the sort of man he was. There are choices, therefore, which would be irrational, if judged *ex ante*, and rational, if judged *ex post*. If Adam prefers sleepy holidays, he would be irrational to spend time or money skiing; but if he would thereby come to love skiing and despise sloth, he would be rational in retrospect. Larger examples, such as a switch to a devout and holy life, make the point even more clearly, which is that the utility numbers vary with changes in character and dispositions. At a level of magnification where all local sources of utility are viewed as components of different possible lives, the whole basis of rational calculation threatens to collapse.

Economists are likely to shrug this problem off on the grounds that radical changes of preference are too rare to matter. Most of us may want sports cars when young and padded saloons when old, but few of us turn our backs on the internal combustion engine altogether. Yet the problem crops up whenever specific preferences are objects of choice. The scaled-up picture of Adam's life contains many chances for him to engineer his character in at least small ways. Otherwise, psychiatrists would soon be out of business and even advertisers would change their tunes. Equally, there are many moments at which it is not obvious that the rational choice should accord with the balance of current dispositions, as in the case of the gambler with whom we began. Choices whose results feed back on the preference order which produced them are common, if one is looking for them.

The root trouble is a tension between two standpoints. On the one hand, choices can only be made 'now', at some particular moment, when the agent has particular wants and dispositions. On the other hand, rational decision-making involves stepping back from the self of the moment reflectively. Neither standpoint makes much sense by itself. If 'now' were all that mattered, agents would be rational in acting like the foolish grasshopper. If 'now' were merely one moment in a set of possible lives, agents would have too much to consider and become rationally paralysed, like the proverbial centipede asked which leg it should move first. Implicitly, therefore, rational choice theory splits the difference by assuming a lasting core to carry the agent through changes of character.

The Liberal Notion of Autonomy

Here the liberal notion of autonomy comes into its own. J.S. Mill's *On Liberty* indeed has memorable things to say about liberty and the value of tolerance. To this extent its conviction that 'the only freedom which deserves the name is that of pursuing one's own good in one's own way' sits neatly with the classic liberal contention that no-one is entitled to impose values on others. As he puts it elsewhere, 'there is a circle round every individual human being, which no government . . . ought to be permitted to overstep' (1848, Book V, xi, 2). At the same time, however, the centrepiece of *On Liberty* is the chapter on Individuality. Here the individual is told how to become master of his desires by forming his own character. He must develop his faculties and exercise his reason, so that his opinions shall become his own and he shall become a self-directed human being. A revealing contrast is made between trees and machines:

> Human nature is not a machine to be built after a model, and set to do exactly the work prescribed for it, but a tree, which requires to grow and develop itself on all sides, according to the tendency of the inward forces which make it a living thing.
>
> (Mill, 1859, chapter 3)

and a page later:

> A person whose desires and impulses are his own – are the expression of his own nature, as it has been developed and modified by his own culture – is said to have a character. One whose desires and impulses are not his own, has no character, no more than a steam-engine has a character.

Autonomy thus starts to pre-select the 'own good' which we are to pursue in our own way. An autonomous person has an 'individuality', which gives the core needed to resolve the tension between standpoints. But 'individuality' is still a general notion, not intended to give any particular shape to 'one's own good'. Different individuals can still develop different characters (see ☐). Yet there is more to character than mere consistency. The task of reason is to make us *reflectively* consistent, whereas a machine built after a model is merely efficient. Reflectively consistent choices stem from a developed character, which has made its desires and impulses its own.

It is not clear, however, that the idea of autonomy as reflective consistency is a stable one. Two lines of thought open up. One is that Mill is very close to painting a *moral* portrait of the autonomous individual, and I shall return to this when we reach the topic of 'positive' freedom. The other is that autonomy involves more than has emerged so far about relations with other people.

The focus so far has been on a single individual, with his own preferences

OF INDIVIDUALITY

It is not by wearing down into uniformity all that is individual in themselves, but by cultivating it, and calling it forth, within the limits imposed by the rights and interests of others, that human beings become a noble and beautiful object of contemplation; and as the works partake the character of those who do them, by the same process human life also becomes rich, diversified, and animating, furnishing more abundant aliment to high thoughts and elevating feelings, and strengthening the tie which binds every individual to the race, by making the race infinitely better worth belonging to. In proportion to the development of his individuality, each person becomes more valuable to himself, and is therefore capable of being more valuable to others. There is a greater fulness of life about his own existence, and when there is more life in the units there is more in the mass which is composed of them.

. . . There is no reason that all human existence should be constructed on some one or some small number of patterns. If a person possesses any tolerable amount of common sense and experience, his own mode of laying out his existence is the best, not because it is the best in itself, but because it is his own mode. Human beings are not like sheep; and even sheep are not undistinguishably alike. A man cannot get a coat or a pair of boots to fit him unless they are either made to his measure, or he has a whole warehouseful to choose from: and is it easier to fit him with a life than with a coat, or are human beings more like one another in their whole physical and spiritual conformation than in the shape of their feet? If it were only that people have diversities of taste, that is reason enough for not attempting to shape them all after one model. But different persons also require different conditions for their spiritual development; and can no more exist healthily in the same moral, than all the variety of plants can in the same physical, atmosphere and climate. The same things which are helps to one person towards the cultivation of his higher nature are hindrances to another. The same mode of life is a healthy excitement to one, keeping all his faculties of action and enjoyment in their best order, while to another it is a distracting burthen, which suspends or crushes all internal life. Such are the differences among human beings in their sources of pleasure, their susceptibilities of pain, and the operation on them of different physical and moral agencies, that unless there is a corresponding diversity in their modes of life, they neither obtain their fair share of happiness, nor grow up to the mental, moral, and æsthetic stature of which their nature is capable.

(Mill, 1859, ch. 3)

and information; who is, so to speak, self-contained within a circle which no government or anyone else should overstep. Let us suggest next that autonomy must be considered in terms of interdependence as well as of independence, and that this applies both to information and to preferences. A rational agent needs reliable or, in the limiting case perfect, information. This is recognized in standard rational choice theory, where he is credited with a subjective probability distribution for possible outcomes, coupled with a learning procedure for adjusting the probabilities. Thus uncertainties which only a trained physicist or economist, for instance, could hope to tackle, are reduced to risks, as if we were betting on which card Nature will turn up next. In effect, this elegant device lets the theory adopt the Cartesian ideal of a solitary mind which winnows its beliefs and accepts only what it knows for itself. But, of course, few of us have the time or skill to check much of what passes for information. There is no dispensing with authorities, who select, interpret and certify the facts which we depend on. Even where rational individuals have a learning procedure, they are still taking much of its input on trust.

Consequently, the assumption that rational choosers have rational beliefs presupposes a benign distribution of power. There is a brisk market in information and one very prone to cartels. Individuals are often up against organized bias, which cross-checks will not easily detect. Indeed, they also have to confront disorganized bias, in the sense of distorted beliefs which have entered circulation and are being reinforced through communication. However, since the idea remains one of objectively rational belief, which must nevertheless be taken largely on trust, autonomy presupposes institutions which reduce distortion. This leads on to liberal ideas of the free society as 'the open society' (a label made famous by Popper, 1945), in which individual rights are protected by keeping power dispersed and information flowing. Unintended distortion is reduced by building criticism into the core of scientific method, as embodied in the institutions of science. Organized bias is kept in check by insisting on open, accountable government with limited powers. Whether or not this solves the problem is a matter for other chapters in this book, but it does at least identify a social dimension to autonomy. Reliable information for the individual depends on warranted trust in others.

It would be a mistake here to tie autonomy to a simple-minded faith in scientific method. Students are often told that in science all beliefs are justified by reason and experiment, and that this is what distinguishes science from ideology. A scientific community always adjusts its beliefs to reality, whereas a millenarian sect, for instance, always finds excuses when its prophecies fail, or lets its members compartmentalize their minds so as not to face up to inconsistency. But this account is vulnerable to the suggestion that science never does and never could justify all its presuppositions and practices, as is clear from the periodical upheavals which mark its history (see Kuhn, 1970). That seems to reveal an unreasoned or 'ideological' element in science, which subverts its claim to be objective and neutral. Conversely, moral, religious and political ways of understanding the world are then no longer automatically debarred from discussing the rationality of ends and hence, it can be argued, opening up an aspect of autonomy which liberals hope to close off by separating facts from values (*see fact/value distinction* (🕮)). Thus the problems of reliable information go very deep.

More practical questions of warranted trust also arise for plans the success of which depends on the behaviour and preferences of other people. In figure 6.1, for instance, it was airily presumed that Adam could marry Eve (or someone or no-one), if he chose. This was a legitimate presumption, in so far as Eve and others are just complex objects in Adam's environment, and are hence rendered predictable by assuming away or discounting for uncertainty. But it ceases to be legitimate as soon as Eve is recognized to be a separate rational agent. More will be said about this in part II of the book, but we should note its bearing on autonomy now.

In defining autonomy as self-direction rather than self-sufficiency, I closed off a line of thought which has attracted some thinkers. There are philosophies of life which bid us be self-contained, rely solely on ourselves and give no hostages, material or emotional, to others. The liberal mainline, however, does not favour detachment from the world and other people, or engagement with them only on terms which avoid emotional risks. It does not incline to self-sufficiency. On the contrary, it has always viewed the circle round every human being as a boundary which can be extended to several human beings with their mutual consent. Mill, for example, explicitly extends individual freedom to freedom of association – the freedom to pursue *our* own good in *our* own way, one might say.

In that case it is no longer plain that figure 6.1 can represent Adam's choices in full, without including some of Eve's. It could perhaps still do so, if mutual commitments, such as marriage, were regarded as exercises in mutual backscratching for individual gain. That would leave a serious informational puzzle about what Adam is to choose, when crucial information about the likely behaviour of other agents depends on what they expect him to choose, as the chapter on GAME THEORY (7) will make plain. But it would mute the complication introduced by the interlocking of preferences. On the other hand, interdependence of the kind symbolized by marriage does seem to be a common fact of life. People commit themselves to others in private and public, in play and work, in love and war. They have loyalties and obligations which they do not regard in the spirit of a commercial contract. Although one might argue that this is all commerce in disguise, as in Becker (1976), that would take some proving. Meanwhile, the suggestion stands that Adam has, or can come to have, some relationships which are integral to who he is or will become.

It may be just possible to absorb this suggestion without overstepping the limits of a 'negative' notion of freedom. The transforming relationships symbolized by ideal marriage are also typical of communitarian living. Communitarian thinking presents us as essentially social and defines a free society before defining the freedom of an individual within it. Such a society is held together by a shared conception of the good, which its members accept as their own good. Autonomy is then the public-spirited kind of freedom with which individuals pursue it, resolving any clash of public and private interest in favour of the former. This freedom can still count as 'negative' provided that the shared conception of the good is only whatever the members declare it to be. In that case the idea just about keeps faith with the central liberal tenet that ends must not be prescribed. Instead of me pursuing my own good and you pursuing yours, with neither dictating to the other, *we* pursue *our* own good in whatever form *we* agree upon. But the position is precarious, as soon as we point out that no society can function without suppressing some forms of dissent.

Certainly this is not easy without some shared conception of the good, if autonomous agents with conflicting preferences are to live together. Does it infringe your autonomy, if I play the trumpet when you want to take a siesta? That depends, presumably, on how we resolve the conflict. The standard liberal view is that no-one's autonomy is infringed by subscribing to a fair and impartial procedure which assumes that the parties have equal rights in the pursuit of reasonable wants. Indeed, such a procedure allows all parties more autonomy than they would have in its absence, as it makes possible many benefits of limited cooperation. This seems only sensible. But it sets one wondering whether rights and reasonable wants can be introduced without an implicit notion of *morally* acceptable behaviour.

In the mean time, the point connects with my earlier remark that Mill comes very close to painting a *moral* portrait of the autonomous individual. In *On Liberty* he goes only as far as prescribing 'individuality'. But in *Utilitarianism*, where he argues the case for utilitarian ethics, the developed individual is presented as one who 'comes, as though instinctively, to be conscious of himself as a being who *of course* pays regard to others' (Mill, 1861, chapter III, his italics). That results from a famous move in the previous chapter (□ p. 265), where Mill contends that true happiness is not to be confused with the satisfaction offered by the lower pleasures, adding:

> It is better to be a human being dissatisfied than a pig satisfied; better to be Socrates dissatisfied than a fool satisfied. And if the fool, or the pig, are of a different opinion, that is because they only know their side of the question.

That could hardly be true, if utility was a matter merely of gross satisfaction. Reflective consistency is being construed so as to rule out a fool's paradise which lasts the fool's lifetime, or a piggish refusal to look beyond the comfort

MORAL FREEDOM

> And indeed, if we examine closely, we shall find that this feeling, of our being able to modify our own character *if we wish*, is itself the feeling of moral freedom which we are conscious of. A person feels morally free who feels that his habits or his temptations are not his masters, but he theirs: who even in yielding to them knows that he could resist; that were he desirous of altogether throwing them off, there would not be required for that purpose a stronger desire than he knows himself to be capable of feeling. It is of course necessary, to render our consciousness of freedom complete, that we should have succeeded in making our character all we have hitherto attempted to make it; for if we have wished and not attained, we have, to that extent, not power over our own character, we are not free. Or at least, we must feel that our wish, if not strong enough to alter our character, is strong enough to conquer our character when the two are brought into conflict in any particular case of conduct. And hence it is said with truth, that none but a person of confirmed virtue is completely free.
>
> (Mill, 1843, book VI, ch. 2)

of the sty. Autonomy is represented by the ever-dissatisfied Socrates. This line persistently attracted Mill. It is memorably summed up in the chapter on 'Liberty and Necessity' in *A System of Logic* (Mill, 1843), where he concluded, 'And hence it may be said with truth that none but a person of confirmed virtue is completely free' (see □).

'Positive' Freedom

Without trying to settle what may be said with truth, we can take this as a cue for turning to 'positive' ideas of freedom. Like instrumental rationality, 'negative' freedom turns on a relation between preferences and means to satisfy them. My remarks about reflective consistency were meant to show that this relation is more complex and harder to achieve than is obvious in elementary cases of rational choice, thus echoing later sections of the chapter on RATIONALITY (1). But they were not meant to challenge its purely internal character. 'Positive' theories, by contrast, see freedom as conformity to an ideal and hold that, in the words of **Kant** (⧉) (1785), 'a free will and a will under moral laws are one and the same'. Typically they contrast the false freedom of the happy slave or fool satisfied with the true freedom of the autonomous moral life. Thus **Rousseau** (⧉), in the famous passage quoted on p. 352 (☐), speaks of moral liberty which alone makes a man truly master of himself, and declares that 'the mere impulse of appetite is slavery, while obedience to a law which we prescribe to ourselves is liberty'.

Any attempt to define freedom as obedience will be suspected of stealing an honorific word for an illegitimate purpose. Certainly, one's hackles rise when a totalitarian state or fundamentalist religious sect announces that it alone has the secret of true freedom and is thereby justified in imposing its commands. Conversely, liberal-minded persons who see an attraction in equating autonomy with moral freedom and hence with obedience to moral laws prescribed to oneself may try to insist that the definition falls just inside the 'negative' range, because it leaves open the subject of what moral laws to prescribe. To test this response (and as background for the chapter on SOCIAL JUSTICE (18)), I shall next sketch out the idea of autonomy found in Kant's ethics.

In the *Groundwork of the Metaphysic of Morals* (1785), Kant argues that a free will is one which 'is able to work independently of alien causes' and yet is not merely arbitrary in its choices. It is guided by reason which, in moral matters, tells us to act on a 'maxim' which we would be ready to prescribe for anyone and everyone with the same choice to make. Thus, if I decide to break a promise to you, I must think of myself telling everyone that such a promise may or should be broken. This commits me at least to acquiescing if you treat me similarly tomorrow, and, if we generalize to all my promises, then it commits me to recommending that the very practice of promise-keeping be scrapped. But, Kant maintains, I cannot consistently will this maxim. Reason puts me in the position of being an impartial judge, seeking universal maxims which can be applied in every case, regardless of who in particular gains or loses. An impartial judge would approve of promise-keeping, not of promise-breaking. To put the point roughly but plausibly, reason bids me do as I would be done by.

If I am coerced by someone else, then my will has 'alien causes', because I am being used as a means to their ends. I am being denied my autonomy as a rational human being. Yet to demand autonomy for myself is implicitly to demand it for each and every rational human being, and thus to commit me to the maxim that one must always treat others as ends in themselves. If I infringe another's autonomy, I have lapsed from this standpoint and so have failed to act as an autonomous being myself. Further reflection on these lines leads Kant to his idea of a free society as composed of autonomous persons who respect one another's autonomy. His name for it in the *Groundwork* is 'a kingdom of ends' and it meshes with his political theory of the *Rechtsstaat*, a just society governed by an impartial legal system which guarantees people's rights.

So far this may all sound like a 'negative' theory, culminating in a classic liberal theory of the state without giving any particular content to the formal notion of respect for persons. Promises must be kept but we were not told which promises should be given. But, Kant argues, if we press the idea of a consistent maxim harder, we can discover which maxims an impartial judge would apply. They turn out, for the most part, to be reassuringly familiar ones; 'tell the truth', 'love your neighbour' and 'exercise your talents', for instance. Yet, as the list grows, a definite picture of the moral life starts to take shape, and the link is forged between the reasons which motivate a free agent and the duties which a moral agent recognizes.

The more definite the picture, the plainer it becomes that we have crossed the line between 'negative' and 'positive' freedom. The border is marked by the proposition that 'a free will and a will under moral laws are one and the same'. It is crossed as soon as one starts to list the moral laws. For a parallel, reflect on the Church of England prayer to 'God, whose service is perfect freedom'. This 'perfect freedom' is on the borderline, abstractly speaking, but becomes 'positive' as soon as the Church spells out what God's service involves. I am not trying to suggest that reflection on autonomy can lead us to pack the pews, or the prayer mats of other religions, since there remains plenty of room for dispute about what a 'positive' notion of freedom implies. But I do offer Kant's line that the rational judgements of an autonomous agent are implicitly universal and impartial as an instructive way of seeing what might be amiss with the happy slave or satisfied fool.

To sharpen the edge of an abstract discussion, consider this facet of the argument about the subjection of women. Many societies cast women in a subordinate role, as evidenced by practices ranging from suttee, through female circumcision, lack of property rights and exclusion from male centres of power to, arguably, the distribution of jobs, educational opportunities and household tasks. Are such disparities a breach of autonomy? There is certainly a case to be made on Kantian lines. Yet many women regard at least some of these examples as no threat to their self-respect and fulfilment, since a domestic life can be a fully autonomous life. Those who think otherwise must try to show that acquiescence is a product of false consciousness, and can do so only in the name of a 'positive' notion of freedom. Meanwhile, if the contrary view is also based on claims about the essential nature of women, the dispute is not between 'positive' and 'negative' but between rival 'positive' accounts.

Conclusion

To sum up, let us relate autonomy to rationality. The theory of rational choice concentrates on internal coherence among preferences, among beliefs and between preferences, beliefs and actions. It is intended to be descriptive in so far as it applies in practice. But, in so far as people in the real world fail to be rational, it is also a normative theory, giving advice on how to do better. This normative element, however, is meant to be morally neutral, of use to saints and sinners equally.

Autonomy too is a normative concept but, as treated in this chapter, one involving more than coherence and effectiveness. At first an autonomous agent seems like a sovereign consumer with a coherent shopping list and a fat wallet in a well-stocked market. To be autonomous is to choose efficiently, thus maximizing the utility of a customer who is always right. Witness the free-market image: the crux is self-direction, not self-sufficiency since, hermits aside, most of us live better through cooperation. But that raises questions about the distribution of power and resources, which call for thought about both information and preferences and put pressure on the distinction between them.

The model agent needs information not only about likely outcomes, considered as future states of his environment, but also about the inner world of others and indeed himself. In particular, he needs to know his own future preferences, since they seem sure to change, partly through his own actions. This suggestion can be resisted by locating preferences deeper in the agent's character and treating an apparent preference for, say, gin to carrot juice as a disposition for enjoyment better satisfied by the properties of gin than of carrot juice. But character too seems prone to change; and a single overall disposition to maximize utility sounds vacuous. That sets the problems about life-choices in figure 6.1, which carry over to any choices whose value depends on whether they are judged *ex ante* or *ex post*. The agent needs a standpoint other than 'now' so that he can be impartial between 'now' and 'then'. This is one condition of what emerges as *reflective* consistency. But the governing idea is still solely that of consistency, with the presumption that a fool satisfied, if harmoniously integrated with other fools through an ideology which deals with **cognitive dissonance** (▨), is both rational and free.

Yet, even if only tentatively, this presumption can be challenged by citing some 'positive' notions of freedom. In so far as freedom, whether individual or communal, is the ability to pursue an own good with a specific content, autonomy takes on moral shape. The happy slave's satisfactions are consoling, but his autonomy is an illusion. Self-direction becomes the moral independence which goes with individuality in Mill, especially if Kant's connection is made between a free will and a will under moral laws. But all this is too speculative to make into a firm conclusion, and is offered only as background for later chapters.

In the chapter on RATIONALITY (1) the subject was divided into 'instrumental', 'procedural' and 'expressive', with the first two offering the firmer ground. Autonomy too can be introduced under these headings. It soon emerges that there is more to it than the ability to satisfy present preferences;

but instrumental rationality too needs to look beyond 'now'. Reasons for moving to 'reflective consistency' have something in common with those for exploring procedural ideas of rationality, but are not only to do with uncertainty. Even at this stage, freedom takes on moral overtones, as in Mill. When a moral content becomes explicit, with freedom as obedience to moral laws, there are echoes of some remarks on expressive rationality. But differences emerge when autonomy is connected with ideas of impartial judgement, duty and justice.

Let us end with two questions. Is the theory of rational choice incomplete without an excursion into ethics and politics, which its technical exponents usually hope to avoid? Conversely, can it yield insights into ethics and politics, so as to illuminate, for instance, the nature of SOCIAL JUSTICE (18)? With these questions on the agenda, we next shift our focus from one individual agent to several, and set about analysing Interactive Choice.

Martin Hollis

Further Reading

J.S. Mill's essay *On Liberty* is crucial for the general topic, especially its central chapter on 'individuality', together with Isiah Berlin's 'Two Concepts of Liberty' in Berlin (1969). These are works primarily concerned with freedom in a political context, whereas this chapter has focused mainly on single individuals and matters of rational choice. But all roads lead back to Kant (1785), of which Hospers (1961, chapter 6) is a useful basic exposition. Three recent books specifically about autonomy are Young (1986), Lindley (1986) and Dworkin (1988). To introduce the idea of reflective consistency, Sen's (1977) article 'Rational Fools' is a lively and subversive comment on the limitations of instrumental rationality, and Frankfurt (1971) suggests ways of giving a rational agent more structure or, as Sen puts it, 'more up top'.

Part II
Interactive Choice

7

Game Theory

Suppose that you wish to build a book-shelf. If you are alone on a desert island, you have to choose which tree to use for the wood and how to attach it to the wall of your hut. This problem might be difficult, but you may also face uncertainty as to the relative strength of alternative materials and how long it would take to build. As discussed in earlier chapters, such uncertainty considerably complicates your choice problem. Nevertheless, you need not consider the actions of individuals on other islands when you decide what to do. Your actions do not affect them and theirs do not affect you. At the other extreme, if you are just a tiny part of a very large competitive economy, you still do not have to take the actions of others into consideration when you choose how to make your book-shelf. You can buy wood, brackets and screws from a shop, and your purchase is too trivial to affect the price they charge or the range of products offered. You can therefore proceed with your decision-making without worrying how manufacturers will react to your actions. Once again, it is as if you are alone on an island, albeit with an excellent mail-order service in book-shelves. Your choice problem is essentially identical.

Next, suppose that you are joined on your desert island by Man Friday, who turns out to be a good carpenter but a lousy cook. You can offer him meals in exchange for a shelf, but how many meals? There are advantages to your cooperating with Friday, but it is a real bore to peel his potatoes. In the absence of a competitive market, how is the rate of exchange between book-shelves and meals established? Similar questions must be asked of the large, sophisticated economy if there are relatively few suppliers of (or demanders for) book-shelves.

In fact, the questions go beyond pure economic interaction. Back on the desert island, you love to tell Friday about your exploits, say, on the hockey field, and he gets tremendous pleasure from informing you about the progress his youngest child is making in shaking a rattle. How do we limit each other's CULTURAL EXCHANGE (11)? On moral issues, you were brought up to believe that gentlemen wear trousers and are upset by Friday's nakedness. He sees your trousers as an offensive hint of imperialism. When hunting, you agree that it is better for one of you to be directing operations, but how do you develop a political structure to apportion power? Neither of you fully trusts the other, but how many guns do you throw into the sea in exchange for how many of his spears? You both like a clean environment, but who should pick up the litter? Such questions touch on the full range of economic, social and political interactions, yet none can be answered with reference only to the method of individual decision-making discussed in earlier chapters, because your welfare is dependent on Friday's actions, and his on yours. Game theory has been developed to provide an answer to how perfectly rational people should act in such circumstances.

A *game* is defined as a situation in which the actions of one person perceptibly affect the welfare of another and vice versa. These effects can be classified according to the degree to which there are motives for cooperation and for rivalry. Sometimes, everyone gains from cooperation (for example, it is far better that all drivers drive on the same side of the road!). Sometimes, there will be pure rivalry without any benefits of cooperation (for example, a dispute over the ownership of a particular piece of land). On other occasions, and most interestingly, there will be a mixture of motives: part conflict and part cooperation (for example, neighbouring powers have a mutual interest in reducing their military spending, but each may also see a national benefit to having more than the other). Whatever the case, the basic method of game theory is to argue that individuals try to predict what others will do in reply to their own actions, and then optimize on the understanding that others are thinking in the same way. Thus, game theory provides a particular and not uncontentious perspective on social action: individuals are both optimizers and perfectly rational in the sense developed later in this chapter. Whether this view of social interaction is descriptive of how people actually do behave, or is prescriptive of how rational people would, or even should, behave, is a question to which we shall return later.

The next section introduces some essential assumptions and terminology of game theory. With this as background, we then develop the key ideas behind solving games, and suggest what game theory tells us about human behaviour. The following sections introduce time into the analysis, and review some recent work on the importance of information. The last section provides a more critical analysis of the calculating, optimizing approach of formal game theory.

The Rules of the Game

On one level, game theory is just a mathematical technique, and as such it requires that problems must be set out with rigorous formality. Do not be put off by this: the level of numeracy necessary to understand most of this chapter is no more than the ability to count! Nevertheless, we shall be building a powerful logic, and this requires that before any specific game can be properly analysed, six basic *rules of the game* in question must be specified. Before a game theorist can set to work on a problem, she must know who the players are, what strategies are available to them, whether binding agreements are feasible, the consequences of all possible combinations of strategies, the extent of information available to each player, and whether this is common knowledge. As will be seen, this is a much deeper requirement than simple knowledge of, say, the rules of chess or poker.

First, we need to know who is making the decisions. This is not because different individuals have different personalities that would make them act differently. Personality does not affect what is the rational thing to do. We need to specify the decision-makers only to identify whose actions each player must take into account. All decision-makers are called *players*, whether they are individual consumers, firms, politicians, trades unions, lawyers, or whoever. For illustrative purposes, it is often convenient to look at two-player games, but all the basic ideas generalize to games involving more players.

Players are able to make *moves* (or *actions*). An example from chess would be to move the Queen's pawn forward one square. A *strategy* is a plan of actions. In chess this can be very complicated, with different actions depending on what your opponent has chosen (for example, the Sicilian defence). A well-defined strategy requires a full set of contingent rules that the player could, if necessary, instruct someone else to implement. In economics, a simple strategy for the government would be to raise interest rates if inflation is rising and reduce them if it is falling. An alternative strategy would be to set monetary policy so as to maintain a fixed exchange rate. In order to formulate a strategy, the players must know the sequence in which they are allowed to make moves (for example, in chess, white starts and then alternates with black). They must also know whether they are going to play the game repeatedly against the same set of players, or whether it is to be played only once (that is, a *one-shot game*). The set of feasible strategies forms the second element of the rules of the games (see **feasible set** (🔑)).

The third element relates to the ability to form coalitions. A *coalition* is a group of players who are able to make binding agreements to implement agreed strategies. In a *cooperative game*, any subset of players is able to form a coalition (see **core** (🔑)). This chapter is concerned only with *non-cooperative games*, in which players are not able to make binding agreements with each other, but must act independently. Connecting cooperative and non-cooperative games is the theory of BARGAINING (8), which analyses the non-cooperative stage of negotiation prior to the implementation of a cooperative strategy.

The fourth part to the specification of a game is the *pay-offs* of the players. Each player will have a set of objectives, such as wealth and security, and a pay-off is a measure of how well those objectives are met in any given outcome of the game (see **utility function** (🕮)). It is only in the fact that players form their own preferences that personality enters the theory of games. It may be that one player values the welfare of another (either positively or even, spitefully, in a negative way!). If so, the utility derived from sympathy and spite must be included in the overall measure of how well objectives are met. Sometimes, a cardinal measure of utility is necessary, particularly when mixed (random) strategies are used, and cardinality is assumed in the next section. While cardinality does not require interpersonal comparisons of utility, it does require quantification of how much better one outcome is than another for a particular person. However, for many purposes it is sufficient to know only the order of preferences; for instance, that Israel prefers arms reductions to an arms build-up if the Arab countries follow suit, but is happiest if the Arabs unilaterally cut their weapons, while the worst outcome is a unilateral cut against an Arab build-up. This example also illustrates how pay-offs depend on the combination of strategies chosen by each of the players.

A standard form of presentation of these rules of the game so far specified is the *normal form* (or *strategic form*) which relates summary strategies to pay-offs. For two-player games, the normal form is usually written as a matrix, with elements representing pay-offs. For instance, if the Arab countries have a similar ranking of outcomes to Israel in the arms reduction game, and we write preferences such that 4 is higher ranking than 3 and so on, then table 7.1 represents the normal form of the game just discussed. Throughout this chapter, the row player's (for example, Israel's) pay-off is given first, and the column player's (for example, the Arabs') pay-off is second. This game is, in fact, identical to the classic game known as the Prisoner's Dilemma.

Table 7.1 The Arms Reduction game.

| | | Arab countries | |
		Build-up	Reduction
Israel	Build-up	2, 2	4, 1
	Reduction	1, 4	3, 3

The fifth element to the rules of the game specifies the *information* available to the players. How much does each know about their own and other players' available strategies and pay-offs? The first category of information distinguishes *complete information* from *incomplete information*. Basically, a game is one of complete information if all players know the rules of the game, including the pay-offs and strategies available to all other players. Complete information is not quite as restrictive as it first seems. It does not require players necessarily to know what moves others have made before them, so information need not be *perfect*. For instance, in many interesting games players have to decide on their moves simultaneously (that is, before either knows what the other has chosen). Nor does complete information require that there be no uncertainty, as long as each player knows the **probability distributions** (⑨) that others attach to the various possible states of nature that might transpire (for example, how each country assesses the chances of a missile being launched by mistake due to technical faults). These assessments (probability distributions) need not be the same for everyone, as long as each player knows how the others view the chances. The bulk of this chapter and, until recently, of applied game theory considers only games of complete information. Anything less than complete information is incomplete information. It used to be thought that nothing could be said about the outcome of such games, but work by Harsanyi and others has shown how progress can be made. A particular development, discussed on p. 121, considers *asymmetric information* games, in which some players have private information (for example, about their own work effort or pay-offs) while others can only imperfectly estimate that information on the basis of either their own pay-offs (for example, company profits) or the informed group's actions (such as a strike).

The final component of the rules of the game sets out what information is *common knowledge*. Common knowledge is information which is known to all players, which each player knows the others know, which each knows the others know he knows, and so on. There can be no element of doubt. The extent of common knowledge is absolutely crucial for solving games because it allows players to put themselves in the place of others, think through what they will do, and act accordingly. Everywhere except on pages 124–29, we will be making the strong assumptions that both the rules of the game and the rationality of other players are common knowledge. The appropriate notion of rationality will be developed in the next section.

This completes a fairly exhausting specification! It might even be said that the prime talent of the social scientist, and perhaps even of the individual decision-maker, is in clarifying these issues exactly. Indeed, some would argue that one of the greatest achievements of the use of game theory is in making us think clearly about the rules of real world games, and that the theoretical solution of such games is almost secondary. However, for the game theorist the fun is about to begin. How do rational decision-makers process the specified rules of the game? In the answer lies the key to understanding interactive choice.

Solving Games

Consider the **Prisoner's Dilemma** (see □). This is an example of a two-player one-shot game, with each player having a choice between two simple strategies (confess, or not confess). It is a non-cooperative game because they cannot get together to make a binding agreement to keep quiet. Both prisoners understand the consequences of their actions and these are summarized in their pay-offs. Inasmuch as either feels any sympathy for the other, or has fears about reprisals, these are included in the pay-offs. There is complete, but imperfect, information. It is complete because both know the strategies and pay-offs available to each other, yet imperfect because decisions have to be made before the other's choice has been revealed. All of this is common knowledge. What is the rational outcome of this game?

What we need is a theory of social action, which Weber defines as 'action which takes account of the behaviour of others and is thereby orientated in its course' (Weber, 1949, p. 5). More formally, we require a *solution concept* (or *equilibrium concept*), which is a behavioural rule that rational players can use to process the given rules of the game in order to choose the best possible strategy, given that other players are applying the same behavioural rule. Game theory looks for behavioural rules which can solve games by embodying the weakest notion of rationality consistent with finding a solution. Some games can be solved by relatively modest rules, such as dominance, but as we proceed through this section, we shall encounter games which require more sophisticated, and more controversial, rules of rationality. The key concept will be Nash equilibrium, although game theorists are constantly arguing for even more subtle refinements in their search for what constitutes 'perfectly' rational behaviour.

We begin with an apparently uncontroversial behavioural rule. It seems quite reasonable to argue that if there exists a strategy that is never as good as another feasible strategy, whatever the other player does, then the former will not be chosen by a rational player. In the jargon, strictly dominated strategies will be rejected. Looking at the pay-offs for the Prisoner's Dilemma, it should be clear that to not confess is strictly dominated, leaving confess as the *strictly dominant strategy*. Whatever prisoner 2 does, 1 does better by confessing, and vice versa. Some people find this result uncomfortable, because if both prisoners kept quiet, each would do better than in the dominant strategy equilibrium. Surely, they argue, rational human beings should be able to achieve **Pareto optimality** (📖)? But, given the inability to make

THE PRISONER'S DILEMMA

This [game] is attributed to A. W. Tucker, and it has received considerable attention by game theorists. The payoff matrix is:

$$
\begin{array}{c}
 \quad\;\; \beta_1 \qquad\quad\; \beta_2 \\
\begin{array}{c} \alpha_1 \\ \alpha_2 \end{array}
\left[\begin{array}{cc} (0.9, 0.9) & (0, 1) \\ (1, 0) & (0.1, 0.1) \end{array} \right].
\end{array}
$$

The following interpretation, known as the prisoner's dilemma, is popular: Two suspects are taken into custody and separated. The district attorney is certain that they are guilty of a specific crime, but he does not have adequate evidence to convict them at a trial. He points out to each prisoner that each has two alternatives: to confess to the crime the police are sure they have done, or not to confess. If they both do not confess, then the district attorney states he will book them on some very minor trumped-up charge such as petty larceny and illegal possession of a weapon, and they will both receive minor punishment; if they both confess they will be prosecuted, but he will recommend less than the most severe sentence; but if one confesses and the other does not, then the confessor will receive lenient treatment for turning state's evidence whereas the latter will get 'the book' slapped at him. In terms of years in a penitentiary, the strategic problem might reduce to:

	Prisoner 2	
	Not Confess	Confess
Prisoner 1: Not Confess	1 year each	10 years for 1 and 3 months for 2
Prisoner 1: Confess	3 months for 1 and 10 years for 2	8 years each

If we identify α_1 and β_1 with not confessing and α_2 and β_2 with confessing, then – providing neither suspect has moral qualms about or fear of squealing – the above payoff matrix in utilities has the right character for the prisoner's dilemma. The problem for each prisoner is to decide whether to confess or not. The game the district attorney presents to the prisoners is of the non-cooperative variety.

(Luce and Raiffa, 1957, pp. 94–5)

binding agreements, it follows logically that a rational player will not confess. The individual rationality of dominant strategies is compelling, even
though the outcome is collectively 'irrational'. This apparent paradox is a
particular example of the *free-rider problem*. A wide range of public-good
problems, such as contributions to a police force, lighthouses, street lighting
and charities, or fishing, tree felling and grazing of common land or water,
each has the same basic structure. Independent, rational individuals will
decide to ride free on the generosity or abstinence of others. Since everyone
has similar incentives, the result is under-provision or over-exploitation.
This is, of course, a major justification for group decision-making and enfor-
cible contracts, whenever they are feasible (see ORGANIZATIONS (10) and
PLANNING (16)).

In games without a strictly dominant strategy, we can sometimes apply the
slightly modified rule of iterated dominance. In game A (see table 7.2), there
is no single dominant strategy for either player, but there is a dominated
strategy on which we can bite. For Adam, who must choose between top (T),
middle (M) and bottom (B), B is dominated by T, whatever Brian does. Brian
can now argue that Adam will never play a dominated strategy and, ruling
B out of the strategy set, reveals right (R) as dominated by centre (C). Given
that R will not be played, M is dominated by T, and this leaves left (L) dominant for Brian. Thus, Adam will play T and Brian will play L. This process
of successive elimination of dominated strategies until only one strategy combination is left is called *iterated dominance*. Its implementation clearly
requires more thought and computational ability than does simple dominance, but with that reservation it does seem a reasonable procedure for
rational players to follow.

Table 7.2   Game A.

		Brian		
		L	C	R
	T	2, 2	4, 1	4, 0
Adam	M	1, 0	3, 3	7, 2
	B	1, 0	3, 2	1, 4

Suppose that Adam's pay-off to {B, L} had been 2 instead of 1. B would
no longer be strictly dominated and the iterations could not have begun.
However, we might still wish to argue that since T is still at least as good
as B whatever Brian does, and strictly better for at least one circumstance (in
this case, when played against either C or R), then B is still not a rational
strategy to play. This is the criterion of *weak dominance*, and it is this weaker
form that is most usually found in the literature on iterative dominance. We

shall return to weak dominance in another context later in this section. For now, though, be warned that iterated weak dominance can hold hidden perils. In particular, there can be more than one such solution to a game, in which case the one chosen will depend on the order of deletion of weakly dominated strategies.

Many games of interest to social scientists cannot be solved by iterated dominance, because A's best action depends on what B chooses to do. It is in such circumstances that we invoke what is undoubtedly the most important concept in game theory – Nash equilibrium. A *Nash equilibrium* is a set of strategies, one for each player, such that given the strategies being played by others, no player can improve on her pay-off by adopting an alternative strategy. This concept is so fundamental that it is often called simply the equilibrium point. Nash equilibria can be found by calculating each player's *best replies* to each of the strategy combinations that might be played by others, and identifying those strategy combinations that are best replies to each other. Best replies always reject strongly dominated strategies, but do not necessarily exclude weakly dominated ones. The calculation of best replies can be illustrated using game B (see table 7.3). If Alice were to choose T, Beth's best reply would be to play C, because a pay-off of 5 is greater than either 4 or 3, which she would receive by playing L or R respectively. And if Alice were to choose B, Beth's best reply would be R. Turning to Alice's best replies, these are B against L, T against C, and B against R. Thus, the Nash equilibrium is {T, C}, because that is the only strategy combination in which each player is making a best reply to the other. Notice that compared with {B, L} a modified free-rider problem has emerged.

Table 7.3   Game B

| | | | Beth | |
		L	C	R
Alice	T	3, 4	2, 5	1, 3
	B	4, 8	1, 2	0, 9

Even in this very simple game, the calculation of the Nash equilibrium is a non-trivial task. Therefore, it requires more than casual justification as a model of human behaviour. Probably the most compelling reason to believe in the Nash equilibrium as an attractive solution concept is to view it as a *self-enforcing agreement*. Imagine that Alice and Beth, leaders of two political groupings meet prior to two simultaneous committees. Alice chairs the planning committee on which her party has a majority, and Beth chairs the finance committee on which her influence is decisive. The main item on the planning agenda is whether a bypass should be located north (T) or south

(B) of the village. The finance committee has to choose between three alternative compensation schemes (L, C and R). Alice proposes that she will vote for B on the understanding that Beth steers her committee towards L. Beth agrees that this would be reasonable, and they depart for their meetings. As soon as Alice has left the room she breaks into a cold sweat. Can Beth be trusted? If the southern route is to be chosen, it is to Beth's advantage to choose R, in which case Alice receives zero. Their agreement is not self-enforcing, because there is an incentive for at least one player to deviate from the agreed strategy. Alice thinks it is safer to go for the northern route to cut her losses. Beth had left the room feeling quite satisfied with their agreement. She was willing to sacrifice a little political advantage in order to achieve a reasonable outcome all round. But she, too, misses a heartbeat as she begins to wonder how Alice is thinking. Does Alice really trust Beth? And what would she do if she does not? If Alice chooses the northern route, Beth had better choose C. It is not only that it is in Beth's own interests to break their agreement, but that she thinks that Alice thinks that she will, and so *she* cannot trust Alice. {T, C} is the only self-enforcing agreement that each can trust the other to implement. Thus, the Nash equilibrium can be seen as the only sustainable outcome of rational negotiation in the absence of externally enforceable agreements. It should be stressed that this is not the only possible rationale, and it can certainly be argued that rational players have no need to meet, because they can work through each other's thoughts.

For one particular class of games there is a complementary rationale for believing in Nash equilibrium outcomes. A *constant-sum game* is one in which the pay-offs of the players always sum to a constant, whatever combination of strategies is chosen. An example is given as game C (see table 7.4), in which all pay-offs sum to 5. Constant-sum games are formally identical to *zero-sum games*, because the units in which utility is measured can always be changed by a positive linear transform (see RATIONALITY (1)) so that they sum to zero (for example, by subtracting 2.5 from each pay-off in game C). The results in this paragraph also extend to the wider class of two-person *strictly competitive games* of pure rivalry, such that one person's gain always entails the other's loss, although not necessarily by the same amount. The Nash equilibrium of game C is given by {M, R}, but suppose

Table 7.4   Game C.

			Ben	
		L	C	R
	T	2, 3	1, 4	2, 3
Alan	M	4, 1	3, 2	3, 2
	B	5, 0	4, 1	1, 4

that instead of optimistically searching for best replies, each player pessimistically believes that the other will try to be as nasty as possible, so that the best he can do is to limit the damage. In particular, Alan can consider each of his options and note the worst pay-off that could arise in each case (that is, 1 if he plays T, 3 for M and 1 for B). The best of these (that is, 3) gives him his *security level*, which is the best he can guarantee himself regardless of Ben's strategy. Similarly, Ben's security level is 2. If both players play the strategies associated with their security levels, that is the strategies which maximize their minimum pay-offs, then the equilibrium outcome is known as the *maximin* (or, identically in the case of zero-sum games, the minimax). In game C, this gives exactly the same strategy combination as the Nash equilibrium. This equivalence turns out to be quite general in zero-sum games.

However, the equivalence of Nash and maximin does not carry though to more general games that are not strictly competitive. For instance, the maximin in game B is {T, L}, while the Nash equilibrium is {T, C}. So, which solution concept should be adopted by rational players? The answer must be that Nash has much stronger claims. It is quite appropriate to expect rivals to be unrelentingly nasty if they will always gain by being so, but surely not when they would be harming themselves. For instance, in game B, Beth has no incentive to play L when she can do better by playing C; which is, of course, just another way of saying that L is not her best reply to either of Alice's strategies. We shall not consider either maximin or zero-sum games, further.

Until very recently, most game theorists have accepted Nash strategies as the only reasonable option for rational players. However, Bernheim (1984) and Pearce (1984) argue that this is too strong a definition of rationality, and there are other strategies that may be *rationalizable* in the sense that they can be supported by a logical and consistent set of beliefs about how other players are thinking. For instance, game D (see table 7.5) has a unique Nash equilibrium {M, C}, but all strategies are rationalizable in the following sense. Angie thinks Brenda will choose R because she might think Angie will play B, on the assumption that Brenda will play L because Angie plays T; and if Angie is expected to play T, it is rationalizable that Brenda will choose R. So in this circle of players trying to out-guess each other, T is a

Table 7.5 Game D.

| | | Brenda | | |
		L	C	R
	T	0, 7	2, 5	7, 0
Angie	M	5, 2	3, 3	5, 2
	B	7, 0	2, 5	0, 7

rationalizable strategy because Angie can tell a coherent story about why Brenda might choose R. Similar loops can be constructed to justify B, L and T. The Nash strategies M and C are necessarily rationalizable, because Angie can play M given she expects Brenda to play C, and she expects Brenda to play C if Angie plays M. Of course, rationalizable strategies that are not also Nash equilibria will result in at least one of the players being disappointed that she was out-guessed, but does that make her irrational? It might be argued that if game D was played regularly (against a different opponent each time, if we are to avoid the issues discussed in the next section), players would learn not to make 'mistakes'. But if Angie and Brenda each out-guess their opponent half of the time by using their non-Nash strategies they receive an average pay-off of 3.5, which exceeds the Nash equilibrium pay-off of 3. So what is the incentive to learn? What this really reveals about a Nash equilibrium is that it requires players not only to *have* the same information as given by the rules of the game, but also to *use* that information in exactly the same way; that is, they must each believe that the other thinks exactly as they themselves do. Thought processes must be common knowledge. This may or may not be how people actually think, but I shall assume it to be true for the remainder of this chapter. The strongest (but not the only) justification for this assumption is once again when players are able to meet before play and reach a non-binding agreement. Non-Nash rationalizable strategies do not form self-enforcing agreements.

In all the games discussed so far, there is exactly one pure strategy Nash equilibrium (a pure strategy is one that maps a determinate plan of actions). Rational players can thus pick their Nash strategies, and their choice problem is solved. However, there are many interesting games in which this uniqueness property does not hold. Sometimes there is no simple pair of strategies that constitutes a Nash equilibrium, and in other games there are many such pairs. We begin by considering the former.

In the game of Matching Pennies (see table 7.6), two players each have the choice of calling heads (H) or tails (T). Alf wins by calling the same as Bert, and Bert wins by calling different. For Alf, the best reply to H is H, and to T is T; but for Bert, the best reply to H is T and to T is H. Put another way, there is no agreement that the two players could come to, using only the *pure strategies* of H or T, that would be self-enforcing. (Incidentally, any choice

Table 7.6 Matching Pennies.

		Bert	
		H	T
Alf	H	1, −1	−1, 1
	T	−1, 1	1, −1

is 'rationalizable' in this game.) Thinking loosely about such a problem, Alf might argue that either call is as good as the other. That is certainly true if he believes that there is an equal chance of Bert choosing H or T. But what if Alf expects Bert to display some bias in favour of H? Clearly, however small Bert's bias is, Alf should pick H since this maximizes his expected pay-off. Now, what if Bert anticipates this? He will choose T, but then Alf would prefer T too, and so on. The only way they can prevent themselves from being out-guessed by an opponent who thinks as they do, is to choose H or T with equal probability. This use of random choices over two or more pure strategies is called a *mixed strategy*.

A random choice does not necessarily mean that pure strategies must be chosen with equal probability, as in Matching Pennies. Other games would require a probability mix with a bias towards one strategy rather than another. For instance, suppose we play Modified Matching Pennies (see table 7.7), raising the pay-off to Alf from choosing H by 1, so that he receives 2 by calling H when Bert also does, and zero by calling H when Bert calls T (perhaps Alf gets poetic pleasure from calling H, and this pleasure is common knowledge). This modified game still has no pure strategy equilibrium, but like nearly all games of interest to social scientists, it does have a mixed strategy equilibrium. It turns out that Alf should continue to call H and T with equal probability, but Bert should raise his probability of calling T to 3/4. Alf has an expected pay-off of 1/2, but Bert's expected pay-off remains zero. It may seem surprising that Alf's temptation to call H has resulted in Bert's behaviour changing, but this is because each has to randomize so as to make the other indifferent between H and T. It is straightforward to verify that with any other probability mix at least one player would have an incentive to change his strategy. Another example of a mixed strategy equilibrium is given by the game of chicken (see □ p. 106).

Table 7.7   Modified Matching Pennies.

		Bert	
		H	T
Alf	H	2, −1	0, 1
	T	−1, 1	1, −1

The computational difficulty of calculating optimal mixes, and the intellectual oddity of people rolling proverbial dice in their heads before adopting a strategy, combine to create a widespread belief that if no pure strategy equilibrium exists, then we should conclude that the problem has no rational solution. The mixed strategy disbelievers can sometimes point to another difficulty. Suppose that Alf were to deviate from the mixed strategy

CHICKEN

Two Hell's Angels, Ace and Brett, decide to resolve a dispute by riding towards each other down the middle of the road. The first to turn away loses. If both continue straight ahead, they will crash and risk serious injury. The pay-offs to each course of action are as follows:

		Brett	
		Straight	Turn
Ace	Straight	$-15, -15$	4, 0
	Turn	0, 4	1, 1

What strategies should each Hell's Angel adopt? Two pure strategy Nash equilibria are immediately apparent. If Brett turns away, Ace should continue straight ahead, in which case Brett indeed does best by turning away. Similarly, Ace turning and Brett continuing straight is an equilibrium. However, consider the following probabilistic (or mixed) strategy. Suppose that Brett is known to have a die which he will roll, unseen by Ace, before making his run. If and only if he rolls a six, he will continue straight; otherwise he will turn away. Ace knows this and calculates that if he himself chooses to continue straight there is a 1/6 chance of a crash and a 5/6 of his winning. The expected pay-off (*expected value*, 🔟) is $(1/6)(-15) + (5/6)(4) = 5/6$. Similarly, he calculates the pay-off to turning also to be 5/6, so Brett's strategy has made Ace indifferent between his options. If Brett were to use any other probability mix, this indifference would no longer hold, Ace would prefer one pure strategy or the other, and Brett's best reply would result in one of the pure strategy equilibria. But that is not the case with the one-in-six mix. However, for this to be an equilibrium strategy, it must be a best reply for Brett to play it against what Ace is doing. This will be true if and only if Ace also rolls a die (either actually or metaphorically) and adopts a similar strategy. Thus, it is a mixed strategy equilibrium if each Hell's Angel chooses to continue straight ahead with probability 1/6. Each has an expected pay-off of 5/6, and a one in 36 chance of ending up in hospital. This sophisticated analysis also leaves Ace and Brett with another problem. Which equilibrium should they choose, and how?

equilibrium, say by playing H with probability one in Modified Matching Pennies. It is easily checked that this will not alter either player's expected pay-off as long as this deviation is not noticed by Bert. But if it is noticed, and Bert raises his probability of playing T to 1/3, *both* players improve their expected pay-offs (to 2/3 for Alf and 1/3 for Bert). Of course, we need to go further and ask why Bert does not exploit Alf's strategy and play T with probability 1; and pushing that line of questioning takes us back to the 'optimal' mix as the only equilibrium. However, in the sense that deviations from equilibrium are not necessarily self-correcting, mixed strategies can be unstable.

This instability is by no means always the case, and it would be nihilistic to reject mixed strategies out of hand. In zero-sum games, such as the original Matching Pennies, they seem an entirely appropriate model of human behaviour; and, as will be seen in GAME THEORY APPLIED (9), this is also true for a range of socially interesting non-zero sum games. Furthermore, Harsanyi (1973) has shown that with a small amount of incomplete information, individual players may act as if rivals are randomizing, even though each knows that the others are actually playing pure strategies. For instance, suppose that Matching Pennies is to be played just once, and each player has a preference for either heads or tails. Each knows only his own preference, but ascribes a 50 per cent chance to the other having a mild *ceteris paribus* preference for H (or for T) and an equally mild dislike for the other. All this is common knowledge. In effect, the pay-offs in the table are averages of positive and negative preference (more formally, they are **expected values** (📖)). Given that your best prediction is that the other player is equally likely to choose H or T, you can freely choose your marginal preference as a pure strategy. In this way, mixed strategies emerge as a result of our ignorance about our rival's best (pure) strategy. Since fully complete information is an extremely strong assumption, this argument has a potentially wide applicability to one-shot games. In games which are repeated, mixed strategies can realistically represent the proportion of times a particular pure strategy is played although, as is shown in the next section, repetition introduces a wider set of strategic possibilities. The moral of this discussion, including that of the previous paragraph, is that mixed strategy equilibria should be carefully considered on their merits in the context of the particular game under consideration.

Games with *multiple Nash equilibria* also present problems for rational choice, this time in choosing which equilibrium the other players will expect. For instance, as for Chicken, in the Battle of the Sexes game (□ p. 109) there are two pure strategy Nash equilibria (plus a third Nash equilibrium in mixed strategies), but this does not really help the two lovers in deciding where to meet. What we require is a stronger notion of rationality that enables us to choose between Nash equilibria. Consider game D1 (in table 7.8), which is a variant of a general *coordination game*. Ada and Betty are driving in opposite directions along a narrow country lane. When they meet, they can either swerve to the left (L) or to the right (R). If they fail to coordinate strategies, they crash. There are two pure strategy Nash equilibria (both go L and both go R) plus one in mixed strategies (each swerves L or R with equal probability). What will be the outcome? There is little within the structure of this problem to help the players. They might just as well do

Table 7.8   Game D1.

		Betty	
		L	R
Ada	L	0, 0	−2, −2
	R	−2, −2	0, 0

anything. Of course, if they could meet beforehand and establish an agreement, or convention, that they would drive on one side or the other, then that would be mutually beneficial and self-enforcing. If the game is repeated, then a convention might evolve over time (Sugden, 1986b). But what if the game is one-shot? What if such a meeting is not possible?

Schelling (1960) introduced the concept of a *focal point*, which both players can recognize as a way of solving their choice problem in the presence of multiple equilibria. A focal point is an outcome that can claim salience in the minds of all players; for instance, if swerving to the R shakes the nerves rather more than going L. Game D2 (in table 7.9) is sometimes called assurance, and gives the revised pay-offs. The Nash equilibria remain exactly as before (except that, somewhat surprisingly, the optimal mixed strategy equilibrium now involves going L with a probability of only 1/3, yielding an expected pay-off of only −4/3). Of these equilibria, {L, L} gives a superior pay-off to both players (that is, it is **Pareto optimal** (▣)). Pareto optimality would seem to be a very good reason to focus on one particular equilibrium, and we might expect rational players to select the Pareto optimal Nash equilibrium if one exists. Of course, this is *not* the same as claiming (wrongly) that players would choose a Pareto optimal point which is not a Nash equilibrium. Nevertheless, once a sub-optimal equilibrium has been established, for whatever historical reasons, it may not be easy for independent players to move to the better equilibrium (see J.S. Mill's insightful analysis of 'The Nine-hour day' □ p. 145).

In game D3 (table 7.10), our two drivers have nerves of steel, but realize that the law supports driving on the left. It is only in the event of a crash that legal considerations enter the pay-offs. {L, L} is no longer Pareto optimal, but

Table 7.9   Game D2, the Assurance game.

		Betty	
		L	R
Ada	L	0, 0	−2, −2
	R	−2, −2	−1, −1

BATTLE OF THE SEXES

Boy and girl are very fond of each other, and enjoy each other's company. Boy also enjoys watching a football match (M) on Saturday afternoons, but girl prefers to watch a film (F). [If you find this example too gender stereotypical, boy might prefer the movie (M), and girl might prefer a fight (F).] Each knows that each other's pay-offs are as follows:

		Girl	
		M	F
Boy	M	3, 2	1, 1
	F	1, 1	2, 3

Thus, if they fail to meet, each is miserable (pay-off = 1); if they meet at the other's preferred venue, they are contented (pay-off = 2); and if they meet at their own preferred venue, they are happy (pay-off = 3). They are unable to contact each other this Saturday afternoon, so where should they meet?

There are two pure strategy Nash equilibria {M,M} and {F,F}, which is to say that if boy goes to the match, it is girl's best reply to do the same and vice versa; and, similarly, if each expects the other to go to the film, it is best for both to do so. There is also a mixed strategy equilibrium in which boy is twice as likely to go to the match as to the film, while girl is twice as likely to go to the film as to the match. More formally, each goes to their own preferred venue with probability 2/3. This might be achieved by rolling a die and going to the other's preferred venue only if a five or six comes up. Each then has an expected pay-off of 5/3.

How far does this formal analysis get us? It does demonstrate that some possible strategies are not rational. For example, if boy was expected to toss a coin and go to the match if it came up heads, girl would exploit the strategy. Given a 50 per cent chance that boy will be at each venue, there is no doubt that girl does best by going to the film. This gives girl an expected pay-off of 2 (that is, the mean of 1 if the coin comes up heads and 3 if it is tails). Given girl's reasoning, boy's best reply is not to toss the coin, but to go to the film. However, the Nash equilibrium analysis still leaves three rational strategies available, and provides no method of choosing between them. The battle of the sexes is discussed further in the text, but before reading on, think deeply as to how *you* would resolve this problem.

it may still be a focal point in the sense that it has a lesser penalty if you guess the 'wrong' equilibrium. This brief analysis of focal points further extends the idea that players can duplicate each others' thought processes. Apart from Pareto optimality and the cost of getting it wrong, other possible

Table 7.10   Game D3.

		Betty	
		L	R
Ada	L	0, 0	−2, −3
	R	−3, −2	0, 0

sources of focal points that arise from the structure of the game include symmetry, qualitative uniqueness and equity (each of which might favour the mixed strategy equilibrium in the Battle of the Sexes, even though it is Pareto sub-optimal).

This discussion of the last three games has used no information that is not specified in the rules of the game. In more realistic situations, away from the abstractions of a pay-off matrix, players may be able to draw on the context of the problem, cultural factors, history and experience in order to choose between equilibria. Even with pay-offs as in game D1, if Ada and Betty were driving in Scotland they might well feel that each would recognize left as the way to swerve; and the same two drivers might go right while on holiday in France. But what if they were in France and each clearly saw that the other was a British driver, with GB plates visible on the oncoming car? To be useful, a focal point must have a uniquely compelling claim to be recognized by both players, and this mutual recognition must be common knowledge.

Focal point theory adds many insights to our understanding of game situations, but its formal development has, to date, been rather limited. That cannot be said of another strand to the literature which has attempted to refine the concept of Nash equilibrium in order to eliminate 'unreasonable' equilibria. More will be said of these in the next two sections, but one idea can be introduced now. Consider game E (in table 7.11), which has two pure strategy Nash equilibria {T, L} and {B, R}. A promising line of argument is to claim that {B, R} is unreasonable because, for Bella, L weakly dominates R. There are two very different ways in which to justify the rejection of weakly dominated strategies. We could propose it as an axiom of rationality. A problem with this view will be discussed shortly. Alternatively, we can appeal to the possibility of mistakes. Suppose that Ann and Bella had got

Table 7.11   Game E.

		Bella	
		L	R
Ann	T	2,1	0,0
	B	1,2	1,2

together to agree on {B, R}. This is a self-enforcing agreement only as long as we do not allow either player to entertain even the slightest doubt that the other will play her agreed strategy. But what if Bella thinks that Ann just might make a mistake in implementing her strategy? (For instance, her hand could tremble when trying to push button B and she might push T by accident). Bella would be left with a zero pay-off. Although everyone might agree that this possibility is exceedingly unlikely, Bella can costlessly 'insure' against it by playing her weakly dominant strategy L. Now Ann will appreciate this and, following the logic of Bella playing L, she will not find it in her best interests to play B, and so will switch to T. Unfortunately for Bella, the temptation she finds to 'defect' from B leaves her with a worse pay-off. In the jargon, {B, R} is not a *trembling hand (perfect) equilibrium*.

At first sight, this seems entirely reasonable as a criterion for eliminating unattractive equilibria. However, consider game F (in table 7.12, and attributed to Kreps). There are two pure strategy equilibria, {T, C} and {B, L}}. {B, L} is clearly Pareto optimal and a strong focal point, but T weakly dominates B, and so {B, L} is not a trembling hand equilibrium. As a theory of perfectly rational play, the dominance argument is actually too strong in this case, because R is a self-evidently irrational strategy and so should not enter the considerations of rational players. Furthermore, this 'mistakes' argument is questionable on the grounds that, with so much at stake, accidental play of R is unlikely to concern the decision-makers too much. You may decide for yourselves what you would do if faced with this game in real life.

Table 7.12 Game F.

	L	C	R
T	50, 0	5, 5	1, −10 000
B	50, 50	5, 0	0, −10 000

It is time to take stock and ask a question that has been lurking in the background of this discussion of solving games. What question, or questions, are answered by game theory? There are at least three candidates:

1 What strategies *would* be chosen by hypothetical, perfectly rational, self-interested players?
2 What *do* real decision-makers actually do in situations of interactive choice?
3 What *should* people do in such situations?

The first can be accepted as uncontroversial, but if (1) alone were true, then game theory should remain a fairly esoteric branch of mathematics. The reason for its current popularity is that more and more social scientists are claiming that it gives real insight into question (2). Some applications are given in GAME THEORY APPLIED (9), and in numerous branches of economics (such as oligopoly theory and macroeconomic policy analysis) and some branches of politics (such as choice of party manifesto), game theory has been able to provide a much deeper understanding of behaviour than was previously possible. Even if decision-makers do not explicitly search for best reply equilibria, they often seem to act as though they do. On page 126, we shall also briefly discuss an evolutionary argument that, somewhat surprisingly, supports the sophisticated behaviour discussed in this section. As usual, the 'should' questions are the most controversial, and (3) is no exception. What makes this one such a minefield, though, is that the best advice is dependent on the rationality of the other players. If the others are not fully rational game theorists, then a theory of how one should behave, based on the assumption that they are rational, could be seriously misleading. For instance, returning to game B, in which Alice and Beth naively agreed {B, L}, who would benefit from their talking to well-trained strategic advisers on the way to their respective committee meetings? And even if they had not met beforehand, might they have (irrationally) focused on {B, L} in the absence of deep, game-theoretic thought? The harder you think about it, the more compelling the Nash equilibrium becomes; but then how hard do most people think about their decisions?

Introducing Time

The games discussed so far have all involved simultaneous decision-making. Very often, however, there is a well-defined sequence in which decisions are made. This raises a whole new set of strategic possibilities as moves are made to influence the future behaviour of other players. It opens up a world of threats, promises, reputation and investment. First, we need a simple way in which to represent games that explicitly involve time. This is conveniently accomplished by using a *game tree*, which is a map of individual moves in a game. In formal terms, this specification of a game by individual moves, as opposed to summary strategies, is called the *extensive form*. The game tree for the Battle of the Sexes (□ p. 109) is drawn in figure 7.1 as game G1. Decision nodes are represented by circles, and the terminal dots precede the pay-offs. Boy (B) is first to move, choosing either M or F. Only once boy has chosen does girl (G) get her chance to choose. As drawn in G1, the dotted oval depicts the fact that even though boy has chosen, girl does not know what he has chosen; only that a decision has been made. Thus, she does not know whether she is actually at the upper or lower decision node. In this way, the game tree has been drawn to include effectively simultaneous

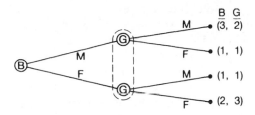

Figure 7.1 Game G1.

decision-making, and the analysis is no different to what has already been described. Game G2 (figure 7.2) is identical to G1, except that it changes the informational structure of the Battle of the Sexes to make girl aware of boy's prior choice. Thus, in the absence of dotted lines around girl's two decision nodes, and depicting lack of information about what has happened in the past, the game is transformed into one of perfect information. Each makes their decision in full knowledge of exactly what the other has done. The question is, does this change in information, which makes decision-making truly sequential, alter the rational outcome of the game?

The first point to note is that the two pure strategy Nash equilibria remain. If boy goes to the match (M), girl's best reply is to go to the match; in which case the match is boy's best reply. And if girl goes to the film (F), boy's best reply is the film; in which case the film is also girl's best reply. However, the latter has an unattractive property in that it is supported by an implicit *threat* which would not be in girl's own best interests to carry out: that is, although if girl says she is going to the film and boy agrees to go too, they would each be making best replies to each other, if boy were actually to go to the match, girl would reply by joining him and boy would be better off. Girl's threat is not *credible*. More formally, {F, F} is not a *subgame perfect Nash equilib-rium*, which is to say that once we reach the subgame represented by the right-hand branches in the top half of the game tree, the threat to play F is no longer a best reply (equilibrium strategy). Subgame perfection would

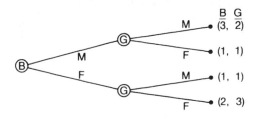

Figure 7.2 Game G2.

seem to be a very reasonable restriction on rationality. Although the idea was only formalized, somewhat obscurely, by Selten (1965) and, rather more accessibly, in Selten (1978a), it rapidly became *de rigeur* for economic models in the 1980s. In games of perfect information, such as G2, a pure strategy subgame perfect equilibrium always exists; and as long as there are no ties in the pay-offs, so no-one is indifferent between strategies, it is unique – and so there is no problem of choosing between equilibria. These results do not necessarily hold, however, if information is not perfect (as, for example, in game G1).

Is there any way in which girl could act strategically to make her threat to go to the film more credible? Schelling defines *strategic behaviour* as an action 'that influences the other person's choice, in a manner favourable to one's self, by affecting the other person's expectations on how one's self will behave' (Schelling, 1960, p. 160). Game G3 (figure 7.3) modifies the Battle of the Sexes to allow girl to buy her film ticket beforehand. (We assume that it is established practice for each to buy their own ticket wherever they go, and that these costs are already included in the pay-offs.) The top half of the game tree is exactly as in G2, but the bottom half represents the conse-quences of girl having already bought her film ticket for £1.50. Boy's pay-offs are unaltered, but girl will have wasted the cost of her film ticket if she ends up going to the match. (It is important that she cannot re-sell the ticket for its purchase price; otherwise the pay-offs would be identical in each half of the tree.) Consider what happens if girl buys her film ticket and boy goes to the match. Girl's best reply is now to go to the film, because a pay-off of one is better than the 0.5 she would receive by going to the match. Given that girl has bought the ticket, if boy goes to the film, they follow the bottom

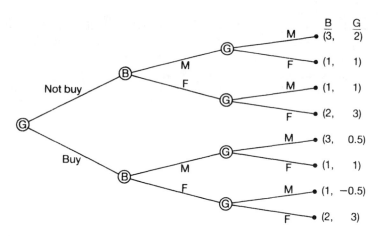

Figure 7.3   Game G3.

branch of the game tree and he receives a pay-off of 2; and if boy goes to the match he receives only one. Thus, conditional on girl having bought her ticket, he will join her at the film. Since girl prefers this outcome (she receives 3) to the outcome if she does not buy the ticket (she would end up at the match and receive only 2), the subgame perfect equilibrium is for her to buy the ticket and then for both to go to the film. This is an example of how a *commitment* can strengthen your position even if, or rather because, it makes certain outcomes worse for you and none any better. Note that boy's pay-offs are unaltered by girl's commitment, which works by affecting his expectation of how she will behave. It also illustrates a *first-mover advantage*, in that if boy has the first move, he does better, but if girl gets to move first, that is to her advantage. This is often, but by no means always, the case, and a rather trivial example of second-mover advantage would be matching pennies, if the rules were changed to allow sequential calls.

A second way in which time is important in game theory, apart from revealing the sequence of decision-making, is when the same one-shot (or one-period) game is repeated by the same set of players. Such *repeated games* are sometimes called *supergames*, though the latter term is best avoided since it is defined differently by different people. The crucial possibilities that repetition opens up are for (i) punishment and reward, and (ii) learning and reputation-building. The former idea is developed in the remainder of this section, and the latter is discussed in the next.

Suppose that the villains in the Prisoner's Dilemma are regularly apprehended by the police. Suspend disbelief for the moment, and further suppose that each prisoner expects to face this situation an infinite number of times. Is it possible for one prisoner to credibly promise to not confess and/or credibly threaten to confess in the future in order to encourage cooperation now? One way in which to achieve this is to adopt the following *trigger strategy*: not confess (cooperate) in the first round and all subsequent rounds unless the other prisoner confesses, in which case confess in all subsequent rounds (or, more generally, revert to the one-shot Nash equilibrium). What is the best reply to an opponent playing such a strategy? Confess gives a one-period gain of 0.1 (1 less the 0.9 that could be had by not confessing) but at the expense of losing 0.8 (0.9–0.1) in the next and all subsequent periods. If pay-offs in all periods are valued equally, it clearly pays to not confess. Is the threat, implicit in the trigger, credible in the sense that it is in the trigger strategist's own best interests to confess in the round following a rival's confession? The answer is yes, because confess is a Nash equilibrium in the one-shot game (in fact, it is the dominant strategy) and one-shot Nash equilibria are always sustainable in a repeated game. Thus, trigger strategies constitute credible threats that sustain cooperation when played against each other. More formally, for the infinitely repeated Prisoner's Dilemma they result in a subgame perfect equilibrium, and the same basic idea can be applied to a wide range of games which have strategy combinations with Pareto superior pay-offs to the one-shot Nash equilibria.

Unfortunately, for those who feel there should be a single most rational thing to do, repetition also opens up a whole new set of possible equilibria. Trigger is not unique as a subgame perfect equilibrium. For example, permanent confession is also a best reply to itself. In fact, the *Folk Theorem* states that, in the absence of discounting, the set of subgame perfect equilibria in *infinitely repeated* games (that is, games which are repeated for an indefinite number of rounds) includes any strategy which gives an average pay-off no worse than what could be secured if rivals did everything in their power to harm you. In the case of the Prisoner's Dilemma, this means anything at least as good as permanent confession. In order to single trigger out of this set we would have to argue its virtues as a focal point, perhaps because it both secures high average pay-offs and is very simple to understand.

The discussion so far has assumed that pay-offs in the future are as valuable as pay-offs in the present (that is, no discounting). This may not be true, for two basic reasons. First, there may be **time preference and discounting** (🔖) of the conventional kind and, second, there may be an expectation that the game will end, with some fixed probability, in any given period. Either way, if discounting of the future is too severe, the current one-shot game regains its paramount importance. For example, trigger strategies cannot sustain the cooperative outcome if the temptation of a high current pay-off to confess exceeds the discounted value of future cooperation. Nevertheless, Abreu (1986) shows that, in general, there may be even more severe punishments than permanent reversion to the one-shot equilibrium, and these can credibly sustain more cooperation than trigger. The general conclusion is that infinite repetition can facilitate cooperative outcomes unless the future is heavily discounted.

A crucial feature of infinitely repeated games is that they always look the same in every period. You never seem to get any nearer the end, and this fact turns out to be deceptively important. Consider a *finite repetition* of the Prisoner's Dilemma (in other words, repetition for a *known* number of rounds). Suppose that the game is repeated 10 000 times. In the last period, the game is exactly the same as the one-shot case, so both players will confess. In the penultimate period, each knows that the other will confess in the final period and so the best reply is to do the same now. There is no credible threat of punishment because the worst will inevitably happen. But if this argument applies to period 9999, it also applies to period 9998, and so on. Following this process of backward induction through to period 1, the only subgame perfect equilibrium is to confess in each period. Neither trigger nor any other alternative strategy is sustainable. This has become known as the *backward induction paradox*, because it is surprising that a game which is repeated 10 000 (or any other fixed number of) times cannot sustain cooperation, whereas one which is repeated an indefinite number of times can (even with a high probability of termination at the end of each period). The crucial difference is that backward induction can only bite on a definite final period, but once it has bitten it is fatal to rational cooperation. The paradox is compounded by the fact that while infinite repetition is implausible as a specification of social games, it is the theoretical results of infinite repetition that are intuitively appealing and which appear to have empirical validity – we often do observe cooperation in repeated situations. Another backward induction paradox is given by the *Chain Store Paradox* (see □), although in that game the surprise is that formal game theory does not predict aggressive behaviour.

There have been a number of attempts to scythe through the finite

THE CHAIN STORE PARADOX

A chain store has branches in twenty towns. In each of these towns there is a single potential competitor, a small businessman who might raise money at the local bank in order to establish a second shop of the same kind. At the present time, none of the twenty small businessmen has enough personal capital to be able to obtain sufficient credit from the local bank; but as time goes on, one after the other will have saved enough to increase his personal capital to the required amount. Let us number the towns and businessmen from 1 to 20 in the order in which they accumulate sufficient capital. As soon as this time comes for each businessman, he must decide whether he wants to establish a second shop in his town, or whether he wants to use his personal capital in a different way. If he chooses the latter possibility, he stops being a potential competitor to the chain store.

If a second shop is established in a particular town, then the chain store has to choose between two price policies for that town. His response may be 'cooperative' or 'aggressive'. The cooperative response yields higher profits in that town, both for the chain store and the entrant (say, profits of 2 each compared with zero each if aggressive); but the chain store's profits are even greater in that town if there is no entry (chain store profits of, say, 5). If the chain store is going to be aggressive, it is better for the businessman contemplating entry to invest elsewhere (earning a profit of 1). The question is: Can the chain store build a reputation for aggressive response to entry (for example, in towns 1–5) in order to deter entry in the later towns? The paradox is that, counter to most people's intuition, if everyone is rational, it cannot.

In the last town, (town 20) the game can be represented as follows:

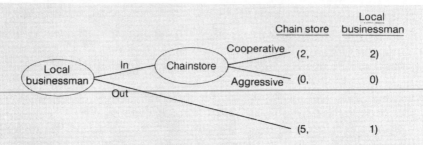

Whatever has happened in the past, if the local businessman decides to enter this market, the chain store's best response is to be cooperative (earning 2 rather than 0). Since there is no town 21, there is no longer any point in building a reputation for belligerence. This cooperative response would yield 2 for the local firm, and since this is better than the pay-off of 1 if he stays out, the business will enter. More formally, {in, cooperation} is the subgame perfect equilibrium. Next consider town 19. Local businessman 19 correctly reasons that the chain store will definitely cooperate in town 20, so it has no reason to develop its reputation in town 19. Thus, if the businessman enters, just as in town 20, the chain store's best reply is to be cooperative; so the local firm will enter. But then the same reasoning applies to town 18 and so on back to town 1. Given that there is a known number of potential entrants, there is nothing the chain store can do to prevent entry.

(adapted from Selten, 1978)

repetition paradox, more or less within the rational decision-making paradigm of formal game theory. One way in which cooperation can be sustained within finitely repeated games is if there are multiple one-shot Nash equilibria. This is *not* the case in either the Prisoner's Dilemma or the Chain Store Paradox, but in other games with a wider range of feasible strategies there can be two one-shot equilibria, with one Pareto dominating the other (that is, it gives both players a better pay-off). A sustainable trigger strategy might then be to cooperate until the other player defects, but revert to the worse one-shot equilibrium in all subsequent rounds in the event of defection before the last period; and to cooperate until the penultimate round, then go to the better one-shot equilibrium in the last period if the other player has also cooperated until then. This can be a self-enforcing agreement because, even in the penultimate period, the combined pay-off to one period of cooperation plus one period of the better one-shot Nash equilibrium can exceed that of one period of 'beating your rival to it' plus one period of the worse one-shot pay-off. Since real life is generally much more complex than the simple illustrative games used in this chapter, multiple one-shot equilibria may be common and so facilitate cooperative behaviour over a period of time. Nevertheless, this cannot explain the backward induction paradox for games with a unique one-shot equilibrium.

Another way out of the paradox is to argue that people are only approximate optimizers. For instance, with the Prisoner's Dilemma pay-offs (see □ p. 99) and repetition ten times without discounting, the pay-off to not confess in the first period, finding you have been made a sucker, and then confessing thereafter, is 0.9, or an average of 0.09 per period. If this is perceived as being so close as to make no difference to the 0.1 per period that can be expected from permanent confession, then it is known as an *epsilon-best reply* (Radner, 1980). And if both players are willing to play their epsilon-best replies, a cooperative epsilon-equilibrium will emerge, as they are willing to try for cooperation even though they do not necessarily expect others to follow suit. Although this begs a number of questions, such as how much non-optimization rational players will tolerate, it does give an explanation for cooperation early in a repeated game, but defection towards

THE NORM OF RECIPROCITY

A norm of reciprocity is, I suspect, no less universal and important an element of culture than the incest taboo, although, similarly, its concrete formulations may vary with time and place.

Specifically, I suggest that a norm of reciprocity in its universal form, makes two interrelated, minimal demands: (1) people should help those who have helped them, and (2) people should not injure those who have helped them. Generically, the norm of reciprocity may be conceived of as a dimension to be found in all value systems and, in particular, as one among a *number* of 'Principal Components' universally present in moral codes.

. . . the basic character of the reciprocity norm imposes obligations only contingently, that is, in response to the benefits conferred by others. Moreover, such obligations of repayment are contingent upon the imputed *value* of the benefit received. The value of the benefit and hence the debt is in proportion to and varies with – among other things – the intensity of the recipient's need at the time the benefit was bestowed ('a friend in need . . .'), the resources of the donor ('he gave although he could ill afford it'), the motives imputed to the donor ('without thought of gain'), and the nature of the constraints which are perceived to exist or to be absent ('he gave of his own free will . . .'). Thus the obligations imposed by the norm of reciprocity may vary with the *status* of the participants within a society [as well as the *culture* of that society].

(Gouldner, 1960, p. 171)

the end, which is an often observed pattern of behaviour. For instance, in the last period the difference in pay-offs between not confess as a sucker (and receive zero) and confess (and receive 0.1) may no longer be perceived as being close (in per period terms), so not confess is the unique best reply.

The game-theoretic approach allows players to have feelings of sympathy or spite and, as stated earlier, these must be incorporated in the pay-offs before analysing the game. However, it is a quite different matter to claim that one player is able to create an obligation for another to reciprocate an act of generosity (or revenge). This would be to allow the history of chosen strategies to endogenously modify the pay-offs, as opposed to simply allowing players to have an exogenous predisposition to take account of the welfare of others. Such arguments fundamentally undermine game theory. Many sociologists would claim that the norm of reciprocity (see □) is present to some extent in all cultures. Acts of kindness in the past create an obligation to undertake a roughly equivalent reciprocal act in the future, and so may sustain cooperation over time; and vengence tends to follow the biblical norm of 'an eye for an eye and a tooth for a tooth'. We shall return to this type of 'tit-for-tat' behaviour, but meanwhile the next section returns to strict game-theoretic reasoning in order to focus on an important role for information.

Incomplete or Asymmetric Information

So far, we have been examining an idealized world of complete information. Even though players may not know what moves others have made (so information need not be perfect), the available strategies and pay-offs of all players have been common knowledge. (Our one deviation from this assumption was in Harsanyi's justification for the implementation of mixed strategies.) Mother Nature may intervene in such games, but if she does all players have common knowledge about how everyone assesses the consequences. Furthermore, it has been common knowledge that all players are rational and are following optimizing strategies. It is obvious that, in reality, people are less than completely informed about other people's pay-offs, and are less than perfectly confident that rivals have had a rigorous training in game theory. One sturdy defence of complete information is that modelling in both the natural and social sciences requires a certain amount of abstraction in order to bring out the fundamental forces at work. For instance, the physics of a frictionless world gives insight into many problems. Nevertheless, we must ask: Does the introduction of a small amount of incomplete information completely overturn the complete information analysis? (Recall the drastic difference that long but finite repetition makes compared with infinite repetition.) Also, does incomplete information help explain aspects of

Table 7.13 Game H1.

		Bunty	
		L	R
Amy	T	2, 2	1, X
	B	1, 2	2, X

uman behaviour that are not explicable by complete information models? In order to get some purchase on these questions, we need to be able to mit the extent of incompleteness. In game H1 (table 7.13), Amy does not now Bunty's pay-off to playing right (R). Amy can calculate that her own est reply to left (L) is top (T), and to R is bottom (B). She can also see that unty will choose L if X is less than 2 and R if X exceeds 2. But this is insuffi- ient information on which to make a rational decision. The game theorist ; apparently left high and dry. However, is it realistic to believe that Amy as absolutely no information on X? Suppose that Bunty is a leading fashion esigner. She can either produce a range that is similar to last year's (L) or o for a radical (R) new design. Amy is less talented but can produce good opies. She has discovered Bunty's radical designs, and Bunty knows this and Amy knows she knows, and so on), but Amy does not know whether he fashion buyers like the radical designs. Bunty does know how much they re willing to pay, and is able to keep this value X as private information. oth must start production before finding out what the other is producing. he natural thing for Amy to do is to make an estimate of X. More formally, he can attach a subjective probability distribution to a range of possible alues. For instance, she might think that X falls anywhere in the range $0 \leqslant X \leqslant 3]$ with equal probability. Thus, X has an expected value of 1.5, nd Amy can reason that on balance Bunty is more likely to choose L, and o she should follow suit and choose T. Now, this example is rather trivial n that Bunty has a dominant strategy, and this reduces Amy's problem to he sort of decision theory discussed (and criticized!) in HOW PEOPLE :HOOSE (3). However, it does illustrate how game theorists are able to nodel games of incomplete information. The key assumption that is iecessary to make them tractable is that players are able to identify the range if possible pay-offs and attach a probability distribution to them. Games in vhich one player has more precise information than another, but for which irobability distributions are common knowledge, are known as games with :*symmetric information*. It is this class of game which is examined in this ection.

This approach, which is originally due to Harsanyi (1967, 1968), gains eal force when games have a sequence of moves so that learning can take place. The idea of learning through the actions of others is particularly clear in repeated games. For instance, even if Amy never observes X, she can infer from Bunty's actions what its likely magnitude truly is on the basis of Bunty's observed choice. In game H1, if X is fixed over a number of repetitions of the game, Amy can infer with certainty that if Bunty chose L in the first round, then $X \leqslant 2$, and if she chose R then $X \geqslant 2$. This can be deduced because Bunty's pay-offs are independent of Amy's actions. In all future rounds, the game becomes one of effectively complete information. However, if there is interdependence between Amy's actions and Bunty's pay-offs, some fascinating possibilities open up.

Consider game H2 (table 7.14), which is to be played twice. Amy believes, before round 1, that there is a 50 per cent chance that the radical design will be successful, in which case $X = 6$, and a 50 per cent chance that it will fail, in which case $X = 0$. Bunty knows the true value of X, so in the second round she will choose R if $X = 6$, and L if $X = 0$. But what about round 1? Suppose that $X = 6$: it may still pay Bunty to choose L in order to persuade Amy that $X = 0$ and so secure {T, R} in the second period. A naive Amy might think, in period 1, that the expected value of X is 3 ($= [0+6]/2$) and so R is most probable, in which case she should play B. If Bunty then chose L in round 1 Amy might revise her estimate of X down to zero, and play T in round 2. This bit of deception by Bunty would have netted Bunty 2 in round 1 plus 6 in round 2, a total of 8, which exceeds the $3 + 3 = 6$ that would have been attained by choosing the complete information best reply R in each round. The most astute of you will be protesting by now. If Amy is as clever as Bunty, she will have thought through Bunty's little ploy and taken into explicit account her incentive to dissemble. Of course, this in turn means that Bunty must take this into account, and so on. In order to solve this circle of reasoning, game theorists have appealed to **Bayes's rule** (🔖) to process information from the past, combined with subgame perfection to eliminate strategies which would not be credible in the future. Variations on this basic Bayesian solution concept have different names, but the one used most frequently is *sequential equilibrium*, and is due to Kreps and Wilson (1982a). The same basic technique can also be used to solve certain types of imperfect (but complete) information games, although these 'signal jamming' games are not discussed any further here (see Tirole, 1988).

Table 7.14   Game H2.

		Bunty	
		L	R
Amy	T	2, 2	1, X
	B	1, 2	X/2, X/2

The calculation of sequential equilibria is computationally burdensome, but the intuition of players taking strategic actions in order to manipulate the beliefs of others, and those others responding rationally by appreciating that their beliefs are being massaged, does add an important note of realism to our modelling of social interaction. One important application of this fundamental idea is in the theory of *reputation*. In some finitely repeated social situations, it will be in a player's best interests to appear to be less than perfectly rational, in the sense that he may wish to avoid the logical consequences of backward induction. Sometimes he may wish to build a reputation for belligerence, while on other occasions a reputation for cooperation may be more attractive. Let us briefly consider an example of each.

First, a reputation for cooperation would be attractive in the finitely repeated Prisoner's Dilemma. Kreps *et al.* (1982) show that cooperation can be sustainable if there is even a small amount of incomplete information. This may take one of several forms. For instance, one player may attach a small positive probability to the possibility that the other player is not perfectly rational, but is following a simple rule such as 'tit-for-tat'. Tit-for-tat is a strategy which is cooperative (in other words, 'not confess') to begin with, and remains cooperative until the other player defects (that is, confesses). Following a defection, tit-for-tat defects in the next period and continues to defect until the other player returns to cooperation, after which tit-for-tat would return to cooperation, and so on. Thus, it differs from trigger by allowing cooperation to re-emerge after a breakdown. Like trigger, tit-for-tat cannot be a 'perfectly rational' subgame perfect equilibrium strategy in a finitely repeated game because of the same backward induction argument. Now if a perfectly rational player believed that it was certain that his rival was playing a tit-for-tat strategy, his best reply would be to cooperate until the penultimate period, and then confess in the last. What Kreps *et al.* show is that even with a tiny probability that one of the players is tit-for-tat, rational cooperation is sustainable in the early rounds of a finitely repeated game, and only breaks down in the last few rounds. Basically, suppose that only player 1's full appreciation of backward induction is in doubt: then even if he is in fact fully rational it pays him to cooperate initially to reinforce player 2's doubts. Player 2 appreciates that player 1 is probably doing this, but as long as he is, he might as well go along with the deception. At some random date, one or other will finally crack and defect, so as not to be suckered. A closely related model is developed in more depth in GAME THEORY APPLIED (9). Briefly, an equally effective alternative to this reputation for less than perfect rationality can arise if rationality is common knowledge, but there is incomplete information about pay-offs. For instance, there might be a remote possibility that one player may not have a dominant strategy to defect in the one-shot game. In fact, even if one player thinks that the other player thinks that he might just not be rational, or might just not have a dominant strategy to defect, this doubt can facilitate the cooperative outcome in early rounds. Thus, the paradoxical results of backward induction are not robust to the introduction of a small amount of incomplete information.

An example of reputation building for belligerence can be developed from the Chain Store Paradox (□ p. 117). Kreps and Wilson (1982b) show that as long as potential competitors believe that there is a small possibility that the chain store would find it attractive to act aggressively in the one-shot game (for example, as it would be if the pay-off to aggressive behaviour was 3 instead of 0) then, even if untrue, it would still pay the chain store to actually be aggressive against early entrants in order to build a reputation for belligerence. Potential entrants should appreciate this incentive and so not trouble the chain store, at least until there were very few potential entrants left so that the value of such a reputation was small.

The game-theoretic analysis of incomplete information appears to add a note of realism both in the assumption that information can be held asymmetrically, and in the prediction that decision-makers can rationally build reputations for either cooperation or aggression. However, should you attempt to study any of the references cited in this section, it will soon become clear that the mathematical reasoning behind these results is incredibly sophisticated, and undoubtedly beyond the formal comprehension of nearly all decision-makers. The final section examines the consequences for interactive choice of behaviour that is intended to be rational, but which is limited by imperfect computational ability.

Bounded Rationality

Game theory has made a huge contribution in adding to our understanding of political, economic, social and military behaviour. A number of such applications, relating to individual choice and the consequences of human action, are developed in GAME THEORY APPLIED (9). Other chapters develop applications to BARGAINING (8) and the design of ORGANIZATIONS (10). However, despite its achievements, game theory does impose a remarkably sophisticated (unrealistic?) degree of calculating rationality on the analysis of problems involving social interaction. The remainder of this chapter provides a more critical view of some of the stronger assumptions of game theory, and introduces some alternative models of interactive choice.

Many people view game theory as a very technical, mathematical subject, populated by esoteric 'fixed point theorems' and 'convex hulls'. The latter are certainly of interest to the game theorist because it is academically interesting to know, for instance, under what rules of the game an equilibrium will exist.

However, such niceties are not generally of interest to the players themselves, who can usually proceed with no more mathematical sophistication than has been necessary to understand this chapter. Of course, this is non-trivial, but it is at least arguable that firms, politicians, generals and other important decision-makers have a strong incentive to get things right, and so are willing to invest the time and effort necessary to think through their rivals' positions before making a choice.

Nevertheless, simpler decision-making procedures might be appropriate either when decisions are perceived as being less important, or when the size of the computational problem exceeds the abilities of the players. Consider the problem posed by the Prisoner's Dilemma repeated 10 times. Experimental evidence suggests that cooperation is sustained in early rounds and only breaks down towards the end (see Roth, 1988, for a review). Two possible explanations within the analytical framework of game theory have already been discussed. The first, based on epsilon-best replies and approximate optimization, still requires the players to calculate the full consequences of each strategy. The second, based on incomplete information, requires a doctorate in Bayesian statistics if it is to be properly implemented (although approximate, intuitive implementation does not seem outrageously unlikely). Neither tackles the problem of bounded computational ability. How might this be modelled? One possibility is that players only calculate the consequences of their actions two or three periods ahead. On its own, of course, this makes backward induction even easier to see and so makes defection more likely. But if players see the problem as, say, 'two periods and the game continues' then it may be treated as effectively infinite until the end is 'in sight'. How people truncate large unwieldy problems is a gap in our understanding of human psychology.

A more radical alternative view of bounded rationality is to see what happens if players adopt simple behavioural rules. Since there will always be a large number of candidate rules, we need a mechanism to evaluate which rules will be chosen. It is natural to follow the lead of Charles Darwin and propose that rules, like genetic mutations, are naturally selected by survival of the fittest. In the realm of human behaviour this evolutionary process need not involve fertility and death (although it might in the case of warfare). Instead, observation and imitation of successful rules, or promotion to positions of greater decision-making power for those using successful rules, can equally well account for survival of the fittest.

This gives a mechanism for choosing between rules, but we have yet to specify how rules emerge in the first place. One possibility is that people apply their powers of reasoning, and incorporate their experience of similar situations in the past, in order to build a relatively simple rule on which to act when they come across similar situations in the future. In order to simulate the results of such behaviour, Axelrod (1984) challenged game theorists and the wider academic community to meet in a repeated Prisoner's Dilemma tournament. Players had to write their rules as computer programs, which were matched against each other in turn. Notice that because players were not allowed to revise their programs in the light of experience, they were able to effectively commit to a strategy that game theorists might consider irrational, in that it was not subgame perfect. Some of the submitted programs were very sophisticated, but the winner was the shortest (four lines of Fortran) and simplest – tit-for-tat. This strategy was submitted by Anatol Rapoport, a political scientist who has written and experimented extensively on the Prisoner's Dilemma. Tit-'for-tat's success was announced and the challenge was re-issued. The first tournament involved 200 repetitions: the second had a constant probability of ending, and so in game-theoretic terms it was infinite. Once again, tit-for-tat won. Interestingly, despite knowledge of the earlier results, only Rapoport submitted the winning program. Clearly, successful rules are not always imitated! But what made tit-for-tat so successful? Axelrod put it down to four attributes of the strategy:(i) it is *nice* in that it begins by cooperating; (ii) it *reciprocates* both nice and nasty behaviour very quickly; (iii) it is *not envious* of others who might try to snatch a quick profit; and (iv) it is *simple*, while more complex rules aimed at exploitation do badly when playing themselves. It is possible that a set of social rules based on this underlying morality might prove to be successful in a wider range of situations. However, this is speculation.

Axelrod's computer simulation approach combines calculated rule formation with natural selection. It is possible, however, to reduce even further the computational abilities of players and ask what happens if random rules, or mutations, meet each other in a tournament. Survival of the fittest will favour a rule which does well when played against itself because, otherwise, as the rule invaded the population, it would become weakened by lack of success. Furthermore, in order to invade the population in the first place, it must not be exploitable by rival rules. At the more formal level, the biologist Maynard Smith (1982) has defined an *evolutionarily stable strategy (ESS)* as one which (i) is a best reply to itself and (ii) if any other strategy is as good when playing the ESS, then the ESS does better against itself than the other does playing itself. Notice that requirement (i) is simply a definition of a symmetric Nash equilibrium in a symmetric game (that is, one in which two players have the same strategy sets and pay-offs), and (ii) is a refinement which is similar in spirit to a trembling hand. An interesting general application of this approach is in the theory of animal contests. Suppose that two animals are in dispute over territory or food, and there are only two types of rule that they might follow: 'A "hawk" fights without regard to any convention and escalates a contest until it wins or is seriously injured. A "dove" fights conventionally, never escalating: if its opponent escalates, it runs away before it is injured; two doves can settle a contest but only after a long period of time.' Following Maynard Smith (1982), suppose that serious injury has a payoff in terms of Darwinian fitness of -20. A victory pays 10, and a long contests costs 3 evolutionary points. If hawk meets hawk or dove meets dove, each has a 50 per cent chance of victory. In **expected value** (▤) terms, the pay-off if hawk meets hawk is $\frac{1}{2}(10)+\frac{1}{2}(-20) = -5$ if hawk meets dove, hawk receives 10 while dove gets 0; and if dove meets dove, the expected pay-off for each is $\frac{1}{2}(10)-3 = 2$ The unique ESS turns out to be to play hawk with probability 8/13 and dove with probability 5/13. Put another way, if behaviour is genetically carried, the population can be expected to evolve such that 8/13 are aggressive and 5/13 are passive. Any deviation from these proportions if, say, more hawks were born, would lead to a greater chance of hawk meeting hawk, resulting in attrition of the hawks until the ESS proportions return. What is really striking is that this model of random mutations, without any remnants of individual choice, brings about exactly the same equilibrium as is predicted by game theory, in which sophisticated players calculate best replies and then replicate each others' thought processes before making equilibrium decisions. This can be seen by writing down the pay-off matrix:

	Hawk	Dove
Hawk	$-5, -5$	$10, 0$
Dove	$0, 10$	$2, 2$

The structure of the game is formally identical to Chicken (□ p. 106) and, as for Chicken, there are two pure strategy and one mixed strategy optimizing equilibria. However, only the mixed strategy is evolutionarily stable. An example taken from the animal kingdom is given in the box (□ p. 128). The application of ESSs to economic and social situations, and their significance for the emergence of conventions, are explored in depth in Sugden (1986b).

Although our discussion of behaviour has progressed from the sophisticated down to the crudest possible hawk versus dove rules, there does, perhaps, remain a gap in our analysis of interactive decision-making in that there has been no explicit, creative role for the imagination. Of course, imagination is necessary to set up a model of the problem requiring a decision. When two motorists meet at a junction, they do not process every detail of car colour, the weather and the age of each driver, nor do they consider all conceivable strategies such as doing a U-turn, deliberately crashing into a wall, or letting down their tyres! Instead, a small number of potential strategies is selected (for example, stop or continue) and pay offs are

GAMES FOR DUNG FLIES

Female dung flies lay their eggs in cowpats, and so males congregate at cowpats and try to mate with the arriving females. Parker found that the rate at which the females arrive at a cowpat decreases as the cowpat gets stale. In game terms the male is presented with a choice of two tactics as the cowpat he is patrolling gets stale. He can leave in search of a fresh cowpat or he can stay. The success of the male's choice of tactic of course depends on the behavior of other males. If most of the other males leave as soon as the cowpat gets stale, then he should stay, because although relatively few females will be arriving, he will have little or no competition in mating with them. On the other hand, if the other males stay, then he should leave. In other words, the only evolutionarily stable strategy is a mixed one in which some males leave early and others stay. Game-theory analysis predicts that with this strategy when the system reaches an equilibrium, early-leaving and late-leaving males should have the same average mating success. Parker's data yield precisely that result. It is not known, however, whether the evolutionarily stable mixed strategy of the dung fly is achieved by some males' consistently leaving early and others' consistently leaving late or by individual males' varying their tactics.

(Maynard Smith, 1978)

weighed up on the basis of a few key characteristics (such as the speed of the cars, the width of the road and traffic law). This process of abstraction, or model formation, might be seen as a computational problem of eliminating obviously dominated strategies, but that would trivialize the rapidity with which we formalize problems sufficiently to make decisions. It also ignores the fact that two people can often use the same data to frame a problem in very different ways. Discussion and argument may then lead to a convergence of their views, but that only reinforces the point that they imagined it to be different in the first place.

Selten (1978b) picks up on this role for imagination, and places it in the middle of three levels of decision-making. The first level is that of routine, in which rules are followed without too much thought. The second level is that of the imagination, in which rough scenarios are compared. The third level is that of reasoning, in which the full paraphernalia of game-theoretic logic is deployed. Initially, a routine level decision must be made as to whether to analyse the problem at the higher levels. Suppose that all three levels have been activated. Does that necessarily mean that the optimum derived from reasoning, the highest level, will be the chosen strategy? Selten argues that this will not necessarily be so, because the imagination has structured the problem in the first place and there is no guarantee that it has specified it correctly. The imagination, or 'gut feeling', may (quite rationally?) overrule reason. With this subversive thought in mind, the following chapters examine some applications of rational, reasoning game theory.

Bruce Lyons

Further Reading

The classic text by Luce and Raiffa (1957) still provides one of the more readable and critical introductions to game theory. Rasmusen (1989) tackles some difficult topics very clearly, and Fudenberg and Tirole (1989) is more approachable and general than the title suggests. The introduction to Binmore and Dasgupta (1986) provides a reasonably accessible treatment of some of the deeper issues. However, each of these references requires a certain amount of mathematical sophistication on the part of the reader. The first part of Lyons and Varoufakis (1989) takes some of the topics dealt with here a little further (but beware of some dreadful typographical errors on pages 103 and 122). Most readable of all are Dawes and Thaler (1988) on why people cooperate, and Sugden (1986b) on evolutionary stability as applied to a wide range of social institutions.

8

Bargaining

The history of this book is as follows. A representative of the publishers visited the University of East Anglia and approached the authors to write a book on 'The Theory of Choice', a broad research area in which each of us was working. We considered this to be a valuable project and so wrote a proposal, to which the publisher responded with an offer of royalties plus various guarantees on distribution. We found the offer quite reasonable but felt that the royalties might be a little higher, and so proposed a counter-offer. The publishers agreed and a contract was signed. Authors and publisher then proceeded to fulfil the terms of the contract, and you are reading the result. This example of negotiation prior to a mutually beneficial joint venture is illustrative of a whole range of bargaining situations. In this chapter, I apply the method of GAME THEORY (7) in order better to understand how the benefits of joint action are shared between participants.

The simplest model of a bargaining game is where two people are offered a pie, but can consume it only if and when they are able to agree how to share it. If they fail to agree, the pie will be taken away. The *bargaining problem*, then, is to agree shares, and the incentive to agree is that the pie cannot be enjoyed without agreement. It turns out that this apparently simple example is rich enough to illustrate the key issues in strategic bargaining. However, a word of caution is required before we proceed. The intention, as with all game theory, is to understand how rational people would solve the bargaining problem. As argued elsewhere in this book, however, not everyone acts with this form of instrumental hyper-rationality all of the time. Whether or not they act as game theory predicts may, in fact, depend on the social context in which the bargaining problem is presented. It might matter to the outcome whether negotiations are between a firm and union over wages, two superpowers over an arms agreement, a buyer and seller of a second-hand car over price, a husband and wife over domestic chores, or an author and publisher over a book. Each application is analogous to the abstract example of splitting a pie (although in the first two examples, the size of the pie may depend on the bargained outcome) and game theory treats them all as fundamentally identical. However, the social context is very different in each case. We shall return to the social dependence of bargaining outcomes in a later section.

There are two ways in which game theorists analyse bargaining. The first, developed here, investigates the *process* by which agreements come about. Negotiation procedures are specified and the outcomes at which rational people would arrive can be derived. A fundamental problem with this approach is that, even granted the hyper-rational agents postulated by game theory, there are any number of procedures that can be followed, and we might be in danger of coming up with little more than an arbitrary bundle of possible snapshots. Fortunately, it turns out that a range of quite different negotiation procedures arrive at a division of the pie that can be characterized in the same straightforward way, although the source of bargaining power may differ in each case.

The alternative game-theoretic approach to bargaining is to avoid specifying a procedure, but instead suggest three or four general principles (or axioms) as to how we would expect rational people to share the pie. Remarkably, this quite different, cooperative approach can give exactly the same answer as confrontational, non-cooperative negotiation. These similarities are the subject of the next section, throughout which, we consider an abstract world in which individuals are rational and extremely well informed. For such a world, the analysis never predicts wasteful conflicts such as strikes or wars. No-one ever walks away from the negotiating table without an agreement. Unfortunately, the real world is otherwise, and the causes of such conflict are considered in the subsequent section. A brief final section reviews some experimental evidence which attempts to establish whether people really do bargain in accordance with game theoretic rationality, or whether they are more likely to observe a social norm such as 'fairness'.

Rational Negotiation

In real-world negotiation processes, people will often adopt attitudes, feign anger, act as if disinterested, discuss tangential issues, curse, shout and/or thump the table. None of these human traits belongs in this section.

Although social psychology can tell us something about why people do these things, deception and threats are unlikely substantially to affect the outcome for well-informed bargainers. By stripping away these fleshly tendencies, it is easier to see how the skeleton works. Of course, the flesh is interesting, but it will be better understood once we fully appreciate the bare structure. Throughout this section, we assume that there are two people bargaining over a pie. Each has complete information in that each knows how the other values any partition of the pie, and knows the mutual consequences of prolonged negotiation or eventual failure to agree. With this same informational structure, Nash (1953), Zeuthen (1930) and Rubinstein (1982) analyse three quite distinct negotiation procedures, each serving to illuminate some aspect of bargaining.

An elderly maiden aunt, Ada, who had a wicked sense of humour, had a niece called Ann and a nephew, Ben, as her only surviving relatives when she died. Her will dictates that Ann and Ben, who share no familial love, must send sealed bids for a share of her estate to the executor's office to arrive on a specified date. Once these bids have arrived, there can be no re-negotiation of claims. If the bids sum to more than the value of the estate, everything is given to the local dogs' home. Otherwise, each receives what they bid, and the dogs' home gets the residue (if any). This very simple structure serves to introduce some key sources of bargaining power, such as control of the sequence of bids, risk aversion and disagreement costs.

In the language of the chapter on GAME THEORY (7), it is a strictly competitive, simultaneous-move game; and it has multiple Nash equilibria. If Ann demands a proportion x, then Ben's best reply is $(1 - x)$, so *any* partition of the estate that has $0 \leqslant x \leqslant 1$ and sums to 1 is an equilibrium. Of course, if one bargainer could commit to a bid before the other, and let the other know it, then this indeterminacy vanishes. If Ann can commit herself first, she will offer Ben only enough to make him better off with agreement than without (perhaps a nominal £1). This illustrates the first source of bargaining power, which is enjoyed by those who can influence the sequence of bids (see AGENDAS (17)). But it also illustrates why rational bargainers will do everything they can not to be left with a take-it-or-leave-it offer. Ben will race Ann to make the first, and his last, offer. Nevertheless, in the absence of an asymmetry that gives one person the advantage, the initial indeterminacy remains.

One way in which players might try to narrow down the range of rational outcomes (equilibria) is to look for a focal point, which is to say a partition of the cake that particularly commands the attention of both bargainers (see GAME THEORY (7)). One such possibility is equal shares. Another is to follow some convention such as that the male or the older person shall receive twice as much. Which is chosen will depend on historical experience, culture and other social conventions. An alternative and more neutral way in which the range of outcomes can be reduced is to build on the idea that one person might be more desperate to reach an agreement than the other. In effect, this is the route followed by Nash (1953) in what has become known as his 'demand game'. Incorporating even an extremely small possibility that Ann and Ben may fail to agree results in their choosing a unique division of the estate. If Ann's utility from receiving a share x is written as $u_1(x)$, and Ben's utility from a share $1 - x$ is written as $u_2(1 - x)$, and if the consequence of their failure to agree is that Ann and Ben would receive $\bar{u}_1$ and $\bar{u}_2$ respectively, it turns out that Ann should bid the value of x (obviously with $0 < x < 1$) which maximizes

$$[u_1(x) - \bar{u}_1] [u_2(1 - x) - \bar{u}_2]$$

and Ben bids $1 - x$. A relatively simple proof using elementary calculus is given in Sutton (1986). What this expression says is that the outcome of the demand game maximizes the product of Ann's utility *gain* and Ben's utility *gain* – the *Nash product*. For instance, if Ann and Ben receive nothing without agreement, so that $\bar{u}_1 = \bar{u}_2 = 0$, and if utility is linear in shares of the estate (see **Risk Aversion** (⧉)), the Nash product boils down to maximizing $x[1 - x]$, which results in $x = 0.5$. All the hard work in reaching this equal shares result hardly seems worth it! But what if Ann is risk-averse or, equivalently, if she values the first 10 per cent of the estate much more than the next 10 per cent and so on; while Ben remains risk-neutral or, equivalently, values each 10 per cent equally? Maximizing the Nash product shows that Ben will bid for more than a half, and Ann for less. For example, if Ann's utility is given by the square root of x, so that a doubling of her share would raise her utility by only 41 per cent, she will bid and receive only $1/3$ of the estate, while Ben receives $2/3$. Observe that if Ann is a poor single parent, and Ben is a wealthy foreign exchange dealer, their attitudes to risk (extra wealth) *are* likely to look something more like this, and he will receive the lion's share. Bargaining does not necessarily arrive at 'fair' outcomes but the theory does tell us something about the nature of POWER (15). This second source of bargaining power is derived from having a more relaxed attitude to risk.

This source of bargaining power depends on the strong informational requirement that each player knows the shape of the other's utility function. In some situations, Ben may have been able to observe Ann's actions in the past (or vice versa) and so deduce her (or his) attitude to risk. If this becomes common knowledge, then the Nash product outcome is quite plausible. However, such observation is often not possible, and even if it is, then Ann has an incentive to misrepresent her preferences when she knows she is being observed. In fact, if misrepresentation is free of cost, each bargainer will do best by proclaiming that (or acting as if) they are risk-lovers or, if that is not possible, risk-neutral (that is, have linear utility) and the estate will be shared equally. If at all possible, then, Ann would not wish to reveal her true risk aversion (see Crawford and Varian, 1979, for a formal proof that this form of misrepresentation is the dominant strategy).

Attitudes towards risk are not the only factors that enter the Nash product. *Status quo* utilities, which is to say those obtained in the event of no agreement, also play a key role. If we stay with the case of linear utilities, (that is, no risk aversion) the Nash demand game gives Ann a share $x = [1 + \bar{u}_1 - \bar{u}_2]/2$. For example, if the aunt has added a codicil to the will giving Ann 1/4 of the estate in the event of no agreement, but has made no such provision for Ben, then rational bargaining gives Ann 5/8 of the estate. The intuition is similar to the case of risk aversion; because a deal means less to Ann, Ben is compelled to bid for less than half. Thus, disagreement utilities provide a third dimension to bargaining power.

The importance of disagreement outcomes raises the possibility of strategic behaviour, with the bargainers threatening each other as to what they might do in the event of no agreement being reached. For instance, Ben might threaten that he would set fire to Ann's house. If believed, this has the effect of reducing her disagreement outcome, $\bar{u}_1$, and so improving Ben's equilibrium share. Of course, Ann has an incentive to make similar threats, and the greater share goes to the person who can make the most horrible, yet believable, threats. There is an important constraint on such threat-making behaviour. Threats have no impact unless they are credible; that is, unless they would be in the threatener's own best interests to carry out if negotiations did break down and the decision to carry out the threat had to be made. If they are not, they are unlikely to affect the outcome of the bargain (see Schelling, 1956). Thus the threat to burn down Ann's house is probably not credible, because arsonists are sent to prison. Similarly, a superpower threatening an escalation of the arms race in order to influence the outcome of arms reduction talks could not credibly threaten to commit 90 per cent of national income to defence.

At this point, you might feel at the same time enlightened by the discussion of the Nash product, but wary that so much is built on such an implausible negotiation procedure as the Nash demand game. An appropriate response to this worry is to analyse a range of alternative and more realistic bargaining processes, and see whether they undermine or reinforce the earlier insights. For instance, Zeuthen (1930) focuses on the way in which concessions come about. Suppose that a firm and a union are bargaining over wages and, to keep things simple, that employment is predetermined. Unlike the demand game, bids summing to more than the size of the pie can be revised down until agreement is reached. The union arrives at the negotiating table with a demand for a 20 per cent increase, and the firm says it is unwilling to give any pay rise this year. What happens? A simplistic view might be that each would concede at the same rate and converge on 10 per cent. But if this process was expected, the union would initially demand 100 per cent (or more!) and the firm would open with an offer of a wage cut, and clearly such a procedure can provide no realistic bounds to the outcome. Zeuthen's insight was to argue that the party who has more to lose from not reaching agreement will be the first to concede. More precisely, he defines the union's risk limit as the ratio of the difference between the utility of its demand and that of the firm's offer to the difference between the utility of its demand and its *status quo* utility (in other words, that if no agreement is reached). The firm's risk limit is similarly defined by exchanging the words 'offer' for 'demand' and 'firm' for 'union'. The party with the lower risk limit, that is the one with more to lose, is expected to make the next concession. The process continues until union and firm agree. Now, this seems to involve much more realism than the simple one-bid bargain over the will. We see bargainers face to face over the table, making demands and counter-offers, finely balancing the gains to holding out against the fear of talks collapsing. We can almost smell the smoke and taste the lukewarm tea. What is even more striking, however, is that, as Harsanyi has shown, this very different negotiating procedure results in *exactly the same* division of the spoils as is predicted by the Nash product. Thus, everything that was said in relation to the Nash demand game – about incentives to commit, relative risk aversion and no-agreement outcomes – holds, without any need for modification, in a world of concessions motivated by fear of failure to agree.

Although Zeuthen's bargaining model has its attractions, and Harsanyi (1977) provides an elegant defence of it as a rational process, it can be accused of being *ad hoc* in the definition of risk limits and in motivating concessions. The last point is crucial. Why do bargainers reach agreement? The obvious answer is because they cannot enjoy the fruits of cooperative behaviour without agreement. But that misses the point. As Cross (1969, p. 13) so clearly put it, 'If it did not matter *when* the parties agreed, it would not matter whether or not they agreed at all'. Why, then, do they agree now rather than tomorrow or next year? Phrasing the question this way forces us to confront the issue of urgency, and two answers are possible. Early agreement may be motivated either by fear that the opportunity for profitable collaboration might disappear, or by a preference for enjoying the fruits of collaboration now rather than in ten years' time. It turns out that the question of which motivation is dominant can have a profound effect on the outcome of the bargain.

An example from international relations illustrates the point. Presidents Gorbachev and Bush are negotiating over reductions in nuclear weapons. The formal structure of the negotiation process is that Gorbachev makes a proposal which Bush can either accept immediately, or reject and, after a delay, respond with a counter-proposal. Gorbachev can either immediately accept the Bush counter-proposal or, after a further delay, offer another share of nuclear weaponary, to which Bush must respond. The process is repeated until agreement is reached. The purpose of this treatment of delay, first proposed by Rubinstein (1982), is explicitly to incorporate time, and so urgency, into the negotiations. Suppose that the urgency to reach agreement is because there is a chance, however small, that domestic political changes might make agreement not feasible in the future; or worse, that the current balance of arms might result in a mutually destructive nuclear exchange, possibly as a result of a mistake. You may no longer be surprised, but it is no less remarkable, that once again, as long as the delay between the offer and counter-offer is sufficiently small, and both bargainers have the same assessment of the risk of the opportunity for a deal disappearing, the equilibrium outcome of this bargaining procedure is exactly the same as that given by maximizing the Nash product. Furthermore, a rational bargainer will make this offer in the first round. Although the prospect of delay motivates agreement, actual delay would be an unnecessary waste because it merely serves to reduce the size of the pie. In the language of GAME THEORY (7), immediate agreement is the unique subgame perfect equilibrium.

Next, suppose that fears of no agreement are set aside, but urgency is derived from the fact that the Soviet economy is being ruined by high defence expenditures and the USA is sacrificing social security spending: thus postponing agreement incurs a cost, which may be different for each leader. The game-theoretic outcome of this negotiating procedure turns out to be sensitive to the specification of these costs. However, suppose, quite reasonably, that the value of any given agreement in the next round of negotiations is only a fraction $\delta < 1$, of its value now. Several interesting results emerge. First, the first person to make an offer has a slight advantage, which increases as δ decreases. For example, if Bush would accept a half share of the missiles in the next round of talks, Gorbachev need only offer him $(\frac{1}{2})\delta$ share now, and he would accept. For the same reason, agreement will be reached in the first round. A simplified example, which illustrates the reasoning, is given in the box 'Fairmen or Gamesmen?' (□ p. 141). Of course, in most negotiations, the time between offer and counter-offer will be small, which is equivalent to saying that δ is close to unity, and this asymmetry disappears. But it does suggest a rationale for the tactic of breaking off talks as a means of reducing your opponent's δ (for example, the Minister of Health offering nurses a small pay rise the day before going on a month's holiday in the Caribbean). Thus delay can be used for strategic advantage. Second, if Gorbachev and Bush have different rates of time preference (different δ's), then the more impatient of the two (lower δ) will receive the smaller share of the gains. A similar point applies when agreement is motivated by the fear of failure, in which case there is an advantage to being less risk-averse. Third, if the period between offers is very small, and both bargainers have similar rates of time preference (or risk aversion), yet again the outcome of negotiations is given by maximizing the Nash product.

Nevertheless, this careful analysis of the motivation behind reaching agreement remains crucial, because the interpretation of the Nash product is quite different in the time preference and risk-of-breakdown models. For example, with agreement motivated by fear of an accidental holocaust, the party that least fears the consequences of such an accident will be able to negotiate the lion's share. But if time preference is the issue, the one whose economy is suffering more, pending agreement, will do less well. Suppose that Bush is the one who feels he has more to lose from an accidental nuclear exchange, and Gorbachev's economy is bleeding more painfully due to excessive military expenditure. Who will secure the more favourable arms agreement? The game-theoretic analysis focuses clearly on the motivation for agreement as providing the key to the answer.

It is time to take stock. Many lessons have been learned concerning the nature of bargaining power: the value of commitment, the first move and the ability to impose delay; the disadvantage of impatience or risk aversion; and the weakness of having high costs during a dispute, or in the event of failure to agree. Furthermore, we have the remarkable fact that, as long as the bargaining procedure is symmetric, the consequences of at least three quite different negotiating procedures can be summarized by the outcome that maximizes the Nash product. This suggests that there might be a set of general principles at work. In fact, Nash (1950) had first looked at the bargaining problem with just such a set of axioms. He suggested four characteristics which he would expect in a rational bargain. First, he accepted von Neumann and Morgenstern's expected utility theory as a model of individual choice (see RATIONALITY (1); see also **utility function** (▨)). An important implication of this is the following : because this does not permit interpersonal comparisons, it effectively rules out notions of fairness to affect the outcome. Second, he proposed that whatever the shares, bargaining is efficient in that the gains are shared in full; in other words, we have **Pareto optimality** (▨). Third, suppose that two people are bargaining over something which can be shared many different ways, and the agreement reached is to give the first person x. Nash proposed that the outcome should remain such that the first person still receives x, whenever the bargaining problem is modified only by the unavailability of some of the previously discarded options. It is as if people search locally for proposals, ignoring more remote possibilities. This has become known as the 'independence of irrelevant alternatives'. Finally, there should be symmetry between the bargainers in the sense that although they may receive different shares of the cake, the outcome should not depend on their names, age, sex or anything else not summarized in their utility functions. Nash's achievement was to show that, provided that a unique solution exists, maximization of the Nash product gives the *only* outcome that is consistent with these four 'reasonable' conditions.

Some people have argued that one or other of the conditions is not, in fact, reasonable. For instance, Pareto optimality assumes efficient bargaining, and perhaps that is too strong. However, it turns out that nothing changes if the second condition is replaced by one that claims, much more weakly, that each person should receive more than she would in the event of no agreement being reached. More substantively, the independence of irrelevant alternatives has been criticized, and replacement conditions for this *can* result in different outcomes (Kalai and Smorodinsky, 1975; Gauthier, 1986). But this need not worry the student of non-cooperative bargaining unless these alternative conditions for a 'good bargain' can somehow be implemented by a realistic negotiation process. Here there are, as yet, no plausible stories to tell. Each of the stylized bargaining procedures in this section fall within the scope of the Nash axioms as long as the specified process is symmetric; and that, fundamentally, is why they result in the same bargained shares.

Conflict

There remains a significant gap in our discussion of bargaining. We have considered in detail who receives what share of the cake, but we have said nothing at all about the circumstances under which there may be failure to agree. Unfortunately, wars, strikes and protracted negotiations remind us that failure is not unknown. So why does damaging conflict arise? We can begin by observing the circumstances under which it does not. If all bargainers are perfectly rational and perfectly well informed, there can never be a reason for a destructive fight as long as there is potential for a mutually beneficial agreement. There is no reason for such bargainers to postpone an agreement that could be reached today because, for reasons already discussed, postponement is costly. A given share today is better than the same share tomorrow. Thus, a bargaining procedure that generates a unique equilibrium share of the pie *must* also predict immediate agreement. Nevertheless, several severe cracks can appear in the imposing edifice of no-conflict bargaining theory.

The first arises from incomplete information. Think back to Ann and Ben, deciding how much of the inheritance to claim. Suppose that Ben has no knowledge of the codicil that gives Ann 25 per cent if they fail to agree, and demands a 50–50 split. If Ann knows that Ben does not know, and cannot inform him of the truth, she can do no better than also to demand 50 per cent. But if Ann believes (falsely) that Ben knows about the codicil, she will demand 5/8, and they will fail to agree. If Ann knows that Ben does not know, she might try to inform him that her reservation utility is higher than he thinks. But a telephone call would lack credibility (why should Ben believe her?) unless backed up by, say, an independent solicitor, whose pay-offs are independent of the negotiated outcome. Alternatively, in a world of continuing negotiations, Ann might decide to demand a higher share initially, incurring costs of delayed agreement, in order to convince Ben that the codicil does, indeed, exist. Whether or not such signalling behaviour is credible, and the extent to which it can lead to 'rational' conflict, depends quite sensitively on the exact nature of incomplete information as well as the procedure in which negotiations take place. Nevertheless, it seems clear that a major justification for lengthy negotiations is that both sides are trying to inform (or misinform) each other.

In reality, bargaining problems are rarely isolated, but are linked over time and/or across parties. The consequences of this year's wage round can depend on what happened last year, and so last year's negotiations will have been conducted with an eye to the future. A union will often be negotiating with several employers, or a firm with several customers, at the same time. Politicians negotiate a range of policies during each Parliamentary session. In each case, the bargainer can carry her reputation from one set of talks to another. To observe that 'if I concede too much to you on this issue, I would be expected to do the same elsewhere' can be an effective way of raising your cost of concession and so raise your share of the gains. In part, this is just to say that the bargaining game is often wider and more complex than it first appears. But the notion of reputation is also tied closely to incomplete information, and thus to the risks of conflict. Information on your opponent's position in another negotiation is likely to be scarce, and your opponent has every incentive to pretend to be a tough nut even when, in truth, she has a soft centre (see GAME THEORY APPLIED (9)). If you were never to test your opponent's strength through costly conflict you would never know if you could negotiate for more next time.

The discussion so far has centred around procedures that generate a single rational division of the cake. However, some bargaining situations will not arrive at a unique outcome, and if there are multiple equilibria, or if people use mixed strategies, conflict must be expected as a result of the inability to coordinate perfectly. In other, perhaps more realistic, situations, actions that lead to a 50–50 share may be focal amongst multiple equilibria. But a 50–50 share of what? Utility gains? That is the game theorist's answer, but is it the way in which actual bargainers behave? Might they not have other notions of what is 'fair'; for instance, sharing monetary gains rather than utility gains, or bringing in extra 'irrelevant' information on the worthiness of each bargainer? Or, perhaps, if they find that the rational thing to do is too complex to calculate, might they try to latch onto a non-optimizing share that the sophisticated game theorist finds hard to understand? Once such a range of possibilities is opened up, the potential for conflict rapidly expands.

Another limitation of our discussion is that it has centred on just two parties bargaining with each other. The addition of more people to squabble over the spoils raises large new issues. Some of these, such as the possibility of coalition formation, are discussed elsewhere (see **core** (🔍)). Here, we have space only to scratch the surface of one question, that of what happens when one person negotiates with a group; for instance, the owner of a firm with a union of workers. One possibility is to *assume* solidarity in the group, in which case the question reverts to two-person bargaining. Another is to assume *no* solidarity and investigate, for instance, the asymmetries between workers with jobs and those without, to see whether bargaining or competitive outcomes result (Shaked and Sutton, 1984).

A third possibility is to ask how solidarity might emerge and be sustained endogenously in a bargaining situation. Akerlof (1980) draws on the fact that individuals enjoy being held in high esteem by their colleagues, as well as enjoying the material pleasures of *Homo economicus*. The esteem in which they are held depends both on their personal adherence to a group code of conduct, and the number of colleagues who uphold such beliefs. Thus, if sufficient people abide by the code, it can be worth sacrificing short-term pleasures, which would erode the value of the code, in order to benefit from future respect. For instance, individuals may prefer to join a strike, rather than free ride, so long as a sufficient number of others join in. Such a theory can help explain why, if called on to strike, union members act as one. But a small extra step can lead to a deeper theory of conflict. A code of practice, such as loyalty to the union, which is never tested would wither in the mists of time, possibly to the extent that a union could no longer rely on its members to join in a strike. This fact would not be missed by employers, and was recognized by Hicks when he observed that 'weapons grow rusty if unused . . . The most able union will embark on strikes occasionally' (1932, p. 142). Therefore, this sociological theory of conflict sees strikes and skirmishes as a necessary reinforcement of group norms, which serve to improve the group's bargaining position between battles. This provides a reminder that game theory, for all its undoubted virtues in clarifying the notion of bargaining power, needs to be supplemented with an account of social context before being applied to specific real-world situations.

Experimental Evidence

The game-theoretic approach to bargaining is rich in its predictions, and there is now a considerable body of experimental literature designed to test it as a theory of actual behaviour. In a typical experimental situation, people at computer terminals make offers to, and accept or reject offers made by, an anonymous person at another terminal. Anonymity is essential in order to eliminate any influence of friendship, fear of reprisal, and so on. The sums of money involved are normally very small, but subjects do receive what they negotiate. This very brief review can do little more than introduce some results from two sets of such experiments. In each case, the shares predicted by rational choice game theory can be compared with an alternative 'fair shares' hypothesis. In the first experiment, fairness dictates an equal division and game theory predicts inequality; while in the second experiment, fairness suggests an unequal division and game theory predicts equality.

The first experiment is described in 'Fairmen or Gamesmen?' (see □). Binmore *et al.* (1985) confronted 82 anonymous pairs of people with this problem: 37 per cent bid close to 50 pence (plus or minus 5 pence) in stage I, and only 20 per cent bid close to 75 pence. In 13 per cent

---

FAIRMEN OR GAMESMEN?

Suppose that the bargaining process is as follows, with only two possible opportunities for agreement between Ann and Ben.

In stage I, 100 pence can be shared. Ann proposes that Ben should receive x, leaving $100 - x$ for herself. Ben can choose either to accept, in which case they each receive what Ann has proposed; or Ben can choose to reject the proposal, in which case they move to stage II.

In stage II, the value of the pie to be shared is reduced to just 25 pence. Ben proposes that Ann should receive y, leaving $25 - y$ for himself. Ann can choose either to accept, in which case they each receive what Ben has proposed; or Ann can reject the proposal, in which case each receives nothing.

What will the outcome be? If Ann and Ben are both '*fairmen*', motivated by a social norm of equal gains, then Ann should propose that each receive 50 pence in stage I, and Ben should accept. On the other hand, if both are '*gamesmen*', seeking the best possible outcome for themselves, then Ann should propose that she receives 75 pence in stage I, and Ben should accept the remaining 25 pence.

The *gamesman's* reasoning follows backward induction. Suppose that stage II were ever reached. Then the best Ben could do is to offer Ann just 1 penny (that is, the minimum necessary to make her better off than with no agreement), leaving 24 pence for himself. If Ann is rational, she would accept this offer as better than nothing. Anticipating this analysis of stage II, the best Ann can do in stage I is to offer Ben 25 pence, leaving herself with 75 pence. If Ben is rational, he will accept this offer as better than the best he could expect by postponing agreement until stage II.

(adapted from Binmore, Shaked and Sutton, 1985)

of cases, there was failure to agree. These results do not appear to give much support to game-theoretic rationality. However, when the roles of those who had made first and second offers in the first trial were reversed, only 17 per cent opened with an offer close to 50 pence, and 62 per cent bid for close to 75 pence. Thus, there was a strong shift towards *gamesman* behaviour as subjects became more experienced and more aware of the significance of the structure of the bargaining situation.

The second set of experiments is analysed in 'Bargaining Over Lottery Tickets' (see □). Roth and various colleagues (Roth, 1988) found that two divisions of the lottery tickets, 20–80 and 40–60, were equally popular. In 17 per cent of cases, there was failure to agree. Once again, fairness seems to be a dominant motivation in the one-off experiment. Next Roth repeated the bargaining experiment for 25 trials, telling subjects that they were playing against different people each time. In fact, this was true in all cases for the last 10 trials, but only for a control group was it true for all 25. The

BARGAINING OVER LOTTERY TICKETS

One hundred lottery tickets, only one of which is a winner, must be shared between Ann and Ben. If Ann wins, she receives £4; while if Ben wins, he receives £1. The bargaining process is such that each person must bid simultaneously so that there are no asymmetries in bargaining power. Although the tickets can be shared, the prizes cannot.

If Ann and Ben are both *fairmen*, motivated by the idea of equality of gains, they might reason that Ben should receive more tickets to compensate for his lower potential prize. In particular, equality of expected prizes is obtained by Ann receiving 20 tickets and Ben getting 80 (each then has an expected gain of 80 pence: see **Expected Value** (□)). While *fairmen* would agree on a 20–80 share, *gamesmen* should share the tickets 50–50.

Gamesmen reason as follows. Ann has an expected utility gain of $pu_A(£4)$, where p is her probability of winning (that is the number of her lottery tickets divided by the total number to be shared), and $u_A(£4)$ is the utility she attaches to winning £4. Similarly, Ben has an expected utility gain of $[1 - p]u_B(£1)$. Now, any symmetric bargaining process which satisfies the Nash axioms will result in the p which maximizes the Nash product, $pu_A(£4)$ $\times [1 - p]u_B(£1)$. Thus, game theory predicts $p = \frac{1}{2}$. Attitudes to risk do not matter in the case of this discontinuous lottery, because there is no opportunity to trade more lottery tickets for a reduced prize, and this means that the utility of the prize is a fixed amount for each person. Expected utility can only be adjusted by changing the probability of winning, and Ann and Ben both have expected utility that is proportional to the number of tickets received.

remainder played against a computer for the first 15 trials. For half of these subjects, the computer was programmed only to make and accept offers in the region of a 20–80 split; and for the other half, the computer made and accepted offers only around 50–50. The first finding was that the control group converged to an average share of 45–55, which is a significant shift towards *gamesmen* behaviour as compared with the one-off trial. In the group that had been conditioned to a 50–50 split, subjects continued to offer and accept the same equal shares, with great stability thereafter. However, in the group conditioned to the 'fair' share of 20–80, there were considerable fluctuations around a mean of 30–70 in the last 10 trials, although with no clear trend towards equal shares. Thus, socialization does seem to have a persistent effect, although it is much more stable if it reinforces the game-theoretic outcome.

It appears that game-theoretic rationality does guide many people's choice, at least in bargaining situations which they understand well enough. But this is far from the whole story. At the very least, it takes repeated confrontation with a situation before most people can appreciate the implications. This helps to explain the existence of professional negotiators, not only as bloody-minded businessmen or hard-nosed trades unionists who have personal preferences which enhance bargaining power, but as cunning tacticians who can exploit an opponent's weakness. However, the experiment reveals a deeper problem for an individualistic theory of rational choice. The influence of conditioning suggests that the social context of a particular bargain influences behaviour in an important way. Finally, in each of the experiments described here, the subjects had complete information on the pay-offs and strategies available to both themselves and their opponents. Yet there was still around 15 per cent failure to agree. It is evident that pride, or some related emotion, is capable of motivating people to reject 'unfair' offers, even when they would be better off to accept.

Bruce Lyons

Further Reading

For a clear, intuitive statement of the tactics of bargaining, the classic essay by Schelling (1956) remains unsurpassed. Sutton (1986) and Binmore and Dasgupta (1987, chapter 1) provide excellent, complementary, technical introductions to bargaining theory. Binmore, Rubinstein and Wolinsky (1986) give a precise explanation of how properly to interpret the Nash product, and the second half of Lyons and Varoufakis (1990) gives more detail on the theory of conflict (see also Varoufakis, 1991). Roth (1988) provides a comprehensive survey of the experimental literature.

9

Game Theory Applied

Were you ever attracted by the famous piece of advice from the 1960s, that you should never trust anyone over 30? Or have you ever questioned the portrayal in westerns of cowpokes as persistent law breakers? Game theory can provide a surprising warrant for the advice, the stereotype and much else.

This chapter gives applications of two games, the first of which is the Prisoner's Dilemma (□ p. 99), which is ubiquitous in social life. 7 Game Theory indicates how legion are its applications. Consequently, I shall focus in more detail in the next section on one variant of this classic game – the mutual aid game. This has particular relevance for understanding of the development of clubs: that is, any group, from a friendly society to the Mafia, which offers services to its members on the basis of subscriptions. The second is the Chain Store game (□ p. 117), so called because a game with this structure of pay-offs was first extensively studied in a connection with a chain store facing competitors in several different local markets. The discussion in the third section is specifically concerned with the insights which the formal analysis of repeated versions of this game generates with respect to reputation-building behaviour in the arenas of international relations, domestic politics and the market for second-hand cars.

Prisoner's Dilemma: Mutual Aid and the Mafia

The provision of public goods and the conditions for participation in collective action are inescapably bound up with attempted solutions to the Prisoner's Dilemma. For instance, consider the decision as to whether or not to join a trade union. Why join a union when, even if you do not join, you will still benefit from any wage increases which the union negotiates? J.S. Mill describes a similar predicament with respect to the reduction of the working day (see □). But if all people follow this logic and do not join the union, it will not exist, and you will not enjoy such

THE NINE-HOUR DAY

There are matters in which the interference of law is required, not to overrule the judgment of individuals respecting their own interest, but to give effect to that judgment: they being unable to give effect to it except by concert, which concert again cannot be effectual unless it receives validity and sanction from the law. For illustration, and without prejudging the particular point, I may advert to the question of diminishing the hours of labour. Let us suppose, what is at least supposable, whether it be the fact or not – that a general reduction of the hours of factory labour, say from ten to nine, would be for the advantage of the work-people: that they would receive as high wages, or nearly as high, for nine hours' labour as they receive for ten. If this would be the result, and if the operatives generally are convinced that it would, the limitation, some may say, will be adopted spontaneously. I answer, that it will not be adopted unless the body of operatives bind themselves to one another to abide by it. A workman who refused to work more than nine hours while there were others who worked ten, would either not be employed at all, or if employed, must submit to lose one-tenth of his wages. However convinced, therefore, he may be that it is the interest of the class to work short time, it is contrary to his own interest to set the example, unless he is well assured that all or most others will follow it. But suppose a general agreement of the whole class: might not this be effectual without the sanction of law? Not unless enforced by opinion with a rigour practically equal to that of law. For however beneficial the observance of the regulation might be to the class collectively, the immediate interest of every individual would lie in violating it: and the more numerous those were who adhered to the rule, the more would individuals gain by departing from it.

. . . Assuming then that it really would be the interest of each to work only nine hours if he could be assured that all others would do the same, there might be no means of attaining this object but by converting their supposed mutual agreement into an engagement under penalty, by consenting to have it enforced by law.

(Mill, 1848, Book V, ch. 11, sec. 12)

a high wage. Or consider a simple decision about pollution. Do you throw a piece of litter on the ground or not? You like a clean environment, but one piece of litter is not going to make a difference, and who needs a sticky sweet paper in their pocket? But, if everyone makes the same calculation, there will be litter all over the place. Reflections such as this reveal how central the Prisoner's Dilemma is to social life.

In this section, we concentrate on a particular decision where the dilemma arises (which can be found in Sugden, 1986b). Suppose that individuals live in an environment which exposes them to a danger, such as illness or robbery, valued at $-d$. The illness (or robbery) is likely to occur with some known frequency: let us assume that the danger strikes one individual in each time period and so, in a population of n individuals, the probability of being the victim is $1/n$. Furthermore, suppose that the individual must decide whether or not to cooperate (that is, to help a person from the group who is ill), which costs c, or to defect (that is, to ignore the person who is ill) which costs zero. The person who is ill enjoys the benefit bN, where N is the number of people who cooperate, and $b > c$ because the aid from someone is more highly valued by an ill person than the cost of giving aid to someone when you are well. Individuals are treated as alike in the sense that they have the same pay-offs in the same circumstances (the values of b, c and d).

Table 9.1 captures the implied expected pay-offs from this arrangement in a two-person version of the game ($n = 2$). It reveals the basic Prisoner's Dilemma, and this generalizes to the n-person case.

As in the two-person game, the defect strategy dominates the cooperate strategy in the n-person game, and so there is a unique equilibrium where everyone defects.

However, things are different when the game is repeated without a definite end. We shall assume that, in each play, there is some probability, p, that the game will be repeated. It is easy to check that 'defect' remains a Nash equilibrium in this game because it is always the best reply to itself. However, it is no longer the only equilibrium. To appreciate this in the n-person case, consider a tit-for-tat strategy which partitions players into two groups: those who are in good standing and those who are not; and specifies a cooperative move if the ill person is in good standing – otherwise it specifies defection. People in good standing are those who

Table 9.1 Mutual Aid game

		A	
		Co-operate	Defect
B	Cooperate	$(b - c - d)/2, (b - c - d)/2$	$(-c - d)/2, (b - d)/2$
	Defect	$(b - d)/2, (-c - d)/2$	$(-d)/2, (-d)/2$

cooperate when the illness attacks someone in good standing. In other words, playing tit-for-tat now puts you into 'good standing' for the next round.

Now, let us suppose that everyone is in good standing. The decision that you make in this round of the game will determine whether you are in good standing until the next opportunity that you have to make this decision. This could be the next round, but it need not be so soon, because the illness may strike you next period, and likewise in the time period after that, and so on. Indeed, to be specific, there is a probability p/n that the game will be repeated next period and that you will be ill, and a probability p/n that the same thing will happen again in the period after this, and so on. Hence, if you choose to defect in this period and cease to be in good standing, then the expected return over the time until you get the opportunity to make the decision again between cooperating and defecting is:

$$(-d)\left[p/n + (p/n)^2 + \ldots\right]$$

If you decide to cooperate in this period and put yourself into good standing, then the expected return, again over the time until you get the opportunity to make the decision again, is:

$$-c + \left[(n-1)\ b - d\right]\left[p/n + (p/n)^2 + \ldots\right]$$

Whenever this expected return exceeds the earlier one, then the individual will decide to cooperate now. This condition reduces to:

$$p > [nc] / \left[(n-1)\,b + c\right]$$

When this condition holds, it is easy to see that tit-for-tat is another Nash equilibrium in the game. If all others follow tit-for-tat, then the condition implies that your best reply is to cooperate, and since this is what the tit-for-tat strategy specifies, this strategy must be a best reply to itself.

Thus, it should cause no surprise to find that a group, confronted by a common but random danger, plays the tit-for-tat strategy, since it is a Nash equilibrium in the game. Individual behaviour would be perfectly instrumentally rational. In fact, it would resemble that of a club in which each individual helps other individuals. Furthermore, in an evolutionary setting we might expect to see the emergence of such a club because the equilibrium is evolutionarily stable (see Sugden, 1986b) and it offers obvious advantages over the Nash equilibrium where all defect. This carries with it the interesting implication that we need not appeal to some guiding hand, some impersonal and coercive force to explain the creation of a club which overcomes the problem of cooperation contained in the Prisoner's Dilemma. Such clubs could emerge as an example of ANARCHIC ORDER (12).

Indeed, it has been argued that this analysis contains the seeds of a plausible account of the emergence of a state which is charged with protecting private property [see Nozick (1974) and Sugden (1986b), and for a related account Schotter (1981)]. The common but random danger might be attacks on property and the tit-for-tat equilibrium is formalized between individuals through the services of the state. Equally, even if the common danger might owe something to the existence of the Mafia itself, it is easy to see how, in the absence of the state, an organization such as the Mafia might emerge spontaneously as an alternative embodiment of the tit-for-tat equilibrium. This thought was famously expressed by Pasquale Villari in his *Lettere Meridionali*, published over a century ago:

> The Mafia has no written statutes, it is not a secret society, hardly an organisation. It is forced by spontaneous generation.

Such a claim can sound decidedly odd, but it is the power of game theory to illustrate precisely how an organization – in the sense of a set of shared practices – such as the Mafia, can emerge as a self-sustaining arrangement between individuals. Anyone concerned with 'fighting the Mafia' would do well to understand this logic: otherwise it might be tempting to think that the organization will disappear simply through the prosecution of its leadership.

The formal analysis of this section also offers support for such suggestions, such as those found in Olson (1965), that cooperative action is much more likely to arise in a settled society because the prospects of the game being repeated (and hence the condition on p. 147 being satisfied) are much higher. It is here, perhaps, that we find the seeds of the cowpokes' predicament. For travellers, like cowpokes, the probability of playing the game again with same group of townsfolk is probably low and so the tit-for-tat strategy, and with it participation in a system of law and order, is likely to be less attractive to them than it will seem to the sedentary townsfolk. Cowpokes are as brutish and instrumentally rational as everyone else: they just happen to be facing the wrong set of incentives!

Nuclear Deterrence, Lame-duck Presidents and Second-hand Car Salesmen

For much of the postwar period, peace in Europe was thought to depend on a nuclear strategy known as Mutually Assured Destruction (MAD). Broadly, it was argued that a small conventional NATO force in Western Europe need not fear the much larger numbers of Warsaw Pact forces, because the temptation given to the East to invade would be offset by the threat of a subsequent nuclear exchange, which would yield 'mutually assured destruction' for the superpowers.

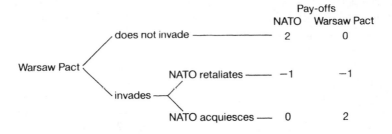

Figure 9.1.

This hypothetical interaction between NATO and the Warsaw Pact can be captured by the game shown in figure 9.1, in extensive form. It has the same structure as the so-called Chain Store game.

The pay-offs are cardinal representations of the preferences of each party, with the worst option for both being an invasion followed by nuclear retaliation producing MAD (− 1 may be a slight underestimate!), while the best outcome for NATO is no invasion, and the best for the Warsaw Pact is an invasion followed by acquiescence.

Set out in this manner, the game theorist would quickly infer that MAD does not constitute a credible threat, and the subgame perfect equilibrium concept points to an invasion followed by acquiescence as the likely result. In short, the game theorist would conclude that there was something badly wrong with conventional wisdom during this period. This is an interesting result for at least two reasons.

First, it was precisely this appreciation which lay behind the switch from MAD to the strategy of 'Flexible Response'. This new strategy relied on the existence of intermediate and tactical nuclear weapons in Europe, which would enable NATO to counter an invasion without recourse to an intercontinental exchange of nuclear missiles. Thus NATO's retaliation in the form of a tactical nuclear strike might plausibly yield a pay-off of 1 rather than the − 1 under MAD, and hence constitute a credible threat which forestalls invasion in the game. This is the doctrine that Europe lived under until the changes in the Warsaw Pact in 1989–90 which have been hailed as the 'end of the cold war'.

Second, there is the interesting question of how 'peace' was maintained for much of the postwar period when the MAD doctrine was in place. One possibility is simply that NATO delusions about the deterrent effects of MAD did not matter because, in fact, the Warsaw Pact countries had no desire to invade Western Europe. Their pay-off from invasion followed by acquiescence was mistakenly thought to be 2; it was actually less than 0, and so the equilibrium in the game did not involve invasion.

Another intriguing possibility is that there was some doubt in the Warsaw

Pact about the pay-offs to NATO. Specifically, suppose that the Warsaw Pact believed that there was some probability, p, that NATO would actually prefer a nuclear exchange, and the consequent mutually assured destruction, to acquiescence (that is, the 'better dead than red' syndrome): or some possibility, if you like, that people making the decisions in NATO were literally 'mad'. Then, when p is greater than 2/3, the Warsaw Pact will decide not to invade. In fact, President Nixon was in no doubt that this was a crucial element of the peace, declaring that 'the real possibility of irrational US action is essential to the US–Soviet relationship'. Indeed, Bob Haldeman informs us that Nixon privately, and rather appropriately, called this his Madman theory of international relations. The problem with this theory, as Shawcross (1979) remarks when discussing the US invasion of Cambodia, is that 'reputations for irrationality have to be established, and that can be done only by irrational actions'.

Shawcross is right, of course, when individuals use **Bayes's rule** (⧉) to revise beliefs. However, rather than develop this potentially sobering reflection on US foreign policy during that period, I shall switch to another application, where we can examine in more detail the role of reputations within games of this sort. Return to figure 9.1 and cast NATO as the President and the Warsaw Pact as Congress: the pay-offs now relate to a typical interchange between the executive and the legislature over, say, the budget. Congress must decide whether to amend the proposal which comes from the President ('invade') or accept it ('not invade'), and if Congress does amend the proposal, then the President must decide whether to fight the amendment or accept it. Given the costs of delay to both parties and the likelihood of Congress having an amendment which it prefers to the original proposal, the pay-offs are not implausible, especially if the President is 'pragmatic' and believes that some compromises are inevitable. However, it is conceivable that the President could be 'principled' to the point where compromise over an amendment from Congress is worse than the delay which follows a disagreement. Let us suppose that Congress entertains a probability assessment (p) that the President is 'principled' (that is, 'tough'/ 'mad') in this way and so prefers a fight to acquiescence.

Finally, let us assume the game is repeated a finite number of times because the President can serve a maximum of two terms, eight years, and there are a limited number of proposals which can be considered in any year. In these circumstances, there is the possibility of a 'pragmatic' President building a reputation for being 'principled', and this can deter amendments in early plays of the game even when there is little doubt in the minds of Congress that the President is 'pragmatic' (in other words, p is small). This result is derived from the sequential equilibrium concept, developed by Kreps and Wilson (1982b) to cover repeated asymmetric games of this sort (see also GAME THEORY (9)).

The first thing to notice is that, if Congress entertains doubt in the form of a probability assessment that the president is 'principled' which is greater than or equal to $2/3$ by the last play of the game, then an amendment in the last play is not certain. Once an amendment in the last play is not certain, the backward induction process cannot take hold to produce amendments followed by acquiescence in all plays, and other results become possible. Second, it is perfectly possible with reputation-creating behaviour (that is, with a 'pragmatic' President behaving as if he or she were 'principled' through fighting amendments) for the probability in earlier plays of the game to be considerably less than $2/3$, and for Congress still to entertain an expectation that it might rise to $2/3$ by the last play of the game. The final part of the Kreps and Wilson analysis revolves around recognizing that, with Bayesian updating of probability assessments, reputation-building is risky. The 'pragmatic' President can only build a reputation for 'principle' by tempting Congress to amend; since without an amendment, there is never any new evidence to warrant a revision in the probability assessment. But a 'pragmatic' President will never tempt Congress to amend if it always fights an amendment. Thus, there must be some positive probability of a 'pragmatic' President acquiescing: and hence reputation-building must be risky if it is to stand a chance of being effective. As it is risky, the President will delay such behaviour until it is absolutely necessary to keep the reputation on course for the critical terminal value. The rest is mathematics. When the current probability assessment is above the value necessary to keep it on course for reaching $2/3$ (actually $[2/3]^n$ in this case, where n is the number of plays remaining), the President does not need to tempt Congress and he or she will fight every amendment. Congress realizes this and will not issue amendments. It only amends with a positive probability when reputation-building has become necessary, since only then is there some positive probability of acquiescence by the President.

In figure 9.2 are depicted the various phases of the game when p_0 is the prior probability assessment of 'principle' which Congress brings to the game, and where the last play of the game occurs at time $t = \tau$.

In the early stage of this game (from 0 to k), before reputation-building becomes necessary, Congress will not force amendments, thus corresponding to what is sometimes called a honeymoon period in politics. Towards the end of the game (in periods after k), it becomes increasingly likely that amendments will be made and that a 'pragmatic' President will acquiesce. Once this happens the President is revealed as 'pragmatic', and there are amendments followed by acquiescence thereafter, thus corresponding to what is sometimes referred to as a lame-duck Presidency.

As a final illustration, imagine a second-hand car salesman, who knows the quality of the cars he is selling, facing a choice when someone enters the lot: to sell a good car or sell a 'lemon'. An 'amoral' salesman prefers

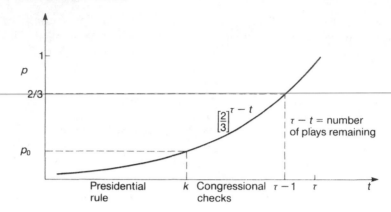

Figure 9.2.

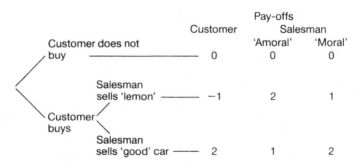

Figure 9.3.

to sell a 'lemon', because both types of car sell at the same price and a 'lemon' costs the salesman less than a good car; while a 'moral' salesman prefers to sell a good car because he does not like to deceive a customer. The customer does not know the quality of the car. Unsurprisingly, he or she profits most by purchasing a good car, and prefers no car to the purchase of a 'lemon' because 'lemons' are just a waste of money. These preferences are captured by the following pay-offs in figure 9.3, the extensive form of this game.

In a one-shot version of the game, provided that the probability of the salesman being 'moral' exceeds $1/3$, the customer will enter the lot. The salesman clearly benefits from having a reputation for being 'moral' in this sense, because otherwise he will sell no cars at all. Indeed, without this level of trust in the better nature of the salesman, no transaction will occur, even though both would be made better off by the sale of a good car. This is the substance of Akerlof's (1970) famous analysis of market failure when individuals do not enjoy such reputations; and the game-theoretic presentation follows Dasgupta (1988).

The interesting insight which we gain into the functioning of such markets, with the aid of Kreps and Wilson's game-theoretic analysis, is that the probability assessment that the salesman is 'moral' can be considerably less than ⅓, and yet trading will still occur as long as the game is to be repeated a sufficient number of times. In this instance, repetition occurs most plausibly because the salesman interacts with a number of different consumers, and provided that we assume that the upshot of sales is public knowledge, then the analysis that follows is as sketched earlier for the case in which the repetition occurs between the same parties. To be specific, it will be in the interest of an 'amoral' salesman to behave as if he were 'moral', because the reputation for morality enables car sales to occur.

A surprising further insight is that the likelihood of an 'amoral' salesman behaving amorally rather than morally is higher in the later stages of the game, when reputation-building has become necessary, than in the earlier stages. This is surprising since it has the following implication. Suppose that salesmen only repeat this game a finite number of times because they grow old and retire, and that salesmen typically start to do business at the same age. The age of the salesman becomes an index of how long he has been in business, and of how much longer he will remain in business. Then, when you have the same probability assessment of the 'morality' of two salesman, other things being equal, it is actually the younger one who you are more likely to trust not to sell you a 'lemon' more than the older one. Or – at the risk of oversimplification – never trust anyone over 30!

Of course, some care is required with this generalization, since other things are rarely equal. For instance, when there are property rights in reputations then the 'old' salesman may continue to nurture a good reputation, because he will then be able to sell his garage for more when he retires. Nevertheless, game theory does provide a surprising reminder that there was more to the 1960s than sex, drugs and rock and roll!

Conclusion

This chapter has given examples, using the prisoner's dilemma and chain store games, of how game theory might be applied to social interactions. In doing this, it has been suggested that game theory has a capacity both to generate results which are surprising and to provide a fresh understanding of some of the common intuitions which we hold about such interactions.

Shaun Hargreaves Heap

Further Reading

Bacharach (1976) provides a good introduction to game theory, together with a variety of illustrations drawn from economics. Rasmusen (1989) does the same at a more advanced level, while Shubik (1982, 1984) has applications which range more widely over the social sciences. The Prisoner's Dilemma has been exhaustively studied by Axelrod (1984), and the use of game theory is one of the distinguishing features of the so-called rational choice marxism of Roemer (1982); for an introduction see Roemer (1988) and Elster (1985). Schelling (1960, 1978) is a seminal contributor to the interpretation of a variety of social interactions as repeated games, and his ideas have been refined and developed by Schotter (1981) and Sugden (1986b). The limits of this approach to social life are discussed in Hodgson (1988) and Hargreaves Heap (1989). Selten (1978b) is responsible for the original discussion of the chain store game, and Kreps and Wilson (1982a) is the seminal reference for reputation-creating behaviour in the context of repeated games.

10

Organizations

In even the most libertarian of free-market economies, individuals voluntarily surrender their freedom of action in order to form and join organizations. The most imposing example is the state itself, and that is a subject of the third part of this book. In this chapter, we concentrate on less total but still ubiquitous organizations, particularly firms, which individuals are free to join and leave. Other examples to which the same broad analysis can be applied include trades unions, clubs, charities, universities, schools, professional organizations and even, some would argue, the family. The next but one chapter, on ANARCHIC ORDER (12), describes the remarkable success of a market economy in coordinating activities, so why do we observe 'islands of conscious power in this ocean of unconscious cooperation like lumps of butter coagulating in a pail of butter-milk' (Robertson, 1930, p. 85)? Max Weber's (1910) answer was that bureaucratic organization can be particularly efficient in that it permits specialization within a disciplined hierarchy, supported by an impersonal, meritocratic reward system. In a pure bureaucracy, individuals mechanically follow rules and procedures to the furtherance of the organization's stated aims. There are two major problems with this idealized view. First, it fails to take full account of individuals in the hierarchy, who may try to manipulate the system to their own ends. Second, there is no explanation of why certain activities are conducted within organizations, such as firms, while other specialized tasks are coordinated by markets, with or without formal contracts.

Three broad themes are developed in this chapter. The first closely parallels **Hobbes's** (⏳) theory of the state and explains organizations as an

A NEW VIEW OF SOCIETY

Any general character, from the best to the worst, from the most ignorant to the most enlightened, may be given to any community, even to the world at large, by the application of proper means; which means are to a great extent at the command and under the control of those who have influence in the affairs of men.

. . . The will of man has no power whatever over his opinions; he must, and ever did, and ever will, believe what has been, is, or may be impressed on his mind by his predecessors, and the circumstances which surround him.

efficient response to the failure of free markets of individuals. The second theme derives from Marx and sees capitalist organizations as vehicles for the exercise of power. The Hobbesian view, and to a lesser extent that of modern marxists, maintains that human behaviour within organizations is fundamentally similar to that outside them. People act as *Homo economicus* and respond to group wishes only inasmuch as incentives, information and authority encourage them to do so. In the final section of this chapter we discuss group values, rules and cultures, which can develop within organizations and may be manipulated by those in authority (see □).

Some Problems with Markets and Formal Contracts

The advantages of joint action in the form of specialization and exchange are ubiquitous and well understood. They were central to the writings of classical economists such as Smith and Ricardo. The advantages of specialization derive from savings by not having to switch between tasks (for example, workers can usually produce more if they do not continually move from machine to machine), from gains by concentrating on activities in which particular individuals have a relative advantage (for example, it would be wasteful for doctors to build their own houses, even if they were good bricklayers), and from learning specialist skills and investing in specialist machinery. If many people can efficiently specialize in the same task, then market competition is an effective way of promoting specialization.

However, many specialized tasks are idiosyncratic to specific relationships. For example, a producer of steel panels for cars might be able to produce at lowest cost only by locating his factory next to the car producer he is selling to, by investing in machinery that is commissioned specifically to make panels shaped to the car producer's design, or by training personnel to understand the details of the maker's individual requirements. Such specific investments are particularly important for efficient production in continuing, frequent, long-term relationships. Once the panel maker has invested in specific assets, he becomes unique and his relationship with the car producer is fundamentally transformed into one of bilateral monopoly, even if there were many potential suppliers prior to the investment. Significantly, the *status quo* regarding bargains over the gains from trade is altered by the existence of specific assets which have a much reduced value outside the particular relationship (see BARGAINING (8)); and fears that this will be exploited in the future may discourage mutually beneficial specific investment (for example, the steel panel maker may invest in a less efficient general technology because, although this raises costs, the ability to sell to someone else improves bargaining power). The notion of specific investments can be interpreted much more broadly than this example of inter-firm transactions. In different contexts the relevant specific asset might be academic reputation, time spent building a network of friendships, or career sacrifice in favour of a partner's prospects. The problem in each case is to design an institutional environment that is supportive of specific investments.

That task would be straightforward if information were a freely available or easily traded commodity. Long-term contracts could be signed and verified, and investments could be made without fear of future renegotiation. But information is not like that. Some people have more of it, and others have different bits. The same might be said of any product, were it not for the crucial extra twist that by its very nature we can never know how much of what bits of information other people have. Trade in information is thus very different from trade in apples and cars. Of course, people can choose to' reveal what information they hold, but it is fundamentally unverifiable that they have told the truth, the whole truth and nothing but the truth. It is, therefore, open to abuse, or what Williamson calls *opportunism*, which is to say 'self-interest seeking with guile . . . more generally . . . the incomplete or distorted disclosure of information, especially to calculated efforts to mislead, distort, disguise, obfuscate, or otherwise confuse' (Williamson, 1985, p. 47). The veracity of this view of human nature is taken up later, but it was certainly shared by Machiavelli (see □ p. 158).

A central paradigm for the difficulties caused by opportunistic behaviour is the *agency* relationship in which two people wish to embark on a mutually beneficial project. The value of the project depends on an outcome (for example, effort, quality or the state of demand) that is observed by one person but not the other. Call the uninformed party the principal, and

PRINCELY VIRTUES

It now remains for us to see how a prince should govern his conduct towards his subjects or his friends. I know that this has often been written about before, and so I hope it will not be thought presumptuous for me to do so, as, especially in discussing this subject, I draw up an original set of rules. But since my intention is to say something that will prove of practical use to the inquirer, I have thought it proper to represent things as they are in real truth, rather than as they are imagined. Many have dreamed up republics and principalities which have never in truth been known to exist; the gulf between how one should live and how one does live is so wide that a man who neglects what is actually done for what should be done learns the way to self-destruction rather than self-preservation. The fact is that a man who wants to act virtuously in every way necessarily comes to grief among so many who are not virtuous. Therefore if a prince wants to maintain his rule he must learn how not to be virtuous, and to make use of this or not according to need . . .

Everyone realizes how praiseworthy it is for a prince to honour his word and to be straightforward rather than crafty in his dealings; nonetheless contemporary experience shows that princes who have achieved great things have been those who have given their word lightly, who have known how to trick men with their cunning, and who, in the end, have overcome those abiding by honest principles.

(N. Machiavelli, *The Prince*, chs xv and xviii)

the informed person the agent. Thus, the agent has an informational advantage over the principal. Examples of principal and agent include the owner of a firm and the manager, the insurance company and the policyholder, the employer and the worker, and the patient and the dentist. Unfortunately, the identity of particular parties as principal or agent is often unclear. For instance, an employer may be ill informed as to the qualities of a potential employee, but the latter may be equally ignorant of the working conditions offered by a particular employer (even though the jaundiced view described in Nietzsche's *Joyful Wisdom* (see □) is probably not typical!). Furthermore, once there are more than two parties involved in a network of relationships, this raises new possibilities for coalitions acting together against other groups. Nevertheless, the simplified principal–agent model does clarify two categories of opportunistic behaviour by the agent that the principal must beware of.

First, suppose that an agreement has been reached of the following form: the principal agrees to compensate the agent in exchange for

A PRINCIPAL–AGENT PROBLEM

People want to live and have to sell themselves; but they despise him who exploits their necessity and purchases the workman. It is curious that the subjection to powerful, fear-inspiring, and even dreadful individuals, to tyrants and leaders of armies, is not at all felt so painfully as the subjection to such undistinguished and uninteresting persons as the captains of industry. In the employer the workman usually sees a crafty blood-sucking dog of a man, speculating on every necessity, whose name, form, and character are altogether indifferent to him.

(Nietzsche, 1882, Book 1 section 40)

her performing some task with a specified level of effort (for example, running a firm, protecting property, controlling quality or caring for teeth). If either the outcome of the task is not observed by the principal, or the outcome depends not only on effort but also on some factor unobservable by the principal (such as the state of demand, the presence of thieves, the breakdown of machinery or the incidence of decay), then the agent may wish to misrepresent information (for example, by saying that conditions are more adverse than in fact they are) and expend less effort than agreed (by, for example, failing to lock their bicycles or working only a six-hour day). This problem of an agent shirking on effort is known as *moral hazard* or *ex post opportunism* (since the problem arises after agreement to work together). It can be reduced by the principal monitoring the agent, but such monitoring is typically difficult and costly.

Second, suppose that effort can be perfectly monitored, but agents vary in their inherent abilities, or in the quality of the service that they are providing. If the principal cannot observe quality, he might assume the worst and offer compensation only commensurate with the poorest quality agent. If he does, then he is unlikely to attract a high-quality agent into partnership, and the value of the project will be reduced, or it may even be abandoned. Offering better terms is not going to deter the least able from wishing to join the project, although it might attract some better-quality agents and so improve the chances of recruiting someone more able. This problem of less appropriate agents being unduly attracted to the principal's offer of participation is known as *adverse selection* or *ex ante opportunism* (since the problem is to choose the right agent before an agreement is reached). Examples include high-risk drivers being more likely to want comprehensive insurance, and providers of a poor service being more likely to bid the lowest price for a contract.

What institutions might develop in order to mitigate, or even solve, the agency problems? One possibility is that we rely on ethics, including promise and trust, in the hope that individuals act in the social good even when it goes against their own private interests. However, as Arrow points out, 'most of us operate in some middle realm where we admit social claims, sometimes forget about them for long stretches of time as we go about our daily private role, sometimes rise to an occasion, sometimes fall miserably short, as we assert our individuality in contexts that are not totally appropriate' (Arrow, 1974, p. 16). Regrettably, then, trustworthiness cannot be relied on, even though most of us try to instil into our children the virtues of truth-telling. It is sometimes possible to distinguish the body language of trustworthiness, but blushing and averted eyes are unreliable indicators.

Somewhat more predictable may be signals which involve agents in choosing to undertake a costly act of self-selection. A signal is useful if a positive attribute, such as trustworthiness or ability, is jointly produced with another, observable characteristic which cannot be easily produced on its own. For instance, we may know that Quakers do not tell lies or that only clever people can obtain a good degree; so, even if trustworthiness and inherent ability are not directly observable, the principal need not worry too much if sufficiently good signals are visible (see Akerlof, 1987; Spence, 1974). Cynics might even go so far as to argue that religious and educational institutions actually develop in order to fulfil such a function. Other organizations certainly are formed with the explicit purpose of monitoring a code of ethics. Members of professional bodies and some industry associations submit themselves to peer group scrutiny in order to signal trustworthiness to potential principals. Some such organizations do manage to build a reputation for the good behaviour of their members, but a fundamental problem is that it is often no easier for members to monitor each other than it is for the principal to monitor his agent, and there is a consequent unwillingness to impose the ultimate and often sole sanction of expulsion. Furthermore, signalling institutions are expensive, and it would be extremely inefficient if the only purpose of a three-year university education was to signal natural ability that was there all along!

Given the frailty of reliance on moral principles, and the costs of signalling, the agency problem might be better resolved by writing a cunning, legally enforceable contract. For example, insurance companies frequently compensate less than 100 per cent of the value of stolen goods or subtract some 'excess' from the insured loss. Not only does this provide a direct incentive to be more careful (in other words, it reduces the moral hazard), but if a variety of contracts is offered, the higher risk individuals will tend to choose contracts with a higher premium and smaller excess, and so risk categories can be separated by self-selection (in other words, by reducing adverse selection). Another possibility is the use of contingent contracts.

For example, if external conditions are such that very low productivity will be observed only if there is machine failure *and* a worker is lazy or incompetent, then the contract can include a clause that imposes a severe penalty on the worker (such as dismissal or a very large fine) if very low productivity is ever observed. Only competent workers would agree to such contracts, and they would not risk being caught shirking in case adverse conditions did prevail and the severe penalty was imposed.

There is now a vast economic literature on optimal contract design, but several worrying conclusions still emerge: the optimal contract is very sensitive to the details of the particular situation being analysed; even in very simple situations, both the computation of the optimal contract and its specification can be extremely complex; there is often no feasible contract that will replicate the desirable properties of a world without moral hazard or adverse selection problems; even if there is, the information necessary to verify it is often unavailable to a court of law; and in order to write a complete contingent contract, the principal needs to know the probabilities of all possible external influences on the agent's effectiveness, but such knowledge is unrealistic and unforeseen circumstances do occur (see RISK, IGNORANCE and IMAGINATION (4)). In the light of such difficulties, it is not surprising that most relationships are *not* governed by legally enforceable contracts. Even when they are, real contracts rarely attempt to specify a full set of contingencies to be adjudicated by the courts in case of disagreement. Instead, a clause allowing for arbitration is preferred. Arbitration permits the resolution of conflict in unforeseen circumstances, but there remains the fundamental problem of the agent's ability to manipulate the information available to the arbitrator.

Before proceeding with the argument, it may be helpful to recap. Efficient production often requires investment in specific assets which are more valuable to a particular pair of traders. An agency problem develops when the parties involved are differentially informed because this permits opportunistic behaviour, and human nature is such that ethics such as promise and trust are weak constraints. The role of formal contracts is restricted by, amongst other things, the limited nature of our ability to specify all contingencies – bounded rationality.

Organizations as Governance Structures

It is in this context that Coase (1937), Klein *et al.* (1978) and Williamson (1975, 1985) have argued that formal organizations develop with the direct purpose of reducing *transaction costs*; which is to say the costs of exchanging goods and services. These are due to opportunism in the presence of bounded rationality and specific assets. In what follows we shall focus on the firm, which is, with the single exception of the family, the most pervasive form of organization in developed economies.

The key agency relationship that the firm seeks to facilitate is between input supplier and final producer. Inputs might be components for assembly, services such as advertising and accountancy, or labour services. Suppose first that the input being supplied is non-specific: that is, the supplier has made no idiosyncratic investment which reduces costs when the input is sold to a particular principal, but which has a lower pay-off if that relationship is broken and the product or service must be sold elsewhere (recall the example of a steel panel maker selling to a car producer). In this case of no specific assets, even in the presence of opportunism and bounded rationality, there is no need for formal organizations such as firms to exist. At the first sign of opportunistic behaviour by either party, the relationship can be broken at no cost. Thus, suppliers of standardized components or building labourers with very general skills have no incentive to be tied into the long-term relationship implied by the existence of a firm.

However, if production *is* cheaper when an investment is made in specific assets, then fears of opportunism arise in an open market. Once I have invested in a specific asset, you might try to reduce the price offered for my services. You might promise me that you will not renege on an agreement made before I invest – you might even give me a contract – but as long as I fear that the contract is not watertight I will hesitate to invest (for example, for fear that you may try to argue that you will go bankrupt if I fail to renegotiate a lower price). Transaction cost theorists argue that only by pooling our interests in a joint organization – a firm – will we be able to encourage efficiency-enhancing specific investments. The firm is seen as a *governance structure*, an organizational alternative to courts of law, within which the integrity of an agency relation is decided. It permits very vague 'relational' contracts to be executed within a discipline imposed by the benefits of remaining part of such a system, and the fear that personal opportunism may lead to sanctions, or even expulsion (for example, I agree to work 40 hours a week for you, doing anything I am told, within loosely specified bounds, in return for a fixed wage). It is not that individuals become any less opportunistic within an organization, but the incentives, information and decision-making authority change as compared with market transactions. However, joining an organization which has the direct purpose of suppressing opportunism has its natural down side. The individual profit motive is also suppressed in favour of bureaucratic direction and imperfect performance monitoring, and this can reduce efficiency and the incentive to innovate. Thus, the firm is seen as a balance between creating the right incentives to invest in efficiency-enhancing specific assets, and the costs of losing the direct impact and consequent benefits of the personal profit motive. This is not unlike the view of society described by 'Schopenhauer's Porcupines' (see ☐).

This view of why firms exist can also be applied to explain their internal structure. Here, we have space to mention only three implications: divisionalization, internal labour markets and the composition of the Board of Directors. Most large diversified industrial corporations are now operated as a collection of semi-autonomous divisions, or profit centres, responsible to a relatively small headquarters with a staff that has powers to gather and process information which is not normally available to external capital markets. Consequently, opportunistic behaviour by divisions can be reduced while preserving as much as possible of the benefits of the profit motive. Furthermore, the headquarters serves as an internal capital market which can make informed strategic investment decisions. Most large firms also operate an internal labour market, with young managers entering the firm at a low grade and being offered regular salary increments plus the chance of promotion without competition from outsiders. Not only does this allow effective screening of ability at an early stage (avoiding adverse selection for senior posts), but it also secures a commitment to (and from) the firm, which encourages investment in specific human assets. Finally,

PORCUPINE SOCIETY

One cold winter's day, a number of porcupines huddled together quite closely in order through their mutual warmth to prevent themselves from being frozen. But they soon felt the effect of their quills on one another, which made them again move apart. Now when the need for warmth once more brought them together, the drawback of the quills was repeated so that they were tossed between two evils, until they had discovered the proper distance from which they could best tolerate one another. Thus the need for society which springs from the emptiness and monotony of men's lives, drives them together; but their many unpleasant and repulsive qualities and insufferable drawbacks once more drive them apart. The mean distance which they finally discover, and which enables them to endure being together, is politeness and good manners. Whoever does not keep to this, is told in England to 'keep his distance'. By virtue thereof, it is true that the need for mutual warmth will be only imperfectly satisfied, but, on the other hand, the prick of the quills will not be felt. Yet whoever has a great deal of internal warmth of his own will prefer to keep away from society in order to avoid giving or receiving trouble and annoyance.

(Schopenhauer, 1851, sec. 396)

the composition of the Board of Directors in almost all companies is dominated by shareholder representatives. At first sight, this may seem odd because workers, managers, and even customers and external suppliers appear to have a greater investment in specific assets than do shareholders, who typically hold a very diversified portfolio with a relatively small interest in any one firm. Surely shareholders are in least need to control the firm so as to minimize opportunism. Put another way, why do workers not hire capital rather than capitalists hiring workers? Williamson's answer is that shareholders are, in fact, uniquely vulnerable to opportunistic expropriation. They supply capital which is converted into specific physical assets, yet, because they are diversified to absorb financial risk, they cannot easily or cheaply monitor opportunistic behaviour in any one firm. Furthermore, they invest for the life of the firm (they can only sell their shares to other shareholders) and are last in line in the event of bankruptcy. This vulnerability means that they would be unwilling to invest in the firm, or would require a substantial premium on their investment, if they did not have a dominant representation on the Board of Directors. It is actually in the best interests of workers to let financial interests have supervisory control of the firm, even though such directors may have little managerial or entrepreneurial talent!

The transaction cost approach can also be applied to social institutions, such as golf clubs. Golf clubs frequently embrace social activities such as drinking, dancing and playing cards as well as playing golf, and these activities are greatly enhanced by friendships and the development of a particular 'congenial milieu'. The latter are specific assets which, Klein *et al.* (1978) argue, are best protected by mutual ownership of such clubs, which is what we typically observe. Members are not allowed to sell their 'membership to anyone 'unsuitable', as they would be able to if they were shareholders in a public corporation; nor are they vulnerable to opportunistic opening of membership to 'undesirables', as they might be under ownership by non-members; but mutual ownership permits select entry of only those who will help create the 'right' atmosphere. A similar argument can even be applied to explain the 'Mutual Ownership of Marriage' (see □)!

It is, perhaps, unsurprising that this view of organizations as an efficient response to devious human nature has not gone unchallenged. The next section tackles the deeper issues of human nature, but first consider the presumption of efficiency. Marxists, for instance, criticize the efficiency view for missing the crucial importance of POWER (15) as a rationale for organizations. Few would dispute that firms might be formed to exercise market power against consumers of their product; and state organizations, such as the Monopolies Commission in the UK and the Federal Trade Commission in the USA, are set up to deter such exploitation. Most people

THE MUTUAL OWNERSHIP OF MARRIAGE

An extreme case of this general problem is a marriage. If each mate had a transferable share salable to a third party, there would be far fewer marriages with highly specific investments in affection and children. If a relationship is not one of specialized interest (specialized to a particular other party) or if it required no investment by any member, then the marriage relationship would be more like a corporation. As it is one of highly specific investments, marriages have historically been mutually owned entities, with permission of both parties generally required for alteration of membership. Government arbitration of this relationship to prevent postinvestment opportunistic behavior by either party can contribute toward lower bargaining costs and investments of resources (recoverable dowries) by both parties to improve their respective postinvestment bargaining positions, and, most importantly, create confidence that opportunistic behavior will not be successful. The legislative movement to 'no-fault' divorce suggests that modern marriages may have less specific assets than formerly.

(Klein, Crawford and Alchian, 1978)

are also familiar with arguments relating to trades unions as vehicles for creating bargaining power for workers, although they can also be explained as efficiency enhancers designed to protect specific investments in human capital by their members (see Freeman and Medoff, 1979; Williamson, 1985). However, marxists argue further that firms have been developed, at least in part, to facilitate a redistribution of wealth away from labour in favour of the owners of capital. Thus, the fact that capital hires labour is understood in a quite different way, and with quite different implications, to the efficiency reasons discussed above. The firm, as an instrument of capitalist power, selects technologies so as to maximize *profitability*. This need not be the same as maximizing *efficiency* because profits can be gained at the expense of employed labour, as well as by raising prices or minimizing non-wage costs. For example, a machine or production line may be chosen so as to extract the maximum possible effort out of workers, who might have preferred a more relaxed life even if it meant lower wages; or the firm might invest in costly activities designed to monitor effort, with small gains to capitalists and large losses to workers.

If workers attempt to collude to neutralize such tight surveillance, one capitalist reaction is to create different classes of workers, possibly based on race, gender, seniority or age, and put one group in a privileged position over the others. By giving some workers more to lose, such discrimination can destroy worker unity – a divide and rule strategy well understood by the British during Imperial rule in India. A further strand to capitalist power is created by paying workers within the organization more than they could receive outside, in order to make an effective weapon of the threat of dismissal for less than maximum effort. If all firms did this and if there was no unemployment, then the threat would not work because dismissed workers could take an equally well-paid job elsewhere. But as long as there is a reserve army of the unemployed, the threat of dismissal is effective; and unemployment will exist because firms do not take on unemployed workers at less than the current wage, since it would under-mine the power of the threat of dismissal.

This system of surveillance technologies, divisive groupings of workers and the reserve army of unemployed is made possible because the firm is an authoritarian, not a democratic, organization. Workers sell their labour, and with it give the employer authority to extract whatever effort he can, subject only to very vague limits and the ability to quit (which can be very costly due to specific investments in friendships, housing near the job, and so on). The system is robust against new forms of organization, such as worker cooperatives, not only because of their difficulty of raising capital, but because the system moulds people's attitudes such that they become opportunistic and cliquish, and so capitalist attitudes and orga-nizations are self-perpetuating. Notice that, although this modern marxist view holds out the prospect of more cooperative behaviour in some form of socialist organization, the Hobbesian view of human nature remains intact under capitalism. But is this really true? Does behaviour within non-socialist organizations remain rigidly individualistic? Many sociologists think not, one going so far as to claim that the view developed in this section 'evokes the menace of the novel and film *The Invasion of the Body Snatchers*, in which aliens occupy human forms, but all that we value about human behaviour – spontaneity, unpredictability, selflessness, plurality of values, reciprocal influence, and resentment of domination – has disappeared' (Perrow, 1986, p. 257).

Behaviour in Organizations

Two aspects of behaviour in organizations require particular comment. One is the use of rules and routines, but we begin with the evolution of group values. At the beginning of the twentieth century, F.W. Taylor developed a 'scientific' school of management now known as time-and-motion study. It was based on very simple, mechanistic study of the indi-vidual, paying particular attention to the physiology of manual labour. ('Speedy' Taylor had earlier applied his skills to the game of baseball,

THE HAWTHORNE LIGHTING EXPERIMENT

In order, then, to study the effects of altered illumination on work (on the assumption that the better the light, the better the work), two groups of employees were selected. In one, the control group, the illumination remained unchanged throughout the experiments while in the other the illumination was increased in intensity. As had been expected, the output in the latter group showed an improvement, but what was quite unforeseen was that the output of the control group went up also. As the lighting in this case had not been altered, the result was naturally puzzling to the investigators, who then proceeded to reduce the illumination for the test group. When this had been done, output went up once more. Obviously some factor was at work which increased output regardless of either greater or less intensity of light in the workshop, and further experiments became necessary in order to discover the nature of this unknown factor.

(Brown, 1954, p. 70)

and was responsible for the introduction of overarm, as opposed to underarm, pitching.) In the spirit of scientific management, and trying to optimize the physiological environment of operatives, in the 1920s the management of the Hawthorne plant of the Western Electric Company near Chicago began experimenting with lighting conditions. They were puzzled by the results of the Hawthorne Lighting Experiment (see □), and Elton Mayo was called in to carry out further experiments. The working conditions of a small group of six women were altered in a carefully controlled way. Each change was sustained for one to three months, and the experiments took many years. Output went up when each of the following were introduced: piece rates, rest breaks and a shorter working day. But output also rose when working conditions were finally returned to the *status quo*! At the end of this first set of experiments, output was 25 per cent higher than at the start. Similar experimental findings have since been replicated on many occasions.

Mayo's interpretation of his results was that the experimental changes were secondary to the fact that the experiments were taking place at all. The interest of management in commissioning the study, and the communication involved, forged a team spirit in the work group. The point is that friendship, reciprocity and obligation begin to modify human behaviour in a group away from the rugged individualism of HOMO ECONOMICUS and towards HOMO SOCIOLOGICUS (5). Team spirit need not always be channelled in favour of common organizational goals (such as output in the Hawthorne study). Subgroups may develop norms of behaviour in support of their own interests (for example, not working too hard in a crisis for fear that a supervisor may expect more effort at *all* times in the future). In part, group norms are supported by group sanctions (such as withdrawal of friendship) but, more deeply, individual preferences might actually be changed by membership of the group.

Leaving aside group norms and values for the moment, consider some of the complexities of decision-making in organizations. Issues relating to group decision-making by committees are developed in part III of this book, but here I focus on how individuals within an organization can make rational decisions in the presence of limited information, rapidly changing external conditions, imperfect knowledge of what others within the organization are doing, and bounded rationality. This environment which – as I argued earlier – makes formal contracts of limited use, also encourages the use of rules and procedures as a means of allocating responsibilities, directing attention to potential problem areas, and making routine decisions. The hope is that even though such procedures do not optimize, they should at least give a satisfactory level of performance. Rules and routines also serve an important function as organizational memory. Individual personnel change, but their experience in dealing with problems can be 'remembered' in the routines that they set up in the past. Of course, this is a very imperfect memory. The reason for rules is often lost in history, so they may continue to be applied long after they have become inappropriate, and it is typically very difficult to change procedures in a long-established organization.

Putting together these social influences on behaviour, the modern jargon for the set of group beliefs, values, norms, language, rules and routines found in firms is *corporate culture* (and non-corporate organizations such as clubs, charities, and families will equally have their own 'culture'). Different firms evolve their own distinctive cultures, often heavily influenced by the lead of the organizational founding father, and reinforced by a verbal tradition of anecdotes (for example, about the office junior who had the initiative to hire a helicopter on Sunday to meet the delivery date; or for a firm with a different corporate ethic, the executive who scoured the waste bins every night for discarded paper clips in order to save money). The role of senior management in a modern corporation is not so much to give orders as to set values, goals and priorities, and influence, in a more or less subversive way, the corporate culture (see □). Walt Disney and Ray Kroc (of McDonalds) went as far as to set up their own corporate 'universities' to inculcate the right culture; and, years after their deaths, Disney Corporation problems are still tackled by posing the question 'what would Walt do?', while McDonalds staff worldwide learn Kroc's priorities of 'Q.S.C. & V: quality, service, cleanliness and value'.

ORGANIZATION MAN

The organization trains and indoctrinates its members. This might be called the 'internalization' of influence, because it injects into the very nervous systems of the organization members the criteria of decision that the organization wishes to employ. The organization member acquires knowledge, skill, and identifications or loyalties that enable him to make decisions, by himself, as the organization would like him to decide.

(Simon, 1945, p. 103)

Does this more sociological view of organizations, in which individual preferences are endogenous and can even be manipulated, invalidate the individualistic theory of organizations outlined in the previous section? I think not. It is true that organizations are more than mere governance structures for implicit contracts. But cultural revolutions are notoriously difficult to enforce, and *Homo economicus* is too powerful a beast to tie down for long. Individualistic opportunism has proved too fruitful an assumption in organization theory to be abandoned just yet.

Bruce Lyons

Further Reading

A very good collection of readings written by economists is edited by Putterman (1986). The efficiency view is thoroughly explored by Williamson (1975, 1985), although Klein, Crawford and Alchian (1978) provides an easier introduction. Chapters 2 and 3 of Schmalensee and Willig (1989) provide an advanced, up-to-date review of the theory of the firm. A minor classic on the marxist view is Marglin (1974), although the treatment here is taken from the excellent synthesis by Bowles (1985). Perrow (1986) provides an historical introduction to organization theory from the sociological point of view, and Pugh (1984) edits a good collection of management readings. A recent review on organizational memory and learning is provided by Levitt and March (1988), while Nelson and Winter (1982) is good on rules, routines and the implications for industrial organization.

11

Cultural Exchange

'All contacts among men rest on the schema of giving and returning the equivalence', declared the sociologist Georg Simmel (1908, p. 387). This bold claim is the foundation of Social Exchange theory which, in its recent main line, is an attempt to understand all social intercourse by analogy with market transactions. Indeed, put more boldly still, it is an attempt to regard specifically economic intercourse as a special case of the universal practice of exchange for mutual benefit. Why do people (sometimes) give away their possessions, their blood and even their lives? Social exchange theory deems the question to be misstated. These are not free gifts. Look closer and the donors will always be found to receive, to have received or to expect to receive something of equivalent value in return.

If this can be established, the basic ideas explored in the chapters on RATIONALITY (1) and GAME THEORY (7) can be extended and applied without limit. One might suppose, offhand, that economics has little to say about the domestic, ethical, cultural and political aspects even of market societies, and still less about more strongly norm-governed worlds, such as those studied by historians and anthropologists. But then reflect how very general the basic analytical approach has been. Although we began where economists begin and used economists' examples of market choices, the story so far has been much broader. It has applied to any rational individual, with ordered preferences and sufficient information to calculate the expected utility of various ways to set about satisfying them. It has applied to any interaction or 'game' the outcome of which can be analysed as a sum of rational individual choices. Even its motivating element, utility maximization or – more blandly still – preference satisfaction, belongs to a general psychology covering far more than market behaviour.

The road is wide open. For instance, why do people, often with little or no Christian conviction, send out Christmas cards? They are not moved by simple Yuletide exuberance. Last year's list is unearthed and the names of those who did not reciprocate are deleted, while recent new acquaintances are added, particularly where the prospect of further contact is welcome. The children in the house, who have been saying that the ritual is silly, are coaxed into sending a few and are thus initiated. Cards received from those missed out are instantly reciprocated, except when the overture is deliberately rebuffed. What look like gifts are, in short, exchanges. But what exactly is exchanged? Well, no doubt there is variety since, for example, official or business compliments of the season differ from reminders to old friends that one is not dead. But the broad social exchange theory answer is that the cards symbolize a relationship which the sender values and affirms, provided that the receiver affirms it too. This answer relies on the more basic thought that, when people make a free exchange, each is moved by his own preferences, coupled with an expectation that he will receive something of enough value to warrant the cost involved. Otherwise they would not do it.

Christmas cards are a tiny example of an underlying reciprocity which social exchange theory claims to discern in every realm of life. The 'schema of giving and returning the equivalence' has been strikingly applied in the analysis of, for instance, friendship, marriage, charitable activity, race relations, democratic politics and international affairs. Witness these examples, it is contentious in its suggestion that there is an 'economic' core to matters of love and hate, war and peace, honour and ethics. But how contentious this is depends partly on how broadly we construe the ideas of utility and preference that are central to the standard theory of rational choice. This chapter is meant to help in probing this aspect of *Homo economicus*. It will also help to focus the widespread suspicion that the broader the construal the more vacuous the theory becomes, because the real explanatory work is then done by social norms, which account for the preferences of individuals, rather than by the preferences thus generated. A bold riposte is to demonstrate how rational choice and game theory can together account for the emergence of norms. Whether this can be done turns crucially on the relation between non-cooperative and cooperative games, as other chapters will show. Meanwhile, we have chosen cultural exchange as a topic, because it puts instructive pressure on the notion of exchange and hence on the rationale for game theory.

The Exchange of Gifts

'Cultural exchange' is best defined initially by reference to traditional societies that practise what anthropologists term 'gift-exchange'. A person presents another with what appears to be a gift, the value of which depends partly on what it expresses. Sooner or later, the other returns a gift with the same feature. The pair of apparently separate gifts constitutes an exchange, because together they affirm a relationship and its place in the seen and unseen worlds of the culture. Cultural exchange is thus *expressive social exchange*, in contrast to instrumental exchange where each person sets out to acquire something more useful to him than what he parted with. Gift-exchange is what Marcel Mauss in his (1925) study *The Gift* called a 'total phenomenon', involving all aspects of social life in a way which strengthens the social bond. One famous example is the *kula* rings which used to exist in the Western Pacific, where gifts of red and white shells circulated from island to island in the course of more instrumental trading expeditions (Malinowski, 1920, 1922). Another is the *potlach* or ceremonial gift-giving feast among North American Indians, where vast amounts of private possessions were given away or publicly destroyed. To the modern mind it is puzzling to find a practice of giving or even exchanging gifts which seem pointless, cripplingly extravagant or both. The explanation offered by Mauss and others is that such 'gifts' are the key to a total system of reciprocal obligations.

Obligations certainly are crucial, but this explanation may suggest that the participants are so deeply absorbed in the social fabric of relationships that they are mere vehicles of established norms. To bring out the point that, in both traditional and modern cultural exchange, this is not so, we shall study a more detailed example. It is taken from Homer's *Iliad*, composed in the eighth century BC and recounting the siege of Troy some 500 years earlier – a world that is clearly 'traditional' rather than 'modern'. The *Iliad* is set in the tenth weary year of the siege, and opens with a quarrel between Agamemnon, commander of the attacking Greek army, and Achilles, the leading warrior on the Greek side. Trouble is sparked when Agamemnon commandeers a captured Trojan woman who was part of Achilles' prize from an earlier battle. Honour and feelings outraged, Achilles withdraws from the siege, which starts to go very badly for the Greeks. At length, Agamemnon is driven to admit to being in the wrong and sends emissaries. They offer Achilles a truly Homeric gift; gold, cauldrons and fine horses, the return of his captive and seven more women, the promise of a shipful of treasure and 20 women when Troy falls, and of seven cities and the hand of one of Agamemnon's daughters on return home. Achilles refuses. When he does return to the war later, it is to avenge his friend Patroclus, who has been killed in, and perhaps because of, his absence. The *Iliad* ends not with the fall of Troy but with Achilles grudgingly letting the Trojan King Priam reclaim the body of his son Hector, whom Achilles has slain in revenge.

There is a good case for holding that the story makes sense only against a background of gift-exchange and what it signifies. The quarrel arose because Agamemnon demanded the Trojan woman as a gift to which he had a right. But, because he did not have that right, he violated Achilles' honour, and so put himself under an obligation to make amends. The gift offered to Achilles was more than enough for the purpose, however, and Achilles had an obligation to accept it and return to the siege. By refusing, he left a duty unpaid – a matter pertinent to the gods' not preventing the fight between Hector and Patroclus. When he returned to the war, he did at length accept Agamemnon's gift and that entitled him to meet Hector in single combat. But he should have allowed Hector due burial, and that he did so only after Priam had abased himself as a suppliant is a sign that character is not the mere extrusion of governing norms.

'Giving and returning the equivalence', in Simmel's phrase, thus supplies the broad 'schema' for 'all contacts among men', rather than explaining all details. The schema for gift-exchange has to do with the proper performance of roles, whose incumbents are expected to act freely and virtuously in discharging their various obligations. It is an essential background for understanding actions which break the rules of exchange or which have no direct connection with them. It can thus be made the key to 'traditional' social life without thereby turning social actors into the creatures of social norms, or even insisting that every action is one side of a successful exchange. On the other hand, the idea of 'equivalence' seems too modern and precise. In a traditional society, entitlements and obligations vary with social position. Obligations incurred in dealings with one person or group are often discharged in dealings with another. Any overall 'equivalence' is – at best – exceedingly loose, especially as there is no precise tariff, such as a modern system of prices, which measures debts and different ways of discharging them (see □ p. 119). The relations between Achilles and Agamemnon are not only one-to-one and are not contractual.

Exchange Theory

The foregoing suggests that traditional cultural exchange is not suited to social exchange theory – yet a case can certainly be made. Peter Blau, for instance, has always argued that there is a general concept of exchange, within which the balance between economic and social elements varies without upsetting the principle (see, for example, Blau, 1964). In a useful encyclopaedia article, he asserts that 'economic exchange may be considered a special case of the general phenomenon of exchange, with social exchange being the residual excluded category'. Both are governed by the basic principle that 'men enter new associations because they expect doing so to be rewarding', and continue or expand their contacts for the same reason. Rewards may be intrinsic, as in love, or extrinsic, as in seeking advice, and the theory 'is intended to encompass all striving for rewarding experiences'. Anyone who does a favour creates an obligation; anyone who benefits acquires a duty to reciprocate. Social and economic exchanges both 'manifest the marginal principle in social life' (Blau, 1968).

By such an account, Homer's world has different institutions from ours but the same reward-seeking inhabitants. Add an exchange-theory analysis of how institutions emerge as devices for securing a mutual flow of rewards, and we have a formidable social theory indeed. But suspicion lingers that Achilles and Agamemnon are not marketeers in armour. Thus consider Mauss's conclusion to *The Gift* (□). Here a radical difference between 'traditional' and 'modern' is discerned in the fragmenting of what was once a 'total' way of life. Modern man is an 'individual' who can separate his activities into compartments, and pursue interests which are his alone. That was not possible before the Renaissance and the rise of a suitable idea of people as individuals (compare with Mauss, 1938). By this test Agamemnon was not seeking any species of profitable investment in future rewarding experiences, nor was Achilles' refusal an intemperate exercise in hard bargaining.

The underlying dispute is not just historical (see ORGANIZATIONS (10)). It applies within 'our Western societies' too, wherever people act without seeming concerned to receive in exchange (Blau, 1968). For instance, blood donors in the UK seem to give blood willingly, without receiving cash, or anything more than a friendly cup of weak tea, in return. Blau would no doubt insist that some reward, such as social approval, must be involved. But Richard Titmuss, in his profound study *The Gift Relation-*

> It is only our Western societies that quite recently turned man into an economic animal. But we are not yet all animals of the same species . . . *Homo economicus* is not behind us, but before, like the moral man, the man of duty, the scientific man and the reasonable man. For a long time man was something quite different; and it is not so long now since he became a machine – a calculating machine.
>
> (Mauss, 1925)

ship: from Human Blood to Social Policy (1970), is adamant that the National Blood Transfusion Service is a system of gifts between strangers, with 'no explicit or implicit right to a return gift or action' and depending on 'creative altruism'. Although no donors were 'purely altruistic' in the sense of 'complete, disinterested, spontaneous altruism', all came forward with 'some sense of obligation' and although their approval and interest was 'perhaps encouraged by a vague sense that the system might benefit them one day', this did not amount to attempting to secure a good for themselves: nor, if they were clear-headed, could it have done, as the 'free-rider' exposition in GAME THEORY (7) demonstrates. The altruism is 'creative' in that 'the self is realised with the help of anonymous others': not a *quid pro quo* but an element in Titmuss's idea of a flourishing society, and one which leads on to his conclusion that 'modern societies now require more rather than less freedom of choice for the expression of altruism in the daily life of all social groups' (Titmuss, 1970).

Blood donation is here presented as a case of 'gifts between strangers' which are common and necessary. Social exchange theory retorts that in all such cases an equivalent return is sought in some form or other. The discussion here may seem to suggest that the issue is an empirical one of what in fact motivates people, whether all contacts are in fact exchanges and whether these questions actually have a single universal answer. But a little thought will show that every social action *can* be described as 'striving for rewarding experiences', with cultural contacts included by recognizing cultural rewards. The rough value of these rewards can then be assessed by applying the assumption that rational agents are induced to incur costs only if they gain greater benefits. Thus social exchange theory can encompass everything, even if at some risk of turning out to be circular, and its merits need to be settled on other grounds.

Obligation

Can the concept of obligation be analysed consistently with, ultimately, the basic concepts of rational choice theory? The simplest attempt is to argue that, although obligations can and do motivate, they never do so directly. Even in Homer's world, where actors are born into social positions with firm obligations attached, there is still room for choice. Agamemnon chooses not to do his duty. He chooses to create some fresh obligations by making promises and then chooses not to honour them. If he can choose not to do his duty, then he also chooses when he does do it. So, even though obligations form the fabric of a traditional culture, they motivate only when the agents choose to act on them. Rational choice theory slots neatly into the gap, with even traditional actors motivated directly by cost–benefit calculations. (Homer's heroes are very conscious that the gods operate a rough system of rewards and penalties for mortals.) In modern societies the gap is more obvious, and social exchange theory fills it to perfection.

However, moral philosophy has other accounts of the relation of obligation to action. The one friendliest to rational choice theory is **utilitarianism** (🗐), in which a moral agent does what promotes the greatest happiness of the greatest number. Here the agent must somehow be reasoned into maximizing the utility of more people than himself (since he counts for neither more nor less than one) but at least his reasons, or good reasons, for action are always forward-looking, as in rational choice theory. Obligations have no independent place or power in this future-oriented scheme. In other moral theories consequences matter less, or not at all. Thus in the work of **Kant** (🗐), as noted in the chapter on AUTONOMY (16), a moral agent does his duty solely because it is his duty, and is unmoved by inclination, prudence or even the resulting welfare of mankind. Where he has created the duty, as when he has made a promise or incurred a debt, this very fact is a reason for action. Some reasons are, we might say, backward-looking.

There is a strong case for regarding backward-looking reasons as essential to moral action. One way to conduct it proceeds as an attack on act-utilitarianism, the version of utilitarianism which holds that the agent should make each particular decision on its particular merits. In this version the agent is not to tell the truth on any occasion when a lie would do more good, is not to repay a debt when the money could be put to better use, and so on. Critics object that a society of overt act-utilitarians would collapse, because essential practices such as truth-telling and promise-keeping would cease to be reliable. Act-utilitarians reply that, since such practices are useful, the agent will of course weigh the impact which his lie would have on them. But the critics are not satisfied, since they argue that these practices have to be placed 'off limits' to rational calculation, if they are to be truly reliable. This means making them unassailable by forward-looking reasons. Rule-utilitarians concede the point. In this version the agent is to act in accordance with the rules whose observance by all would produce the best consequences. These rules are thus to be treated as if they prescribed duties which are to be carried out whatever the consequences. Although the ultimate ground for the rules is utilitarian, the effect is to introduce backward-looking reasons into an otherwise forward-looking moral psychology.

Critics conclude, unsurprisingly, that the act-utilitarian version has a fatal flaw which the rule version cannot remedy without conceding the game. Without trying to umpire, I can at least identify the crux of the matter, which is whether or not the gap between obligation and action can be filled solely with forward-looking reasons. The case just sketched for denying it in moral philosophy is readily translated into an accompanying moral psychology, where agents respect normative expectations for non-consequential reasons (see HOMO ECONOMICUS, HOMO SOCIOLOGICUS (5)). This crux echoes one which featured in the discussion of the Prisoner's Dilemma (□ p. 99) and the free-rider problem in the chapters on GAME THEORY (7) and GAME THEORY APPLIED (9). If the motivation of each prisoner is solely to maximize the pay-off to himself, then Pareto-inferior outcomes result. Can they not see this and rationally adopt cooperative strategies? Well, they can rationally strike the necessary bargain, but it will not help them while each retains a dominant reason to defect. It might 'stop the rot' if each could regard his having given his word as a conclusive reason to keep it, thus putting utility calculations 'off limits'. But this would require backward-looking reasons to operate in a framework in which all reasons for action are forward-looking. Indeed, even the striking of a bargain, conceived as creating a mutual obligation, presupposes an alternative mode of thought.

Obligation thus threatens to cause a radical snag, especially if social exchange theory claims to analyse cultural exchange in a traditional society, whose social fabric depends on backward-looking reasons. This leads on to a further doubt. Achilles and Agamemnon, as described by Homer, do not think of themselves in the terms that are basic for rational choice and exchange theories. Kings and warriors are not universal 'individuals', and Homer has no single word for 'person' which applies independently of social position and role. Can such theories possibly be right, if they are so far removed from the concepts and self-definitions in the heads of their subjects? Once the question is raised, it can quickly be extended to the study of our modern world too. For, although an economic model of social action as exchange is at least in circulation nowadays, it is doubtful whether it is generally accepted. At any rate, 'creative altruists', who include most of us some of the time, do not share it. Indeed, granted the previous snag, neither traditional nor modern worlds could function if the inhabitants thought of themselves and their dealings with one another solely as economically rational individuals, exchanging for gains in utility. Therefore the analysis has to bypass the actors' own story and trace the explanation of action to unconscious motives, and to hidden pressures which the economic and social system puts on its units to engage in utility-maximizing behaviour. That takes it far from its starting point which was, after all, a theory of *choice*. We need much more persuading that social actors can be so radically mistaken about the character of their obligations and, indeed, themselves.

In summary, obligation does not 'rest on the schema of giving and returning the equivalence'. If it did, duty would never be done at a loss except through miscalculation. Yet this is often the case. The retort might be that examples of high-minded action nevertheless presuppose a general, if diffused, *schema* of reciprocity. But, even so, obligation is not the only moral concept. People not only act 'beyond the call of duty', as the saying goes, but display virtues and concern for what is morally good, whose conceptual roots seem not to be those of duty at all. Whenever someone returns good for evil, dies for a worthy cause or is kind to a stranger, even the schema of giving and returning the equivalence seems absent. There is more to motivation than the forward-looking logic of rational choice can easily admit or, indeed, do without. Some people, I dare say, send Christmas cards just to wish others a Happy Christmas.

Martin Hollis

Further Reading

Heath (1976) is a useful introduction to social exchange theory in relation to rational choice, with references to the anthropological discussion of gifts by Malinowski (1922) and Mauss (1925). Titmuss (1970) is fascinating, not only about blood donation but also in terms of its wider significance. Social exchange theory, for the purposes of this chapter, has much in common with what Frohlich and Oppenheimer (1978) call *Modern Political Economy*, or the application of rational choice theory and game theory across the board.

12

Anarchic Order

Living things are marvellously intricate and elegant solutions to design problems, problems that are far beyond the grasp of human engineers. This used to be taken as evidence for the existence of a divine Designer. But we now know that living things are not the product of any designer; they are the unintended consequence of a blind process of evolution. The deepest insight of economics is that we depend for our survival on a network of exchange that in this respect is like a living thing or an ecosystem: it is highly ordered, but no-one has ordered it.

This network is made up of many independent agents, each seeking some kind of profit through interaction with others – there is no guiding intelligence or central plan. The idea that the order we observe in an economic system is spontaneous, the unintended consequence of many independent actions, is most famously expressed in Adam Smith's *Wealth of Nations* (1776). For **Smith** (▣), the predominant (but not the only) motive for the individual is self-love (see □): that is why we appeal to the brewer's and the baker's own interests when we try to provide for our dinners. Economic order, then, is the unintended consequence of self-love. But, Smith also says, this unplanned order generally *works to our benefit*. His metaphor of the invisible hand (see □) suggests that it is as if this order were the product of a benevolent designer.

The idea of spontaneous order is fundamental to economics: the economist's standard approach to understanding social phenomena is to treat them as the unintended consequences of the actions of individuals, and to assume that each individual acts rationally in terms of his own preferences. In this respect, modern economics is undoubtedly Smithian. But

SELF-LOVE

Man has almost constant occasion for the help of his brethren, and it is in vain for him to expect it from their benevolence only. He will be more likely to prevail if he can interest their self-love in his favour, and shew them that it is for their own advantage to do for him what he requires of them. . . . It is not from the benevolence of the butcher, the brewer, or the baker, that we expect our dinner, but from their regard to their own interest. We address ourselves, not to their humanity but to their self-love, and never talk to them of our own necessities but of their advantages.

(Smith, 1776, pp. 26–7)

THE INVISIBLE HAND

Discussing barriers to international trade, Smith argues that, other things being equal, a merchant will prefer to employ his capital in his own country rather than abroad. A merchant will know more about the laws and customs of his own country, and about whom he can trust; thus domestic trade involves fewer risks than foreign trade. By favouring domestic trade, he uses his capital in a way that 'give[s] revenue and employment to the greatest number of people of his own country'. But:

By preferring the support of domestick to that of foreign industry, he intends only his own security; and by directing that industry in such a manner as its produce may be of the greatest value, he intends only his own gain, and he is in this, as in many other cases, led by an invisible hand to promote an end which was no part of his intention. Nor is it always the worse for the society that it was no part of it. By pursuing his own interest he frequently promotes that of the society more effectually than when he really intends to promote it. I have never known much good done by those who affected to trade for the publick good. It is an affectation, indeed, not very common among merchants, and very few words need be employed in dissuading them from it.

(Smith, 1776, p. 456)

the thought behind Smith's metaphor of the invisible hand is much more controversial. How far the market works to our benefit is probably the most impotant issue of debate among economists.

Most economists take the fundamental institutions of the market as given: they assume that property rights are well-defined and secure, and that contracts are enforceable. The protection of property rights and the enforcement of contracts are seen as jobs for government. From this viewpoint, the spontaneous order of the market exists within a framework of institutions which may themselves be the product of human design. Indeed, modern economists are fond of drawing 'policy implications' from their work. A policy implication is a recommendation as to how the government, by imposing a tax here or redistributing property rights there, should change the framework within which individuals pursue their own interests.

However, it may be possible to see the market as a spontaneous order in a more fundamental sense. Our dependence on exchange is not a peculiarity of a particular age or culture: trade seems to be a constant feature of human history. (It was the trade in flint axe-heads that enabled our remote hunting ancestors to live far away from any flint beds.) When there are gains to be made by trading, trading networks tend to spring up – even when governments try to suppress them. (Think of prostitution, or of the trade in cocaine.) So perhaps the institutions of property and exchange are themselves the unintended outcomes of the pursuit of individual interests.

More generally, the market might be thought of as a microcosm of anarchic social order. If the market could be shown to work to our benefit, then this might be taken to be a demonstration that social order does not always require design, that life without government need not be (as **Thomas Hobbes** (🖾) thought) solitary, poor, nasty, brutish and short. The greater are the possibilities of anarchic order, the less we need government. The more it is true that social order is spontaneous and self-regulating, the less room is left within which government can manoeuvre, and the greater are the difficulties in attempts to reform long-established institutions. Important political principles are at stake here.

The Evolution of Social Order

It is useful to begin by considering some very simple cases of spontaneous order. As a first example, think of the problem faced by two drivers who approach one another on collision courses at a crossroads. What follows is not intended as a stylized history of how rules of priority at crossroads actually came into existence in any particular society. Rather, it is intended as a model of how such rules *could* have come into existence and, more generally, as a model of the evolution of order in human relations.

The problem faced by the drivers can be modelled as a game. Each driver must choose one of two strategies, 'maintain speed' or 'slow down'. For each driver, the best outcome is the one in which he maintains speed and the other slows down, but the opposite state of affairs (slowing down

Table 12.1   The Crossroads game.

		Player B	
		Slow down	Maintain speed
Player A	Slow down	0, 0	2, 3
	Maintain speed	3, 2	−10, −10

while the other driver maintains speed) is only slightly inferior. The outcome in which they both slow down is worse than these ('After you, Claude'; 'No, after you, Cecil'), while the outcome in which they both maintain speed is worse still. To allow a game-theoretic analysis, we can assign some fairly arbitrary utility numbers, to give the game shown in table 12.1. This game is similar in structure to the Battle of the Sexes (□ p. 109). Clearly, both drivers want to coordinate their behaviour. But how are they to do this?

First think of what would happen in a community of road users who repeatedly played this game with one another, and who thought of the game as being entirely symmetrical. In this case, the community would settle down in an equilibrium in which, on average, drivers slowed down exactly 80 per cent of the time. But why should this be? Suppose that you are a driver, and you discover that 80 per cent of the other drivers you encounter at junctions slow down. Then the expected utility from slowing down yourself is $(0.8 \times 0) + (0.2 \times 2)$, that is, 0.4. The expected utility from maintaining speed is $(0.8 \times 3) - (0.2 \times 10)$, which is also 0.4. Therefore you will be indifferent between slowing down and maintaining speed. If the probability that the other driver will slow down were greater than 0.8, it would pay you to maintain speed; and if that probability were less than 0.8, it would pay you to slow down. But this is true for everyone. So if more than 80 per cent of drivers slow down, there will be a tendency for drivers to gravitate towards the 'maintain speed' strategy, thus reducing the proportion of drivers who slow down. Conversely, if less than 80 per cent slow down, there will be a tendency for the proportion of drivers who slow down to increase. The situation in which 80 per cent slow down is, in this sense, a stable equilibrium.

In the language of game theory, this is a Nash equilibrium in mixed strategies. If we think of A and B as each playing 'slow down' with probability 0.8 and 'maintain speed' with probability 0.2, we have a state of affairs in which each player's strategy is a best reply to the other's. This equilibrium is stable in the evolutionary sense: A and B are playing evolutionarily stable strategies (see GAME THEORY (7)).

This state of affairs is not particularly desirable for anyone: drivers coordinate their behaviour only 64 per cent of the time. (In 32 per cent of cases they both slow down and, unfortunately, in 4 per cent of cases they both maintain speed.) It seems unlikely, however, that this would continue indefinitely. Suppose that some people realize that the game is not quite symmetrical: in every instance, one driver is approaching from the right and the other from the left. Suppose further that, for whatever reason, some of these people come to believe that although on average 80 per cent of drivers slow down, drivers approaching from the left are slightly more likely to slow down than those approaching from the right. For someone who believes this, the best strategy is always to maintain speed when approaching from the right and always to slow down when approaching from the left. But if some people adopt this strategy, it will indeed be true – even if initially it was not – that drivers approaching from the left are more likely to slow down. This tendency is self-reinforcing: the more people follow the convention 'Give way to the right', the more it pays other people to follow it. Sooner or later everyone will realize that it is his interest to follow this convention.

I have provided no reason why the convention that becomes established should be 'Give way to the right' rather than 'Give way to the left'. Nor have I given any reason why it should be based on the left–right asymmetry rather than some other (such as the asymmetry between major and minor roads, or between larger and smaller vehicles). In large part, *which* convention evolves is an accident of history. But what is significant is this: provided that the players of the Crossroads game recognize *some* asymmetry, there will be a tendency for a convention to evolve which tells one driver to slow down and the other to maintain speed.

The Crossroads game, then, provides a model of spontaneous order. Each driver acts on his own beliefs and preferences. The unintended consequence of these independent actions is a pattern or order in social behaviour (drivers on the left give way to drivers on the right). And this order works to everyone's benefit. If we assume that each person approaches crossroads from the right just as often as he approaches them from the left, then everyone benefits equally.

This is a very simple model, but it captures the essence of some significant forms of spontaneous coordination. Think of how buyers and sellers make contact. In markets in which traders do not have shops or offices, there are usually conventions about how to make transactions: if there were no such conventions, trade would be impossible. There are conventional times and places for prostitutes and ticket touts, as well as taxi-drivers and market traders, to meet their respective customers; there are conventional days on which to place different kinds of advertisement in conventional newspapers. To take a very different example, consider languages: we are able to communicate with one another because we use the same arbitrary associations between sounds, symbols and meanings. These are conventions that have evolved spontaneously.

As these examples suggest, spontaneous order often works to our benefit. But sometimes it can lead to patterns of behaviour that are inefficient from everyone's point of view. Keeping with the example of behaviour on the roads, consider a roundabout (traffic circle). It is easy to see that traffic will flow most smoothly if everyone follows the convention that drivers on the roundabout have priority over drivers entering it. (Otherwise, the roundabout may become blocked.) Once established, this convention would be self-enforcing, for the same reason that 'Give way to the right' was self-enforcing in the original crossroads game. But other rules for assigning priority, although less efficient, can be equally stable. For example, if a minor road crosses a major road at a roundabout, there could be a convention that traffic entering the roundabout from the major road has priority over traffic on the roundabout. In the long run, all drivers would be worse off from following this inefficient convention; but, in following it, each driver would be acting quite rationally (given his expectations about the behaviour of the others). This is exactly what happened in the early years of roundabouts in the UK: it was only because of the intervention of the Ministry of Transport that the efficient convention became established.

Conventions may also distribute benefits in ways that seem morally arbitrary. **David Hume** (⊞) (1740, p. 490) argued that rules of property constitute a spontaneous order that 'arises gradually, and acquires force by a slow progression, and by our repeated experience of the inconveniences of transgressing it'. What he had in mind can, perhaps, be modelled by the game of Chicken (see table 12.2). Imagine two people who come into conflict over something that they both want. Each can choose either to be conciliatory (the 'Dove' strategy) or to be aggressive ('Hawk'). If both play Dove, they divide the disputed object equally. If one plays Dove and the other plays Hawk, the Hawk threatens to fight, the Dove gives way, and the Hawk takes the disputed object. If both play Hawk, neither gives way and so there is a fight, which (on average) is damaging to both. This game is presented in table 12.2, again using some fairly arbitrary numbers.

Table 12.2 Chicken.

		Player B	
		Conciliatory (dove)	Aggressive (hawk)
Player A	Conciliatory (dove)	1, 1	0, 2
	Aggressive (hawk)	2, 0	−2, −2

The structure of this game is very similar to that of the Crossroads game. In each game, there are two Nash equilibria in pure strategies. In the Crossroads game, 'slow down' is the best reply to 'maintain speed' and vice versa, so that if one player chooses one of these strategies and the other chooses the other, there is a state of Nash equilibrium. Similarly, in Chicken, Dove is the best reply to Hawk and Hawk is the best reply to Dove. However, there is a significant difference between the two games. In the crossroads game, both players are better off in (pure-strategy) Nash equilibrium than if they play symmetrically: they may thus be said to have a common interest in coordinating on *some* Nash equilibrium, even though they have conflicting preferences *between* these equilibria. But in Chicken if, say, A plays Hawk and B plays Dove, B is worse off than she would have been had they both played Dove. (For more discussion of Chicken, see GAME THEORY (7).)

If there is any asymmetry between the two players in a typical game of Chicken, it is possible for a convention to evolve, prescribing which player should be the Hawk and which the Dove. For example, the rule might be that whichever player is in possession of the disputed object at the start of the game should be the Hawk. Notice that this is a *de facto* rule of property. The possessor is prepared to fight to obtain the disputed object, and the other player is willing to let him have it rather than fight: it is as if both recognize that the possessor has some special claim to it. The asymmetry between possessing and not possessing does in fact seem to be an important element in *de facto* property rights, as Hume (1740, pp. 501–13) pointed out. Interestingly, many animal species seem to be genetically predisposed to use this particular asymmetry to resolve conflicts (Maynard Smith, 1982, pp. 97–100).

The implication seems to be that the institution of property can emerge spontaneously, as an unintended consequence of individual action. This is clearly a form of social *order*. It may be true that any rule of property is better for everyone than no rule at all. (This is plausible, but need not be the case: some people might do better in a free-for-all than with a rule of property that consistently favoured other people.) But even so, the existence of one rule rather than another has distributional consequences. And these distributional consequences, like the rule itself, may be accidents of history: they may not be ones that we would judge to be good in terms of any independent moral standard.

The Market as Spontaneous Order

In general, then, spontaneous order need not work to our benefit; but it often does. How about the spontaneous order of the market economy?

Is Smith right to suggest that, within the rules of the market (that is, given the laws of property and contract), the interaction of self-interested individuals tends to promote the good of society as a whole?

If we are to think sensibly about the workings of a whole economy, we must use some theoretical model. Any model will seem absurdly simplified and abstract but, if we want to ask general questions about the benefits or disbenefits of the market system, there really is no alternative. Most modern analysis of the workings of markets is based on a model originally presented by Léon Walras (1874) and subsequently refined by, among others, Arrow and Debreu (1954). Here there is room only for a quick sketch. Imagine a world with two types of economic agent, consumers and firms. There are many goods. Each consumer has preferences over different bundles of consumption goods and leisure; these can be represented by utility functions. Each firm has a 'production function' which specifies how it can transform labour and raw materials into consumption goods. Each good, and each type of labour, has a market price, which is taken as given by every agent. Firms seek to maximize their profits by buying labour and raw materials, transforming them into consumption goods and selling them. Any profits are distributed as dividends to consumers. Consumers seek to maximize their utilities by selling labour and raw materials and buying consumption goods.

Now consider any list of prices, one for each good and type of labour. For each consumption good there will be demands (by consumers) and supplies (by firms). Similarly, for each raw material and for each type of labour there will be demands (by firms) and supplies (by consumers). The market for a particular good or type of labour is said to *clear* if there is neither excess demand nor excess supply: the total amount demanded is exactly in balance with the total amount supplied. There is a state of *competitive equilibrium* (or Walrasian equilibrium) if all markets clear simultaneously. Another way of putting this is to say that in equilibrium, the plans of all agents are consistent with one another. Each agent decides independently, in the light of its own objective and the list of market prices, how much of each good to buy and sell. But all these independent decisions mesh together in such a way that every plan can be carried out.

Given certain important assumptions (of which, more later), three important results can be proved about competitive equilibrium. The first is that every economy has a competitive equilibrium: there is some list of prices at which all markets clear simultaneously. This is quite remarkable: it means that it is possible to coordinate the plans of many independent agents by means of a price system.

The second result (sometimes called the *first fundamental theorem of welfare economics*) is that any competitive equilibrium is Pareto-efficient (or Pareto-optimal, or economically efficient). An allocation of resources is Pareto-efficient if there is no way of rearranging things so that some person is made better off while no-one is made worse off (see **Pareto optimality** (⊞)). We must recognize that Pareto-efficiency is compatible with distributions of welfare that are quite unjust. (For example, a slave economy would be Pareto-efficient if it was impossible to free the slaves without making the former slave-owners worse off.) Nevertheless, a Pareto-efficient economy *is* efficient in a genuine sense. One way of formalizing the sense in which it is efficient is to use the concept of a **social welfare function** (⊞). An allocation of resources is Pareto-efficient if it maximizes *some* social welfare function in which each individual's welfare has a positive weight. (The efficient slave economy maximizes a social welfare function that gives a high weight to the welfare of the slave-owners and a low weight to the welfare of the slaves.) This result, too, is remarkable. It says that an economy that is coordinated only by a price system can work as though every transaction had been determined by an omniscient central planner who had chosen to maximize some social welfare function.

The final result is more relevant to a discussion of economic planning than to one of spontaneous order, but I give it for completeness. This is the *second fundamental theorem of welfare economics*; that every Pareto-efficient allocation of resources can be achieved by means of *some* competitive equilibrium. Imagine an omniscient planner who chooses a social welfare function and then seeks to maximize it. He is confronted with a given set of consumers, each with his utility function, and with a given set of firms, each with its production function. He also has to take as given the total amounts of labour and raw materials available to the economy. In principle, this information is sufficient to allow the planner to compute exactly how the economy must be organized so as to maximize the social welfare function; and having computed all this, he might then give the appropriate directions to every agent. The second fundamental theorem tells us that the same result could be achieved by means of a price system, provided that the planner was free to make lump-sum transfers of purchasing power between households.

So far, nothing has been said about *how competitive equilibrium is reached*. This issue is crucial. If we are to treat competitive equilibrium as the expected state of affairs for a market economy, we must appeal to some forces that tend to move a market economy from disequilibrium to equilibrium. An early attempt to deal with this issue was made by Walras, and an adaptation of his approach is still much used by economists. This uses the model of an auction. First consider how a single object, say, a painting, is auctioned. The auctioneer begins by calling out a relatively low price. More than one person is willing to buy at this price –

there is excess demand. The auctioneer keeps raising the price until only one person is left in the bidding. Now demand is in balance with supply. In this microcosm of an economy, then, the rules followed by the auctioneer provide a means of reaching equilibrium.

Walras's insight is that a whole economy can be modelled as an enormous auction. Imagine an auctioneer who calls out a list of provisional prices, one for each good and type of labour. Each agent takes these prices as given and chooses its demands and supplies so as to maximize utility (in the case of a consumer) or profit (in the case of a firm). These demand and supply decisions are reported to the auctioneer, who then works out for each good whether there is excess demand, excess supply or exact balance. If demand and supply are everywhere in balance – if all markets clear – then the price list is declared final and each agent carries out its planned transactions. Otherwise, no trade takes place and the auctioneer revises the price list by raising the price of any good in excess demand and lowering the price of any good in excess supply. This process of *tâtonnement* – of groping for equilibrium – continues until a price list is found at which all markets clear. Such a price list is a competitive equilibrium.

The **Walrasian auctioneer** (🛈) may seem an extravagant fiction, but the idea is to try to capture in a simple model the impersonal market forces of supply and demand that lie behind changes in prices. As a first approximation, it is perhaps legitimate to assume that a market economy works *as if* it were presided over by an auctioneer. This model helps us to understand one significant aspect of the market system: its use of decentralized information. In any economy, vast amounts of information about production functions and preferences are necessarily private to individual consumers and firms. No single mind or computer program could handle all this information, even if (which seems unlikely) consumers and firms could be relied on to reveal it with honesty. But this is the information that a central planner would need in order to calculate a Pareto-efficient allocation of resources. In the Walrasian model, this information remains private. Each firm knows its own production function, each consumer knows his own preferences, and all agents know the list of market prices. But no-one needs to know any more than this. Everything that any agent needs to know about other agents is contained in market prices. Market prices adjust in response to the independent decisions of many individual agents, each of which is choosing its demands and supplies in the light of its own objective. In this sense the spontaneous order of the market can achieve feats of coordination that would be beyond the ability of any planner.

What Makes Markets Work?

A major weakness of the Walrasian theory is that its account of the price system lacks any motive power. Why, we might ask, do goods have prices? Why does each good have only one price rather than many? Why do prices rise when there is excess demand and fall when there is excess supply? The model of the auctioneer seems to suggest that a price system could be administered by officials following a set of simple rules (just as ordinary auctions are). These officials, of course, would not presume to know anything about preferences or production functions. They would merely publish lists of prices, collect information about demand and supply, and adjust prices until markets cleared. Indeed, socialist economists in the 1920s and 1930s, drawing up master plans for central planning, sometimes proposed a bureaucratically administered price system of this kind as part of the planning mechanism (see, for example, Lange and Taylor, 1938; see also **market socialism** (⚐)).

But would such a price system really work? There is a tradition of economic thought, usually called 'Austrian' and deriving particularly from the work of **Friedrich Hayek** (⚐) (1948) and Israel Kirzner (1979), which answers 'No'. According to this school of thought, the market is a spontaneous order in a more fundamental sense than can be captured in the Walrasian theory (see also RISK, IGNORANCE AND IMAGINATION (4)).

Consider a simple example. Imagine an island economy. In the sparsely populated north of the island there are many springs which supply naturally aerated water. Some local people drink this water, but there are so few of them that the owners of the springs have never found it worthwhile to charge them. In the densely populated south, the people drink tap water and various bottled drinks, but have never thought of aerated water as a possible drink. Think how this would look in a Walrasian model. Aerated water must be treated as a distinct good, entering into each person's utility function. It must have a single price (net of any transport costs). According to our story, this price is zero. The auctioneer reports to everyone in the south that aerated water has a price of zero (plus transport costs from the north) and invites bids. Within this model we cannot make any sense of the idea that the southerners have never thought of drinking aerated water: to say that they have well-defined preferences is to say that they already know whether or not they want to drink it. In the light of their preferences, they report their demands. These demands, we shall suppose, sum to a large volume of water. The auctioneer responds by raising the price of aerated water. When the spring-owners hear of the new price, they open up bottling plants.

This story ought to be about the *discovery* of an opportunity for mutually beneficial trade between the north and the south. That aerated water is a good at all is a discovery of some importance; until this is realized by someone, there can be no trade. The Walrasian story simply assumes that the auctioneer knows what is a good and what is not. It also fails to explain how people come to realize that they have a taste for aerated water: it assumes that they already know this. Because all the relevant facts are taken to be already known, the opening up of a new line of trade appears automatic: as soon as households in the south develop a preference for aerated water, the price of this good will start to rise and trade will begin. But suppose that we take the Walrasian theory literally and imagine that the price system is presided over by a competent and professional auctioneer. It might never occur to her to list a price for aerated water. Alternatively, she might be a perfectionist, and try to list prices for anything that could conceivably be a good (aerated spring water, free; ordinary spring water, free; dirty river water, free; sea water, free; and so on). Then the typical consumer, receiving a book rather like a telephone directory in which prices were listed for thousands of completely useless commodities, would probably never realize that aerated water was something that he would enjoy, were he to try it. And so the opportunity for trade might pass unnoticed.

In a real market economy, the motive power is provided by *entrepreneurship*, by which we do not just mean the activities of a small number of businessmen and women, but the more general idea of alertness to possibilities for gain. On our island, the first person who transports aerated water from the north to the south and persuades southerners to try drinking it will make a useful profit for herself. Until this happens, an opportunity for profit is waiting to be discovered. No doubt many people will pass the opportunity by, and later wonder why they never thought of such an easy way of making a profit. No doubt other people will back hunches that prove to be ill-founded, wasting their resources trying to open up markets in goods that no-one wants. But if there are alert people, looking out for ways of making gains, we should expect a tendency for such opportunities to be discovered.

According to this view, the Walrasian auctioneer represents another level of spontaneous order, working below the surface of the price system as it is usually modelled by economists. In this spontaneous order, information is discovered by agents who are seeking profit for themselves. Because people are alert to the possibility of buying cheap and selling dear, disparities in prices are evened out: this is why we can assume that each good has a single price. Similarly, firms' production functions are not a given feature of the world, but are the result of a process of discovery motivated by the profits to be had from producing a good more cheaply than before, or from producing a new good that households can be induced to buy. For these processes of discovery to work, it is not necessary that everyone is motivated by the desire for gain. It is sufficient that some people are so motivated, and that there are no restrictions on trade. Suppose, for example, that all the firms in an industry are complacently using an inefficent method of production, passing on the costs to the consumers in the form of high prices. Then, if there is freedom of entry into the industry, an alert outsider can make a profit by moving into the industry, adopting more efficient methods of production, and undercutting his competitors.

Some of this sense of the market being driven by individuals' pursuit of gain is captured in a model of the economic system that derives from the work of **Francis Edgeworth** (1881) (📖). Edgeworth pictures the economy not as an auction, but as a bazaar; an arena in which everyone is free to haggle with everyone else. The flavour of this approach can best be conveyed by thinking of a pure-exchange economy. Consider a marketplace in which many people congregate. Each person comes to the market endowed with particular quantities of various goods, and with a preference ordering over possible bundles of consumption. Each person wants to come away from the market with a bundle of consumption goods that ranks as high as possible in his preference ordering. To achieve this end he must make exchanges with other people, who are similarly trying to benefit themselves. The only constraint on the system is the law of property: no-one may be forced to trade against his will, but if two or more people agree to trade, no outsider may prevent them from doing so.

Edgeworth asks what outcome can be expected, given that each person pursues his own interest in a rational way. Edgeworth's analysis of this problem is a pioneering work in what has come to be known as cooperative game theory. In the language of modern game theory, Edgeworth uses the concept of the **core** (📖) of a game. Consider any possible pattern of trade, T, and ask whether this could be the outcome of rational bargaining. First, suppose that there is at least one trader who is made worse off by T than if he had refused to trade at all. Then, if this person were to realize this, he would refuse to become involved in T. Therefore, T could not be the outcome of rational bargaining: the individual who would be made worse off would *block* it. Now suppose instead that there is a group of two or more traders who could all do better by refusing to go along with T, instead trading only among themselves. Then, again, if they were all to realize this, they should refuse to go along with T – they should block it. The core of a bargaining game contains all those outcomes that cannot be blocked by any individual or group. If the core of a game contains only one outcome, there is a presumption that this would be the outcome of rational play. Notice that it is alertness to the possibility of gain that provides the force that leads bargainers to core solutions. To say that an outcome is blocked is to say that it contains some unexploited opportunity for gain by some individual or group; the idea behind the concept of the core is that such opportunities will not remain unexploited.

Edgeworth conjectured that, with a sufficiently large number of traders, the core of the bargaining game would contain only the competitive equilibrium. This striking result has since been proved (Debreu and Scarf, 1963). The implication is that markets with large numbers of traders work as though organized by a Walrasian auctioneer. Although no-one need consciously think in terms of prices, the pattern of trade that results from rational bargaining can be described in terms of a single list of prices. It is *as if* each individual takes these prices as given and then chooses an optimal set of demands and supplies. In other words, the price system itself is an unintended consequence of individual action. But is it a good consequence?

The Welfare Properties of Competitive Equilibrium

It has already been said that although competitive equilibrium is efficient, its distributional consequences might be judged to be morally arbitrary. This depends on how one thinks about SOCIAL JUSTICE (18). It has also been said that the proof of the efficiency of competitive equilibrium depends on certain important assumptions. It is now time to 'come clean' about some of the most significant of these.

One of these assumptions is that every agent takes prices as given: no agent expects its own actions to have any perceptible effect on market prices. This is reasonable enough if there are many agents involved in buying and selling each good, each responsible for only a small proportion of total trade. If an agent can influence prices by its own actions (for example, if a firm can raise the price of the good it sells by withholding supply from the market) then Pareto-efficiency cannot be guaranteed. The corresponding implication for Edgeworth's model of the market is that if any agent is responsible for a significant proportion of total trade in a good, there will typically be many core solutions, each involving a different distribution of the gains from trade. Admittedly, each of these core solutions will be Pareto-efficient. (This is an implication of the definition of the core of a game: a Pareto-inefficient outcome can be blocked by a coalition containing all the players.) But it is far from obvious that even perfectly informed individuals will settle on *a* core solution when many such solutions exist: each may try to hold out for an outcome that favours himself, with the result that potential gains from trade are not realized.

A second assumption is that the production functions of firms do not have increasing returns to scale. (There are increasing returns to scale if, when all inputs are increased in the same proportion, output increases in more than that proportion.) If there are increasing returns to scale in the production of a particular good, then it may not be possible to have an equilibrium in which that good is supplied by firms which take the price as given and maximize profit. The problem is that if the price of the good is sufficient to induce any production at all, it may induce far more than households demand.

A third assumption is that there are no **public goods** (⬚) or **externalities** (⬚). It is crucial that each agent's decisions about production and consumption, buying and selling, have no effects on other agents – other than those effects that are transmitted through the price system. When public goods or externalities are involved, individually rational action can lead to unintended consequences that no-one wants: these are instances of the Prisoner's Dilemma (□ p. 99).

Further problems arise when we try to take account of *time*. Economic agents act on plans that involve the future as well as the present. Suppose that your car is becoming old. It is now 1991, and you plan to buy a new car in 1993. As part of this plan, you refrain from consumption in 1991 so as to build up a stock of savings. The amount you choose to save depends on your expectations about the price of cars in 1993. Meanwhile, car manufacturers are already making decisions that will influence the number of cars that are produced in 1993 (setting up their production lines, placing orders for steel, and so on). These decisions will depend on the manufacturers' expectations about the prices at which they will be able to sell cars in 1993. Is there any reason to suppose that we are all basing our plans on the same expectations about the 1993 price of cars? Even if we are, is there any reason to suppose that this is the price that will actually emerge when we all act on our plans? Perhaps the car manufacturers are underestimating the 1993 demand for cars. If so, then in 1993 there will be an excess demand for cars at the previously expected price, and so the price of cars will be higher than expected, and your 1991 decisions will be revealed as misguided. (Unable to afford the car that you planned to buy, you might realize that you ought to have saved more in 1991.)

When we prove that competitive equilibrium is Pareto-efficient, we assume that all agents know the equilibrium prices and base their plans on those prices. This assumption is built into the model of the auction: in an auction, no trade takes place until an equilibrium price has been established. In contrast, in the car-production example, trade in 1991 commodities takes place before the prices of 1993 commodities are known.

At the theoretical level, it is possible to generalize the Walrasian model to take account of time by introducing futures markets. Suppose that in 1991 there are markets not only in all present-dated commodities but also in all future-dated commodities (1993 cars, 1994 washing machines,

1998 chocolate bars, and so on). Then we can imagine a gigantic auction *in 1991* which would establish equilibrium prices for all commodities and for all future dates. Such an equilibrium would be Pareto-efficient. But the flight of fancy involved in assuming the existence of such an array of futures markets is too great to make this result of much practical interest.

The thought that all trading could take place at one point in time conflicts with the fundamental experience of human life that as time passes, people are born, grow to adulthood and die. Some of the agents who will be supplying labour and consuming goods in, say, 30 years' time are not yet alive; others are too young to take serious economic decisions. A satisfactory model of the workings of a market economy over time must allow for the existence of overlapping generations, and restrict trade at any time to those people who are currently alive and of a suitable age.

Such models have been constructed. They do not, as some critics of the market would suspect, imply that if present generations are selfish, no provision will be made for future ones. For example, suppose that the interval between planting a tree and harvesting it is 100 years. A person who plants trees today will not live to see them harvested, but he can plan to sell the growing trees to a younger person in, say, ten years' time. That person, in turn, can plan to sell to someone still younger in another ten years' time; and so on. If timber can be expected to command a market price in 100 years' time, then trees have a market value from the day they are planted. Even though the consumers of the timber have yet to be born, the market gives us an incentive to cater for what we predict their preferences to be.

However, this kind of relationship between generations has its costs. In a market economy, land and capital goods are privately owned. If people are self-interested, they will not wish to be holding wealth at their deaths, and so at any time those people who are relatively old will be selling their assets to those who are relatively young. This in turn means that the relatively young must be forgoing consumption in order to buy assets, while the relatively old are financing additional consumption from the sale of those assets. But if this pattern of trade and consumption is to occur in a market economy, the prices of assets must be sufficiently low to induce the young to buy them. Equivalently, the interest rate must be sufficiently high to induce the young to make the required volume of savings. Thus, even if there is no economic growth and even if people have no pure time preference (see **time preference and discounting** ($\boxed{?}$)), the rate of interest must be positive. It can be shown that the resulting distribution of consumption over the life cycle is sub-optimal: each generation would be better off if assets were passed down from generation to generation without payment. Such transfers can and do take place in market economies, through gifts and bequests; but they depend on non-selfish motivations.

Summing up, then, it is far from clear that the spontaneous order of the market always produces consequences that we should judge to be good. This opens up an agenda for debate about the proper role of government in economic affairs. If the market fails to generate the outcomes that we regard as optimal, we may be able to improve things by collective action. This is not to say that we always can improve things in this way. That depends on what outcomes we can expect to emerge from the political process. Political processes, just like markets, involve the interaction of many individuals, each with his or her own information, beliefs and preferences. Political interactions, like market ones, may produce unintended consequences -- not all of which we may like.

It should not be surprising that the outcomes of markets are not always desirable. These outcomes are unintended. Unless we believe that the world is the handiwork of some divine Designer -- unless we can believe in an invisible hand that is something more than a metaphor -- we have no reason to expect that the institutions that evolve will always conform with independently derived moral judgements. But at the same time, we must recognize that although the market is unplanned, it *is* ordered. It allocates resources in a way that makes use of knowledge that is dispersed among millions of separate individuals. No panel of specialists, however technically skilled and however powerful their computers, could possibly acquire or process this information. So we should not be too ready to believe that we can improve on the spontaneous order of the market by deliberate planning.

Robert Sugden

Further Reading

The idea that game theory can be used to model the evolution of social conventions is developed in Schotter (1981), Taylor (1987), Axelrod (1984) and Sugden (1986b) and, at a more philosophical level, in Lewis (1969). Maynard Smith (1982) provides an advanced survey of the use of evolutionary game theory in biology; Dawkins (1976) is a very accessible introduction to this area. The theory of general equilibrium and the fundamental theorems of welfare economics can be found in most advanced microeconomics textbooks; for example, Varian (1978). Boadway and Bruce (1984) and Sugden (1981) provide introductions to welfare economics.

Part III
Collective Choice

13

Social Choice

In a collective choice the decision of some is binding on all. If a family is deciding whether to go to the seaside or the country for their day out, then the choice is collective if all members of the family go to the chosen destination even when some members would have preferred the alternative. If a group of friends is deciding whether to eat Indian, Chinese or Italian, then the choice is collective if all go along with the selected alternative whatever their personal preferences. If a group of workers accept a pay settlement, then their choice is collective even when some would have preferred to go on strike. A collective choice, as distinct from the result of a series of individual choices, therefore has the characteristic that it holds for all members of a given group.

Politics is the realm of collective choice *par excellence*. When governments pass laws, enter into foreign treaties or adopt a policy, they do so in the name of all members of the political community. As Friedman (1962, p. 15) once expressed it, the characteristic feature of action through political channels is that it tends to require or enforce substantial uniformity. It is not impossible in political decisions to provide for exceptions or minority interests, for example by exempting conscientious objectors from the obligations of military service or by making special educational provision for religious minorities, but even in these cases the decision still bears the hallmark of a collective choice, since the definition of conscientious objection or the specification of special education is something that is decided by the authority of government. Unlike commercial transactions, where suppliers have an incentive to seek out the special characteristics of niche markets, governments will usually act in ways that impose common rights and obligations upon all citizens. Indeed, the defining idea of the modern state might be taken as common legislation for all citizens on equal terms.

Politics has this characteristic because the principal agent of modern politics, the state, claims to be sovereign. Austin captured the essence of sovereignty in his famous definition: 'if a determinate human superior, not in a habit of obedience to a like superior, receives habitual obedience from the bulk of a given society, that determinate superior is sovereign in that society, and the society (including the superior) is a society political and independent' (Austin, 1832, pp. 193–4). Replace Austin's 'determinate human superior' by the core institutions of the modern state, and you have the essence of contemporary claims to political authority. To accept the sovereign authority of the state is to accept limitations on the freedom of individual action and judgement. You may dislike or disagree with a law, but if it has been duly passed you cannot reserve the right to say that it is not a law, nor can you deny that it is in some significant sense the collective choice.

To accept a process of collective choice in politics is therefore to accept the overriding of one's judgment in determining public action. Why would a rational individual submit to collective choice in this sense? It is easy to see why in some social groups individuals go along with collective choices that are not their own but which they nonetheless accept as binding. Children go on days out with their parents because they normally lack the power to implement an alternative, and one of the characteristic signs that children have started to grow up is that they insist on individual choices that are different from the family's collective preferences. Similarly, friends or workers may decide that they are better off going along with the group for a variety of reasons – including a sense of social solidarity – rather than opting out, even if they believe that the group should have adopted another course of action. The decision to accept the collective choices of politics seems more fundamental, however, since it affects the basic conditions in which one leads one's own life. Rational individuals would presumably want to ask why there should be any sovereign collective choice processes at all in society and what conditions such processes should satisfy. These two questions, the *rationality* of collective choice in politics and its *reasonableness*, form the subject of this chapter.

The Origin of Collective Choice

Why is there such a thing as collective choice in society? The usual answer to this question is that, in the absence of the enforcement of collective choices by government, there would be anarchy. But what is wrong with anarchy? The usual answer to this question is that anarchy inevitably leads to unnecessary death, destruction of property and a loss of human welfare. Yet this familiar answer is too hasty (see ANARCHIC ORDER (12)). Examples of the breakdown of governmental authority, for example the civil war in Nigeria in the late 1960s or Lebanon in the 1980s, are certainly gruesome, but they do not provide an argument against anarchy, since they essentially spring from groups seeking to monopolize the coercive force of government. Rather than being instances of the problems of anarchy, then, they can be interpreted as an argument for the claim that no institution should possess the supreme authority of a sovereign state. Is it possible to go beyond conventional expressions of prejudice therefore, and analyse the conditions under which the establishment of a sovereign government might seem a rationally preferable alternative to anarchy?

Anarchy may be defined as a state of society in which no association in society plays the role of a sovereign. Contract theorists of the seventeenth century thought there might be such a state of society which they dubbed 'the state of nature'. In the most famous description of the state of nature, Thomas Hobbes described it as a condition in which human life was 'solitary, poor, nasty, brutish and short' (Hobbes, 1651, p. 82; □ p. 325). Hobbes rather cleverly shows that we do not have to suppose that the

THE CONTINUING THREAT OF WAR

It may seem strange to some man, that has not well weighed these things; that nature should thus dissociate, and render men apt to invade, and destroy one another: and he may therefore, not trusting to this inference, made from the passions, desire perhaps to have the same confirmed by experience. Let him therefore consider with himself, when taking a journey, he arms himself, and seeks to go well accompanied; when going to sleep, he locks his doors; when even in his house he locks his chests; and this when he knows there be laws, and public officers, armed, to revenge all injuries shall be done him; what opinion he has of his fellow-subjects, when he rides armed; of his fellow citizens, when he locks his doors; and of his children, and servants, when he locks his chests. Does he not there as much accuse mankind by his actions, as I do by my words? But neither of us accuse man's nature in it. The desires, and other passions of man, are in themselves no sin. No more are the actions, that proceed from those passions, till they know a law that forbids them: which till laws be made they cannot know: nor can any law be made, till they have agreed upon the person that shall make it.

(Hobbes, 1651, ch. 13)

state of nature is a distant historical fiction; even in existing civil societies, it is an ever constant threat (see □ p. 201). Given this characterization of life without government, it is not surprising that Hobbes, in the *Leviathan*, was prepared to contemplate an authoritarian imposition of sovereign authority upon society in order to achieve the benefits of social cooperation. Yet Hobbes was not content merely to state the need for sovereign authority, but wished to show how it followed from the logic of individual choice in the pre-political state of nature.

Hobbes supposes that the state of nature is a world stripped of morality. Human beings are conceived simply as matter in motion, and the fundamental law of their nature is self-preservation. In accordance with his materialist programme, Hobbes insists upon redefining the moral vocabulary that his society inherited from previous political philosophies, so that the concept of a right is defined in terms of the power of laying possession to things. Since there are no moral restrictions in the state of nature, Hobbes supposes that in this state everyone has a right to everything, including the use of one another's bodies. In short, in their constant struggle for survival, human beings are always seeking to appropriate from each other the means of survival, and there is no prior limit placed upon what these means might be, so that they may even extend to the bodies of others. Hobbes might appear to be arguing that might is right, and to be asserting that the stronger will always govern the weaker, but it is just at this stage that his argument takes a characteristic twist. He asserts it as an axiom of human nature that all human beings are equal in the (striking) sense that they all have the capacity to kill one another. For Hobbes, sovereignty cannot be understood simply as the superior assertion of power by one set of people over another, since no such arrangement could be stable in the face of the evident equality of power that humans possess in respect of one another.

The argument can be rephrased in the parlance of modern game theory, by saying that the state of nature for Hobbes is a Prisoner's Dilemma in which the equilibrium strategy for each player is defect (□ p. 99). Individuals who act cooperatively in the state of nature run the risk of being suckers, because others will be tempted to 'free ride' on their compliance. Yet, since everyone can see that free-riding is individually advantageous when others are complying, everyone has an incentive to free ride in this sense (see GAME THEORY (7), pp. 98–100).

Hobbes's solution to this dilemma is to suppose that a binding social contract will be necessary in order to induce social cooperation: '. . . covenants, without the sword, are but words, and of no strength to secure a man at all' (Hobbes, 1651, p. 109). By affixing penalties to non-compliance, the sovereign effectively changes the returns to non-compliant behaviour, making it less attractive than compliant behaviour. This fact changes the reasoning that individuals engage in concerning the social contract. The role of the sovereign is not simply to change the pay-off for each individual. The effective exercise of sovereign power is also intended to have the further effect of ensuring to all the contracting parties that others will abide by the terms of the contract. It becomes rational for everyone to comply with the terms of the social contract, because each person knows that everyone else is under threat of penalty from the sovereign. The role of sovereign power is therefore to supply some assurance to each individual that others will keep to their side of the bargain. Thus, the point of Hobbes's argument is not to portray the possibility of political authority as resting on force, but by revealing the 'logic of Leviathan' (Gauthier, 1966) to persuade individuals to understand how it is in their rational self-interest to accept an obligation to abide by the decisions of the sovereign.

The Force of Hobbes's Argument

Hobbes's account of political obligation, when understood in the light of modern game-theoretic concepts, is a sophisticated account of how rational individuals could come to form a political community. An analysis of the logic of Hobbes's argument therefore provides a good case study of the rational choice approach to the understanding of politics and social co-operation. If flaws and difficulties can be found in the Hobbesian approach, then they should be revealingly instructive about the analytical problems that rational choice theory faces.

In terms of modern game theory, the Hobbesian argument essentially turns on the claim that the problem of political obligation can only be solved by the creation of a cooperative political game, instead of the non-cooperative game played in the state of nature. Luce and Raiffa express, with customary succinctness, the definition of a cooperative game: 'By a *cooperative game* is meant a game in which the players have complete freedom of preplay communication to make joint *binding* agreements' (Luce and Raiffa, 1957, p. 89). Note that there are two elements in Luce and Raiffa's account of a cooperative game: preplay communication and binding agreements. Both of these elements are essential to a Hobbesian account of the social contract. Negotiation over the social contract constitutes the preplay communication, and agreement to establish an absolute sovereign creates the conditions for binding agreement under which players will be assured that the terms of the contract will be kept. When the Prisoner's Dilemma is played non-cooperatively in the state of nature, mutual defect is the equilibrium outcome. When it is played by means of a cooperative agreement to establish a sovereign who will punish defection, the equilibrium outcome is mutual compliance. At least, this is the Hobbesian claim.

How far is it true, however, that the state of nature Prisoner's Dilemma game can only be solved by transforming the game into one of a cooperative nature? One approach has been to question Hobbes's line of reasoning by noting that the Hobbesian contract may not solve the problems inherent in the state of nature but merely displace them on to another level. The Hobbesian contract solves the dilemma of the state of nature between individuals and social groups by creating a state with sovereign power. This has the effect of ending the state of nature in the relationship between individuals by recreating the same relationship between nation states in the system of international relations (Taylor, 1976, p. 131). It is a commonplace of international relations to point out that nation states are located in a state of nature with respect to one another. Moreover, the organization of the modern state is such that it typically amasses great destructive power in the form of nuclear, chemical and conventional weapons. Perhaps, it may be argued, the Hobbesian approach does not solve the problem of the war of all against all, but merely displaces it on to this higher level where its potentially destructive threats are even greater.

Such problem displacement might be tolerable if it were the only way of avoiding the destructive effects of anarchy at the level of individuals, but here the anti-Hobbesian offers a riposte. The state of nature might not be so nasty, brutish and short once we see the logic of voluntary cooperation in a *repeated* Prisoner's Dilemma. The claim here is both negative and positive. The negative part of the claim is to assert that Hobbesians are mistaken in modelling social interaction as a one-off Prisoner's Dilemma. Social interaction is better modelled as an iterated Prisoner's Dilemma in which the players undertake repeated plays. The positive part of the claim is that in an iterated Prisoner's Dilemma mutual cooperation is the equilibrium strategy provided that certain conditions are met (see GAME THEORY (7), pp. 115–16 and GAME THEORY APPLIED (9), pp. 146–48). Transposing this claim to the Hobbesian state of nature, the argument is that, contrary to Hobbes's own assumptions, individuals could learn to cooperate to their mutual advantage without the intervention of the state. Anarchy is a viable possibility. The problem of mutually destructive competition in the state of nature can be solved by cooperation to mutual advantage within the game, and does not need preplay communication leading to a binding agreement before the game.

Does the possibility of providing a model under which anarchic cooperation is rational in the state of nature undermine the Hobbesian argument for a sovereign, and hence show that collective choice is unnecessary for societies considered as independent entities? It would be altogether too hasty to draw such an inference. In the first place, the abstract possibility of cooperation does not show how mechanisms can be established by which cooperative strategies would emerge. The most likely candidate for such a mechanism would be some sort of evolution by which cooperative strategies were favoured in the process of selection, while non-cooperative strategies were rejected or filtered out. Axelrod's (1984) experiments in which computer programs encoding different strategies for playing a Prisoner's Dilemma game were pitted against one another in a round robin tournament, and in which 'tit-for-tat' came out as the all-round winner, provide some insight into the processes by which the appropriate long-sightedness might evolve within a population. Yet, evolutionary processes work by differential rates of reproduction of the favoured and non-favoured character traits, and conscious beings are unlikely to wait around long enough to see whether their preferred trait is favoured by selection; they are much more likely to want to push the pace along by imposing some norms of behaviour by conscious choice of conventions. Second, societies that were experimenting with the evolutionary emergence of norms would be vulnerable to the superior organized force of societies in which a sovereign was already established. In other words, the superior military force of a society in which authority had been given to a sovereign would make anarchic societies vulnerable to attack, and therefore provide them with a motive to establish their own sovereign. So, although the anarchist riposte qualifies the Hobbesian argument, it fails to show that it is entirely redundant. Self-interest in avoiding the anarchy of the state of nature provides a motive for the establishment of a sovereign authority within a society so as to establish processes of collective choice among individuals. However, the way in which those processes are to be constructed and constrained is something that requires further examination.

The Problem of Preference Aggregation

Suppose that a sovereign authority has been established. The anarchist argument has shown that the state of nature is not such a miserable place that individuals would be willing to hand over unrestrained control of their lives to the sovereign authority. They will want to ensure somehow that their views are taken into account when the sovereign formulates policy. In other words, having been persuaded by the rationality of collective choice, individuals would still want to ensure its reasonableness. Let us suppose that the sovereign is benign and genuinely wishes to reflect the preferences of the citizens in the making of policy. It might seem that if the sovereign were benign there should be no difficulty over this. All the sovereign has to do is to consult the preferences of the people when a significant choice for the society arises. Unfortunately, as we shall now see, this is not such a straightforward task, for as soon as there is a certain level of disagreement among the people about the course of action to be followed, it becomes impossible for the sovereign to design constitutional arrangements for consulting the people that satisfy certain apparently reasonable conditions.

In order to understand how the difficulty can arise, let us consider a simple two-way choice. Suppose that a society is confronted with a choice between two policies, x and y, and that these are the only policies involved. These policies are mutually exclusive in the sense that if policy x is implemented, then it will not be possible to implement policy y, and vice versa. The sovereign wishes to exercise authority in a way that reflects popular preference, but finds that there is disagreement in the population, with some voters preferring x to y and some preferring y to x, while others are indifferent between them. Given this difference of opinion, how should the sovereign decide?

One approach that might seem attractive is to ascertain the number who prefer x to y as distinct from the number who prefer y to x, and leave out of account those who are indifferent on the grounds that they do not mind whether x or y is chosen. The sovereign then might contemplate adopting the following collective choice rule:

$$N(x > y) \text{ is greater than } N(y > x) \quad \rightarrow \quad x > y \tag{1}$$

where $x > y$ means that x is collectively or socially preferred to y and $N(x > y)$ means the 'number who prefer x to y', and so on.

If it turns out that the numbers are balanced on each side, then the sovereign can adopt the rule:

$$N(x > y) \text{ equals } N(y > x) \quad \rightarrow \quad x = y \tag{2}$$

where $x = y$ means that, from the social point of view, the two alternatives are of equal value. Were the sovereign to adopt these rules, then the social choices would be made by the method of majority decision (MMD). Someone who is attracted to the MMD can point out that it satisfies a number of interesting conditions. First, it is *anonymous* in the sense that it is only the numbers, and not the names, of individuals that determine the social preference relation. Second, it is *issue neutral* in the sense that no alternative is favoured by virtue of its intrinsic properties, but only in virtue of the numbers who favour it. Third, it is *positively responsive* to changes in individual preference, in the sense that if one individual's preference shifts in favour of an alternative then the social choice should shift in favour of that alternative (see □, pp. 208–9, for an illustration of these conditions).

Why should someone think that these conditions make the MMD more appealing? One reason is that they seem to encapsulate a form of political equality. No-one's preferences are favoured because of who they are, and no issue is favoured because the sovereign process deems it to be intrinsically significant. Moreover, the decision-making process will shift in the direction of an individual's change of mind irrespective of who that individual is. It can also be shown that the MMD is the *only* collective choice rule that satisfies all of these conditions when individuals are allowed to order their preferences over alternatives in any way that they please (May, 1952).

We seem to have solved the problem of the benign sovereign without any difficulty. All the sovereign has to do is consult the majority preference. Not only will a preference be expressed, but the process will also incorporate a form of procedural political equality. Unfortunately, this illusion of there being a solution can be easily shattered once we allow that the society may be confronted by more than two alternatives. In that circumstance we can find the following preference profile in the case where there are just three individuals to consult:

$$x >_1 y >_1 z$$
$$z >_2 x >_2 y$$
$$y >_3 z >_3 x$$

where $x >_1 y$ means that individual 1 prefers x to y, and likewise for other individuals and alternatives.

If we apply the MMD to this profile we generate an inconsistency at the social level. In the choice between x and y the majority prefers x; in the choice between y and z, the majority prefers y; and in the choice between x and z, the majority prefers z. If we write out the social preference that results from the application of the MMD to these pairwise comparison, we find it looks like this: $x > y > z > x$. (A simple analogy is the children's game in which paper wraps rock, rock blunts scissors and scissors cut paper.) The sovereign will simply be drawn round in a circle. This is Condorcet's Paradox (see **Condorcet winner** (📖)), and it shows how the application of the principle of majority rule to well-formed individual preferences can lead to inconsistency at the collective level.

Can we stop our sovereign going around in circles? One train of thought might run as follows. The MMD will not preserve transitivity at the collective level. Since the MMD is the only rule that satisfies the conditions of anonymity, neutrality and positive responsiveness, it follows that no rule can satisfy these three conditions and transitivity while being responsive to the full range of preferences that individuals might exhibit. If we wish to preserve responsiveness to the full range of preferences that individuals might exhibit and prevent the sovereign from going round in circles, it follows that we must require something less stringent than these conditions imply.

ILLUSTRATION OF ANONYMITY, NEUTRALITY AND POSITIVE RESPONSIVENESS

Consider a society of five individuals. The preferences of the first individual are written $x >_1 y$, for the second $x >_2 y$ and so on. The social preference relation is written $x > y$, $y > x$ or $x = y$ depending on the results of applying the collective choice rule. We can then illustrate the three conditions as follows.

Anonymity. Suppose in a statement of individual preferences that we shuffle the individuals, but keep the preference relations identical; then the collective choice rule should not change. Suppose, therefore, that:

$$\begin{bmatrix} x >_1 y \\ x >_2 y \\ x >_3 y \\ y >_4 x \\ y >_5 x \end{bmatrix} \quad \text{implies } x > y$$

Anonymity will require that:

$$\begin{bmatrix} x >_1 y \\ x >_2 y \\ y >_3 x \\ y >_4 x \\ x >_5 y \end{bmatrix} \quad \text{still implies } x > y$$

In other words, we have altered the names of the individuals holding the preference, but nothing else, and so the social choice should remain the same.

Neutrality. Suppose that in two preference profiles that there two pairs of alternatives that are ranked in the same way by individuals. Neutrality requires that the social choice process rank them equivalently. Suppose, therefore, that:

$$\begin{bmatrix} x >_1 y \\ x >_2 y \\ x >_3 y \\ y >_4 x \\ y >_5 x \end{bmatrix} \quad \text{implies } x > y$$

Neutrality will require that:

$$\begin{bmatrix} w >_1 z \\ w >_2 z \\ w >_3 z \\ z >_4 w \\ z >_5 w \end{bmatrix} \quad \text{implies } w > z$$

In other words, if we change the labelling of the alternatives, if should not make any difference to the ranking process. Note that the condition of the independence of irrelevant alternatives is simply a special case of neutrality, in which identical labelling should mean that rank ordering is identical.

Positive responsiveness. Suppose that an alternative rises in one individual's ranking without falling in anyone else's ranking; then positive responsiveness will require that it rise in the social ranking. Suppose, therefore, that:

$$\begin{bmatrix} x >_1 y \\ x >_2 y \\ x >_3 y \\ y >_4 x \\ y >_5 x \end{bmatrix} \quad \text{implies } x > y$$

Positive responsiveness will require that:

$$\begin{bmatrix} x >_1 y \\ x >_2 y \\ y >_3 x \\ y >_4 x \\ y >_5 x \end{bmatrix} \quad \text{implies } y > x$$

In other words, because y has risen in one person's ranking and not fallen in anyone else's ranking, it should rise in the social ranking.

One such milder set of requirements has been suggested by Arrow (1963a) (see □ p. 210). Arrow posed the following question: Given collective rationality and universal domain, is there a collective choice rule, other than the MMD, that satisfies the conditions of the Pareto principle, non-dictatorship and the independence of irrelevant alternatives? We already know, from its violating the condition of collective rationality, that the MMD does not satisfy all the conditions simultaneously. The devastating conclusion of his General Impossibility Theorem is that there is no collective choice rule that simultaneously satisfies these conditions (see **Arrow's Theorem** (🕮)).

The problem that Arrow identified is both deep and pervasive. In order to understand its significance, consider just two individuals, Jack and Jill, who have the following preferences:

$$\text{Jack:} \quad x >_{\text{Jack}} y \quad \& \quad y >_{\text{Jack}} z$$
$$\text{Jill :} \quad y >_{\text{Jill}} x \quad \& \quad y >_{\text{Jill}} z$$

Jack prefers x to y and he also prefers y to z. Jill prefers y to x and, like Jack, she also prefers y to z. Given this information, the question arises as to whether it is possible to construct an ordering that will represent a collective choice for both Jack and Jill. It turns out that we cannot construct

ARROW'S 'REASONABLE' CONDITIONS OF COLLECTIVE CHOICE

1 *Collective rationality.* The collective choice should be represented by an ordering of all alternatives. An ordering is complete: every pair of alternatives can be ranked against each other, even if the ranking is one of indifference. The ordering should also be transitive, so that for any alternative, x, y and z, if x is preferred or indifferent to y and y is preferred or indifferent to z, then x is preferred or indifferent to z.

2 *Universal domain.* The function mapping a statement of individual preference into a statement of collective choice should be capable of taking as its domain of operation all logically possible orderings by individuals.

3 *Pareto inclusiveness.* This is a weakened version of positive responsiveness. Positive responsiveness says that if one individual comes to favour an alternative more highly, then that alternative should rise in the social ordering. Pareto inclusiveness says that if all individuals prefer x over y, then society would prefer x over y.

4 *Independence of irrelevant alternatives.* This is implied by neutrality. Independence makes the social choice depend on how alternatives rank in individual preference orderings by restricting the social preference between two alternatives to information solely on how individuals rank these alternatives.

5 *Non-dictatorship.* This is a weakened version of anonymity. Anonymity says that a named individual should not be able to determine a social choice in any circumstance. Non-dictatorship says that no named individual should be able to determine the social choice in all circumstances in the sense that the social ordering coincides with the ordering of that individual whatever others may think.

such an ordering without making that ordering coincide in all respects with the preference ordering of just one of the individuals. When the collective ordering coincides with an individual ordering in exactly this way, Arrow's condition of non-dictatorship is no longer satisfied. To see why not, we have to look in some detail at the possible ways of constructing a social ordering from Jack and Jill's individual preferences.

If we say that social choice procedures should respect the Pareto principle, then we shall want the social ordering to include a preference for y over z, since both Jack and Jill prefer y to z. We might now try the following argument. Since Jack and Jill differ over the relative merits of x and y, they cannot both get their way. The social ordering cannot reflect both persons' preferences. Suppose that the social ordering were to reflect the preference of one of them. For that particular pair of alternatives the

person concerned would be decisive over that pair. Let Jack be decisive
for x over y, and let Jill be decisive for the pair x and z. Can we find a
social ordering that somehow will respect the differences of preference
that Jack and Jill have? The answer is 'no' if we want to respect both the
Pareto principle and the principle of transitivity; for if Jack is allowed to
decide x versus y, then with the aid of the transitivity principle he will
also ensure that his preferences for x over z will be decisive, even though
we have already stipulated that Jill's preferences should be decisive over
this pair. Having made Jack decisive over one pair of the alternatives, we
find that the final social ordering coincides with his preferences entirely.
In Arrow's language, Jack has become a social choice 'dictator', a dictator
in the sense that we should have only to consult his preference ordering
to find out what the social ordering should be. We seem to have found an
inconsistency in the assignment of decisiveness to the two individuals.

Can we avoid the inconsistency by starting at some other point and making
Jill decisive? Suppose that we say that Jill's preference in relation to x and
z should be decisive whatever else happens. Suppose that Jill prefers x to z;
then Jack is still determining the social ordering in the sense that it coincides
completely with his preferences. Suppose that Jill prefers z to x; then we seem
to be involved in a contradiction, for if z is preferred to x by Jill's decisiveness, and y is preferred to z by Pareto, then transitivity will mean that y is
preferred to x. In other words, the price for preventing Jack from being the
social choice dictator is that we have made Jill the social choice dictator.

To avoid this outcome, we might say that the social ordering should
be indifferent whenever there is a conflict of preference of the Jack and
Jill type. So, in the above case, we say that the social ordering is one of
indifference between x and y, because Jack and Jill have opposing preferences. But this suggestion, when conjoined with the Pareto and transitivity
requirements, also leads to a contradiction: if x and y are declared socially
indifferent and y is preferred to z by the Pareto principle, then x will be
preferred to z by the principle of transitivity. But this means that if Jill
prefers z to x (which she may well do), we are treating the choice between
x and y on the one hand and x and z on the other in some different way.
When we are confronted with a situation in which Jack prefers x to y
and Jill prefers y to x, we declare the alternatives to be socially indifferent,
but when we are confronted with a situation in which Jack prefers x to z
and Jill prefers z to x, we declare Jack's preferences to be decisive. There
is no obvious reason why we should treat these two similar situations
differently. The fact that we appear to run into difficulty in this simple
case of preference divergence suggests a problem. There appears to be a
contradiction lurking in our conditions for a suitable social choice procedure: we can seek to respect the diversity of preferences that individuals
exhibit, in which case we lose the coherence that the social choice process

produces from a social ordering, or we can have coherence in the social choice process at the collective level, but only at the cost of making one person a dictator.

The great achievement of Arrow's General Impossibility Theorem was to show that this sort of problem is endemic to all processes of social choice that satisfy his apparently reasonable conditions (for a sketch of the proof, see **Arrow's Theorem** (🕮)). If we allow individuals to have any preference orderings over the available alternatives, if we seek to respect the Pareto principle and we want to find a social ordering, then we are likely to be faced with a difficulty. Conflicts of preference mean that some subset of individuals will have to be decisive for some pairs of alternatives; and if social choice over any pair of alternatives is determined simply by individual preferences over those alternatives, then a contradiction will soon emerge.

Implications

There is, in the words of Riker (1982, p. 129), a 'theoretical invulnerability' about Arrow's theorem. What this means is that if you accept the way the problem is posed and you accept the definitions and premises that Arrow proposes, then you are logically committed to the conclusion that there is no collective choice procedure that simultaneously satisfies collective rationality, universal domain, the Pareto principle, the independence of irrelevant alternatives and non-dictatorship (or what may be called the *cupid* conditions, for ease of reference). This does *not* mean that no existing collective choice procedures operate satisfactorily. As long as individual preference profiles are restricted in various ways, the way in which public choice systems aggregate preferences may lead to no problems. For example, if Schattschneider (1960) is right, and there is a natural process by which all political choices eventually resolve themselves into a contest between two alternatives, then the standard procedures of majoritarian democracy will be adequate to the task of choosing coherently between the alternatives while giving equal weight to all voters' preferences. We can even have more than two alternatives provided that the condition of universal domain is restricted by making voter preferences single-peaked over alternatives (see DEMOCRACY (14)). The problem is, as these examples illustrate, that the satisfactory operation of collective choice institutions cannot be guaranteed to avoid a breach of one of the Arrow conditions.

From one point of view it should not be surprising that there is an inconsistency in the Arrow conditions, since some of them are attempting to secure representativeness in the process of collective choice by ensuring that there are no dictators, that the Pareto principle is respected and that any combination of preferences is allowed, and others are seeking to ensure that there is some coherence to the collective choice process by requiring collective rationality and consistency in the aggregation of preference profiles. These twin requirements of coherence and representativeness come into conflict. Coherence requires decision-makers to know their own minds all things considered, but representativeness pushes towards the inclusion of considerations that may make knowing one's own mind impossible. From this intuitive point of view, the invulnerability of Arrow's theorem should not, on reflection, seem so surprising.

However, it can be argued that the Arrow result displays a theoretical invulnerability in a stronger sense (also defended by Riker), in which the reasonableness of the conditions is difficult to question. Consider the requirement of collective rationality, which a number of people have questioned on the grounds that there is no reason to suppose that society has a mind analogous to that of individuals, and that transitivity is a property of ordering minds, not of impersonal social processes. The lack of an analogy between the mind and society is well taken, but it is questionable whether this shows that a requirement such as collective rationality can be dispensed with. The process of collective choice is about obtaining some sort of result. In order to obtain a result, a logical structure needs to be imposed on the set of feasible options; otherwise there is no point in seeking to derive collective choices from individual preferences. That logical structure will have to resemble something like an ordering if the available feasible set is to be reduced in any way to produce a choice set (see **path independence** (🔍)). Moreover, weaker requirements than transitivity also produce problems, revealing that the conflict between coherence and representativeness is deeply embedded in the structure of collective choice. Thus if transitivity is weakened to quasi-transitivity, requiring only transitivity of strict preference but not of indifference then, although we lose the Arrowian dictator, we gain an 'oligarchy'. An oligarchy is a subset of choosers who, if all the members agree, can impose a choice or, if they do not agree, each member of the subset individually can veto a choice (Kelly, 1978). The moral is that to secure some sort of choice the coherence must come from somewhere, and it will come for a subset of individuals if preferences are sufficiently diverse.

The other condition that has been subject to attack as being unreasonable is the independence of irrelevant alternatives. As we have seen, the effect of this condition is to restrict the collective choice function from operating on anything other than ordinally defined pairwise alternatives. If only ordinal rankings are thought to make sense in the context of social choice, because there cannot be interpersonal comparisons of utility, then it is difficult to deny Arrow the independence condition. The condition of the independence of irrelevant alternatives has the effect of making social choice depend solely on information regarding individuals' preferences over pairs of alternatives. Information on strength of preference is thereby excluded, including the sort of cardinalization provided by a von Neumann–Morgenstern utility function (see RATIONALITY (1)). For some this restriction on the type of information seems unduly strict. Yet it is worth remembering that the independence of irrelevant alternatives is a *weaker* version of neutrality, which is one of the conditions that characterize majority rule (Sen, 1970, p. 72). The implication is clear. If the only problem with using majority rule in some circumstances is that the condition of collective rationality is violated, then there can be no objection to the relevance of the condition of the independence of irrelevant alternatives.

If we grant Arrow the most contentious of his conditions, are we forced to conclude that the theorem is theoretically invulnerable, and that Arrow has shown that it is meaningless or arbitrary to impose collective choice procedures in any circumstances where a society is faced by more than the most straightforward of binary choices? This has certainly been the response of some, of whom Riker (1982) is the most eloquent. Riker argues that Arrow's theorem, and the host of related results that it has attracted, show that the notion of a popular will is meaningless, and therefore that the democratic aspiration to make government policy conform to the will of the people can never be realized. We should give up the aspiration to direct the sovereign and concentrate instead on trying to chain the Leviathan of government. Limited government, in which the state refrains from taking positive measures, is the most appropriate response to the dilemma that Arrow has posed.

However, there are two reasons at least for not moving to such a conclusion too quickly. The first of these is to acknowledge the full implications of the Arrow result and to note that no institutional devices satisfy the Arrow conditions, including markets, which are the usual alternative to politics as a form of social coordination. This can easily be shown by considering a two-person two-commodity world. Let there be two individuals, Jack and Jill, and let there be two possible joint commodity allocations for the pair, labelled x and y. Suppose that the commodity allocation is such that Jack prefers x to y and Jill prefers y to x (as will happen if the commodity allocation is zero-sum). It is possible that both x and y are in the **core** (⬚) of the economy, and the alternative chosen by the market will depend upon the initial endowment of each person. Hence the market can take two situations, both with identical preference profiles, in the one case selecting x over y and in the other y over x, in violation of the independence condition. If we wish to restrict the scope of political control because governmental institutions violate the Arrow conditions, we shall find, given the generality of the Arrow result, that alternative institutions also violate the Arrow conditions.

The second reason for not drawing too rapid a practical political conclusion from the Arrow result is that one can question the adequacy of the model of preferences that is built into the approach when we are considering matters of political choice. In the Arrow model judgements about the relative merits of alternative social states are represented in the same way in which tastes are represented in the choice of commodities by consumers. But, whereas with many commodities it makes sense to hold to the principle of *de gustibus non est disputandum*, the same hardly holds true of political judgements. In any political argument that rises above the level of the saloon bar, people offer reasons for favouring their preferred alternatives. These reasons may be more or less cogent or more or less persuasive, but the logic of advancing a political preference must be understood in the light of these underlying reasons, and not simply as claims to have one's preferences satisfied whatever they happen to be (see Thompson (1988), who shows that this is a pervasive feature of political life). In adopting an ordinalist approach to preferences, the Arrowian approach thereby takes over the behaviouralism that provided its motivation and logic. If we question the behaviouralist approach to politics by requiring that due account be given of the reasons that underlie the formation of political preferences, we are in effect saying that not all of the Arrow conditions are reasonable in the construction of a political constitution.

An alternative model of collective choice would be most likely to present it not as a process of preference aggregation, in which there is a mapping from a set of individual orderings to a social ordering, but as a process of dialogue in which reasons are exchanged between participants in a process that is perceived to be a joint search for a consensus (compare Habermas, 1979, p. 186). Such a dialogic concept of collective choice would necessarily work not with fixed preferences to be amalgamated, but with preferences that were altered or modified as competing reasons were advanced in the course of discussion (compare the discussion of expressive rationality in RATIONALITY (1)). Such a process of dialogic exchange would not necessarily preclude the occurrence of paradoxes of collective choice, since differences of judgement might remain after debate and dialogue, leaving voting as the only practicable way of overcoming disagreement. Yet, in this context, the paradoxes would be seen not as the proof that the popular will was a meaningless concept, but as revealing the as yet unresolved imperfections of a process of discussion that characterized an adequate concept of collective choice.

Albert Weale

Further Reading

A good introductory level text to the topics covered in this chapter is provided by McLean (1987). The social choice logic of Hobbes's political thought is clearly laid out in Gauthier (1966) and is treated with great mathematical sophistication in Taylor (1976). There are many works on the philosophy of political obligation, but a good introduction is provided by Horton (1992).

Arrow (1963a) provides the original discussion of the General Impossibility theorem, while Sen (1970) sets the theorem in context and still provides the best introduction to the formal elements of the theory. Kelly (1978) offers a useful summary of results that extend and deepen Arrow's original theorem. Riker (1982) offers a clear interpretation of the application of Arrow's theorem to political institutions.

14

Democracy

One difference between a democratic government and an authoritarian government is that in a democracy the government is supposed to be responsive to popular preferences in the choices that it makes about public policy. Democracy is something more than government in the interests of the people; it also involves government according to the wishes of the people. Benign authoritarian forms of government may well succeed in acting in the interests of the people, but they lack mechanisms to ensure that they act in accordance with the wishes of the people. (Frederick the Great of Prussia was once alleged to have said, 'Of course, there is freedom of speech; the people say what they like – and I do what I like.') To be *democratic*, as distinct from being merely *benign*, a system of government ought to be responsive to popular preferences.

Liberal Democracy and Political Markets

Since people typically hold a variety of views about the direction that public policy should take, one of the functions of democratic institutions is to aggregate the diverse preferences of citizens into a public choice among the available policy alternatives. It is not difficult to show that the processes by which this aggregation is accomplished are important in themselves: that is, for a constant set of preferences, different rules of aggregation will produce different results. For example, in 1978 opponents of Scottish devolution managed to insert a clause in the Parliamentary bill that established a referendum on the question, under which 40 per cent of the registered electorate had to agree to the devolution proposals before they could be implemented. In the event there was a majority of those voting in favour of the proposals, but the numbers supporting devolution did not match the required proportion of the electorate, and so the devolution proposals were lost. With the same voting majority, had the 40 per cent rule not applied, the proposals would have gone through, and Scotland would have had its own devolved assembly. Voting rules provide one aspect of the institutional processes for amalgamating individual preferences into a public choice, but there are many others. For example, it can be argued that one of the reasons why environmental issues played such a large part in German politics in the 1980s, but only a relatively minor part in British politics in the same period, is due not to any difference of cultural perception between the two countries over the importance of the environment but to the German system of proportional representation, which put the German Greens in a near pivotal position in forming provincial and national governments.

Within the rational choice tradition of political analysis, considerable effort has been devoted to formalizing the conditions under which liberal democratic institutions can perform their essential task of representing popular preferences. The strategy of analysis has been twofold. The first stage has been to analyse the conditions under which governments will reflect majority popular preferences. The second stage has been to ask what happens if these conditions are relaxed. It turns out, as we shall see, that the conditions that will secure responsiveness are rather stringent, so that only a mild loosening of the conditions is required to destroy the capacity of political institutions to respond to majority preference.

The basic elements of liberal democratic politics are that parties compete with one another for the right to govern the country, and that the party or coalition that secures a winning share of the popular vote earns the right to govern until the next election. Elections are therefore the critical device for transmitting popular preferences into party, and ultimately governmental, programmes. This suggests that in order to provide a model of how liberal democracy might work to aggregate preferences, we should look at a simplified representation of electoral processes. The guiding principle of the rational choice approach goes back to a remark of Schumpeter: 'Politically speaking, the man is still in the nursery who has not absorbed, so as never to forget, the saying attributed to one of the most successful politicians that ever lived: "What businessmen do not understand is that exactly as they are dealing in oil so I am dealing in votes"' (Schumpeter, 1943, p. 285). The analogy here is between an economic marketplace and a political marketplace. Under certain conditions within an economic market, the individual pursuit of self-interest by consumers and producers leads to an equilibrium with optimal properties (see ANARCHIC ORDER (12)). If there is a political marketplace, we can ask under what conditions the pursuit of their own ends by voters and political parties leads to a political equilibrium. The initial identification of the conditions under which this equilibrium is achieved was due to Downs (1957), and it is primarily a portion of his work that we shall be summarizing in the next section.

Conditions of Competitive Equilibrium

Within an economic market we assume that entrepreneurs maximize profits. Analogously, the Downsian approach is to treat political parties as unitary agents and to assume that their primary motivation is to win office. This assumption has the effect of sharply reducing the extent to which parties are motivated by ideological assumptions. As Downs puts it: 'parties formulate policies to win elections, rather then win elections in order to formulate policies,' (Downs, 1957, p. 28). Office-seeking political parties engage in competitive agenda-setting. They will identify themselves with policies if they find this an effective way of seeking office.

Voters are also to be thought of as rational. This means that they can order all alternatives according to their own scale of values. In voting they choose the party whose proclaimed policy position is closest to their own. How these different policy positions are identified is of crucial importance. As a first approximation, the Downsian assumption is that policy positions can be laid out one-dimensionally, along a left–right spectrum. Voter preferences are assumed to be single-peaked in this one-dimensional spectrum. Thus, if we represent the left–right spectrum on a horizontal axis, and the level of preference on a vertical axis, no-one's preferences have more than one top-point or peak. The difference between single-peaked and non-single-peaked preferences is illustrated in figure 14.1. Single-peaked preferences exhibit what one might think of as a typical or normal form. If you are left-wing in your political views, you prefer the centre to the far right, whereas if you are centrist your distaste for extremes shows itself in declining preferences for both left- and right-wing alternatives. Non-single-peaked preferences are those we might associate with certain versions of extremism. You may prefer the left to the right, or vice versa, but you may like centrism least – either full-blooded socialism or full-blooded capitalism, and worst of all a mixed economy.

What form will a political equilibrium take in this Downsian world? The *median voter theorem* (see Austen-Smith, 1983, for a clear exposition) states: *provided there is no abstention by voters, voters are rational and have single-peaked preferences in a one-dimensional issue space, the*

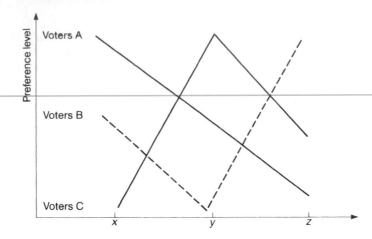

Figure 14.1 Single- and non-single-peaked preferences for groups of voters. Preference orderings over *x*, *y* and *z* are as follows:

Voters A: *x   y   z*

Voters B: *z   x   y*

Voters C: *y   z   x*

Voters B have non-single-peaked preferences. With this non-single-peaked profile, there is no *Condorcet winner*.

winning party in a two-party contest will take up a policy position that coincides with that of the median voter.

The concept being used here of the median voter can best be understood by means of an example. Suppose that the left–right spectrum is defined in terms of a commitment to government intervention in the economy, so that the further right a policy position is on the spectrum the less public expenditure is involved, and the further left a policy position is on the spectrum the more public expenditure is involved. Hence the proportion of the economy that is taken in public expenditure provides an underlying metric within ideological space. Voters will be located on this spectrum in terms of their most preferred level of intervention. Suppose that there are 99 voters, each with views about the most desirable level of public expenditure, and suppose that we identify each of these voters in terms of their ideological position. We now count 50 voters from the left in terms of their position in ideological space and 50 voters from the right. Our count will lead to the same person: namely, that individual who is in the middle of the ideological spectrum, or the median voter.

It is important to note that the median voter is not necessarily located at the point midway between zero public expenditure and 100 per cent public expenditure. If opinion in the electorate is skewed generally to the right, then the median voter prefers less than 50 per cent expenditure; and if it is skewed to the left the median voter prefers more than 50 per cent. The median voter is identified by reference to the relation between his or her preferences and the preferences of all other voters, not by reference to the underlying terms in which the ideological space is defined. The median voter is that voter we identify when we have counted half the voters, starting from the left or from the right. It is that voter who fixes the policy position of political parties when they are competing with one another. To see why, consider what would happen if this were not true. A party to the left of the median voter would take all the votes to its left and all the votes to its right up to a point midway between the party and the median voter. By occupying a median position the other party could easily win. Indeed, no matter how closely the left-wing party approached the median position without actually occupying it, the right-wing party could win simply by standing firmly on the median. By parity of reasoning, the same logic applies if the left-wing party is at the median point, and the right-wing party beyond it. Hence the median point is one that is uniquely proof against any alternative strategy and is therefore the sole equilibrium. Note that this is so regardless of how popular preferences are distributed along the left–right spectrum. The median voter result does not assume that voters are clustered in the middle of the political spectrum. It assumes only that each and every voter casts a rational vote. The pull towards the median voter is illustrated in figure 14.2.

The median voter point is a **Condorcet winner** (⧉), in that it can beat any other alternative taken in a pairwise competition. Although the alternative that constitutes the Condorcet winner may be the ideal point for only a few of the voters, there is a sense in which it is a natural point of convergence for a majority when they consider that alternative against any other. For this reason it may be said to provide a meaningful account of the notion of the 'popular will'.

Clearly, the Downsian world is a highly simplified one, but under certain circumstances it does appear to capture much that is of interest in politics at certain times. Thus, it appears to provide a good account of US and UK politics in the 1950s, when Eisenhower's blandness ruled in the White House and 'Butskellism' was prevalent in the UK. Similarly, it can provide a good explanation of why the Labour party began to modify its policy stance in the late 1980s, as part of its first serious attempt to regain office after 1979. Perhaps more importantly, the model might help show how political responsiveness of the government to the preferences of the people could occur through a set of political institutions. The Downsian model provides a world in which the political equivalent of Adam Smith's invisible

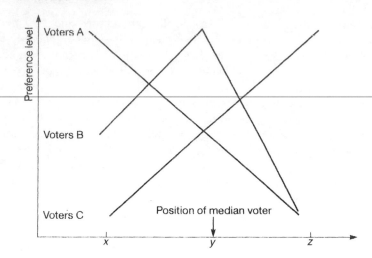

Figure 14.2 The median point as a majority equilibrium. Preference orderings over x, y and z are as follows:

Voters A: x y z

Voters B: y x z

Voters C: z y x

With this single-peaked profile, y is the *Condorcet winner*.

hand operates: in pursuit of their own interests voters and political parties promote the public interest, since the governing party adopts a policy in accordance with the popular will, that is the will of the median voter. Before drawing this conclusion, however, we should enquire how sensitive the median voter theorem is to the assumptions from which it is derived. In the next section, we shall examine the assumption of one-dimensional competition.

A World of Two Dimensions

Suppose that we relax the assumption that policy competition takes place in only one dimension and imagine that it can take place in two. This is not an unreasonable relaxation. Policy competition in more than one dimension is clearly typical of the real world. Political parties differ about the degree of government intervention in the economy as measured by public expenditure, but they can also differ in terms of the degree of regulation that they favour in respect of personal morals. The Thatcher administration in the UK showed that those who are *laissez-faire* in their economics can still be authoritarian in their views about the government enforcement of censorship in broadcasting (Brittan, 1989, pp. 49–50). Consequently, we should not expect a perfect correspondence between economic and social interventionism, and political parties can be expected to campaign independently in two dimensions.

Apart from changing our assumption about the number of dimensions in which party competition takes place, all the other assumptions underlying the median voter theorem remain in place. Political parties set their programmes competitively. Voters are rational. There is no voter abstention. Is the stability of our one-dimensional world retained in the two-dimensional world? In general, the answer is 'no'. To see why not, consider figure 14.3. There are three policy alternatives x, y and z, but they are not strung out along one dimension: y is in the median position along one dimension, but is distant from the two other alternatives along the second dimension. Despite this difference, there is still an incentive for political parties to move towards y in their policy position, since otherwise they will not secure a majority. However, as they are both drawn towards y, one of them will realize that there is a position y' midway between x and z in the first dimension that will provide a majority against y. Inspection will show, however, that there will be a position between, say, x and y which would provide a majority against y'. And so it can go on. There is no majority preference policy position that can defeat all the others taken in pairwise competition. In short, there is no Condorcet winner.

The instability illustrated in figure 14.3 comes about because of the way in which voters are distributed across the policy space. Is there a distribution of voters that will make party competition more stable than this hypothetical case suggests? It turns out that there is, but it is so constrained that it is impossible to believe that it would ever be found in the real world. Essentially, the distribution must be such that one voter occupies the median of both dimensions, and remaining voters are strung out in such a way that they are all diametrically opposed to one another around this median point and exactly paired with one another (for a clear exposition of this instability, see Riker, 1982, pp. 181–8). What this means is that, in practice, in two-dimensional issue space there is always a silent majority to which a party can appeal to oust an incumbent party from office at an election.

Since parties are more vulnerable to competition in a two-dimensional world than in a one-dimensional one, a standard strategy of political competition is to open up a new dimension as a basis on which to appeal to the electorate. Thus, the Conservative Party maintained its dominance during the 1980s in UK politics in part by exploiting the split in the Labour party over nuclear weapons. (Riker (1986) provides a set of rich and

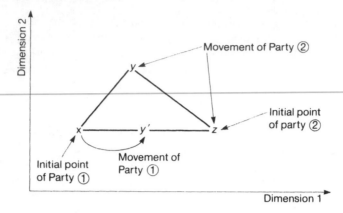

Figure 14.3   The breakdown of equilibrium in two-dimensional issue competition. When three equal-sized blocks of voters order their preferences in terms of which point is closest:

Voters A: x y z
Voters B: y x z
Voters C: z y x

Initially, Party 1 beats Party 2 because Voters A + B prefer x to y. When Party 2 moves to y, it wins because Voters B + C prefer y to x. When Party 1 moves to y', it wins because voters whose first preference is either x or z prefer y' to y.

entertaining stories of the ways in which splitting the opposition has been accomplished in various historical situations.)

There is no reason why dominance by one party must be a permanent feature of political competition. Indeed, the typical existence of silent majorities in two dimensions means that office-seeking political parties should be able to find some combination of issue positions that would defeat existing office-holders. However, the existence of this possibility breaks the link between the public choice of the winning party and the profile of popular preferences that is responsible for ensuring that the party is elected. The electoral connection ceases to be an institutional device sufficient to make governments responsive to the popular will, defined as majority rule. Indeed, in one sense we have lost the notion of a popular will.

Irrational Voters

The first variation on the median voter theorem that we have explored is a change in the dimensions of party competition. However, that is not the only variation to explore. Suppose that we relax the requirement of there being no voter abstention and allow individual voters to decide whether or not they will vote. What effects can we predict from this relaxation?

From the point of view of rational choice theory the act of voting has costs, if only the opportunity cost of the time spent in going to the polling booth. What benefits can the individual voter expect to set against the costs? If the act of voting is thought to be instrumentally effective, then it should be possible to show that a stream of benefits will flow to the individual voter as a consequence of voting. These benefits will take the form of a party differential, that is the advantage that a set of voters derive from having its more preferred to its less preferred party in office. Such benefits might include tax concessions or increased spending on public programmes preferred by particular citizens. In some cases these benefits may be quite substantial and so it would seem that there is no difficulty in understanding how voting can be an instrumentally effective action. Yet there is a difficulty, because the party differential will arise for a voter when one party rather than another gets into office. Typically, however, any one voter's preferred party will secure office without any particular individual supporter voting for that party. In other words, even with only a moderately large electorate, it will seem to the individual voter that the probability of his or her action making any difference to the result will be quiet small. Once the party differential is multiplied by this probability to produce the expected utility arising from the act of voting, the utility gain might be expected to be very small, and probably negative. In other words, what appeared to be an instrumentally rational action fails to be so on inspection.

Here a further difficulty arises. It is commonly assumed in rational choice theory that all agents assume that every other agent is rational. If one voter can reason that it is not worth going to the polls, so can every other voter. But if a large number of voters reason in this way, then the voting calculus for any particular individual begins to change, since the larger the number of people who stay away from the polls the greater the probability that any one individual's act of voting will be decisive. In the limit, if everyone stays away from the polls except for one individual, then that one individual will be fully decisive. With a greater probability of being decisive, the expected utility of voting increases and we should anticipate that the benefits of voting will outweigh the costs. At this point another phase of the cycle begins. Since the value of voting is now positive, citizens will rationally come to see its value, and the effect of this is to induce a greater propensity to vote in the population. Yet this in turn will recreate the original dilemma and lead people to think that the act of voting is not worthwhile after all. As Downs puts it, 'each citizen is trapped in a maze of conjectural variation' (Downs, 1957, p. 267). It is impossible to know what each voter should rationally do, since each voter is locked into interdependent reasoning of the form 'I think that others will think that I think that others . . .'.

It is difficult to see how any individual voter can escape from this maze, and therefore difficult to see how rational choice theory is capable of explaining the levels and intensity of popular participation in mass democratic societies. In theory there should be a mixed strategy equilibrium (see GAME THEORY (7)), with each voter using some probabilistic device to ascertain whether he or she should vote on any particular occasion. But this raises the problems alluded to in the discussion of game theory; namely, the computational difficulties associated with calculating optimal mixes. Of course, at one level it is not difficult to see how the problem is solved in practice, since the act of voting comes to acquire a significance that is deeper for the individual than would be implied by regarding it as merely being instrumental, and so the act comes to express a desire to comply with the ethic of voting, to affirm allegiance to a democratic system, and to affirm a partisan preference (Riker and Ordeshook, 1973, p. 63), thus bringing in the notion of norms and the character of *Homo sociologicus* rather than *Homo economicus*. These intrinsic satisfactions of an act fall strictly outside the rational choice framework; and so our experiment of relaxing the assumption of voter abstention has served to highlight one of the limits of the rational choice approach.

Conclusion

What lessons can we learn from this review of rational choice approaches to the analysis of liberal democratic instituions? The general thrust of the analysis has been to stress the inefficiency of political institutions in translating the preferences of the citizens into a coherent statement of social choice in any world that is at all complex – that is, in any world which resembles the one that we live in. If we want governmental actions to reflect and implement the will of the people, understood as an amalgamation of individual preferences, then we will inevitably be disappointed, since it is impossible to construct a process of party competition that will elicit such a will.

Of course, at one level, it is not surprising that liberal democratic institutions do not elicit a popular will, understood in terms of preference amalgamation, since we know from Arrow's Impossibility Theorem that no institution satisfying certain rather mild conditions can perform this function (see SOCIAL CHOICE (13)). We should not expect any political institutions to perform the logically impossible. Moreover, it may be worth noting that we would not expect to judge political institutions solely by their ability efficiently to translate preferences into a social choice. There are other values that we expect political institutions to satisfy apart from efficient preference amalgamation; for example, procedural fairness, lack of corruption and tolerable problem-solving capacity (see SOCIAL JUSTICE (18)). Even if we could circumvent the Arrow result – which we cannot – we would not necessarily want to if it meant compromising those other values. Liberal democratic institutions need to be judged by criteria that are more broadly based than those captured in rational choice theories of political behaviour.

Albert Weale

Further Reading

Held (1987) provides a succinct and readable account of theories of democracy, and Lively (1975) raises some interesting philosophical questions. Dahl (1956) is still worth reading. Barry (1978) is a good introduction to issues of rational choice and democracy, while McLean (1987) provides a good discussion of current public choice approach to democracy. His earlier work (McLean, 1982) examines voting behaviour, bringing together both survey evidence and rational choice analysis. Downs (1957) still remains stimulating, not least because he is so often misquoted and it is fascinating to see the original. Riker (1982) provides an extensive summary of the research indicating the breakdown of the median voter theorem in two dimensions, and the tales related in Riker (1986) show how adept politicians have been throughout history in exploiting potential splits among their opponents. A useful and compact statement of the median voter theorem is provided by Austen-Smith (1983). The problem of voter abstention has received much discussion: an interesting contribution is provided by Benn (1972).

15

Power

Power is everywhere. Governments exercise it by raising taxes, imposing laws, commanding armies, or building schools, hospitals, roads and bridges. Similarly, large private corporations exercise power by redeveloping city centres, deciding where to locate their investment or production, or expanding their activities into new markets. The rich exercise power through purchasing the control of newspapers or football teams, and they symbolize their power through the ownership of fast cars and luxury yachts. Even ordinary citizens can occasionally exercise power on a significant scale, as President Johnson discovered in 1968 with the opposition to his conduct of the war in Vietnam, and President Mitterrand discovered in 1986 with the mass opposition to his government's plans to reform the French school system. Nothing is more obvious about societies than that choices are made or unmade by the exercise of power.

This has implications for the theory of choice. The focus of conventional economic approaches in the rational choice tradition is that of individuals making choices in the context of others making choices. Thus, individual buyers and sellers in a competitive market are regarded as price-takers rather than price-makers, because their choices are made within limits set by the sum of the choices made by all the other agents in the system. Yet it is clear, even in relatively competitive markets, that different agents have a varying capacity to buck market trends and avoid the adverse consequences of action. For example, those with scarce factor talents will be better placed than those with common factor talents. Moreover, when for technical or institutional reasons agents acquire monopoly status, their power to affect market outcomes and appropriate a share of consumer surplus is greater than agents who do not have monopoly status. Thus, by focusing upon the choices that agents make within the constraints to which they are subject, we risk missing the processes by which those constaints are constructed and maintained, and hence failing to see how individual choices are not merely coordinated within limits fixed by others but shaped and determined by the choices of others.

Although the existence of power may seem an obvious feature of society, when we seek to understand the phenomenon in the social sciences, all that is solid seems to melt into air. The exercise of power can accomplish great things, but as Tawney (1952, p. 60) once said, 'power is both awful and fragile: to destroy it nothing more is required than to be indifferent to its threats, and to prefer other goods to those which it promises'. Analytically, things become yet more difficult when we try to identify what is common to the various manifestations of power. The very ubiquitousness of power stands in the way of understanding it. What links power acquired through the spending of money, the possession of authority or the will of a charismatic leader? The only common element that would appear to link these diverse forms of power is the ability to cause things to happen. But if the notion of power is reduced merely to the generalized ability to cause things to happen, it becomes identical to the notion of cause, and all we are left with is the claim that the analysis of power is the analysis of causes of things that happen, which hardly seems an illuminating insight or a fruitful way in which to understand how choices are made.

In order to avoid this outcome, the analysis of power needs to identify the characteristics or attributes that mark out the possession of power from its non-possession. In this approach, the exercise of power is not simply any way of causing things to happen, but is constituted by specific ways in which social outcomes are produced. A closely related question is whether an adequate definition of power allows us to measure its distribution. Although we commonly say that power is unequally distributed in society, there are important analytical questions about the extent to which we can go beyond this intuitive observation to a more precise specification of how and to what degree power is unequally distributed among agents in different societies. Therefore, once we have considered the definitional question of how power is to be identified, a second question involves the issue of measurement, of how we can assess the distribution of power once it has been defined.

The Definition of Power

In everyday discussions of power, we commonly use two distinct forms of expression. On the one hand, we speak about the 'power to' do something, as when we speak about 'the power of the UK Prime Minister to dissolve Parliament' or 'the power that Martin Luther King had to define the strategy of the US civil rights movement in the 1960s'. On the other hand, we also use expressions containing the term 'power over', as in 'the power Margaret Thatcher had over her cabinet colleagues' or 'the power of the Roman Catholic Church over the politics of Ireland'. Associated with these two ways of speaking, we can distinguish two strategies for the definition of power. According to one strategy, it is the notion of 'power to' which is basic, and power is essentially to be thought of as a dispositional ability to bring things about. According to the second strategy, it is the expression 'power over' which is basic, and power is to be defined as a relation that holds between agents (Lukes, 1974, pp. 26–33).

The argument for making the expression 'power to' basic is that we can capture the relational sense by reference to the dispositional sense, but we cannot reduce the dispositional sense to its relational counterpart. For example, we can say that what it means for prime ministers to have power over their colleagues is that they have the power to determine the outcome of cabinet deliberations or bring recalcitrant ministers into line by threatening to use their powers to appoint and dismiss. In other words, we can redefine the power of prime ministers over their colleagues in terms of specific dispositional abilities. By contrast, it is not possible to redefine the power of the Prime Minister to dissolve Parliament in terms of the power exercised over others. It would be a simple constitutional mistake to attribute the power of the Prime Minister to dissolve Parliament to a relation in which he or she stood to other political actors. What seems essential to the exercise of power is the ability to effect outcomes; 'power over' is best understood in terms of that ability, not vice versa (Morriss, 1987, pp. 32–5).

Despite this argument, advocates of the 'power over' view are drawing attention to something significant in the understanding of power, namely that while all forms of power can be understood in terms of ability, not all abilities can be understood as power, at least if we focus upon 'social' power rather than abilities more generally (Barry, 1989a, p. 308). You may have the power, that is the ability, to swim the Channel, but that sort of power is usually not at issue when thinking about your social power; that is, your ability to determine outcomes via your participation in politics or the market. When we focus upon power in the social sciences, we are normally interested in the way in which the exercise of power enables people to get their way in economic relations or in politics. The relational notion of power helps to draw attention to the fact that the abilities in which we are typically interested in the social sciences are those that enable some persons to secure outcomes or advantages when they are in competition with others for scarce resources or the right to determine policy.

Definitions of power have varied in the extent to which they stress dispositional or relational elements of conflict or competition. Weber (1922, p. 152), only hinting at the dispositional element, defined power as the probability that one actor in a social relationship be in a position to carry out his will despite resistance, regardless of the basis on which this probability rests. Tawney (1964, p. 159) defined power as the capacity of an individual or group of individuals to modify the conduct of other individuals in a desired manner while not being similarly modified. Dahl's (1957, pp. 202–3) intuitive idea of power is that A has power over B to the extent that he can get B to do something that B would not otherwise do. Barry (1989a, p. 308) says that your having power entails your having the ability to overcome resistance or opposition, and by this means achieve an outcome different from the one that would have occurred in the absence of your intervention. If the notion of successfully overcoming opposition or resistance is linked with a dispositional conception of power, the analytical problem becomes one of understanding how the disposition is constituted and revealed. In virtue of what do some agents have the ability to overcome the opposition or resistance of others when they are in competition with them?

One way in which power in this sense can be acquired is by the possession of superior physical force. Until David came along, Goliath had this form of power. Yet, despite physical force somehow being 'obvious' as a paradigm of power, it provides only a poor basis for understanding how social and political power is constituted. Hume (1742, p. 110), building on Hobbes's observation that among human beings physical force was approximately equally distributed, put the point with his customary clarity when he said that government was founded upon opinion because even tyrants have to lead those who implement their wishes by opinion rather than

HUME ON POWER

It is . . . on opinion only that government is founded; and this maxim extends to the most despotic and most military governments, as well as to the most free and most popular. The soldan of Egypt, or the emperor of Rome, might drive his harmless subjects, like brute beasts, against their sentiments and inclination: But he must, at least, have led his *mamelukes*, or *praetorian bands*, like men, by their opinion.

(Hume, 1742, p. 110)

force (see ☐). More cynically still, we might note that power is most insidiously exercised when those who are controlled have their consciousness shaped in such a way that they come to assent voluntarily to their condition (see AUTONOMY (6)). Therefore, if we are to understand the basis of social and political power, we shall have to look beyond the exercise of physical force to other factors.

Hume identified the control of opinion as being crucial, but this sort of control can be secured in various ways, for example by persuasion, the use of economic resources or the possession of political authority. In other words, my power to overcome your resistance or opposition is given by my ability to persuade you to change your mind, to provide you with some economic reason for lowering your resistance or to exercise my position of authority, with all that this might imply in terms of institutional support, to order you to do what I want. Real-world instances of conflicts normally involve elements of all three methods of exercising power, and the study of power is at its best when it shows how these elements are brought together in specific circumstances.

Consider, as an example, the Cuban missile crisis of 1962 (see Allison, 1972). The discovery of Soviet nuclear missiles in Cuba posed a challenge to the US President, John Kennedy, in the exercise of his power. The task was to persuade Krushchev to withdraw the missiles despite the evident advantages to the Soviet government in keeping them there. Another task was to assert his authority over his own government machine (for example, US missiles in Turkey had not been withdrawn earlier, despite Kennedy's command that they should be). Eventually, Kennedy succeeded in convincing the Soviet Union to withdraw the weapons by imposing a naval blockade, but this was not simply the exercise of force, since it was recognized among the Kennedy aides that there was a considerable element of bluff in the US decision should the Soviets decide to raise the stakes by seeking to breach the blockade. It could not have worked, in any case, had the US not possessed both the economic resources and the political organization to mobilize forces at short notice.

The Cuban missile crisis provides an example of the sources of power in a situation of confrontation and decision, but we can also observe the interaction of various elements in the constitution of power in the existence of structures of power, which bestow differential power on individuals occupying specific roles. Thus economic resources bestow power upon people by providing them with the means to overcome resistance either by buying the opposition off or by using the resources to mobilize superior political organization. Consider, as an example, the power of different occupational groups to secure public policies to their own advantage. Formally, their power is equal, since there are no political or constitutional restrictions in liberal democracies upon interest groups forming to advance their own economic interests. However, there may be institutional rules and practices that bestow advantages on some groups relative to others. For example, since capitalist property law protects material objects and intellectual property rights, but not the market value of skills, those in possession of marketable human or physical capital will typically find that they are better able to protect their interests as compared to those with skills that are in market decline, for example those skilled in traditional crafts or agriculture who face competition from capital-intensive modes of production.

Rules and institutional practices will therefore bestow differential economic returns to various occupational groups, and these differential returns will provide the basis upon which members of those groups can purchase influence, fund organizations to protect their common interests and assert their common social objectives. Note that in this conception power is still a property of individuals or aggregates of individuals, although the source of differential power is to be found in the existence of specific institutional practices. Some writers (such as Lukes, 1974, p. 24) go further than this, however, and *identify* power with a pattern of rules and institutional practices that systematically biases the operation and outcomes of the social system in favour of some issues and against others. One of the ways in which this bias arises is by inducing in certain agents a false understanding of their own interests (see AUTONOMY (6)), preventing those agents from mobilizing resources to their own advantage. According to this account, power is the existence of differential social advantage as encoded in a given set of institutional practices and rules.

The crucial question to ask about this concept of power is whether it provides us with a way of understanding the phenomenon associated with power that is not available to us when we say simply that individuals have power and that differences in power are (in part) due to the existence of differential resources flowing from the operation of a social system. The main advantage of retaining the concept that power is a property of individuals, or groups of individuals, is that it enables us to retain the distinction between the possession of power and its exercise. A social system must presumably be always exercising its power simply by virtue of its continual operation, whereas individuals or groups of individuals can choose whether or not to exercise their power. There are important substantive social scientific questions that hang upon the distinction between power and its exercise, for example why business groups in Scandinavia have accepted welfare state legislation advanced by social democratic parties with greater willingness than similar groups in Austria and Germany (Esping-Andersen and Korpi, 1984). We are unlikely to find the explanation for this difference purely in the differences in the economic resources available to distinct national bourgeois groups; their attitude towards the use of those resources is also likely to be an important variable in its own right.

Power, then, is the ability of agents to secure an outcome or objective against the opposition of others by mobilization of the resources of persuasion, authority and money (or their functional equivalents). It is a property of individuals, or collectivities of individuals, and its possessors may choose whether or not to exercise it so that the competition is one for an inherently positional good.

Is the conduct of market exchange an exercise of power in this sense? Typically it is not, since traders in a fully competitive market do not achieve their desired outcomes against the opposition of others but with their cooperation. However, there are at least two circumstances in which this characterization breaks down. The first is the straightforward case in which there is an 'unreasonable' imbalance in bargaining advantage in the making of a contract, so that one party is exploiting weaknesses in the other through lack of knowledge or absence of acceptable alternatives. Legal systems typically regard contracts made under threat of force or fraud as void, presumably on the grounds that such contracts are not generally conducive to mutual advantage, so that one party is not securing his or her aims with the cooperation of another. Moreover, there is a tendency over time to expand the definition of reasonable balance in bargaining advantage, so that even contracts signed in good faith are included in the scope of 'unreasonable'. For example, contracts for financial services in England and Wales are void unless procedural conditions are met other than the simple signing of a contract.

The second exception to the view that conventional market exchanges are not exercises of power is when two or more bidders are seeking precisely the same object, so that the competition is one for an inherently positional good. In most markets it does not matter how many other people are in the market, since all that happens is that the sum of demand is increased, so that more is produced of that commodity and less of something else. Bidders are not therefore in competition for particular goods, and no-one gets their way despite the opposition of others. When two people are bidding for ownership of the same newspaper, however, there is an exercise of power, since if one bid is successful the other must necessarily fail. It is for this reason that many takeover bids manifest the qualities normally associated with power politics, and each side seeks to mobilize its resources in competition with its rivals.

The Distribution of Power

So far we have considered the definition of power, and the ways in which it is exercised. However, there are important issues about the measurement of power, and about its distribution. It is clear that power is unequally distributed in society, but it is difficult to know how to provide a precise conceptualization of this inequality. The dominant approach in the literature is to seek to conceptualize this problem through the construction of 'power indices', particularly as they can be formulated in relation to voting in committees or committee-like situations. Since committee voting is a relatively well-defined phenomenon, the hope is to construct a system for measuring power in that well-defined context which can then be used as the basis for a more general account.

The prototype of all power indices is the **Shapley–Shubik index** (). This operates on a voting scheme in which a certain number of voters are needed to form a winning coalition, and it measures the proportion of times that any individual is decisive in turning a losing coalition into a winning one out of all the occasions on which winning coalitions are formed. The logic of this approach is easy to see in a simple example. Suppose that a three-person committee is comprised of individuals A, B and C. Let each person have one vote, and let the committee decide by means of majority voting. Imagine that A and B are divided in their opinions. Then, clearly, individual C will be *pivotal* in determining the result, since the outcome will coincide with the way in which C votes. The Shapley–Shubik index defines a measure of someone's power as the frequency with which they are pivotal in this sense. Given an assumption that individual preferences are randomly distributed, it should be clear in the above example that everyone has a power index of one third: that is to say, each individual can expect to be pivotal on one-third of the occasions on which votes are called.

This may seem a trivial result, but the value of the Shapley–Shubik method can be seen when we consider a system of weighted voting. Suppose, on our three-person committee, that one person has one vote, and the two others have two each, so that three votes are necessary to form a winning coalition. This weighting will have no effect on the power index, since the individual with one vote will be pivotal with the same frequency as the individuals with two votes each. In other words, the power index is a function not of the number of votes at one's command but of the frequency of those votes being pivotal in the formation of winning coalitions. 'Small' members of a voting body may find themselves as powerful as 'large' members.

One of the ways in which the significance of being pivotal is revealed is in terms of the power of small parties in political systems in which the governing cabinet has to be formed from a coalition of parliamentary forces. Small parliamentary groupings are often in a position to extract large concessions for their support, for example in the number and range of cabinet portfolios that their members receive. Thus, the German Free

Democrats have invariably held important portfolios in postwar German governments, despite their small size. Their pivotal position in the formation of German cabinets means that they are able to extract considerable patronage in the process of government formation.

The analytical issue that arises from formal power indices is how far one can generalize from these specific situations. Cabinet formation, being a form of patronage, is not necessarily a prototype of politics in general. When governments are formed, it matters to political parties whether or not they are in or out of the winning coalition but, in many other political situations, this is not the sort of question that is at the forefront of attention. Where the issue is which social alternative is to be chosen, then being pivotal makes no difference. If there is already a winning coalition for a motion of which you are in favour, then it can hardly matter that your voting or not voting is not decisive; you have already secured the outcome that you want (compare with Barry, 1989a, pp. 278–80). Politics does sometimes involve patronage, but it more typically involves decisions on public policies where the actors have preferences over outcomes, where these outcomes have the form of pure public goods which affect everyone equally, and where it makes no difference to the interests of an actor whether he or she has participated in bringing about that outcome.

Where decisions in politics are orientated towards outcomes in this way, the notion that would form the basis for a suitable power index is not that of being pivotal but that of being decisive in Arrow's sense (see SOCIAL CHOICE (13)). Thus, it would be a form of power to be able to determine what the social ordering was to be, since that would be a way of determining policy outcomes. However, once we move outside of the artificial context of highly formalized voting procedures, the notion of decisiveness becomes much more difficult to incorporate into measures of power. Moreover, being decisive in an Arrowian sense is only one of the abilities that one might wish to possess in politics. Being able to persuade others who were decisive to share your ordering would, arguably, be equally, or more, important (see AUTONOMY (6)).

Given the difficulty of moving from formalized voting situations to the attribution of power in other social settings, it seems unlikely that we shall ever be able to measure the distribution of power in the way that the Shapley–Shubik index, or any other measure based upon formal game-theoretic notions, promises. If we regard power dispositionally as the ability to achieve outcomes that one desires against the opposition of others, then the exercise of power involves assembling resources and instruments to achieve what one wills within specific institutional contexts. The description of the processes involved in such exercises of power requires more information than is typically captured in sparsely formulated game-theoretic accounts of social interaction. In consequence, we seem to be left not with precisely measurable indices of power but with categorical judgements concerning which individuals or groups are among the most powerful in society, with the possibility of some rough ordering of actors' political power relative to one another.

Conclusion

Power is clearly an important phenomenon in any society, and when we seek to account for what happens in social choice it is impossible to dispense with the notion for long. However, it presents problems for rational choice theories of social life. Rational choice theories of politics and society necessarily abstract from the institutional context within which interaction occurs, and hence leave out of account a description of the resources upon which agents can call in the pursuit of their plans. Can it be any wonder that in the paradigm of rational choice analyses of society, namely neoclassical accounts of the market, the phenomenon of power is entirely absent?

Albert Weale

Further Reading

The literature on power is large, but the notion is typically treated historically or anecdotally rather than analytically. Morriss (1987) gives an admirably lucid account of the concept, offering a sophisticated account of the disposition view. Lukes (1974) provides a brief and influential account, with illustrations. His 'three-dimensional' analysis of power is criticized among the essays collected in Barry (1989a), which also seeks to develop an economic theory of power. Much discussion in political science has revolved around the debates initiated by Dahl's (1961) discussion of the question 'Who governs?' The original is still worth reading. The literature on the measurement of power outside of formal settings is discussed in Weale (1976).

16

Planning

The institution of government is often seen in the Orwellian guise of Big Brother because it intervenes in the affairs of individuals. With such interventions, it alters the outcomes which otherwise would have resulted from individuals freely interacting with each other, and thus it appears to confound Mill's (1848) famous dictum that 'individuals are the best judges of their own interests'. But, as Mill also recognizes, the label can do an injustice to governments because 'there are matters in which the interference of the law is required, not to overrule the judgement of individuals respecting their own interest, but to give effect to that judgement' (p. 552).

This may sound strange to those who marvel at the order that can be created, apparently without design, when individuals interact freely in markets. It is as if individuals are guided, in Smith's famous words, by an 'invisible hand' ($\Box$ p. 180). However, as ANARCHIC ORDER (12) reminds us, the invisible hand frequently also does mischief, with the result that the individual pursuit of interest produces collectively self-defeating results. In short, markets also fail and this necessitates social choices over the type of government intervention which will remedy those failures ('to give effect to individual judgement'). We shall discuss a variety of reasons for market failure in this chapter, together with the compensating types and techniques of planning that have been employed by governments.

One common source of market failure is the presence of **externalities** ($\boxed{?}$). These arise when there is a gap between the privately perceived costs and benefits of an activity and its true values. In these conditions, private decisions yield an inappropriate level for the activity relative to its true costs and benefits. In the next section we consider a technique, cost–benefit analysis, which has been used by governments to guide decisions with respect to the provision of goods where externalities are significant.

Markets can also fail when the participants are poorly informed. This is equally unmysterious because people are unlikely to avail themselves of all the opportunities for mutually beneficial exchanges when the opportunities have not been fully recognized. However, information failures can be more subtle and complex than this as, for instance, when they arise in economic relationships through the absence of trust. Unemployment is sometimes regarded as an example of an information-related market failure, and it has provoked a lively debate over the appropriate form of government intervention. Keynesians recommend active management of aggregate demand by the government, but this is vigorously opposed by other economists. Some argue against intervention altogether, while others find favour in more wholesale intervention directed at planning production. These types of planning are discussed in the final two sections of the chapter.

When markets fail because of the presence of externalities or inadequate information, the failure is with respect to the efficiency of the outcomes. There are mutually beneficial exchanges which could have been made but which were not undertaken under market arrangements. This contrasts with a different sense of failure, ethical failure, which also motivates government interventions. Markets fail in this sense because the outcomes are judged to be ethically undesirable; the distribution of income is not fair, the rights of some group have not been respected, or some similar ethical assessment has been made.

In practice, it is not always easy to separate one motive from the other, and this is reflected below in the discussion of different kinds of government intervention. Thus, in the section on Keynesian demand management, for instance, there is a brief mention of the measures associated with what is called the welfare state. The welfare state refers to a group of interventions which have been ethically motivated, and these have been closely connected historically with Keynesian demand management. Indeed, they have formed the twin pillars of social democratic politics during much of the postwar period.

Likewise, in the final section, I observe that it is difficult to separate the ethical arguments from the efficiency arguments in the case for planning production, particularly as there is an unfortunate tendency in these debates to elide markets with capitalism and planning with socialism. Indeed, the same difficulty of separation arises in a slightly different way with respect to cost–benefit analysis, because it will be seen in the next section that ethical considerations seem to surface unavoidably even when the objective is to intervene on efficiency grounds alone. However, while the discussion here acknowledges an ethical motive for planning, it does not develop the concept of ethical failure at length, because this is the concern of SOCIAL JUSTICE (18).

Cost–Benefit Analysis

This technique for deciding between alternative courses of action can be used by anyone. However, it has a special relevance for governments when they take actions to avoid a market failure which arises from externalities. Externalities exist when individual costs and benefits deviate from their true social values. For instance, if you pollute the atmosphere by burning refuse, there is no market mechanism which forces you to take account of the costs which you impose on your neighbours. You take account of the cost only in terms of materials that you must purchase, and any personal discomfort, with the result that you are likely to burn refuse more frequently than would be the case if you were to take account of the full costs.

Externalities occur in a particularly acute form with what are called **public goods** (⬚). The characteristic feature of these goods is that their benefits spill over – there are positive externalities. Once the good has been provided, it will benefit many in the community, and yet there is no easy way in which only those who benefit can be charged for the good. For instance, once a system of defence is in place, everyone in the country 'benefits' from it. Once a road has been built everyone can use it. Once a national system of education has been established, everyone benefits, even when they are not sending their children to the schools. In these cases, with benefits that are not accounted for, a purely private decision is likely to lead to the good being underproduced. Each individual realizes that she or he will gain from other people's decisions to purchase a public good, and so each individual decides to purchase less, resulting in collective underprovision.

Let us consider a particular example in which these externalities arise and where the government takes compensating action. The government is deciding where to build a road. There are several alternative routes: one goes through a famous beauty spot; another through a breeding ground for rare birds; while another goes through a traditional site used by travellers; and yet another passes by a large number of houses. Routes also differ according to directness and cost per mile to construct, because they do not share the same civil engineering constraints. Cost–benefit analysis is an attempt to put a monetary valuation on the various costs and benefits of each route, thereby enabling the government to choose the route which offers the greatest net benefit (see also CONSUMER THEORY (2)).

The approach is not without problems. One difficulty, of course, is that many of the costs and benefits are intangible and/or difficult to value in monetary terms. Thomas Balogh had a particularly stark way of expressing the problem when he asked the question: 'What price a little bit of torture?' Fortunately, most governments do not encounter the problem in such an acute form, and considerable ingenuity has gone into developing ways to quantify what at first sight seems unquantifiable.

One strategy uses existing evidence from markets. The change in the value of property adjacent to major road developments in other areas gives some idea of how people have valued the cost of living close to a new trunk road. What people are willing to pay to go to similar nature reserves which charge a fee gives some indication of the value to bird-watchers of an amenity such as the rare breeding ground for birds. The market establishes what is the value of time saved by the most direct routes through the wages which are paid to the people who are likely to use the route, and so on. Even when markets fail to deliver a direct comparison, there are other sources of indirect individual valuation (see **value of life** (⧉)). However, despite the exercise of ingenuity in this area, there remains – as the discussion on the valuation of life indicates – considerable dispute over the precise figures that are to be attached to particular costs and benefit.

Another strategy is to conduct surveys among those groups affected by each route, to try to establish directly how people value the proposed changes. The difficulty with this approach is that there is plainly an incentive to reply dishonestly. For instance, suppose you prefer very strongly to have the road go through the bird breeding ground rather than through your own village: then you are likely to exaggerate, in reply to questions, the compensation which you would have to receive to become indifferent between the two. Sometimes honesty can be relied up on, or there is survey evidence from other localities which was undertaken with respect to hypothetical schemes, and so there was no incentive for the participants to dissemble. There is also a rather cunning proposal for a tax on respondents, known as the Clark–Groves tax, which gives them the incentive to reply honestly. Suffice it to say that, while it is another example of ingenuity, it is also a little cumbersome and potentially very expensive; and this has so far reduced its use to all but a few experimental settings.

Perhaps the largest area of difficulty with cost–benefit analysis is that even when it accurately renders a monetary figure for the merits of each route, it is likely to be incomplete by itself as a guide for government intervention. The logic behind the use of cost–benefit analysis is that it identifies projects which offer potentially Pareto-optimal improvements, and the principle of **Pareto optimality** (⧉) is likely to command the assent of most people. However, the emphasis needs to be placed on the *potential* nature of these improvements. The gains outweigh the losses and, in principle, those who lose could be compensated by those who gain and still leave some people better off. This means that when cost–benefit analysis is treated as the sole guide for government intervention and the project which it isolates is implemented, there is no guarantee that the outcome will actually be a Pareto-improvement. To enjoy the assent which accompanies Pareto-improvements, cost–benefit analysis must be supplemented by a system of compensation which realizes that potential. The failure to compensate in practice, together with the suspicion that figures can always be found to support an original prejudice for one proposal, perhaps helps to explain why cost–benefit analysis is not always held in high esteem.

Keynesian Demand Management and the Welfare State

Unlike the problem of externalities, where too much of some goods and too few of others are produced, markets can also fail to produce enough goods in aggregate to warrant the full employment of the economy's resources. There has been an enduring debate in economics over the cause of such unemployment, and the appropriate policy remedies that governments should undertake.

On the Keynesian side of this debate it is usually argued that unemployment arises from deficient aggregate demand and, accordingly, that governments should manipulate the level of demand through changes in fiscal and monetary policy. Fiscal policy relates to the choice of tax rates and levels of public expenditure, while monetary policy refers to the control of monetary conditions either via control of interest rates, exchange rates or the money supply. The precise source of such aggregate demand failures is a matter of further controversy, and unfortunately this cannot be addressed in detail here. However, to take one strand of the debate, such demand failures can be linked to the poor levels of information held by market participants, on the grounds that inadequate information can make wage and price adjustments sluggish at the same time as it makes the need for such adjustments more likely, because the equilibrium of an economy has become sensitive to swings in sentiment.

This connection can be quite complex, but it is not difficult to see it in outline. First, poor information might forestall appropriate wage and price adjustments. Suppose, for instance, that you are presented with the offer of a particular increase in money wages by your employer, where the employer makes this offer on the basis of the current and expected future state of demand in the economy. You would like to know whether this is likely to constitute a change in the real wage, whether there are similar wage offers elsewhere in the economy, and whether any change is likely to be a temporary or permanent state of affairs before you decide what to do. These are large informational demands, and it would not be surprising to find that you sometimes make a mistake; with the result, for instance, that you interpret the offer as a real wage cut which you refuse when, in fact, had it been accepted it would not have been a cut given the wage and price developments in the rest of the economy. Second, in these circumstances, it may be sensible for the government to manage demand so that the prospective economic conjuncture avoids producing wage offers which may be misunderstood in this fashion (or so that there are rapid revisions in the wage offer to avoid the consequences of a misunderstanding).

This theoretical argument enjoyed ascendency amongst economists for much of the postwar period and, until the global recessions in 1974–5 and 1980–81, most of the major economies were able to avoid situations reminiscent of the mass unemployment of the 1930s. Quite what contribution Keynesianism made to the avoidance of major unemployment in these countries is controversial. For instance, it is not clear that governments acted on Keynes's theory to smooth the business cycle. Indeed, there is some evidence to support the idea that Keynesian demand management techniques were used by governments to manipulate the timing of the business cycle for political/electoral reasons rather than to eliminate it, thus ushering in the phenomenon of the 'political business cycle'. In addition, the underlying theory itself has attracted increasing criticism over the postwar period.

In recent years, first monetarism and then the new classical macroeconomics have given us cause to doubt the wisdom and efficacy of such demand manipulations. The monetarist school typically believe that changes in demand only have a lasting effect on the price level, and that the roots of unemployment are to be found in a real wage which has been set too high as a result of market imperfections such as trades unions (and this necessitates a different type of government intervention). These ideas have gained ground steadily, and few governments would proclaim themselves as Keynesian now in the manner that was popular in the 1950s and 1960s – although the practice of managing demand for electoral purposes does not seem to have weakened to quite the same degree!

The perception of inflation as the major macroeconomic problem in the 1970s was a contributory factor to the decline in public affection for Keynesian demand management policies in some countries. However, this concern has not always led to the adoption of the 'hands-off' approach favoured by monetarists and the new classical macroeconomic school. Indeed, in some countries, it has encouraged another form of state activism with respect to wage- and price-setting, the introduction of incomes policies.

These policies involve control over wages and prices by establishing norms, targets, rules and so on for individuals, businesses and unions to follows. One reason for their introduction is the undesirable consequences which can arise, in the absence of trust between work groups, with a staggered and decentralized system of wage bargaining. In such a system, each work group could be in a Prisoner's Dilemma (□ p. 99) that generates an inflationary bias. Each group can either moderate its wage claim or choose not to. If all can agree to moderate, the outcome is better than non-moderation because inflation slows, but unless there is some mechanism to enforce the agreement it is unlikely to hold because there is an incentive not to moderate when others do, since inflation will still slow and your relative wage will improve. When all groups realize this logic, they will all decide not to moderate, with the result that inflation does not slow.

In effect, this coordination problem is to do with trust. Each work group is unable to trust other groups to recognize and act in the collective interest; and an incomes policy becomes a substitute mechanism for guaranteeing the moderation of wages, which is in the interests of all. To maintain the broad line of argument, such problems of trust can be subsumed under the general heading of information difficulties since they refer to the problem, albeit in a more complicated sense, of the expectations which can be rationally entertained about the behaviour of others.

Furthermore, despite the growing importance of rival theories, it should not be thought that governments have lost interest in managing demand with a view to influencing the overall level of economic activity. A clear recent demonstration of continuing interest is provided by the stock market crash of October 1987, when Central banks in all the major economies of the world rushed to increase the money supply. They had learnt the lessons of the Great Depresion of the 1930s, and wished to avoid a rush into liquidity causing the same type of cumulative collapse. Keynes would have been proud of them!

In many countries after the Second World War, the commitment to Keynesianism was combined with a commitment to the welfare state, to form the twin pillars of social democratic politics. The welfare state often refers to a package of expenditure and tax programmes. On the taxation side, it is associated with a progressive income tax, and significant wealth and inheritance taxes; while on the expenditure side, the hallmark is a special emphasis on public provision in the fields of housing, education and health, and social insurance programmes such as unemployment insurance, pensions and income maintenance.

While some aspects of the distinctive interventions of the welfare state can be understood as a response to the problem of externalities, there was always a stronger sense that markets were failing ethically and that this warranted intervention to promote greater equality. Whether market outcomes are good or bad is, of course, more controversial and is taken up in the chapter on SOCIAL JUSTICE (18). For now, it suffices to point out that the growth of the welfare state at a time when governments were committed to Keynesian demand management was a happy coincidence. Not only did each support the other by encouraging a general suspicion over market outcomes, but the progressive income tax structure and the growth of income-related government benefits also provided a powerful mechanism for the stabilization of aggregate demand. For instance, when output growth slows down and unemployment starts to rise, the government will automatically collect proportionately less taxes and spend more on its social security programmes, thus propping up aggregate demand at a time when this is required. In much the same way, there was a happy coincidence between the opposition to the welfare state (the 'nanny' state) and the macroeconomics of monetarism and the new classical school in the politics of 'Thatcherism'.

Planning Production

Problems with markets are often regarded as more serious than the externality and demand failures discussed above. The analysis of failure varies, but an inference which is frequently drawn is that the role of markets must be further circumscribed by the conscious planning of production.

The degree of planning varies with the task. At one extreme, there is the indicative planning that has been practised in France, and which is used in Japan. It is certainly true that both countries have mechanisms which enable the government to push and nudge the private sector in one direction or another, but explicit intervention has never been an important part of this sort of planning. Instead, in both countries, it was felt that planning was an exercise for generating information about likely developments in the economy, and that this would enable the private sector to make better decisions. Thus, again, the government's involvement can be regarded as a response to underlying information problems in a market system.

At the other extreme, there are the full-blown planning systems of the Soviet Union and Eastern Europe, and the motives behind such intervention are more complex. These systems are changing rapidly, but in their heyday they presented a model for organizing economic life which is almost the direct antithesis of the market. Central planners would issue orders to all enterprises concerning both what they should produce and where it should go to, and with what inputs from what factories. The technique was known as material balances, and the objective of the central planner was literally to act as a substitute for the market; to ensure that the supply and demand for each commodity balanced.

The development of input–output tables for an economy, tables which plot the physical interconnections between industries, together with the advent of cheap computing power have greatly simplified the task of the central planner. However, the growth of an economy through technological change constantly threatens to make the task more difficult. The economy becomes more complicated at the same time as the historical picture contained in an old input–output table becomes less relevant to current production. In this context, and with the historical record of exceptionally rapid industrialization in centrally planned economies, it is perhaps not surprising that such planning systems have increasingly come to be seen as most effective for economies which are beginning to industrialize. In such economies, the mobilization of labour and the high levels of capital investment which can be achieved under a planning system can produce spectacular gains. In comparison, central planning is regarded as being less suited to a mature and complex economy, where technological change has become the driving engine of growth.

The arguments for wholesale planning are inextricably bound up with the arguments against capitalism. Those regimes claiming to be communist or socialist have until recently been centrally planned economies, and have frequently held up the planning of production as an important symbol of what distinguishes them from capitalism. Hence much of the argument for planning has revolved around an attack on the failures and inequities of capitalism. It is important to understand this, but it is also important to appreciate that the elision of markets with capitalism, implied by this argument, is wrong in significant respects.

Marx himself provides useful counter. He plainly thought that markets suffered from defects in their own right, even if they took their character from the property relations of capitalism. Indeed, it is quite plausible to construe much of his analysis of the origins of unemployment in Keynesian terms, as revolving around information and coordination failures which can exist in markets, albeit in ways which are particular to capitalism. Likewise, in Marx's discussion of the ethical failures of capitalism, markets feature prominently but are not simply another way of describing capitalism. Markets generate unfortunate ethical consequences in their own right, such as the reification of objects, whereby relations between people are falsely understood as relations between commodities. However, the most significant ethical problem in Marx's critique is the one which attaches to capitalism rather than markets. It is the private ownership of the means of production, the defining characteristic of capitalism, that is responsible for the private and exploitative control which a minority enjoy over what is fundamentally a social enterprise, the economy (see **exploitation** (🔢)).

Furthermore, Marx is not alone in distinguishing between markets and capitalism. It has always been recognized, both in the early practice of the so-called communist countries and in the debates within the wider socialist camp, particularly in the 1930s and 1940s when there was a vibrant tradition expounding **market socialism** (📖). The same recognition is an important feature of the contemporary discussions of economic reform in those countries. Thus it is wrong to treat the question of markets versus planning as synonymous with the question of capitalism versus socialism.

To tease out what might be at stake in the specific question of markets versus planning in more detail, and hence understand why governments might opt for planning production, it will be helpful to focus on a discussion that has recently come alive and which, like the one on market socialism, has a history stretching back to the 1930s. This is the debate on the existence of the firm, covered in ORGANIZATIONS (10). It serves no purpose to repeat that discussion here, save to remind us that trust may be a vital ingredient in some economic exchanges, and it may be nurtured more effectively in firms than in markets. What has to be remembered for the purposes of this chapter is that the firm is a non-market method of organizing the economic activity of a number of different individuals. The firm is organized hierarchically, with managers telling different people what to do with a view to coordinating their various efforts. In effect, it is a microcosmic planning institution, albeit one which operates under capitalist property relations!

Indeed, in this context, the continued existence of the 'firm' provides a clear reason for being wary of declarations that the age of planning production is over.

Conclusion

Planning takes various forms, and in this chapter we have focused on cost–benefit analysis, Keynesian demand management and the planning of production; three techniques which have been commonly used during this century by governments to influence the behaviour of the economy. The motives for these interventions have been equally various, but most plausibly it is the desire to rectify a perceived market failure with respect either to the objective of efficiency or some ethical criterion which has been the most important reason. As such, these interventions can be understood as the exercise of social choice, which becomes imperative once it is recognized that the sum of choices at the individual level can produce collectively self-defeating results.

Shaun Hargreaves Heap

Further Reading

Sugden and Williams (1978) offer a comprehensive introduction to cost–benefit analysis, and Sugden (1981) provides a guide to the associated wider issues in welfare economics, together with a description of the Clarke–Groves tax. Marglin (1967) gives a full discussion of a particularly tricky issue in cost–benefit analysis, the choice of discount rate, while Marin (1983) and Schelling (1988) offer helpful introductions to the equally difficult matter of valuing life. Trevithick (1977) is a good introduction to the debates over Keynesian economics which have been prompted by the high inflation of 1970s. Hargreaves Heap (1988) provides a discussion of the conflicting views on the origins of unemployment, which sketches the connection between the Keynesian perspective and the presence of informational problems. The seminal contribution to this view on Keynes was Leijonhufvud (1968), and information difficulties together with coordination problems are key elements in the so-called new Keynesian macroeconomics (see Ball, Mankiw and Romer 1988). Monetarism is inescapably associated with Milton Friedman. Lucas (1972) and Sargent and Wallace (1975) are the seminal contributions to the new classical macroeconomics. Bispham and Boltho (1982) contains a survey of the effects of demand management during the postwar period. The landmark contribution linking Keynesianism with the welfare state for social democratic politics is Crosland (1956), while a recent reassessment is given by Marquand (1988). Ellman (1979) contains a detailed introduction to centrally planned economies, and Nove (1983) takes up the issue of 'Whither socialist economies?' The debate over market socialism in the 1930s and 1940s was sparked by Hayek's (1935) re-publication of von Mises (1920) celebrated denial of the possibility of rational calculation under socialism: the other major protagonists in the dispute were Lange and Taylor (1938) and Lerner (1934, 1937). A contemporary review of the issues can be found in Hodgson (1984) and Le Grand and Estrin (1989).

17

Agendas

Politics has been described as 'the art of the possible', and much of this art lies in the conduct of business. The problem of SOCIAL CHOICE (13) is to find a rule, formula or procedure which always identifies a social or collective preference, whatever the variety of the separate preferences of all individuals concerned. Even if it has a theoretical solution, at least for a limited range of diversity, there are still practical questions of the mechanics of finding or enacting it. Artful politicians are skilled in driving the machinery of decision. This skill can be put to good use, as suggested in the chapter on DEMOCRACY (14), where it can help to engineer the coalitions closest to representing the popular will. But it also gives a power to manipulate for other ends. An agenda is an order of business to be conducted by impersonal rules so as to arrive at a collective decision. There is an art which can bend the rules, adjust the order and influence the business in ways which favour the artful. We shall begin with some illustrations, suggest that no system can ever be immune, comment on the nature of power, challenge the very idea of a neutral decision-making procedure and end with a suggestion that agendas are an artform of creative politics.

Procedures and Tactics

To keep things simple, let us assume that we are dealing with constitutions the principle of which is majority rule, both as an electoral guide and for any particular decision-making body such as a parliament, senate or committee. At any moment of decision-making a majority vote shall be decisive. This is standard for democracies but commonly applies within narrower forms of government too, whenever those belonging to the ruling elite decide among themselves. We start with an instructive question which faced the Roman Senate in AD 108.

A vivid picture of Roman life at the end of the first century AD is painted in the letters of Pliny the Younger (AD *c.* 61–113). In one letter he describes a case which came before the Senate while he was presiding. A consul had been found dead and it was unclear whether he had been murdered by his servants, been killed by them at his own command or committed suicide. The Senate was to decide the fate of the servants. Some senators (including Pliny) were for acquittal, some for banishment and some for the death penalty. There was no simple majority and Senate rules did not prescribe a definite procedure. Pliny reckoned that, if each Senator were asked to vote for his preferred option and the largest group declared the winner, acquittal would result. However, if the question of guilt was put first and that of penalty afterwards, the result would be banishment. The alternatives are shown in figure 17.1.

Pliny proposed the one-step procedure, on the grounds that those who would combine to vote against a not-guilty verdict did not form a genuine group with a single opinion – 'all different opinions should be counted as conflicting'. He objected to letting one of the three opinions have a 'bye', as when 'one gladiator draws a lot which entitles him to stand aside and wait to fight the victor'. This ruling was accepted by the Senate. However, it did not result in acquittal. The leader of the death faction promptly withdrew his bid, and his supporters switched over to banishment, thus forming a majority.

We should distinguish between the procedural and the tactical questions. Pliny presents himself not as trying to secure an acquittal but as seeking to guide the Senate on the proper way to proceed. This is intended as a neutral question, although it offers tacticians their chance when there is no clear single answer. He presents the death faction as tacticians who were opportunistically uniting with an opinion which they did not share. But he might be wrong about that, as we shall see, since it is not always obvious how interpreting a procedure differs from manipulating it. Let us start with the idea of a neutral procedure.

Figure 17.1.

Assume for the moment that problems of social choice are soluble in theory, in the sense that whatever preferences, opinions or legitimate interests the members of a decision-making body may have, there is a best collective decision to be reached if the correct neutral procedure is followed. For instance, if we believe that the best social choice is one in which the preferences of each individual have been given equal weight, then one plausible neutral procedure is majority rule. In the language of **Rousseau** (⊞) the aim is to arrive at a General Will, expressing what is best for the body of citizens, by a procedure which takes account of what each citizen thinks best. (The reason for mentioning Rousseau will become clear later.) For the moment, define manipulation as the artful enactment of minority opinion by a procedure intended to enact majority opinion.

Now consider the common process of decision-making, in which a meeting opens with a question or motion proposed and ends with a vote to determine whether the outcome is for or against. Amendments to the original motion can be moved and, if carried, mean that a rather different motion reaches the moment of final decision. The laudable aim of allowing amendments is to clarify the proposal, refine it so as to test opinions more precisely and to respond to shifts in thinking occasioned by debate. But the process also gives scope for manipulation. Suppose that an all-male club is thinking about the admission of women. The liberal members are all for it and the diehards flatly against. There is a third group of cautious reformers, who propose the motion that professional women be admitted as members. The diehards, faced with defeat, move an amendment to delete the word 'professional'. This is carried with the help of the liberals, who would have supported the original motion but prefer this one. The motion becomes that women be admitted as members. It is put to the vote and, being too strong for the cautious reformers, is defeated by them in alliance with the artful diehards. Minority opinion has prevailed. (A famous American instance of this tactic is the harmless-sounding amendment to a constitutional reform bill moved by Senator De Pew in 1902, which held up the reform for a decade (Riker, 1986, chapter 2).)

To analyse the example, suppose that the three groups are of roughly equal size and have this order of preferences for admitting women:

liberals	all, professional, none
cautious	professional, none, all
diehards	none, professional, all

Here the original motion to admit professional women is a **Condorcet winner** (⊞), (as explained in DEMOCRACY (14)) and, whatever precisely 'majority rule' implies, should defeat 'none'. In other cases in which there are more than two options and several orders of preference among the participants, deeper questions arise about the meaning of majority rule. But here the diehards have plainly outwitted the rest.

This is one of a whole box of tricks which, given unwary or disorganized opponents, can outwit majorities. Thus the order in which amendments are proposed can affect the final wording and so the fate of a motion. The place of motions on the agenda matters too. Alliances can be reshuffled during a meeting in the light of previous votes, positions declared or promises made. A tea interval is a good moment for horse-trading. Many a minority has got its way by prolonging a meeting and voting through a late motion after opponents have started to go home. In such ways persistence and ingenuity baulk a silent or unwary majority, not only in the legislative forum but also in the wider arena where lobbies and pressure groups go to work on the looser agenda of political life.

This all gives power to whoever organizes an agenda. Items can be added with cunning, and can be put in the order which bests suits the setter. Equally – and more importantly in the wider arena – items can be kept off the agenda. It is one task of political lobbies and, more abstractly, one dimension of power, to prevent opposition from surfacing in the decision-making arena. Battles which would be lost are often won by avoiding them, and control of an agenda can include a choice of which battles should occur. But all is not lost if an awkward item does climb on to the agenda – it does not have to be reached. The more crowded the order of business, the more priorities are needed. As Cornford (1908) advised the young academic politician in his delicious *Microcosmographia Academica*, 'When other methods of observation fail, you should have recourse to *Wasting Time*' (see also □).

Manipulation can be taken a step further, so as to achieve the artful enactment of what seems, but only seems, to be *majority* opinion. Here I become more contentious. The 'rational agent' of the chapter on RATIONALITY (1) has *given* preferences, complete, consistent and conscious. But advertisers, political parties and others can plausibly be said to manipulate preferences. They engineer changes in people's preferences, and in people's beliefs about their preferences. Sometimes, it seems, a sincere majority vote expresses the true preference of only a minority. This is a contentious claim because it relies on distinguishing between people's apparent and real preferences, or perhaps between their wants and their real interests. Otherwise there has simply been a change of preference. There are hard theoretical questions here, for instance about the difference between rational persuasion and manipulation or the relation of desire to belief, some of which are raised in the chapter on AUTONOMY (6). But a distinction between artificially induced wants and real interests is commonplace, and, if allowed, lets us connect control of agendas with further large issues raised in the chapter on POWER (15).

THE CONDUCT OF BUSINESS

This naturally divides into two branches; (1) *Conservative Liberal Obstruction*, and (2) *Liberal Conservative Obstruction*.

The former is by much the more effective; and should always be preferred to mere unreasonable opposition, because it will bring you the reputation of being more advanced than any so-called reformer.

The following are the main types of argument suitable for the *Conservative Liberal*.

'*The present measure would block the way for a far more sweeping reform*.' The reform in question ought always to be one which was favoured by a few extremists in 1881, and which by this time is quite impracticable and not even desired by any one. This argument may safely be combined with the Wedge argument: 'If we grant this, it will be impossible to stop short.' It is a singular fact that all measures are always opposed on both these grounds. The apparent discrepancy is happily reconciled when it comes to voting.

Another argument is that '*the machinery for effecting the proposed objects already exists*'. This should be urged in cases where the existing machinery has never worked, and is now so rusty that there is no chance of its being set in motion. When this is ascertained, it is safe to add that '*it is far better that all reform should come from within*'; and to throw in a reference to the *Principle of Washing Linen*. This principle is that it is better never to wash your linen if you cannot do it without anyone knowing that you are so cleanly.

The third accepted means of obstruction is the *Alternative Proposal*. This is a form of Red Herring. As soon as three or more alternatives are in the field, there is pretty sure to be a majority against any one of them, and nothing will be done.

The method of *Prevarication* is based upon a very characteristic trait of the academic mind, which comes out in the common remark, 'I was in favour of the proposal until I heard Mr—'s argument in support of it'. The principle is, that a few bad reasons for doing something neutralise all the good reasons for doing it. Since this is devoutly believed, it is often the best policy to argue weakly against the side you favour. If your personal enemies are present in force, throw in a little bear-baiting, and you are certain of success. You can vote in the minority, and no one will be the wiser . . . .

(Cornford, 1908, pp. 25–6)

Making Procedures Work

We should not presume, however, that manipulation is invariably a bad thing. It may sometimes be a way of correcting a procedural flaw. Rousseau remarks that 'the General Will is always rightful and tends to the public good; but it does not follow that the decisions of the people are always equally right' (1762, Book II, chapter 3). Dubitable decisions can stem from dubitable procedures. Thus Pliny presumed that, since his procedural ruling was disinterested, the supporters of the death penalty who switched their votes to banishment were insincere. But were they? Pliny's ruling left them no other scope for registering their second preference or heading off the result that they favoured least. So the switch could have been an honest attempt to correct a procedural distortion. A similar line is often taken by tactical voters who support the party of their second choice in the UK's first-past-the-post electoral system, especially if they have reasons of principle for advocating proportional representation as a fairer system. This suggests that there is such a thing as honest manipulation, so to speak, whenever the procedure which funnels a variety of opinion into a single vote for or against threatens to filter some opinions out altogether. What looks, from one point of view, like insincerity or manipulation can, from another, be an attempt to preserve procedural neutrality.

Whether the procedure for setting the agenda, conducting the business and aggregating the opinions works neutrally can depend on the sophistication of the participants. For instance, the example of the diehards outwitting the liberals depends on naivety by the latter. In general, liberal thinkers who put faith in constitutions and defined procedures also insist on informed and independent-minded participants. This is the familiar progressive link between freedom, democracy and education. Whether or not procedures encourage decisions which tend to the public good can depend on how well they are understood. Less familiarly, it can also depend on how an ambiguity is resolved in the idea of taking account of what each participant thinks best. Does this mean that each is to vote for what best suits himself or for what he judges best for all (including him)? For instance, when a ban on smoking is put to the vote, should non-smokers vote for and smokers against? Or is the question one of the public good, where reflective smokers and non-smokers might be found on both sides of the motion? On the one hand, to equate democracy with the personal preferences of the majority is to oppress minorities. On the other, the public good presumably varies with the proportion of non-smokers. As an aid to reflection, it is worth studying Rousseau's view (see ☐). What connects the attractive first paragraph to the alarming idea in the second is the thought that what is in the public interest is in

FORCED TO BE FREE

> Every individual as a man may have a private will contrary to, or
> different from, the general will that he has as a citizen. His private
> interest may speak with a very different voice from that of the public
> interest: his absolute and naturally independent existence may make him
> regard what he owes to the common cause as a gratuitous contribution,
> the loss of which would be less painful for others than the payment is
> onerous for him: and fancying that the artificial person which constitutes
> the state is a mere rational entity (since it is not a man), he might seek
> to enjoy the rights of a citizen without doing the duties of a subject. The
> growth of this kind of injustice would bring about the ruin of the body
> politic.
>
> Hence, in order that the social pact shall not be an empty formula,
> it is tacitly implied in that commitment – which alone can give force
> to all others – that whoever refuses to obey the general will shall be
> constrained to do so by the whole body, which means nothing other
> than that he shall be forced to be free; for this is the condition which,
> by giving each citizen to the nation, secures him against all personal
> dependence, it is the condition which shapes both the design and the
> working of the political machine, and which alone bestows justice on
> civil contracts – without it, such contracts would be absurd, tyrannical
> and liable to the grosset abuse.
>
> (Rousseau, 1762, book 1, ch. 7)

everyone's real interest. Hence the losers, in being forced to comply with the
public interest, are being forced to do what they really want to do.

Deeper Doubts

So far we have been supposing that there are, in theory, ideal procedures
which, if followed dispassionately, lead to the right decision or General
Will. But what if the whole idea of a uniquely best procedure to obtain a uniquely best decision is to be rejected? **Arrow's Theorem** ($\square$), as explained
in SOCIAL CHOICE (13) and DEMOCRACY (14), points this way. It fuels
a wider suspicion that we can never justify a decision completely on the
grounds that it was reached by a prescribed procedure, because we can never
justify one procedure against all others. Let us explore this thought in
two stages.

First, think of an outcome as justifiable if it matches the preferences of each individual as closely as the rules permit, given the preferences of all other individuals. Is there any reason to suppose that there will always be exactly one justifiable outcome? Recall the Battle of the Sexes game (□ p. 109). Here there are benefits to be had from cooperation, but they are not symmetrical. In one solution, boy receives 3 and girl 2, but there is another solution in which it is the other way round. Both players benefit from the emergence of a convention, which involves asymmetry, and the theory gives no reason to distinguish between the solutions. Typically, therefore, it represents the advantages of a division of labour without caring who obtains the greater benefit. In the battle of the sexes it declares both sexes the winner, but ignores what may be a systematic bias to men (or, in theory, women). Similarly, a social choice procedure can be partial in its results although impersonal in its operation. If some further rule is imposed, for instance one which requires equality in all outcomes or invokes a principle of compensation over a series of outcomes, then the problem of justification is compounded. Take away the target – a uniquely correct outcome or General Will – and we are left saying that every procedure involves an arbitrary element.

Now, for the second stage, ask how we might reduce the arbitrary element. Rousseau has an answer to the objection that one cannot assess a procedure by whether it produces a General Will, because there is no knowing what the General Will is without first following a procedure. His answer is that, given open discussion, no vested interests and so on, *whatever* emerges is the General Will. This answer gives a rationale for many liberal attempts to frame an unbiased constitution and secure a free flow of information and debate. But the rationale becomes circular as soon as we drop the idea that there is always a General Will to search for. The procedures cannot be justified by their results if the results are then justified by their emergence from those particular procedures. The question now becomes one of how to justify a process of decision which comes out in favour of some opinions and interests against others, when there is no longer an independent test.

The answer currently in favour introduces the notion of accountability. A group of persons (electors, shareholders or members of a community) appoints a smaller group to conduct their collective business for them. This smaller decision-making group is entrusted with interpreting the ground rules and carrying out policies deemed to be in the general interest. From time to time it is held to account. Its members must then try to show that they have been good and faithful stewards. If they fail, they will be replaced. Accountability does not presuppose a General Will which 'is always rightful and tends to the public good'. It presupposes only that those dissatisfied with what has been done in their name know whom to hold responsible.

We can conclude that politics is indeed the *art* of the possible. The hope of the theory of social choice is that it can become the science of the possible, and this hope is explored further in the chapter on SOCIAL JUSTICE (18). It can be a science, whether or not there is a General Will to aim at, if there is at least such a thing as a fair and neutral procedure. The aim of this discussion is not to dash all theoretical hope, even if the practical problems are immense. It is merely to put in a word for art, in the sense of scope for judgement. Accountability is about whether decisions have been well taken, as distinct from whether they are the right decisions. Even if there are no right answers, the process may still have been well-conducted.

William Riker is a political scientist, whose passionate advocacy of a positive science of politics and of participatory democracy has yielded over the years to a Madisonian belief in representative government. In a 1980 article he summed up the limit which he had finally set to the reach of political science (see □). This shows very exactly why there is bound to be scope for manipulation. But it is not so plain why 'political skills and artistry' are confined to people who 'exploit the disequilibrium of tastes to their own advantage'. Pliny is an early example of someone who tried to use them for the public good.

Conclusion

'Agendas' become a vast topic if one presses the questions about the scope of science and the nature of power. Therefore we will conclude with a comment about the place of agendas in collective choice. The chapters in

POLITICAL ARTISTRY

In the long run, outcomes are the consequence not only of institutions and tastes, but also of the political skills and artistry of those who manipulate agenda, formulate and reformulate questions, generate 'false' issues, etc., in order to exploit the disequilibrium of tastes to their own advantage. And just what combination of institutions, tastes and artistry will appear in any given political system is, it seems to me, as unpredictable as poetry. But given the short-term structural and cultural constants, there is some stability, some predictability of outcomes, and the function of the science of politics is to identify these 'unstable constants'.

(Riker, 1980, p. 445)

this part of the book discuss questions about rational interaction within a framework or set of ground rules – one difference between non-cooperative and cooperative games. The ambition of a complete theory of choice is to start with one rational agent, progress to interactive, non-cooperative choices and end with a guide to collective decision-making which extends even to a theory of SOCIAL JUSTICE (18). But the framework presupposed by cooperative games is problematic. It might not be, if we could identify a unique set of procedures which were neutral between preferences (or opinions or interests) and yielded decisions which tended to the public good. But, even if we could, there is still the point that games take time and are played in stages, thus giving scope for intervention in them by those who set agendas and manage the conduct of business. Since we cannot, this scope reveals an inherent limitation to the very idea of neutrality, and shows why the control of an agenda is one of the arts of the possible.

Martin Hollis

Further Reading

Riker (1986) is a very readable survey of famous examples of political manipulation, together with thoughtful comments on the topic. A fine theoretical treatment will be found in Farquharson (1969). Cornford (1908) is a light-hearted discussion of academic politics, not without more serious intent. For a major discussion of the underlying topics, Riker (1982) is recommended and, for related questions of the nature of power, Lukes (1974).

18

Social Justice

Justice is about the obligations that people have to one another, about the claims that one person may properly make against another. Justice is a part of morality, but it is only a part. Suppose that you have borrowed a thousand pounds from someone, on the promise that you will repay by a certain date. The day comes and you have the money to hand. According to most views of justice, you have an obligation to repay: the other person has a claim in justice against you. In contrast, suppose that you have a thousand pounds in the bank and you are approached by a charity which provides shelter for the homeless. Many people would say that although it would be morally good of you to donate the thousand pounds to the charity, justice does not require you to do so. The distinction between what is good and what is just is brought out in the old saying that one should be just before one is generous.

Social justice is about justice in relation to social institutions: rules of property, taxes and welfare payments, the provision of education and health care, and so on. It is primarily concerned with the claims that people may make against society as a whole, or against a government. Thus we might say that the existence of homelessness is a matter of social injustice; that it is unjust that some people have no shelter while others live in plenty; and that a government which fails to provide for the homeless is failing to meet its obligations to them. Analogously with the case of individual action, not all issues of social policy need be thought of in terms of social justice. For example, you might argue in favour of government subsidies for vocational training, claiming that this policy would foster economic growth; but you might do so without claiming that anyone was *entitled* to have his training subsidized.

This chapter reviews a number of competing theories of social justice. The existence of competing theories is not necessarily a sign of the inadequacy of our understanding of justice. A theory of justice is not a theory in quite the same sense of, say, the theory of gravitation or the theory of consumer demand: it does not yield predictions that can be tested against evidence. According to one view at least, the task of a theory of justice is to postulate a set of fundamental principles from which more specific implications can be drawn. To accept a theory of justice is to be morally committed to its implications. It may be that some people can sincerely commit themselves to one theory and some to another, without either theory being at fault in any sense.

It should be said that this is not the only possible view of the purpose of theories of justice. Some people have the more ambitious aim of trying to uncover what the concept of justice means in a more absolute sense. According to this alternative view, it might be possible to show that some theories of justice, although internally consistent, are wrong; indeed, it might be possible to arrive at *the* theory of justice. It is hard to deny that we can learn *something* from this kind of approach. Justice is a concept which has some meaning and for which we can offer definitions. (I did exactly this in the opening paragraph of this chapter.) Thus we are not free to call things just or unjust as the fancy takes us. Suppose, for example, that I say that social justice does not require me to pay income tax, but that everyone else is required to pay: I offer no reason for exempting myself from tax other than that I am Robert Sugden and everyone else is not. Then it might be a legitimate response to say that I have misunderstood the concept of social justice. My own view, however, is that this kind of approach can never hope to do more than eliminate eccentric propositions about justice (such as the one just discussed). None of the theories that we shall be reviewing seems to me to be eccentric in this sense. Each of these theories, I shall suggest, rests on some intuitions about justice that are deeply rooted in our culture – intuitions that most of us feel. To ask what the concept of justice means is to ask what people mean when they speak about justice. Each theory is part of the answer to this question.

This chapter is part of a book about rational choice. Its aim is to show the connections between theories of rational choice and theories of social justice. Thus we shall concentrate on those theories of social justice that have the strongest links with the theory of rational choice. Effectively, this means that we shall be concentrating on theories that, in one sense or another, are *individualistic*. Individualistic theories represent society as a collection of individuals, each of whom has his or her own ends: society has no purposes of its own, independent of or transcending the purposes of the individuals who comprise it. According to this view, social justice must ultimately be about certain kinds of claim that individuals can make against individuals. Another view is possible, in which we are essentially social animals, so that society is an expression of our humanity and the source of some of our ends – *it* has claims on *us*. This view can be found in the old-style conservative strand of thought which stresses the importance of custom, tradition and established institutions. It can also be found in a strand of socialist thought, deriving from **Jean-Jacques Rousseau** (▣), in which individuals create society, but in so doing are fundamentally transformed: to enter society is to take on a new set of ends (□ p. 352). We shall not be discussing theories such as these; but that is not to say that individualistic theories are the only coherent ones.

Utilitarianism

Utilitarianism derives principally from the writings of **Jeremy Bentham** (▣) (1789) in the late eighteenth century; it was developed by economists and philosophers such as **John Stuart Mill** (▣) (1863), **Francis Edgeworth** (▣) (1888), **Henry Sidgwick** (▣) (1901) and A.C. Pigou (1920) in the nineteenth and early twentieth centuries. For Bentham, the fundamental idea is that the only good thing in the world is pleasure, of which pain is the antithesis (see □). The hope was that all experiences of pleasure would prove to be measurable on a single scale, valid for all people (or even for all creatures capable of feeling), such that pleasures could meaningfully be added across time and across people. For any one person, his good was to be understood as the sum of his pleasures. Similarly, the good of any group of people was the sum of their pleasures. Thus the proper criterion to use to appraise any social institution was to ask whether it maximized total pleasure. The word 'utility', which originally signified the power of physical objects to give pleasure, has come to be used as a term for the pleasure itself: and so the utilitarian criterion can be expressed as the maximization of utility.

Utilitarianism provided the intellectual foundation for many movements for social reform. It gave (or was thought to give) a method for evaluating existing institutions according to rational, scientific criteria, and thus of challenging the *status quo*. There is undoubtedly a flavour of social engineering in utilitarian thought, and this often strikes modern readers as slightly sinister; but there is a humanitarian vision behind it too. It we recall the highrise flats of the 1960s – a classic failure of social engineering – we should also recall the Victorian reformers who, under the influence of utilitarian ideas, provided clean water and sewers for crowded industrial towns.

One significant feature of utilitarianism is that it makes no distinction

BENTHAM'S UTILITARIANISM

By the principle of utility is meant that principle which approves or disapproves of every action whatsoever, according to the tendency which it appears to have to augment or diminish the happiness of the party whose interest is in question: or, what is the same thing in other words, to promote or to oppose that happiness. I say of every action whatsoever; and therefore not only of every action of a private individual, but of every measure of government.

By utility is meant that property in any object, whereby it tends to produce benefit, advantage, pleasure, good, or happiness (all this in the present case comes to the same thing) or (what comes again to the same thing) to prevent the happening of mischief, pain, evil, or unhappiness to the party whose interest is to be considered: if that party be the community in general, then the happiness of the community: if a particular individual, then the happiness of that individual.

The interest of the community is one of the most general expressions that can occur in the phraseology of morals: no wonder that the meaning of it is often lost. When it has a meaning, it is this. The community is a fictitious *body*, composed of the individual persons who are considered as constituting as it were its *members*. The interest of the community then is, what? – the sum of the interests of the several members who compose it.

It is vain to talk of the interest of the community, without understanding what is the interest of the individual. A thing is said to promote the interest, or to be *for* the interest, of an individual, when it tends to add to the sum total of his pleasures: or, what comes to the same thing, to diminish the sum total of his pains.

An action then may be said to be conformable to the principle of utility, or, for shortness sake, to utility, (meaning with respect to the community at large) when the tendency it has to augment the happiness of the community is greater than any it has to diminish it.

(Bentham, 1789, ch. 1)

between what is good and what is just. According to the utilitarian view, social institutions are both good and just if they are such as to maximize overall utility: the only claim that an individual may make against a government is that it must take as much account of his utility in its calculations as it does of anyone else's. Utilitarianism may be thought of as a particularly straightforward attempt to reduce justice to rationality. In the standard theory of rational individual choice, each person maximizes his utility. Analogously, a rational utilitarian government maximizes the total utility of its citizens.

One way of dramatizing this idea can be found in the work of **David Hume** (🖹) (1740) and **Adam Smith** (🖹) (1759). Hume and Smith believed it to be a property of human nature that the spectator of another person's pleasure experiences a sympathetic pleasure, and that the spectator of another person's pain experiences a sympathetic pain. Realistically, they thought that sympathetic pleasures and pains were normally only very faint reflections of the original experiences, and that their intensity depended on the nature of the relationship between the people. Thus you feel more sympathy with the pain of your own child than with that of someone else's, and more sympathy with the accident victim you see than with the one you only hear about (see ☐). But the sentiments of the person principally concerned and those of the spectator 'have such a correspondence with one another, as is sufficient for the harmony of society' (Smith, 1759, p. 22)).

In principle, it is possible to imagine an *impartial spectator*, who has no direct involvement in society but looks on it, as if from a distant vantage

HOW STRONG IS SYMPATHY?

Let us suppose that the great empire of China, with all its myriads of inhabitants, was suddenly swallowed up by a earthquake, and let us consider how a man of humanity in Europe, who had no sort of connexion with that part of the world, would be affected upon receiving intelligence of this dreadful calamity. He would, I imagine, first of all, express very strongly his sorrow for the misfortune of that unhappy people, he would make many melancholy reflections upon the precariousness of human life, and the vanity of all the labours of man, which could thus be annihilated in a moment. He would too, perhaps, if he was a man of speculation, enter into many reasonings concerning the effects which this disaster might produce upon the commerce of Europe, and the trade and business of the world in general. And when all this fine philosophy was over, when all these humane sentiments had been fairly expressed, he would pursue his business or his pleasure, take his repose or his diversion, with the same ease and tranquility, as if no such accident had happened. The most frivolous disaster which could befal himself would occasion a more real disturbance. If he was to lose his little finger tomorrow, he would not sleep tonight; but, provided he never saw them, he will snore with the most profound security over the ruin of a hundred millions of his brethren, and the destruction of that immense multitude seems plainly an object less interesting to him, than this paltry misfortune of his own.

(Smith, 1759, pp. 136–7)

point. Being equally distant from everyone, the impartial spectator sympathetically experiences everyone's pleasures and pains in proportion to their true values. Hume and Smith suggested that ordinary human beings arrive at judgements about justice and injustice by imagining themselves in the position of an impartial spectator. In this way, judgements about the social good are reduced to the rational preferences of one person. Now suppose that we consider rational individual choice in terms of the maximization of utility (an idea that postdates Hume and Smith). Whatever maximizes the total utility of a society must also maximize the utility of an impartial spectator of that society; so the preferences of the impartial spectator are utilitarian.

One of the most difficult problems for utilitarians is to find a satisfactory way of measuring pleasures on a single scale. Even for one person, it is not clear that different kinds of pleasure are commensurable. In what units can we compare, say, the pleasures of a convivial party with those of walking alone among mountains? It is hard to believe that developments in our knowledge of the brain will ultimately show that all human pleasures represent the same physical phenomenon in different magnitudes. It is surely more plausible to think that, at the level of brain chemistry, different kinds of pleasure are incommensurable. Bentham himself recognized that pleasure had a number of dimensions (such as intensity and duration), but offered no satisfactory account of how these were to be combined into a single index.

We might also question whether everything that is desirable, or everything that contributes to a person's happiness, can be reduced to pleasure. Bentham's utilitarianism is robustly hedonistic: one of his most famous remarks is that pushpin – the eighteenth-century equivalent of a video game – is as good as poetry. But many later utilitarians have been reluctant to endorse conclusions such as these. Mill, for example, argues that there are 'higher' and 'lower' pleasures, and that higher pleasures, being superior in 'quality', should be given more weight in the utilitarian calculus (see □). According to Mill, utility must be understood as 'utility in the largest sense, grounded in the permanent interests of a man as a progressive being' (1859, p. 136). Moves such as these can help to defuse the charge that utilitarianism has no place for human rights and puts no value on liberty: the utilitarian can say, with Mill, that the enjoyment of liberty is one of the highest pleasures. But there is an obvious danger here. It is crucial to the utilitarian enterprise that utility is a neutral – or as Bentham would say, scientific – standard of comparison. We should not be smuggling our own ideas about what is good or bad into the judgements that we make about other people's pleasures. In principle, Mill recognizes this. That is why he does not allow 'feelings of moral obligation' to enter into his definition of higher pleasures. But we may still wonder whether Mill's claims about Socrates, the fool and

SOCRATES, THE FOOL AND THE PIG

If I am asked, what I mean by difference of quality in pleasures, or what makes one pleasure more valuable than another, merely as a pleasure, except its being greater in amount, there is but one possible answer. Of two pleasures, if there be one to which all or almost all who have experience of both give a decided preference, irrespective of any feeling of moral obligation to prefer it, that is the more desirable pleasure . . .

Now it is an unquestionable fact that those who are equally acquainted with, and equally capable of appreciating and enjoying, both, do give a most marked preference to the manner of existence which employs their higher faculties. Few human beings would consent to be changed into any of the lower animals, for a promise of the fullest allowance of a beast's pleasures; no intelligent person would consent to be a fool, no instructed person would be an ignoramus, no person of feeling and conscience would be selfish and base, even though they should be persuaded that the fool, the dunce, or the rascal is better satisfied with his lot than they are with theirs . . . It is better to be a human being dissatisfied than a pig satisfied; better to be Socrates dissatisfied than a fool satisfied. And if the fool, or the pig, are of a different opinion, it is because they only know their own side of the question. The other party to the comparison knows both sides.

(Mill, 1861, pp. 259–60)

the pig make sense, except as a statement of Mill's own values: did he *really* know what it was like to be a pig?

Welfarism

Utilitarians have continually struggled to find a satisfactory interpretation of 'utility'; an interpretation that is broad enough to encompass all the things that human beings can desire or value, and that does not presuppose any particular view of what ought to be desired or ought to be valued. One line of development of utilitarianism can be found in economic theory, which tries to cut through these difficulties by interpreting 'utility' as a representation of a preference ordering, and interpreting preference in terms of choice. Then, at the level of individual choice 'maximizing utility' is a synonym for 'choosing consistently' (see RATIONALITY (1)).

If utility is interpreted in this way, interpersonal comparisons of utility seem to have no meaning at all. Most of us feel able to make at least rough and ready interpersonal comparisons of pleasure and pain. But if utility numbers are no more than a mathematical device for describing choices, then there is nothing to make interpersonal comparisons *of*. Suppose that Alice chooses tea when she could have had coffee, while Betty chooses coffee when she could have had tea. If we think in terms of pleasure and pain, we might ask whether the extra pleasure that Alice obtains from drinking tea rather than coffee is greater or less than the extra pleasure that Betty obtains from drinking coffee rather than tea. But the answer to this question has no bearing on their choices; so it can have no bearing on their utility functions – utility numbers have no information content beyond the description of choice. The implication seems to be that utility cannot be added across individuals: there is nothing to be added.

Is it possible to retain anything of the utilitarian conception of the social good while interpreting utility in terms of choice? One way of trying to do this is to treat judgements about the overall good of society as subjective statements, analogous with preferences, rather than as statements about any kind of objective reality. Suppose that you imagine yourself as a *social decision-maker*, with full responsibility to make choices on behalf of society as a whole. Imagine having to choose between two alternative *social states* (that is, complete descriptions of society) x and y: x would favour one group of people while y would favour another. Even though you cannot compare the pleasures and pains of these two groups on any objective scale, you may be able to say that you would choose x rather than y – that, *in your judgement*, x is better than y for society as a whole.

We may now invoke the standard theory of rational choice and say that a rational decision-maker will have an ordering of all possible social states, just as a rational consumer has a preference ordering over all consumption bundles. If the decision-maker accepts certain value judgements – essentially, that the good of society depends only on the welfare of individuals, as judged by those individuals – and if certain technical assumptions are satisfied, then the decision-maker's judgements can be represented by a Bergson–Samuelson **social welfare function** ($\boxed{\exists}$). By construing social welfare judgements in this way, economists have been able to retain much of the theoretical structure of utilitarianism without committing themselves to any assumptions about the measurability of pleasure and pain. This approach is often called *welfarism*, a term coined by Sen (1979).

Harsanyi (1955) has proposed a mental experiment by which anyone can arrive at his or her social welfare function, and which leads to a welfarist analogue of utilitarianism. Harsanyi asks you to imagine having to choose between alternative social states, knowing that you are one of the persons in the relevant society, but not knowing which. More particularly, you know you are equally likely to be any one of those persons. Harsanyi argues that the self-interested preferences you would have in this imaginary position represent impartial judgements about the welfare of society as a whole. Take the case of Alice who likes tea and Betty who likes coffee. Suppose that the two relevant social states are S_1, in which tea is taxed but coffee is not, and S_2, in which coffee is taxed but tea is not. Alice prefers S_2 to S_1; Betty prefers S_1 to S_2. If you are to carry out Harsanyi's experiment, you must imagine that you have a 50–50 chance of becoming each of these two people, and then make a choice between S_1 and S_2. If, say, you choose S_1, then you are judging that S_1 is better than S_2 for Alice and Betty taken together. Notice that this construction, like Hume's and Smith's idea of the impartial spectator, reduces judgements about the social good to the rational preferences of one person.

Harsanyi then applies the axioms of expected utility theory (see RATIONALITY (1)) to imaginary choice problems of this kind. In such problems, the objects of choice (analogous with gambles or 'prospects' in conventional expected utility theory) are social states. Each such social state has to be understood as a gamble with n possible consequences, where n is the number of people in society; a typical consequence takes the form 'being person i in social state x' (for example, being tea-drinking Alice in a society in which tea is taxed). If the axioms of expected utility theory are obeyed, there must exist a utility number for each such consequence; this may be interpreted as the utility of being person i in social state x, as viewed by whoever is carrying out the mental experiment. Furthermore, preferences between social states – that is, social welfare judgements – must be consistent with the maximization of expected utility. Since, by assumption, the person carrying out the experiment is equally likely to become any of the individuals in society, this amounts to saying that social welfare judgements must be consistent with the maximization of the *sum* of the utilities of all individuals.

This, of course, is very much like utilitarianism. The difference is this: whereas utilitarianism relies on our supposed ability to make objective measurements of pleasure, Harsanyi requires instead that we are able to make subjective judgements about whether we should prefer to be one person rather than another. Whether such subjective judgements are any more meaningful than are interpersonal comparisons of pleasure is a matter of debate: we shall return to this question later.

Utilitarianism and the Distribution of Income

Economists have been interested in deriving the implications of utilitarian principles for the distribution of income. Any theory about the workings of a whole economic system must rest on simplifying assumptions: economists say that they are working with *models* of the economy. This is true whether the theory is intended to be descriptive or prescriptive. If we are to say anything useful about how income ought to be distributed in a large society, we have no choice but to work within some kind of model: we must ask what the implications of utilitarianism are for a model economy.

It is possible to derive many insights from a model of an economy in which there are only two goods, *consumption* and *leisure*. As far as preferences and utility functions are concerned, all individuals in this model are identical, each preferring more consumption to less and more leisure to less. Consumption and leisure are each subject to diminishing marginal utility. We shall simplify things still further by assuming a 'separable' utility function of the form

$$u = f(c) + g(l)$$

where u is a person's utility, c is his consumption, and l is the amount of leisure he enjoys. Individuals are able to produce consumption goods by giving up leisure; for each individual there is a given (constant) rate at which consumption goods are produced per unit of leisure forgone. This rate, which may differ between individuals, represents the individual's *productivity*.

Before we can say what a utilitarian government ought to do in this instance, we must ask whether it knows everything that we (the creators of the model) know about the economy. Economists who work with this kind of model usually assume that the government can know how much each person produces – in this model, that person's *income* – but not how productive he is. Thus a person who produces a lot might be very productive and have given up relatively little leisure; or he might be only averagely productive but have given up a great deal of leisure. (To make sense of this, we have to think of leisure as the antithesis of effort, where effort involves more than mere hours of work: hours of work, of course, are fairly easy to observe.) Given this assumption, the only way in which the government can transfer income from more productive to less productive people is by taxing high incomes and by making payments to people with low incomes.

From a utilitarian point of view, such a system of taxes and transfers has two effects which work in opposite directions. Because of the assumption of diminishing marginal utility, any direct transfer of consumption from higher-income to lower-income people increases total utility: the utility lost by the higher-income people is always less than the utility gained by the lower-income ones. This effect favours a policy of equalizing after-tax incomes. However, any tax on income distorts the individual's choice between consumption and leisure, and leads to Pareto-inefficiency (see **Pareto optimality** (📖)). In the extreme case of a tax system which completely equalized after-tax income, there would be no incentive to work and so (given the assumptions of the model) no work would be done and there could be no consumption. The utility-maximizing solution is a system of taxes and transfers which reduces, but does not completely eliminate, income inequalities. How much equalization there should be depends on how great the disincentive effects of income taxation are, and on how quickly the marginal utility of income is assumed to fall.

To modern ears, this conclusion seems uncontroversial. But doubts about the utilitarian view of social justice may begin to surface if we change the assumptions slightly. What if the government *does* know how productive each person is? Now the way is open for the government to order each person to produce a specified amount, this amount depending on his productivity. The total product of all individuals can then be collected and redistributed in any way the government chooses. (This amounts to the direction of labour. Is this not an invasion of individual liberty? Possibly, but liberty has no intrinsic value in a utilitarian theory. All that matters is utility.) Now it follows straightforwardly from the assumption of diminishing marginal utility that whatever total amount of consumption goods is produced must be divided equally among individuals: there are no disincentive effects to worry about. But there will not be a correspondingly equal distribution of leisure. The distribution of leisure is optimal when the cost, in terms of forgone *utility*, of producing an extra unit of consumption goods is the same for all people who are engaged in production. This can be achieved only by requiring the more productive individuals to give up more leisure – even though they receive no extra consumption in return. Therefore, if there were no problem about incentives, utilitarianism would not recommend complete equality: it would recommend a system of inequality which favoured the *less* productive.

If this result seems strange, consider an analogy. Imagine a society in which there is no production and which receives a fixed cash income from some outside source. It has a government, the sole task of which is to use this income to buy consumption goods from outside and to distribute these goods among individuals. Suppose that these individuals' utility functions are identical in all but one respect: some people have a taste for champagne and others for lemonade. Litre for litre, the champagne-drinkers' preferences for champagne are identical with the lemonade-drinkers' preferences for lemonade. Because a litre of champagne is more expensive than a litre of lemonade, the utilitarian solution will give more lemonade to each lemonade-drinker than it gives champagne to each champagne-drinker. Thus the lemonade-drinkers will enjoy more utility: in utility terms, the champagne-drinkers are disfavoured because they have an *expensive taste*.

Now go back to the original problem of people with different productivities. At the level of the whole society, we may think of leisure as a good which can be bought by giving up the consumption goods which would have been produced by the corresponding labour. The cost of a person's leisure is higher, the more productive he is. Each person derives utility from his own leisure, just as each person derives utility from his preferred drink. Therefore to be relatively productive is to have an expensive taste, and thus to be penalized in exactly the same way as the champagne-drinker is penalized.

Some people, myself among them, feel uneasy about the claim that this is just. The unease arises from the thought that an individual has at least some special claim to his own labour, and to the product of that labour. Utilitarianism cannot recognize any such claims.

Rawls's Theory of Justice

Until the 1970s, most theoretical discussions of social justice were based on utilitarian or welfarist principles. That this is no longer the case is in large part due to the influence of John Rawls's *A Theory of Justice* (1971).

Rawls presents his theory of justice as an alternative to utilitarianism. In criticizing utilitarianism, he stresses the way in which it treats the welfare of society as an aggregate of the welfares of individuals. To do this, he says, amounts to adopting 'for society as a whole the principle of rational choice for one man', the one man being the impartial spectator of Hume and Smith. By this construction 'many persons are fused into one'. Thus, for utilitarians:

> . . . there is no reason in principle why the greater gains of some should not compensate for the lesser losses of others; or more importantly, why the violation of the liberty of a few might not be made right by the greater good shared by many.

This objection to utilitarianism is summed up in a much quoted passage in which Rawls says that utilitarianism 'does not take seriously the distinction between persons' (pp. 26–7).

This line of criticism reappears in a slightly different form when Rawls argues that utilitarianism lacks 'psychological stability'. A set of principles of justice is psychologically stable if people living in a society organized according to those principles can be expected to develop the desire to uphold them. Rawls claims that this would not be true of a utilitarian society. Utilitarian principles may demand that, for the greater good of the whole society, some people forgo advantages over the whole of their lives. (Recall the example in which more productive people have to accept less leisure than the less productive, without receiving anything in return.) Rawls (pp. 177–8) says:

> This is surely an extreme demand. In fact, when society is conceived as a system of cooperation designed to advance the good of its members, it seems quite incredible that some citizens should be expected, on the basis of political principles, to accept lower prospects of life for the sake of others.

In this passage we see one of the recurring themes of Rawls's theory: society is to be conceived of as a system of cooperation, designed to advance the good of *each of* its members (not, as in utilitarianism, the aggregate good of its members). In this respect, Rawls's theory belongs with the mutual-advantage theories that we shall discuss later in this chapter. At the core of the theory, however, is an idea rather similar to Harsanyi's. Rawls asks us to imagine that we have to agree on the principles of justice by which our social life is to be regulated, and that we have to do so from an *original position* behind a *veil of ignorance* that prevents us from knowing anything about our personal identities.

Despite this basic similarity, Rawls's theory differs significantly from Harsanyi's. To begin with, Rawls rejects the idea that we can have preferences as between being one person and being another. A proposition of the form 'I should prefer being person i in social state x to being person j in social state y' is, Rawls argues, meaningless. If you really are to imagine *being* person i in social state x, and thus having all of i's preferences, and similarly to imagine *being* person j in social state y, with all of j's preferences, who is the 'I' who expresses a preference between 'being i' and 'being j'? Interpersonal comparisons cannot be subjective, because there can be no 'I' to provide the location for the subjectivity (see **extended sympathy** (🔁)).

However, Rawls does not make recourse to the utilitarian idea of trying to make objective comparisons of pleasure and pain. Instead, he introduces the idea of *primary social goods*. These are goods which any rational person can be presumed to want, irrespective of his preferences, talents and other personal characteristics. The idea is that primary social goods can be used in the pursuit of almost any rationally formed plan of life. The adjective 'social' is used in contrast to 'natural'; a social good is one that 'is at the disposition of society', whose distribution can be a matter of social policy. Natural primary goods, such as intelligence and athletic ability, are also commodities which any rational person would want, but are seen as lying outside the scope of the theory of justice. As far as Rawls's theory is concerned, the most important primary social goods are 'rights and liberties, powers and opportunities, income and wealth' (p. 62). Behind the veil of ignorance, Rawls suggests, the rational thing to be concerned about is the quantity of primary social goods one will have when one emerges into the real world. Thus Rawls's theory of justice is a theory about the distribution of primary social goods, and not about the distribution of utility.

Rawls argues that his 'contracting parties' – the imaginary people located behind the veil of ignorance – would opt for two fundamental principles of justice. I shall not discuss the details of the argument by which Rawls reaches this conclusion. One crucial assumption is that the contracting parties choose in accordance with the maximum principle (see *risk aversion* 🔁). A succession of commentators have questioned this assumption and have argued that, without it, Rawls's veil-of-ignorance construction, like Harsanyi's, would lead to essentially utilitarian conclusions. Nevertheless, many people have been attracted by the two principles, which can be viewed as a theory of justice in themselves. Rawls himself does not see the argument for these principles as depending solely on the logic of choice in the original position. As in the passages quoted above, he sometimes argues for the two principles on the grounds that they express the idea of society as a scheme of cooperation for mutual advantage. At other times, he argues that they correspond with our 'settled convictions', 'we' being the citizens of liberal democracies such as the USA.

Rawls's first principle, which has lexicographic priority over the second (see **lexicographics** (📖)), is that 'each person is to have an equal right to the most extensive basic liberty compatible with a similar liberty for others' (p. 60). Once this set of rights has been defined, it constitutes an absolute constraint on the pursuit of any other social objectives. Simplifying slightly, the second principle (the *difference principle*) is that 'social and economic inequalities are to be arranged so that they are . . . to the greatest benefit of the least advantaged', where 'least advantaged' is to be interpreted in terms of the possession of primary social goods (p. 83).

The contrast between Rawls's theory and utilitarianism comes out clearly in relation to the issue of income distribution. The difference principle allows the more productive to earn more than the less productive, but only if the poorest people in society are thereby made less poor. (The idea is that by providing incentives, we can induce the more productive to work more and pay more taxes, which can then be transferred to the poor.) But it does not allow us to trade off the interests of the poor against those of the better-off: no amount of gain to the better-off can be justified if it is achieved at any cost to the poor. Recall the utilitarian and welfarist argument in which incentives are justified because of the government's limited knowledge of individuals' productivities. According to this argument, if the government's knowledge were not limited in this way, the ideal solution would require the direction of labour. There would be inequality, with the more productive having less leisure (but no more consumption) than the less productive. This inequality would not be permitted by the difference principle, since it does not work to the benefit of the people who are least advantaged (in this case, the more productive people). In any case, Rawls would regard the direction of labour as a violation of his first principle of justice.

Needs and Capabilities

Let us now reconsider the case of the champagne-drinkers and the lemonade-drinkers. Imagine that you are responsible for organizing the purchase and distribution of goods for this economy, and that you have full knowledge of everyone's utility function. You work out how to maximize total utility, and you find that this requires you to spend more on champagne for each champagne-drinker than you spend on lemonade for each lemonade-drinker. (Given the facts as presented, it is perfectly possible that this could be the case. It could equally well turn out that the utility-maximizing solution required more to be spent on the lemonade-drinkers. We need to know more about utility functions and relative prices to work out which type of person receives the higher monetary value of drink.) By assumption, this solution maximizes utility; but is it *just*? We might imagine the lemonade-drinkers saying: 'What have tastes got to do with justice? Our society receives a fixed income from outside. Justice requires this income to be divided equally between us. So it is unjust to spend more on satisfying the champagne-drinkers' preferences than on satisfying ours.'

Notice that Rawls would agree with this complaint. Here the relevant primary social good is income; the difference principle requires that income should be distributed equally. (Because there is no production in this economy, there is no way in which inequalities in the distribution of income could work to the advantage of those who had least income.) How a person chooses to use his income (provided that no harm is done to others) is nothing to do with justice.

In this case, I suspect, many of you will agree with Rawls. But now consider a different version of the same problem. Suppose that the two goods are not champagne and lemonade but braille books and ordinary paperbacks, and that the two groups of people are the blind and the sighted. The blind, we may say, have an expensive taste. Would it be unjust to spend more per person on books for the blind than on books for the sighted? Or, to put the problem more generally, does a person's blindness give her a claim on society for additional income? Rawls's difference principle treats the claim of the blind in exactly the same way as it treats the claim of the champagne-drinkers: income must be distributed equally. For Rawls, the difference between the blind and the sighted (which concerns natural rather than social primary goods) is not a matter for a theory of justice.

If there is a difference between the two cases, how are we to make the theory of justice sensitive to it? One answer is that neither income (or primary social goods) nor utility is the appropriate unit for making interpersonal comparisons. Utility makes the theory of justice too sensitive to tastes (as in the case of champagne and lemonade) and interpersonal comparisons of utility raise too many problems. But income is too crude a measure to take account of differences between people that are relevant for a theory of justice. One possibility is to develop a concept of *need*, so that we can say that the blind need braille books while the champagne-drinkers merely desire or have a taste for champagne. Then we may say that the satisfaction of needs is a matter of justice, while the satisfaction of mere desires is not (or is less important).

Sen (1985) has proposed a slightly different way of approaching this problem. He suggests that we make interpersonal comparisons on the basis of what he calls *capabilities*. To have a capability is to be able, if one so chooses, to do a range of things. The idea is to make the concept of capability as objective as possible. (Were we to speak of the capability to achieve pleasure, we would have returned to utilitarianism.) If, for example, we consider the capability to learn about the world, it is clear that to achieve a given level of this capability will require more expenditure by a blind person than by a sighted one, and so in this case, equality of capability will require inequality of income. One difficulty with this kind of approach is that we need an index of capability (or, if we think in terms of needs, an index of need-satisfaction). No really satisfactory index has yet been constructed.

Justice as Mutual Advantage

Utilitarianism can be seen as a way of reducing issues of social justice to the rational choices of a single impartial agent. As already said, Hume's and Smith's impartial spectators, and Harsanyi's model of rational choice under uncertainty, are ways of dramatizing the basic idea that thinking about social justice means taking an impersonal view of society. But is this really what social justice is about?

In thinking about this, it may help to begin with a case of justice between private individuals. Consider Hume's story of the two farmers (see □). Let us put some (interpersonally comparable) utility numbers to the problem, and say that it costs each farmer one unit of utility to help the other with his harvest, and that each gains two units of utility if the other helps him. Let A be the farmer whose corn ripens first, and B the one whose corn ripens second. If each helps the other, A and B each end up with one unit of utility (two units as a result of the other's help, less one unit as the cost of helping the other). If neither helps the other, each ends up with zero utility. This gives us a game which is similar to the Prisoner's Dilemma (□ p. 99), 'helping' and 'not helping' corresponding with 'cooperate' and 'defect'. The difference is that in Hume's game the players move in sequence, so that A can observe whether B helps him before he decides whether to help B. According to the standard view of rationality, neither player will help the other. (A, who moves second, has nothing to gain by helping B. Therefore B can predict that, whether he helps A or not, A will not help him; so B has nothing to gain by helping A.) This outcome, like the individually rational outcome of the Prisoner's Dilemma, is Pareto-inefficient.

Now imagine that when A's corn ripens, he asks B to help him, promising

HUME'S FARMERS

Your corn is ripe today; mine will be so tomorrow. 'Tis profitable for us both, that I shou'd labour with you today, and that you shou'd aid me tomorrow. I have no kindness for you, and know you have as little for me. I will not, therefore, take any pains on your account; and should I labour with you on my own account, in expectation of a return, I know I shou'd be disappointed, and that I shou'd in vain depend upon your gratitude. Here then I leave you to labour alone: You treat me in the same manner. The seasons change; and both of us lose our harvests for want of mutual confidence and security.

(Hume, 1740, pp. 520–1)

that if B helps him, he will help B in return. If B accepts the theory of rational choice, he will refuse to trust A's promise, on the grounds that it would not be rational for A to keep it. But suppose that B *does* trust A. Having received B's help on these terms, does justice require A to help B? And if so, why?

A utilitarian would point out that if A helps B, A loses one unit of utility, while B gains two. Thus, from an impartial point of view, A's helping B leads to an increase in overall happiness. But this does not seem to capture our sense of why it would be unjust for A not to help B. Even if B had not first helped A, A's helping B would still produce the same net increase in utility; but in this case it seems quite just for A to refuse to help. Or, to remove the element of retaliation, suppose that A grows a crop which he can and does harvest perfectly well by himself. Having neither asked for nor received help from B, does A have an obligation in justice to help B, when B's corn ripens? Alternatively, may A say: 'I can see that my helping you would increase overall utility, but what has that got to do with me?'

In cases such as this, our ideas of justice are perhaps tied in with thoughts of *mutual advantage*. In the problem as described by Hume, the practice of mutual aid – or, equivalently, of keeping promises – works to the benefit of *each* person. The practice is one which each person can approve from his own standpoint, and not merely from the standpoint of an impartial spectator. Of course, this still leaves open the question of whether A has any *motivation* to keep his promise: we shall return to this question later. Nevertheless, there is a clear distinction between the case in which A's helping B is part of a continuing practice that benefits both people, and the case in which A incurs a loss so as to generate a greater gain for B.

According to some theories, Hume's game provides a model for *social* as well as individual justice. The fundamental idea is that society should be thought of as a scheme by which individuals cooperate for mutual advantage. The constraints that social life impose on any particular person are to be justified by showing that, when followed by everyone, these constraints work to *that person's* advantage, and not merely for the good of society as a whole. (This idea is also central to Rawls's criticism of utilitarianism, as shown above.)

To think of society as a cooperative scheme is to compare it with some non-social or pre-social state of affairs, and to say that everyone has gained, or should gain, from the existence of society. It is also to suppose that society should be seen as means by which individuals achieve *their own* ends. As an analogy, consider the relationship between the European Community and its member states. What criterion should we use to judge alternative policies that the Community might adopt? (How, for example, should we judge a proposal to introduce a common currency?) Should the criterion be that of maximizing the overall good of the Community? This would be analogous with a utilitarian conception of justice. Or should we require that any major piece of Community policy works to the benefit of *every* member state (if necessary, by offering *quid pro quos* to member states that otherwise would find themselves as net losers)? This would be analogous with a mutual-advantage conception of justice.

One of the most serious problems for a mutual-advantage theory of justice is to define the pre-social state of affairs, the baseline from which the benefits of cooperation are to be measured. A theory of social justice requires us to consider the obligations of government in general; and this seems to require us to take, as our baseline, a world without government.

The classic statement of the idea of justice as mutual advantage is to be found in Thomas Hobbes's *Leviathan* (1651). **Hobbes** (⏏) begins by describing an anarchic *state of nature* in which men (women do not appear in seventeenth-century political literature) live solitary lives, each pursuing his own interests in a completely unconstrained way. Every man, says Hobbes, has a right to every thing; that is, the right to *try* to take anything he wants. The overriding aim of every man is physical survival; but each seeks his own safety at the expense of the others, and the result is a 'war of every man against every man' (see **Hobbes** (⏏) and the box therein). Hobbes presents a set of 'laws of nature', by which he means principles that it is rational for an individual to follow; rational in the quite uncomplicated sense of promoting that individual's physical survival. Thus it is part of the first law of nature that if a man cannot obtain peace, 'he may seek, and use, all helps, and advantages of war' (chapter 14). But the second law of nature is the crucial one: 'That a man be willing, when others are so too, as far-forth, as for peace, and defence of himself he shall think it necessary, to lay down this right to all things; and to be contented with so much liberty against other men, as he would allow other men against himself' (chapter 14).

The idea here is that it is rational for all men to make peace on equal terms, provided that each can be assured that the others will keep the peace agreement. Hobbes argues that the only way to provide this assurance is to appoint a sovereign with absolute powers to enforce peace. Thus, for Hobbes, it is rational for each man to consent to the appointment of such a sovereign. This provides a justification for absolute government, and this justification is grounded in mutual advantage: according to Hobbes, everyone gains from the establishment of government.

Hume (1740) offers a less bleak picture of the possibilities of a state of nature. Hume argues that some constraints on the pursuit of immediate self-interest would tend to evolve out of a Hobbesian state of nature, even if there were no government. (He suggests that some system of government, initially based on extended families or clans, would also tend to evolve.) Among the constraints to evolve would be rules of property (see ANARCHIC ORDER (12)) and the institution of promises. Each individual would learn by experience that it was in his interest to keep his promises, so as to build up a reputation for future dealings with others. The original motivation for each person to abide by these constraints, Hume claims, is long-term self-interest. This is justice as mutual advantage. However, there is an extra twist to Hume's argument. Because these principles can be seen to work to everyone's benefit, they can be approved from the viewpoint of an impartial spectator. Thus people will come to regard acting on these principles as virtuous, and this will provide them with an additional (but probably relatively weak) motivation to act on them. But Hume, unlike the later utilitarian writers, does not see the appeal to the impartial spectator as a way of justifying practices which benefit some people at the expense of others: the idea of *mutual* benefit seems to be central to his view of justice.

Among modern writers on social justice, James Buchanan (1975) is perhaps the most Hobbesian. Buchanan accepts much of Hobbes's theoretical framework, in particular his grim conception of the state of nature and the idea that people might escape from this state by drawing up a social contract. The most important difference is that Buchanan emphasizes the dangers of giving political power to anyone, and tries to show that rational individuals would build constitutional constraints on government into the social contract.

David Gauthier (1986) is another modern writer in this tradition. Like Hobbes, Gauthier starts with a state of nature and asks whether rational and self-interested individuals could establish a system of social constraints that would work to everyone's advantage. Rather like Hume, he argues that such a system of constraints can be maintained by rational self-interest, even without the intervention of government. But Gauthier parts company with Hume (and with almost all game theorists) in denying that the motive for abiding by these constraints is necessarily connected with the value of reputation. In the case of Hume's farmers, for example, Gauthier argues that it would be rational for A both to make and to keep his promise to B, even if he knew he would never meet B again and that no-one else would ever know whether or not he kept the promise.

One essential feature of a mutual-advantage theory is that there is no place for purely redistributive transfers of income – for transfers which impose a cost on some people so as to benefit others. Most mutual-advantage theories claim that government should concern itself only with the supply of **public goods** (📖). For this reason, these theories tend to appeal to people who see the distribution of income that emerges from the market system as being just.

However, the idea of grounding the theory of justice in nothing other than mutual advantage has implications that most people find hard to accept. Consider the case of someone who is born with a physical handicap so severe that he can never hope to earn his own living. Do the other members of his society have an obligation in justice to support him? Not if justice is a matter of mutual advantage, for he has nothing to offer the others in return. Alternatively, consider our relationship with future generations. Does our society have any obligation in justice to consider the interests of future generations when choosing the rate at which it will release carbon dioxide into the atmosphere? Notice that future generations have nothing to give us in return for our not harming them. As a further example, consider the relationship between the Native Americans and the European settlers in the nineteenth century. The native peoples occupied vast tracts of land which the Europeans wanted and had the power to take. It was in the interests of the Europeans to exterminate them and to take the land for themselves. Would this have been (or was it, for this is uncomfortably close to what actually happened) unjust? Proponents of mutual-advantage theories usually reply that there is more to morality than justice. We may, for example, say that the Europeans' treatment of the Native Americans was inhumane, and for this reason morally blameworthy, even though not unjust. But it is hard to feel entirely comfortable with this answer.

Natural Rights

One way of dealing with this problem is to argue that each person has certain fundamental rights which others must respect; it is only within the constraints imposed by other people's rights that anyone is entitled to pursue his self-interest. These rights are seen as existing in the state of nature: in this sense they are *natural rights*.

The classic formulation of natural rights is provided by John Locke (1690). Locke takes it as self-evident that the world is the creation of God, and that the natural state of life for man – the state in which God originally placed him – is one in which there is no government and no-one has authority over anyone else. But God's purposes require that men accept the constraints of a code of natural law; he has given us the faculty of reason with which to discover what the content of this law must be. Men are, Locke says, 'all the servants of one sovereign master, sent into the world by his order and about his business'; they are 'his property, whose workmanship they are, made to last during his, not one anothers pleasure'. From this Locke deduces that each person has a first duty to God to preserve himself and, subject to this, a duty to do as much as he can to preserve the rest of mankind. Locke takes this to imply the natural law that 'no one ought to harm another in his life, health, liberty, or possessions'. Given human nature as we know it, any law requires a procedure for punishing violations; since no-one has authority over anyone else, everyone must have the right to punish (book 2, ch. 2, pp. 311–13).

Note that this natural law includes a right to property. But how is property rightfully acquired in a state of nature? Locke says that God has given the Earth and all its resources to men *in common*; no-one has any greater right to these resources than anyone else. But if these resources are to be used, they must be appropriated by individuals. The fruit of a tree, for example, must be taken and eaten by particular individuals if it is to feed them. Therefore God must have intended some principle of just appropriation. Recall the premise that there is no government. The principle must therefore be one that can be followed by individuals who may be quite isolated from one another, and who have no collective decision-making machinery. It cannot require each person to have the explicit consent of everyone else for every act of appropriation. (Nor, we might add, although Locke does not consider this possibility, could it require an egalitarian or utilitarian division of resources between individuals: such a division would need a government to administer it.) Locke argues that it is a natural law that a person acquires property in a natural resource by 'mixing his labour' with it; thus the fruit on a tree is common property, but when anyone uses his labour to pick it, it becomes that person's private property. Similarly, a person who encloses a piece of previously common land, and improves it by his labour, becomes the owner of that land (see book 2, ch. 5, pp. 327–33).

This general principle is hedged around with a number of provisos. First, no-one may take more from Nature than he can make use of: 'Nothing was made by God for man to spoil or destroy' (book 2, ch. 5, p. 332). Second, the right to appropriate depends on there being 'enough, and as good left in common for others' (book 2, ch. 5, p. 329). It is clear that Locke is imagining the natural (and original) existence of man to be in a world in which natural resources are abundant but labour is scarce. When one person in this world appropriates a plot of land and improves it, there is more than enough common land remaining for anyone else who wants to do the same. Thus anyone who complains about such an appropriation reveals that he 'desired the benefit of another's pains, which he had no right to, and not the ground which God had given him in common with others to labour on' (book 2, ch. 5, p. 333). Third, the right to the product of one's own labour does not permit one to let another person starve: God 'has given no one of his children such a property, in his peculiar portion of the things of this world, but that he has given his needy brother a right to the surplusage of his goods; so that it cannot justly be denied him, when his pressing wants call for it' (book 1, ch. 4, p. 205). This third proviso seems to be a necessary consequence of Locke's basic idea that everyone must seek to preserve human life.

Locke's purpose in all this is to argue that legitimate government can be founded only on the consent of the governed; he is trying to undercut various arguments that might be made for the legitimacy of absolute monarchy. But some modern writers, particularly Robert Nozick (1974), have tried to use a Lockean approach to address issues of social justice.

Nozick takes Locke's system of natural law as given, admitting that this is a 'yawning gap' in his own argument, but claiming that Locke did not provide 'anything remotely resembling a satisfactory explanation' for this system either (p. 9). We must assume that Nozick considers Locke's religious premises to be unsatisfactory; but it is not clear whether Locke's theory of natural law can be translated into secular terms. Natural rights have to be taken as premises for Nozick's theory of justice.

Nozick then asks whether a system of government could emerge out of a Lockean state of nature, without anyone's rights being violated and, if so, what activities such a government could legitimately pursue. He argues that a *night-watchman state* – a state 'limited to the functions of protecting its citizens against violence, theft, and fraud, and to the enforcement of contracts' (p. 26) – *could* emerge, but that no functions beyond this are legitimate. Nozick differs from other mutual-advantage theorists in denying that the supply of public goods is a legitimate function of government. Here Nozick's argument depends on his denying – for reasons that are difficult to understand – the reality of the free-rider problem (pp. 265–74).

The part of Nozick's argument that has aroused most interest is his discussion of distributive justice. Nozick argues that the distribution of resources in a society is just if and only if it is the result of a process in which no-one's rights have been violated. Property can be justly acquired in the way described by Locke (by the mixing of labour with un-owned natural resources). Each person is then free to transfer his property to anyone else who agrees to take it; thus property can change hands by gift or free exchange. (Nozick does not include Locke's principle that each person has a right to subsistence when others are living in plenty.) Whatever results from this process – essentially, from the workings of a market economy – is necessarily just.

Nozick contrasts this concept of distributive justice with the idea that a distribution of resources is just by virtue of its having some *pattern*, such as maximizing total utility, or giving to each person what he deserves. If each person is free to dispose of his property as he chooses (within the constraints of natural rights), then we cannot expect the resulting distribution to have any desirable pattern. Or, as Nozick puts it, 'liberty upsets patterns' – a

HOW LIBERTY UPSETS PATTERNS

Suppose that the existing distribution of resources satisfies some patterned criterion of justice:

> Let us suppose it is your favourite one and let us call this distribution D_1: perhaps everyone has an equal share, perhaps shares vary in acordance with some dimension you treasure. Now suppose that Wilt Chamberlain is greatly in demand by basketball teams, being a great gate attraction. . . . He signs the following sort of contract with a team: In each home game, twenty-five cents from the price of each ticket of admission goes to him. . . . The season starts, and people cheerfully attend his team's games, each time dropping a separate twenty-five cents of their admission price into a special box with Chamberlain's name on it. They are excited about seeing him play; it is worth the total admission price to them. Let us suppose that in one season one million persons attend his home games, and Wilt Chamberlain winds up with $250,000, a much larger sum than the average income and larger even than anyone else has. Is he entitled to this income? Is the new distribution, D_2, unjust? If so, why? There is *no* question about whether each of the people was entitled to the control over the resources they held in D_1; because that was the distribution (your favourite) that (for the purposes of the argument) we assumed was acceptable. Each of those persons *chose* to give twenty-five cents of their money to Wilt Chamberlain . . . . If D_1 was a just distribution, and people voluntarily moved from it to D_2, transferring parts of their shares they were given in D_1 (what was it for if not to do something with?), isn't D_2 also just? . . . Under D_1, there is nothing that anyone has that anyone else has a claim of justice against. After someone transfers something to Wilt Chamberlain, third parties *still* have their legitimate shares; *their* shares are not changed. By what process could such a transfer among two persons give rise to a legitimate claim of distributive justice on a portion of what was transferred, by a third party who had no claim of justice on any holding of the others *before* the transfer?

(Nozick, 1974, pp. 160–2)

maxim which he illustrates with his story of Wilt Chamberlain, the star basketball player (see □).

Social Justice versus Spontaneous Order

The story of Wilt Chamberlain highlights the difference between utilitarian and mutual advantage conceptions of justice. It is fundamental to the utilitarian approach that we look on society from a single impartial viewpoint. Thus social justice becomes identified with the preferences or choices of some single agent; the impartial spectator, the social decision-maker, the individual behind Harsanyi's veil of ignorance. If, following the received theory of rational choice, we take rationality to imply some form of maximization, then we are led to the idea that a just society must be one in which something – some measure of goodness or justness – is being maximized.

Now suppose instead that we think of justice in terms of mutual advantage. Then we may consider each individual as maximizing something – perhaps subject to the constraints imposed by other people's rights. But each person is maximizing a separate objective. We have no reason to expect that the behaviour of these independent individuals, when taken together, will actually turn out to be maximizing anything (or even, from a social point of view, achieving anything). According to this account, justice has nothing to do with taking a social point of view. One might perhaps say that there is no such thing as social justice, only justice.

This is precisely what Friedrich Hayek (1976) says in *The Mirage of Social Justice* (see □). Hayek (▢) takes social justice to be about the distribution of income and wealth; a distribution is seen as socially just to the extent that it is in accord with some 'preconceived pattern' (such as the principle that rewards should be related to effort or sacrifice, or the principle that income should be related to needs). The core of Hayek's argument is the claim that the market is a spontaneous order; it makes use of more information than any individual planner could possibly comprehend and, because of this, can produce feats of coordination that no economic forecaster could predict and that no planning system could replicate (see ANARCHIC ORDER (12)). But it is a fact of life that the market does not and cannot generate social justice: the market, we might say, upsets patterns. We can ask whether the actions *of individuals* are just or unjust by asking whether they are in accord with rules; but we have no reason to expect that just actions will generate outcomes that satisfy any independent criterion of social justice.

This, of course, leaves us with the question of why we should accept the rules of the market. If the spontaneous order of the market is incompatible with social justice, why is it social justice that we have to give up? Unlike Nozick, Hayek does not claim that the rules of the market are grounded in

THE MIRAGE OF SOCIAL JUSTICE

It is now necessary clearly to distinguish between two wholly different problems which the demand for 'social justice' raises in a market order.

The first is whether within an economic order based on the market the concept of 'social justice' has any meaning or content whatever.

The second is whether it is possible to preserve a market order while imposing upon it (in the name of 'social justice' or any other pretext) some pattern of remuneration based on the assessment of the performance or the needs of different individuals or groups by an authority possessing the power to enforce it.

The answer to each of these questions is a clear no. . . .

The contention that in a society of free men (as distinct from any compulsory organization) the concept of social justice is strictly empty and meaningless will probably appear as quite unbelievable to most people. Are we not constantly disquieted by watching how unjustly life treats different people and by seeing the deserving suffer and the unworthy prosper? And do we not all have a sense of fitness, and watch it with satisfaction, when we recognize a reward to be appropriate to effort or sacrifice?

The first insight which should shake this certainty is that we experience the same feelings also with respect to differences in human fates for which clearly no human agency is responsible and which it would therefore clearly be absurd to call injustice. Yet we do cry out against the injustice when a succession of calamities befalls one family while another steadily prospers . . . And we will protest against such a fate although we do not know anyone who is to blame for it, or any way in which such disappointments can be prevented.

It is no different with regard to the general feeling of injustice about the distribution of material goods in a society of free men. Though we are in this case less ready to admit it, our complaints about the outcome of the market as unjust do not really assert that somebody has been unjust and there is no answer to the question of *who* has been unjust. Society has simply become the new deity to which we complain and clamour for redress if it does not fulfil the expectations it has created. There is no individual and no cooperating group of people against which the sufferer would have a just complaint, and there are no conceivable rules of just individual conduct which would at the same time secure a functioning order and prevent such disappointments.

(Hayek, 1976, pp. 67–9)

any kind of natural rights. He makes the simpler claim that the market is incomparably more efficient at creating wealth than any form of planning. If we want the standards of living that only the market can provide, we must accept that social justice is unattainable.

To modern readers, the choice presented by Hayek may seem too stark. We may accept that there is a trade-off between efficiency and equality; but might we not sacrifice some of the wealth that would be generated by an unconstrained market for the sake of a more equal distribution? Hayek seems to give us no reason of principle for not thinking in these terms (and, indeed, accepts the case for some degree of redistribution of income so as to alleviate genuine poverty: see Hayek (1960, pp. 285–305)). In appraising Hayek's contribution, however, we must remember that his early (and, arguably, his greatest) work was done in the 1930s, when it was widely believed that a system of central planning on the Soviet model could generate *both* efficiency *and* social justice. If it now sometimes seems as though Hayek is fighting a non-existent opponent, that is largely because his early arguments have been so decisively confirmed by subsequent experience.

Why are There so Many Theories of Justice?

It is now time to take stock. This chapter began with the idea that questions of social justice are questions about what is best for society as a whole, and that to think about social justice is to look on society from the viewpoint of an impartial spectator. This idea provides the starting point for utilitarianism and welfarism. However, it is vulnerable to the objection that, as Rawls put is, it does not take seriously the distinction between persons.

This objection leads to the idea that a just society should be seen as a cooperative venture for mutual advantage. But if we are to think in terms of mutual advantage, we must specify some pre-social baseline from which 'advantage' is to be measured: we must say what individuals are entitled to do, or able to do, in the absence of society. Hobbes's answer, that in the state of nature every man 'has a right to every thing', is robust and consistent; but it has unpalatable implications. Rawls's answer, that the baseline should be located behind a veil of ignorance, seems not to make a decisive break from utilitarianism: Rawls's contracting parties are impartial spectators in a new guise. If we are to take the distinction between persons more seriously than this, it seems that we have to endow individuals with rights of some kind.

However, we then have to specify what rights people have. If the list of rights is not to look hopelessly arbitrary, we need a theory that can explain why individuals have those particular rights and not others. The classic theory of this kind is that of Locke, which sees natural rights as part of the procedures by which God's purposes can be carried out in the absence of government. But this brings us back towards the idea of the impartial spectator: natural rights are being justified by their ability to promote the well-being of mankind, impartially viewed. In a somewhat similar way, Hayek's defence of the spontaneous order of the market ultimately rests on the claim that the market system is the best mechanism we have for generating wealth: we are told to respect the institutions of the market because they promote human welfare.

Thus we come round in a circle. Utilitarianism seems inadequate because it considers only the general good and has no secure place for individual rights; but when we try to explain why individuals have particular rights, we find ourselves appealing to notions of the general good.

Some readers may feel satisfied to endorse one particular theory of justice and to reject all the others. But I suspect that many, like myself, will feel pulled in different directions. Each theory seems to be based on some ideas about justice that are deeply rooted in Western culture. Each tries to formalize and generalize the ideas on which it is based. Invariably, it seems, this produces some implications that are hard to accept. The search for a theory of justice is an attempt to reconcile our intuitive ideas about what is just with our desire, as self-styled rational agents, to hold beliefs that can be shown to be consistent and coherent. I cannot help wondering whether this is an impossible task.

Robert Sugden

Further Reading

More detailed surveys of the material covered in this chapter can be found in, for example, Barry (1989b), Buchanan (1985) and Hamlin (1986). Smart and Williams (1973) provides a good starting point for examining the debate between utilitarianism (represented by Smart) and its critics (represented by Williams). The essays in Sen and Williams (1982) are very useful too. But there is no real substitute for reading the classics themselves, particularly Hobbes (1651), Locke (1690), Hume (1740) and Bentham (1789), along with such major modern contributers as Hayek (1960), Rawls (1971) and Nozick (1974).

Keywords

Keywords

Arrow's Theorem

In order to understand the logic of the proof of Arrow's Theorem, we shall need some notation for two key ideas. We write $D(x, y)$ when an individual is 'almost decisive' for x against y. This means that if an almost decisive individual prefers x to y and others prefer y to x, then the almost decisive individual wins. We write $D^*(x, y)$ when an individual is 'decisive' for x against y. The decisive individual wins whether or not others share the same preference. It might seem obvious that, if someone wins when opposed by others, then the same person will win when others agree, but such a conclusion would be equivalent to assuming the positive responsiveness of social choice to individual rankings, and this is not an assumption that needs to be used in the Arrow proof. In fact, the implication is the other way round. If someone is decisive then that person is almost decisive by implication: that is, $D^*(x, y) \rightarrow D(x, y)$, *not* vice versa.

Arrow's proof falls into two parts. The first part consists of showing that, for any triple of alternatives (say x, y, z), if there is someone who is almost decisive for a pair, that individual is decisive for all pairs, given Pareto-responsiveness, independence of irrelevant alternative and collective rationality. The second part consists of showing that there is an almost decisive individual in the required sense for at least one preference profile. The following outline of the proof paraphrases the proof in Sen (1970, pp. 41–6).

Part 1. The proposition to be proved is that if any individual is almost decisive for a pair (x, y), then that person is decisive for all pairs in the triple

(x, y, z). Formally, this amounts to showing that, in the light of the Arrow conditions, the following six implications hold:

$$D(x, y) \quad \rightarrow \quad D^*(x, z) \tag{1}$$
$$\rightarrow \quad D^*(z, y) \tag{2}$$
$$\rightarrow \quad D^*(y, x) \tag{3}$$
$$\rightarrow \quad D^*(y, z) \tag{4}$$
$$\rightarrow \quad D^*(z, x) \tag{5}$$
$$\rightarrow \quad D^*(x, y) \tag{6}$$

As an illustration of how these implications are derived consider how we might show (1). We assume two individuals, Jack and Jill. By the condition of unrestricted domain, we can choose any pattern of preferences as a possible profile for the two individuals. Let us suppose the following:

$$\text{Jack:} \quad x P_{\text{Jack}} y \quad \& \quad y P_{\text{Jack}} z$$
$$\text{Jill:} \quad y P_{\text{Jill}} x \quad \& \quad y P_{\text{Jill}} z$$

Note that individual rationality will mean that Jack will prefer x to z, but that we have said nothing about how Jill ranks x and z. Suppose that Jack is made almost decisive for x against y. By that token, x will be socially preferred to y. Since *both* Jack and Jill prefer y to z, it follows by the Pareto principle that y is socially preferred to z. Thus we have xPy and yPz. By the condition of collective rationality, this implies xPz. All we know, however, are Jack's preferences between x and z. Therefore, whatever Jill's preference between x and z, the social choice will be xPz. This is equivalent to saying that Jack is decisive for x against z. (Note that Jill's stated preferences over x and y, and y and z, cannot have any influence on the ranking of x and z without violating the independence of irrelevant alternatives.) Hence $D(x, y)$ implies $D^*(x, z)$, and proposition (1) is proved.

Having established this result we can sketch how we obtain a proof of propositions (2)–(6).

For (2) assume:

$$z P_{\text{Jack}} x \quad \& \quad x P_{\text{Jack}} y$$
$$z P_{\text{Jill}} x \quad \& \quad y P_{\text{Jill}} x$$

and Jack almost decisive for x against y. By parity of reasoning with (1), $D(x, y) \rightarrow D^*(z, y)$.

For (3), transpose y and z in (2). By parity of reasoning $D(x, z) \rightarrow D^*(y, z)$. Interchange x into z, z into y and y into x in (1). By parity of reasoning with (1), $D(y, z)$ implies $D^*(y, x)$. Since we have already shown that $D(x, y) \rightarrow D^*(x, z)$, $D(x, z) \rightarrow D^*(y, z)$ and $D(y, z) \rightarrow D^*(x, y)$, it follows that $D(x, y) \rightarrow D^*(y, x)$.

For (4), (5) and (6), begin by interchanging x and y in the above results. Hence we can assume:

$$D(y, x) \rightarrow [D^*(y, z) \quad \& \quad D^*(z, x) \quad \& \quad D^*(x, y)]$$

But from (3) we know that $D(x, y) \rightarrow D(y, x)$. Hence we now know that $D(x, y) \square\!\!-\!\!\square [D^*(y, z) \& D^*(z, x) \& D^*(x, y)]$. Thus if Jack is almost decisive for any pair in a triple, he will be decisive for all pairs in that triple.

Part 2. Here we need to show that there is always a decisive individual. The strategy is to assume the opposite and to show that such an assumption leads to a contradiction.

There will always be a decisive set of individuals, since the Pareto condition shows that the set of all individuals will be decisive. In the absence of unanimity, search around for the smallest almost decisive set. Let that set comprise two people, Jack and Another. Suppose the preferences for Jack, Another and Jill are as follows:

$$\text{Jack: } xP_{jack} yP_{jack} z$$
$$\text{Another: } zP_{another} xP_{another} y$$
$$\text{Jill: } yP_{jill} zP_{jill} x$$

Jack and Another have been chosen as a decisive set, so that x must be preferred socially to y. Between y and z only Another prefers z to y, so that if z were socially preferred to y Another would be decisive. But Jack and Another have been chosen as the *smallest* decisive set, so Another alone cannot be decisive. Hence, socially, y must be at least as good as z. We now have x socially preferred to y and y at least as good as z, so by collective rationality x must be preferred to z. But Jack is the *only* individual who prefers x to z. Hence there is a contradiction in supposing that there is not a decisive individual.

APW

Bandwagon Effects

It has often been said that journalists hunt in packs, on the simple premise that a single editor can always fire a single journalist, but all editors cannot fire all journalists. If this is true, then it is an example in which the desirability of a course of action depends positively on the numbers of other people who are expected to undertake the same action. In such circumstances, bandwagons can develop.

To illustrate how bandwagons can roll, let us assume that the relationship between the percentage of people (x) who undertake an action and the percentage expected to do it (x^e) is given by $x = f(x^e)$ in figure 1. Now, consider an initial set of expectations x_1^e and assume that they evolve according to the adaptive expectations ($\boxed{?}$) hypothesis; that is, expectations

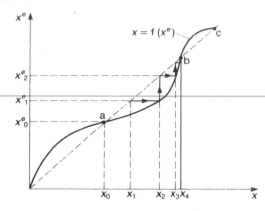

Figure 1.

adapt to experience. Initially, x_2 per cent of the population will undertake the action, which will produce a revision in expectations to x_2^e and once this happens the numbers rise to x_3 per cent, provoking a further upward revision in expectations, and so on. A bandwagon develops whereby more people want to undertake A just because more people are doing it, and so on, until point b is reached with x_4 per cent of the population doing A. At this point the bandwagon stops rolling because expectations match experience. Alternatively, had initial expectations been for compliance below x_0^e, the bandwagon would have rolled in the opposite direction. Fewer and fewer people undertake A just because fewer and fewer people are doing A; and this bandwagon only stops when nobody is left performing A.

The desirability of doing something may rise with the number of other people who are expected to do it for a variety of further reasons. First, individuals may desire the approval of the group to which they belong. They positively value their reputations in the eyes of the group and follow the group's actions to secure that reputation. Customs in traditional societies are often thought to follow this pattern. But, equally, it has been argued that contemporary social customs arise from this source. For instance, Akerlof (1980) argues that the reluctance of the unemployed to cut wages can be explained in this way. There is a social custom which prevents wage-cutting in response to unemployment, and when many abide by the custom the unemployed person does not wish to breach it for fear of a loss of reputation (an equilibrium such as b above). But, if few people are expected to follow the custom, it ceases to be a source of reputation and the unemployed person will cut wages (leading to an equilibrium such as O, at which the custom disappears).

Second, individuals may value an action when others are expected to do it simply because the action has become a coordinating device. Some conventions which arise in ANARCHIC ORDER (12) illustrate this: for instance, it pays increasingly to drive on the left when more people drive on the left.

Likewise, it pays to base your expectation on the same piece of extraneous information as others when there are multiple rational expectations equilibria (see **expectations** (⊞)). Unlike the reputations discussed by Akerlof (1980), which were intrinsically valued, compliance with what others do in these cases has no intrinsic value – it is a means to an end. Equally, it might be argued that individuals in institutions during periods of rapid political change, such as secret police and army personnel in many Eastern Europe countries during 1989–90, can have a similar instrumental attitude towards doing what others do. They may have no special allegiance to one political arrangement rather than another: their major concern is to be on the side that wins, as this will secure their position under the new regime.

Whatever the source of these bandwagon effects, they have been widely recognized in the social sciences (see Jones, 1984) and they are the source of some important insights and issues.

For instance, the presence of bandwagon effects can help explain both inertia in behaviour and rapid change. To appreciate this it should be noted that there are four equilibria (O, a, b, c), in the sense of expectations which are confirmed when acted upon (the self-confirming character of these expectations sometimes leads to the description of these as 'bootstrap' equilibria). Two are stable (O, b) and two are unstable (a, c), in the sense that small departures will either lead back or away from the original equilibrium under a scheme of adaptive expectations. The existence of unstable equilibria is useful analytically, because it provides a simple way of explaining major changes. Should a society find itself at a, then small changes in expectation will lead to dramatic changes in the proportion of the population undertaking the action: it can either rise to a clear majority at b or shrink to zero at O.

But there is more to it than this. Suppose that a society is at b, and there is a negative change in the beliefs about the intrinsic desirability of A, such that at each level of expected compliance with A, between 0 and 100 per cent, the proportion doing A falls. The function balloons out to the left, and the equilibrium proportion at each new b gradually falls. However, as soon as a position such as that depicted in figure 2 by $x = g(x^e)$ arises, under the influence of these gradual changes in belief, b ceases to be a stable equilibrium, and it only requires a small further change or a small change in expectations to produce an abrupt and dramatic move to O or to c. Likewise, one can appreciate inertia by supposing an initial equilibrium at O and allowing for positive changes in belief which shift the function to the right. There is no change in the proportion doing A, despite these changes in belief, until the change in belief has shifted the function to a position such as that given by $x = h(x^e)$ in figure 2.

More generally, the existence of multiple equilibria here, each with very different properties, raises crucial questions about the formation of expectations and the power this may give to those who can influence expectations.

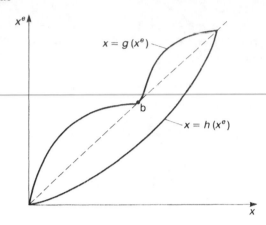

Figure 2.

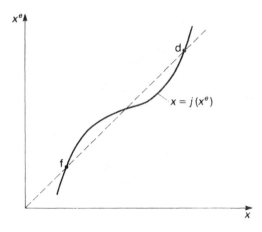

Figure 3.

To sharpen this issue, let us suppose that there is some bedrock support for two political parties (one is *A* and the other is non-*A*), such that some people would vote for *A* even if they expected nobody else to, and likewise non-*A*. In addition, there are some people who are positively affected by the prospect of being on the winning side, so that there are some bandwagon effects. The relationship between the proportion voting for *A* and the expected proportion voting for *A* might look like $x = j(x^e)$ in figure 3. There are two stable equilibria here, *d* and *f*, with very different consequences for the election of *A*. Consequently, how expectations are formed becomes crucial, as a bandwagon can roll in either direction, and considerable power will reside with those who might influence expectations.

SHH

Bayes's Rule

Bayes's rule provides a method for revising probability assessments in the light of new information. It is an extremely powerful rule of inference which, while not applicable to all situations of uncertainty, can provide some surprising insights that are neither readily nor usually appreciated.

To illustrate the rule, let us suppose that an eyewitness to a burglary at night describes the robber, somewhat stereotypically, as a black man of medium build and with height of about 5 foot 10 inches. The eyewitness has normal sight and it is well-known from tests that people correctly identify someone as black or white from that distance and in those lighting conditions on 80 per cent of occasions. Is it reasonable for the police to issue a description of the robber as black?

Naturally, the anwer to this question will depend on the criteria of reasonableness. For simplicity, we shall assume that it is 'reasonable' if there is a more than 50–50 chance that the man was black ($p(B) > 0.5$). In these circumstances, it is tempting to say that the eyewitness's observation, together with the known 80 per cent reliability, clinches reasonableness. But Bayes's rule counsels caution.

Matters are not quite so simple, because the eyewitness's observation is not the only piece of information available to the police. In fact, before the eyewitness came forward with this piece of information, and in the absence of any other information, the police would (or should) have already formed a probability assessment of the robber being black, based on the proportion of the population who are black (= 15 per cent). The question then becomes: How should this prior probability assessment be revised in the light of the new information from the eyewitness?

Bayes's rule covers such cases, and tells us that the probability of B (the burglar is black) conditional on the information A (the eyewitness report that he is black) is given by

$$P(B|A) = P(B \text{ and } A)/P(A)$$
$$= P(A|B)P(B)/[P(A|B)P(B) + P(A|W)P(W)] \qquad (1)$$

where $P(A|W)$ is the probability of A (the eyewitness report of a black robber) conditional on the person being white and $P(W)$ and $P(B)$ are the prior probabilities that he is, respectively, white or black.

Substitution of the details in this example, $P(A|B) = 0.8$ $P(B) = 0.15$, $P(A|W) = 0.2$ and $P(W) = 0.85$, into (1) yields the revised probability assessment of 0.41. In other words, relative to the probability in excess of 0.5 criteria, it is *not* reasonable for the police to issue a statement describing the robber as black.

To appreciate the origin of this result, and the rule in general, it will be helpful to consider 100 sightings of robbers drawn randomly from the population. Of these, 15 are black and, given the 80 per cent success rate of the eyewitness, 12 are identified as black and 3 are identified as white. The remaining 85 of the robbers are white and, given the 80 per cent success rate of the witness, 17 are identified as black and 68 are identified as white. Thus on 29 occasions a robber is identified as black, and in only 12 of those cases is it actually a correct identification. Hence the probability of the person being black when the eyewitness identifies the robber as black is 12/29 (= 0.41).

This is a variation on an example from Salop (1987) and one may suspect along with him that, although Thomas Bayes first developed the rule over 200 years ago, it is not always used by our legal system in the evaluation of information, eyewitness reports, and so on.

Of course, there are instances in which Bayes's rule cannot be applied. For instance, it will be apparent that it cannot be used when the prior probability assessment of some event is zero, as the expression in (1) is not defined in this case. Equally, individuals must entertain some prior probabilities if the rule is to be used, and even when an event is not ruled out (that is, zero probability) there are situations of uncertainty (see **risk and uncertainty** (⊡)) in which prior probability assessments simply cannot be made. Finally, the rule cannot be used to form predictions when the probability distribution of outcomes is not stationary.

Thus, Bayes's rule is not an all-purpose device for generating probability assessments in the light of new information. Nevertheless, the results which it can generate are sufficiently surprising to warrant a suspicion that it is yet to be used as widely as it might be.

SHH

Bentham, Jeremy (1748–1832)

Jeremy Bentham was an uncompromising advocate of the utilitarian approach to morals and legislation, and he was the founder and inspiration of the so-called 'philosophical radicals' who, in the nineteenth century, favoured the democratic reform of British government and administration (see Halévy, 1972).

Bentham himself wrote prolifically – if unsystematically – on a number of subjects, but most importantly on legal and constitutional reform. In *The Principles of Morals and Legislation* he happily admitted that the utilitarian principle was dangerous, but only for those functionaries whose sinister interests led them 'to maximize delay, vexation and expense, in judicial and other modes of procedure' (Bentham, 1789, p. 15). Bentham believed that the application of the **felicific calculus** (⊡) would lead to the greatest happiness of the greatest number. With some elements of the legacy of the philosophical radicals (for example, Victorian sanitary reform) this is almost certainly true. With other elements (for example, the 1834 Poor Law) the case is more doubtful, as Charles Dickens, among others, subsequently demonstrated.

APW

Borda, Jean-Charles de (1733–1799)

In a paper delivered to the French Academy of Sciences in 1770, Borda was the first person to develop a mathematical theory of elections. He argued that single-vote elections, giving success to the candidate gaining the most first-choice votes, will often lead to the wrong decision if there are more than two candidates. For example, eight electors may place A first, seven think B best and six vote for C; therefore A would be elected irrespective of the fact that 13 of the 21 electors might prefer either B or C to A. Borda proposed the method of marks as a better electoral system. Each elector ranks the n candidates in order; then, in the absence of information on the strength of preferences, each first place vote is worth n marks, a second place is given $n - 1$ marks, and so on. The candidate with the most marks wins. Borda showed that this simple system will give exactly the same result as if marks are allocated according to votes in a comprehensive system of pairwise ballots (for example, A against B, B against C, and A against C). He appreciated the danger of strategic voting, with electors disguising their second preferences by placing strong rivals to their favourite at the bottom of their list; but his response was that 'my scheme is only intended for honest men'. The method of marks was adopted by the French Academy of Sciences from 1784 until 1800, when Napoleon Bonaparte objected to the system and it was changed.

BRL

Carroll, Lewis [Charles Lutwidge Dodgson] (1832–1898)

Charles Dodgson was an Oxford mathematician, now best known for *Alice's Adventures in Wonderland* (1865) and *Through the Looking Glass and What Alice Found There* (1872), which he wrote under the name of Lewis Carroll. His inclusion here, however, is for his prescient thoughts on voting systems, committee procedures and political representation. His 1884 treatment of electoral strategies is game-theoretic in spirit and offers shrewd ideas on proportional representation. For discussion, see Black (1958) and Sugden (1983).

MH

Cognitive Dissonance

It is easy to imagine a politician telling an aide, 'go ahead, do it, just don't tell me about it': or, to echo Richard Nixon's phrase from the Watergate tapes, the politician might be saying 'I don't want to know the details'. There need be nothing puzzling about the command. It could be that details threaten an information overload, and the procedurally rational politician does not want to hear them when a broad understanding of the matter will suffice. However, Festinger's (1957) cognitive dissonance theory alerts us to another interpretation.

Suppose that the imaginary politician does not want to know about the specific illegal acts which are to be performed by the intelligence services to shore up democracy somewhere. There is an uncomfortable tension between the illegality of the acts and the worthy objective which they serve; and perhaps 'not knowing the details' somehow helps to lessen this tension for the politician.

> Basically, cognitive dissonance is a state of tension that occurs whenever an individual simultaneously holds two cognitions (ideas, attitudes, beliefs, opinions) that are psychologically inconsistent . . . Because the occurrence of cognitive dissonance is unpleasant, people are motivated to reduce it . . .
>
> (Aronson, 1988, pp. 116–17).

It is, in Aronson's words, a 'remarkably simple theory', yet it has generated important predictions regarding human behaviour which have been extensively tested.

In economics it has been used by Akerlof and Dickens (1982) to explain why there might be sub-optimal use of protective equipment in hazardous industries. Workers in such industries find that the belief that they are sensible and rational conflicts with the belief that the industry is hazardous, and so the dissonance is removed by filtering out the evidence on hazards. With a reduced perception of the risks, the workers do not make full use of new safety equipment when it becomes available.

In psychology two general strategies for reducing dissonance have been distinguished, one internal and the other external. 'Not knowing the details' is an example of an internal strategy, because the individual takes an action to reduce the dissonance. Typical of such actions are those directed at selectively acquiring information which will confirm existing beliefs or previous decisions. Thus, for instance, it has been found that purchasers of new cars (once they have made a purchase) tend, like Akerlof's workers, to steer clear of advertisements for other makes of cars. In a similar fashion, it has been found that beliefs tend to change so as to reinforce the correctness or worthiness of a previous decision. For example, in experiments which are designed to elicit cheating it has been found that individuals who do not cheat tend to develop very hostile attitudes towards cheating afterwards, while those who do cheat become quite tolerant of cheating.

The second strategy broadly involves searching for an external explanation of the tension. If there is something in the decision setting which seemed to force action that caused the dissonance, then the dissonance can be reduced by blaming the situation. For instance, in the cheating experiment, a person paid a lot of money to cheat is less likely to need to find an internal reason for their action (in the form of a tolerant shift in attitudes towards cheating) than someone who cheats when paid a little because the large sum of money provides an external reason for the behaviour.

Typically, the experimental literature has found that individuals will only use an internal mechanism for reducing dissonance when external reasons are weak or unavailable, and this has potentially important implications. For instance, consider how this insight qualifies the so-called economic (rational choice) approach to crime (see □). Cognitive dissonance theory suggests that when individuals find themselves upholding the law 'without really thinking about it' and the punishments are mild, then they are more likely to develop internal reasons for obeying the law than when punishments are large, because large punishments supply an external reason for law-abiding behaviour. Consequently, the economists' rational choice proposal to fight crime by increasing punishments, while deterring crime, may not be the most effective means of crime reduction. Given the costs of law enforcement, a more effective way of fighting crime could be through encouraging internal reasons, self-motivation for obeying the law. Yet, it is exactly the growth of this motivation that cognitive dissonance theory suggests will be undercut by the introduction of significant external reasons for obeying the law in the form of harsher punishments.

COUNTING THE COST OF CRIME

Most economists who give serious thought to the problem of crime immediately come to the conclusion that punishment will indeed deter crime. The reason is perfectly simple . . . If you increase the cost of something, less will be consumed. Thus, if you increase the cost of committing a crime, there will be fewer crimes

(Tullock, 1974, pp. 104–5)

Likewise, Peters and Waterman's (1982) discussion of the reward systems of successful corporations in the management literature seems to turn on a similar line of reasoning (see □). The illustrations can quickly multiply. Nevertheless, there may be something puzzling about the way in which individuals are more rationalizing than rational in this theory. Individuals wish to maintain a good image of themselves, and doubts over self-image (experienced as dissonances) must be removed; yet such dissonance-removing actions seem likely to require a measure of self-deception on occasion for their success. Consider our imaginary politician: to know that you do not want to know the details seems to require a knowledge of the likely details – otherwise why would you want to suppress them? However, if you know the likely details, how can it help to suppress them unless you conveniently forget why you did not want to know about them in the first place? Self-deception of this sort may seem strange at first, but on reflection it is likely to have a familiar ring. After all, who is not acquainted with the bias of 'listening only to what he or she wants to hear'?

SHH

SUCCESSFUL REWARDS

.In fact, if our understanding of the current state of psychology is even close to correct, man is the ultimate study in conflict and paradox. . . .

Now, how do most companies deal with these conflicts? They take great pride in setting really high targets for people . . . These are perfectly rational but ultimately self-defeating. Why do TI and Tupperware, by contrast, insist that teams set low objectives? Why does IBM set quotas so that almost all salespeople can make them?

The answer is surprisingly simple. . . . We all think we're tops. Yet most organizations, we find, take a negative view of their people . . . With their rationalist hat on, they design systems that seem calculated to tear down the workers' self-image . . . The lesson that the excellent companies have to teach us is that . . . their people by and large make their targets and quotas, because the targets are set (often by the people themselves) to allow that to happen. . . .

People tune out if they feel they are failing, because 'the system' is to blame. They tune in when the system leads them to believe they are successful . . .

(Peters and Waterman, 1982, pp. 55–8)

Condorcet Winner

The notion of a Condorcet winner is derived from the work of the Marquis de Condorcet (1743–94) on the theory of voting. A mathematician, philosopher and social scientist, Condorcet's thought was part of that intellectual movement of enlightenment that paved the way for the French Revolution (compare Black, 1958, p. 159). Although a revolutionary, his independence of mind led to his falling foul of the Committee of Public Safety and he took poison on 28 March 1794 after he had been imprisoned.

The Condorcet winner refers to an element in a choice set (candidates, policies, motions, and so on), and is defined as the alternative that can beat all others when taken in a series of pairwise majority votes. In a situation in which there are only two alternatives, the Condorcet winner is simply the alternative preferred by the majority. When there are more than two alternatives, the Condorcet winner is that alternative capable of securing a majority against every other alternative when taken in a pairwise vote. An example is provided by table 1. As table 1 shows, the Condorcet winner may not be the most preferred alternative for a majority, but it must be sufficiently high in individual preference orderings to beat each other alternative.

Table 1 Possible preference profile for three individuals and three alternatives (left), together with votes cast for alternative in row against alternative in column (right). y is revealed as the Condorcet winner, since it is the only alternative to have a majority at each place in its row.

			x	y	z
A:	$x > y > z$	x	—	1	2
B:	$y > x > z$	y	2	—	2
C:	$z > y > x$	z	1	1	—

Many people feel that if a Condorcet winner exists a voting system should select it, on the grounds that it represents a reasonable point of compromise within an otherwise divided electorate. Yet, frequently, real-world electoral systems, for example the first-past-the-post system of parliamentary elections in the UK, fail the test of selecting a Condorcet winner. Moreover, it is easy to find preference profiles in which there is no Condorcet winner to be identified, of which the most famous is the profile discovered by Condorcet himself (table 2). The failure to identify a Condorcet winner leads straight to the heart of problems of SOCIAL CHOICE (13).

Table 2 Condorcet's preferencee profile for three individuals and three alternatives (left), together with votes cast for alternative in row against alternative in column (right). There is no Condorcet winner, since no one alternative secures a majority at each place in the row, and so there is a Condorcet cycle.

			x	y	z
A:	$x > y > z$	x	—	2	1
B:	$y > z > x$	y	1	—	2
C:	$z > x > y$	z	2	1	—

APW

Core

The core is a game-theoretic equilibrium that has been described as 'an uncensored account of frankly rapacious . . . behaviour' (Bacharach, 1976, p. 119). It builds on the idea that decision-makers, or players, will form any coalition that they can in order to achieve the best outcome for themselves. Coalitions may be with any number of players, including the single-membered coalition of themselves alone, and the grand coalition of all players. The image is of players exhaustively contemplating proposals and counter-proposals until no preferred alliance can be found. Once a stable set of coalitions has been found, players within each coalition cooperatively implement their agreed strategies.

However, the core combines this very positive attitude with an extremely pessimistic view of how players outside the coalition will behave. Each conceivable coalition calculates the maximum damage that those outside could feasibly do to its members. The utility pay-off to this worst-case scenario is known as the coalition's security level (see GAME THEORY (7) for the non-cooperative equivalent). Suppose that the players are contemplating a set of coalitions, and associated strategies, that would give any one or any group less than their security levels should they form an alternative coalition. Then the supposed set of coalitions is said to be blocked, or dominated, because the alternative coalition would not agree to it. No group can be forced below its security level. Finally, the core is defined as the set of utility allocations that are not blocked (or dominated). Note that since the grand coalition of all the players is always one alternative, the core must be Pareto optimal (see **Pareto optimality** (⏍) (although not all Pareto optimal allocations need be in the core). In fact, core allocations will often involve formation of the grand coalition, although individual allocations within the grand coalition still crucially depend on the ability to block by forming a smaller alternative coalition.

An example may serve to illustrate why the core is categorized by game theorists as a cooperative concept, despite the unscrupulous wheeling and dealing that motivates it. Change the rules of the Prisoner's Dilemma (□ p. 99) to allow for coalition formation. Since this is a two-person game the only coalitions of interest are the two single-membered coalitions and the grand coalition of both players. Acting alone, given that the non-member does his worst for you, the security level is the result of both confessing 0.1; while, acting together, they can each guarantee themselves 0.9 by not confessing. Thus, the single-membered 'coalitions' are blocked by the grand coalition, which is not dominated and which forms the core. Note that this does not mean that there is no need to worry about non-cooperation in the Prisoner's Dilemma. Not confessing remains a compelling result as long as the constraints and institutions in which the game is embedded mean that coalitions are unable to implement binding agreements or strategies. For the core to be an appropriate concept, each coalition's agreed actions must be implementable without dissembling. In fact, the core of two-person games is rather trivial, and the concept only becomes really interesting when there are more players. However, this introduces new problems. First, as the number of players increases, the number of coalitions to contemplate increases very much more rapidly, so that the informational requirements for calculating all the options become huge. Second, the costs of agreeing and maintaining a coalition may well be large relative to the gains, in which case non-cooperative behaviour becomes more likely.

An important application of the core is in the analysis of exchange economies. Suppose that there are n traders with initial endowments of m commodities, and they each engage in a search for partners with whom to exchange products in order to best satisfy their personal tastes. The core defines the set of equilibrium negotiated outcomes. In general, there will be more than one core solution, as a range of feasible allocations will not be blocked. Interestingly, it can be shown that one of these allocations must be exactly the perfectly competitive equilibrium that results from price-taking behaviour. Thus, the core forges a strong link between barter and market economies. This bridge was first developed by **Edgeworth** ($\square$), who also conjectured (quite correctly) that as the number of traders becomes very large, the core will shrink until it converges on the competitive equilibrium. The latter is a very striking result because the core permits monopolistic coalitions to form: but this implication is that such coalitions will be blocked as long as the economy is sufficiently large.

The above example provides a core with many possible equilibria, at least in small economies. However, there are other interesting cases in which the core is empty, which is to say that there is *no* allocation which is not blocked. This typically arises when the grand coalition fails to add much more value than can be shared between members of a smaller coalition. A classic example of an empty core is given by Sharing a Shilling. It takes its name from the old English shilling, which could be divided into 12 old pence. The shilling can only be shared out if a majority out of the three players (A, B and C) can agree to a division of the money. Consider equal shares of 4 pence each. This seems equitable, but A and B could better (or block) this by agreeing to 6 pence each. But this is still not a core solution because C can offer, say, A 7 pence and herself 5 pence. Now this can be blocked by B offering equal shares with A, and so on. No division cannot be blocked by some coalition, so the core is empty (see Bacharach, 1976, p. 128, for a formal analysis). Riker (1962) argues that political processes can often be captured in a similar way; for example, when winning an election is a prize of fixed value to be shared between all those who supported the victorious candidate. Clearly, it is advantageous to form a coalition of minimum winning size so that participating members obtain the largest possible share of the gains. The insight of core theory is that potentially winning coalitions in such circumstances are inherently unstable, as those outside can offer to replace some participating member, while accepting a smaller share of the gains for themselves and giving more to continuing participants. Generalizing to a prize of victory that is more valuable to some coalitions than others, the core says which particular coalitions are stable.

BRL

Determinism

Determinism is usually stated as the thesis that every event has a cause. What does this mean and imply? According to a very strong interpretation, it means that whatever happens was necessitated by what went before, and could not have happened otherwise. There are no random elements and, it seems, no human free will. In a famous example of a strong determinism, **Marx** (⌘) makes the causes of human actions basically economic and social (see □).

THE REAL FOUNDATION OF SOCIETY

In the social production which men carry on they enter into definite relations that are indispensable and independent of their will; these relations of production correspond to a definite stage of development of their material powers of production. The sum total of these relations of production constitutes the economic structure of society – the real foundation, on which rise legal and political superstructures and to which correspond definite forms of social consciousness. . . . It is not the consciousness of men that determines their existence, but, on the contrary, their social existence determines their consciousness.

(Marx, 1859, Preface)

This interpretation may seem far too strong. According to **Hume** (⌘), causes do not necessitate their effects. Causal laws are only correlations or patterns which we have come to notice and rely on. In that case determinism means only that every event is predictable, given its conditions and a suitable covering law or pattern. That human actions are predictable is no threat to free will. Free actions are caused by the agent's desires and information, whereas non-free actions are caused by other factors, with consequences contrary to the agent's desires. In this context, 'caused' means only 'predictable on the basis of'. Freedom is not only compatible with determinism but, indeed, presupposes it, since free agents need a predictable world, so that they can satisfy desires, which proceed predictably from their own character (Hume, 1748; Mill, 1843; Ayer, 1954).

The strength of this school of thought, which is known as 'compatibilism', lies in its insistence that what is not caused can only be random, and that randomness is no help to free will. There is no comfort to be had from invoking the Heisenberg Uncertainty Principle in physics, or in the economists' distinction between 'deterministic' (fully predictable) and 'non-deterministic' (probablistic, or stochastic, and so not fully predictable) processes. Action is only as free as its consequences are predictable. Free actions are, as said, explicable, not mysteriously random.

Compatabilism equates free action with rational action. It implies that a free action is one where the agent *would have* acted differently in the circumstances, if his desires had been different. Critics, such as Austin (1961) object that freedom requires that the agent *could have* acted differently in the same circumstances. This may seem merely to reintroduce a random element. One can go on to argue, however, that an agent's reasons do not function as causes, without thereby becoming random. Perhaps the most interesting version of this line is in Wittgenstein (1953), where rational agents are thought of as followers of rules. If human experience is textured by rules, which are human handiwork, then action needs to be understood in terms of the agent's understanding of it. Understanding of the social world contrasts with explanation of the natural world, in ways forcefully expressed by Winch (1958).

Here lies disputed territory. Meanwhile, the standard notion of rational choice does seem to make the agent a mere throughput between the conditions which have shaped his preferences (and information) and the behaviour which his internal computer has determined upon. And so there is no quick way to dispose of the old dispute between free will and determinism.

MH

Edgeworth, Francis Ysidro (1845–1926)

Born to an Irish father and Catalan mother, Edgeworth was educated at Trinity College, Dublin and Oxford. He later studied mathematics and law, and was called to the Bar in 1877. He became Drummond Professor of Political Economy at Oxford in 1890 and Editor of *The Economic Journal* from that year until 1911, when Keynes took over. His most important book was *Mathematical Psychics* (1881). Apart from defending mathematical analysis in economics and contributing to the theory of utilitarianism, the book's major contribution was in developing the theory of exchange, focusing on incentives to make and break contracts and form coalitions. These advances were little understood at the time and it is only since 1959, when Shubik linked Edgeworth to modern game theory (see **core** ([🛐])), that the greatness of his contribution has been fully appreciated.

BRL

Envy

Sometimes, when you are eating in a restaurant with someone, the other person's meal turns out to be more attractive to you than the meal you have ordered. This is an occasion for envy. Envy is a propositional attitude, a mental act that we understand by reference to the proposition that it takes as its object. Thus, if you think how fortunate the other person has been and you wish that you had been as fortunate, this is a case of benign envy. Your envy amounts to a desire that you might have enjoyed such good fortune. If, on the other hand, your desire is that neither of you should enjoy the meal because you have been unfortunate, we have a case of malign envy; a desire that someone else is brought down because your situation is not as good as theirs.

It is often claimed that sentiments of envy should be excluded from processes of social choice. Thus, Rawls (1971, pp. 530–41) assumes that there is no envy motivating the parties in the original position (see SOCIAL JUSTICE (18)), and he argues that his theory of justice, if implemented, would diminish the occasion of envy in practice. Similarly, Dworkin (1977, pp. 234–38) seeks to exclude what he terms 'external preferences' from social choice procedures, external preferences being preferences that one person has about how others should live their lives. According to Dworkin's view, social choice procedures satisfying principles of right would prohibit the counting of external preferences, including those based upon envy. Dworkin's case for excluding such preferences amounts to the claim that to include them involves a form of double counting, since the person with external preferences is asking both for his or her preferences to be counted and for those preferences to count in respect of someone else. One difficulty with this argument is that it would seem to lead to an exclusion of altruistic external preferences in social choice procedures, which many find counter-intuitive (Weale, 1983, pp. 38–41).

A more contentious claim is that some principles of social choice are motivated by malign envy. For example, Nozick (1974, p. 240) says that egalitarianism is due to envy. This view ignores the distinction between envy and resentment. The latter, as Bishop Butler (1726, pp. 125–6) pointed out, depends upon a moral assessment, and we may properly ask whether the resentment is groundless or is motivated by a justifiable sense of inequality. What may appear to be envy could simply be justifiable resentment, grounded in a moral evaluation.

If the elimination of justified resentment is a proper ground of public policy, then the connection with envy requires analysis. Nagel (1973, p. 231) has argued against Rawls's difference principle, urging that a consistent schedule of unequal rewards inevitably affects people's sense of their intrinsic worth. Thus, income inequality may undermine self-respect. Detaching the notion of envy from that of resentment has implications, therefore, for the theory of SOCIAL JUSTICE (18) and our account of **fairness** ([?]).

APW

Equilibrium

An equilibrium exists if no decision-maker has any incentive to deviate from her current plans, and if those plans are feasible (see **feasible set** ([?]). Inasmuch as current actions affect future possibilities, people have to form expectations; and if decisions can be revised over time, expectations must be correct for an intertemporal equilibrium to exist. Partial equilibrium refers to a single market in isolation. **General equilibrium** ([?]) refers to a whole economy of interrelated markets, including both sales and purchases by each economic agent. Competitive equilibrium is a special case in which there are sufficiently large numbers of buyers and sellers such that each can treat prices as independent of her own actions.

In recent years an enormous number of refinements have been made to the concept of equilibrium, in two important areas. The notion of intertemporal equilibrium in a world which allows stochastic shocks has been developed largely in the macroeconomic policy literature. This is discussed in rational **expectations** ([?]). Microeconomics, particularly oligopoly theory, has been the main springboard for developments in the notion of Nash equilibrium, in which a small number of cunning, strategic decision-makers must anticipate the strategies of rivals (see GAME THEORY (7)). Nash equilibrium is appropriate in a non-cooperative world in which decision-makers act independently. If coalitions are feasible, then another equilibrium concept is necessary, one of the best developed being the **core** ([?]).

Three key questions are posed in equilibrium analysis.

1 Existence: given tastes, technologies and feasible strategies, does an equilibrium exist? For example, work by Arrow, Debreu and others in the 1950s showed very precisely the conditions (such as non-increasing returns to scale) required for the existence of a general competitive equilibrium.

2 Uniqueness: is there more than one possible equilibrium? For example, equilibrium in a particular labour market may obtain either with low wages and many hours of labour both demanded and supplied, or with high wages and few hours of labour both demanded and supplied (as workers prefer more leisure once they have obtained a sufficiently high income).

3 Stability: suppose that the economy begins from a position of disequilibrium. Will decision-makers take actions that lead the system back towards equilibrium? The most famous example of stability analysis is cobweb theory in a competitive market, in which supply decisions are based entirely on last period's price and demand decisions on current price only; stability then depends on the relative slopes of the supply and demand curves.

It is sometimes argued that the real world is in such a state of flux that equilibrium analysis can tell us nothing about actual economies. This view is particularly strongly held by the Austrian school (see RISK, IGNORANCE AND IMAGINATION (4)). However, although few economists would be so bold as to argue that the world is always in equilibrium, most do hold the view that the world has a strong tendency towards equilibrium. If a unique equilibrium exists, we can investigate how that equilibrium changes in response to altered exogenous or policy variables (such as population growth or taxation). This methodology is known as comparative statics, and is fundamental to much applied economic theory. If there are multiple equilibria then this too can have strong policy implications, such as the possibility of moving from a high-unemployment to a low-unemployment equilibrium. Stability analysis has been a poor relation, partly because it requires quite separate assumptions to add on to basic equilibrium analysis. Samuelson's correspondence principle developed in the 1940s forged an important link with comparative statics, and modern chaos theory holds out promise, but in the intervening years there have been many disappointed hopes.

BRL

Ethical Preferences

When the boycott of South African goods in protest against Apartheid was at its height, economists were often asked why it was working. Why were some people refusing to buy South African oranges, even when they were cheaper and juicier than their rivals. One explanation was that agents can have 'ethical preferences', which make sense of otherwise irrational behaviour. For the opponent of Apartheid, the source of oranges affected their utility. This seems at first to be a simple extension of the idea that the given preferences of a rational agent may stem from any set of what are, ultimately, tastes, provided only that they are consistent. Being South African is as much a quality of an orange as being juicy and – for some consumers – a distasteful quality which they prefer to avoid.

Similarly, electors may rationally turn out to vote, even though cost–benefit calculations should apparently have kept them at home, if they have an ethical preference for being a good citizen; and they may rationally vote against their apparent interests, if they prefer a socially just society. Within the purely economic realm too, one can invoke an ethical preference for honesty to account for people who keep bargains, even when they could have defected. Indeed, it may be hard to explain the lack of free riders otherwise.

Yet this extension of the basic model of rational choice is not so simple. Notice first the strain put on the notion of utility. An agent who prefers a fifth apple to a fourth pear can be held to have tastes which are given, need no reason, are known introspectively and mean that the fifth apple has the greater utility. But what is the common measure when the juiciness of the orange is outweighed by its South African origin? One might reply that it is the psychological strength of the agent's approval or disapproval. But this moral psychology, for all its crudity, would be purely speculative as a theory of what motivates agents who make moral choices. For an agent who can compare anything with anything, utility is no longer a measure. Talk of greater utility becomes simply a way of reporting the bald fact that one thing is preferred to another.

Even if motivation always relates to desires (which is disputable), an obvious point about ethical preferences is that they involve concepts which supply reasons for choice. That an orange is South African is no motive in itself, without the aid of a belief that, for instance, Apartheid violates human rights (and can be undermined by a boycott). On the other hand, such morally charged beliefs do not motivate automatically. People can condemn Apartheid and still buy South African oranges, on grounds which range from other moral beliefs, through unconcern, to the size of the price differential or weakness of will. Hence the moral psychology needed to accommodate ethical preferences is more complex than that of weighing satisfactions in the scale of tastes.

Current thinking favours the idea of a two-tier preference structure, whose first tier ranks the consequences of actions by the subjective value of the goods obtained, and whose second tier ranks these preferences by the test of whether or not the agent is content with them. This gives scope for the familiar tension between what one wants to do and what one thinks right, with an ideally rational agent not choosing according to his first-order preferences unless they are also those which he prefers to have. Ethical preferences are then plausibly regarded as operating on the upper tier as constraints. In a related fashion, when a rational bargainer commits himself to an action which deliberately removes the temptation to compromise by – so to speak – burning his boats, a similar two-tier structure can make it rational to be seemingly irrational.

However puzzles remain. Since people can and do override their ethical preferences, there is some mental process that is not yet accounted for. Nor is it always plainly rational or right to prefer the ethical preference. A guilt-ridden homosexual, for instance, might be wise to override the feelings of guilt. A censorious parent might do better to act lovingly. Yet, whereas it is easy to discover the sense in which it can be rational to burn one's boats, because of long-term gain in utility, it is hard to see why second-tier ethical preferences have any special claim. Nothing in this discussion shows why it is rational to reject South African oranges, just because one's reasons are ethical. However, that is a sign only that further thought is needed.

MH

Expectations

Many actions are forward-looking and depend on expectations about the future. When a business executive is deciding whether to invest in new equipment, she or he must form an expectation of the future level of demand for what will be produced by the equipment. Likewise, the politician who is deciding when to call an election must form an expectation about the likely popularity of his or her party at different future dates. Should you buy your foreign exchange today or wait until nearer to your holiday? Examples proliferate and they beg an important question about how expectations are or should be formed about future events.

One simple rule is to be 'adaptive'. Under this rule, the expectation is revised or adapted in light of previous errors in expectation. Thus, suppose that you are interested in forming an expectation about the rate of inflation (P) next year. You will adjust your expectation from what you held last year depending on how well it fared: if you overestimated last year then you will revise your expectation downwards; and, conversely, you will revise it upwards when last year's proves to be an underestimate. This idea is captured in equation (1), where λ is the coefficient of adaption or error correction, the subscript refers to the time period of the variable in question, and the superscript e refers to the expectation of the variable:

$$P^e_{t+1} = P^e_t + \lambda (P_t - P^e_t) \tag{1}$$

At first sight this seems a plausible and broadly rational scheme to use because you learn from previous mistakes. However, it does have a peculiar property which has led some critics to deny that expectations formed in this

way are rational. Suppose that you have been anticipating the rate of inflation and then there is a sudden rise in the rate. Under the adapative scheme,
the gap between expectations and experience closes by the same proportion,
λ, in each subsequent period. Thus, in general, when λ is less than one, inflationary expectations will only gradually be adjusted towards the new level
of inflation; and during this period of revision your expectation always lies
below the actual rate of inflation. The expectation is wrong: this is not just
a white-noise error, where you sometimes get it wrong in one direction and
sometimes in the other, with no temporal pattern to these errors. Instead,
the errors exhibit a systematic pattern: you always err on the side of
underestimation.

According to the 'rational expectations' hypothesis, your expectations
should not suffer from systematic errors: there should only be white-noise
errors. The reason is simple. You ought to be able to learn about the
systematic component of your errors, and there is every incentive to do so
since you will profit by removing them. If you are making a systematic error,
then information is potentially available which you could profitably use to
avoid making this sort of error. Hence, it is the instrumentally rational
agent's 'eye for the main chance' that comes together with the opportunity
for profit, when errors are systematic, to produce the white-noise-only
rational expectations hypothesis.

This hypothesis, although not exactly in this form, is usually first credited
to Muth (1961). It constitutes a tempting line of argument, but it is not
without its own problems. You may wish to avoid systematic errors, but it
is not easy to act on this in the social world. It is not just a question of allowing time to elapse and new information to be processed with the aid of
Bayes's rule (⧆), as it might be for someone forming expectations about
the landscape as the fog disappears. The objects of expectations in the social
world are frequently not independent of the expectations that we entertain
about them, and this greatly complicates the matter of forming rational
expectations because it means that what we are trying to form an expectation
about does not have a stationary probability distribution.

Two principal problems can be noted, and they combine to suggest that
this account of expectation formation will remain incomplete unless it is
supplemented by other rules of expectation formation and with them other
senses of rational action (see RATIONALITY (1)).

The first relates to the learning process itself. GAME THEORY (7) looks like
a promising area in which to search for insights into the learning process,
because the pay-off to an individual of holding one set of expectations
depends on actual outcomes, and these outcomes depend on the expectations
of others. Furthermore, game theory works with the same instrumental
conception of rational action which underpins the rational expectations
hypothesis. However, when game theory suggests that a Nash equilibrium

will obtain, it offers little help in the matter of learning, because the Nash equilibria in such games are rational expectations equilibria (see Frydman and Phelps, 1983).

Thus, game theory merely points us to situations in which no learning is required! Formally, what is required for insights into the learning process is an analysis of out-of-equilibrium behaviour, which has proved a controversial area in game theory, not least because – by definition – it involves agents behaving in ways which are not rational in the normal instrumental game-theoretic sense (otherwise there would be a Nash equilibrium), and there is little agreement over how to characterize these other sorts of behaviour.

Second, there are a variety of social settings in which the dependence of outcomes on expectations yields multiple rational expectations equilibria (see Hahn, 1980): that is to say, there are many expectations which, if widely held, would reproduce themselves but for white-noise errors. From the perspective of the instrumentally rational agent who is only empowered to hold rational expectations, this corresponds to a situation of uncertainty (see **risk and uncertainty** (⧉)) as there will be no good reason for preferring one potential rational expectation from another. This poses a difficulty for the hypothesis since some explanation is required of how one equilibrium is selected by agents; and, by definition, this will have to involve something in addition to the rational expectations hypothesis.

In these circumstances, it is tempting to revive the adaptive expectations hypothesis and cast it not as competitor but as a potential complement to the rational expectations hypothesis. It might, for instance, be appropriate in some out-of-equilibrium settings and thus help to explain both the learning side of expectation formation and, with it, the selection of equilibrium when there are multiple rational expectations equilibria.

Adaptive expectations may seem plausible in this context, but some care is required. What will matter in cases in which there are multiple rational expectations equilibria is not so much the formal content of the supplementary rule (how 'reasonable' it seems in the abstract), as the fact that it is shared by others. In particular, in cases in which there is a continuum of rational expectations equilibria for example, *any* price could be a rational expectation), then any rule for forming expectations will yield a rational expectation provided that it is shared by others, and it is of no significance how plausible it appears in the abstract (see **bandwagon effects** (⧉)). A continuum of rational expectations equilibria may seem extreme (although see Azariadis, 1981 on this), but they do help to remind us that the adapative and rational expectations hypothesis do not, between them, exhaust all the possibilities for the formation of expectations.

SHH

Expected Value

An expected value is the probability weighted average of the values of all possible, mutually exclusive events. For example, in a raffle with 1000 tickets sold, a first prize of £100 and six second prizes of £10 each, the expected money value of each ticket is $0.001(£100) + 0.006 (£10) + 0.993(£0) = £0.16$. Another example is given by the expected number of heads when two unbiased coins are tossed (see **probability distribution** (📖)), which is $0.25(2) + 0.5(1) + 0.25(0) = 1$. Notice from the first example that the expected value need not be an outcome that could actually occur.

BRL

Exploitation

The most famous – or infamous – theory of economic exploitation is due to Marx, and it arose from conjoining two observations that seemed innocent taken separately, but puzzling taken together. Marx shared the first observation with classical political economy. The classical political economists were struck by the seeming paradox that use value and exchange value were not positively correlated: diamonds, which are of limited use value have a high exchange value; whereas water, which is of high use value, has only a low exchange value. The solution to the paradox, according to classical political economy, is that exchange value is given by the quantity of labour embodied in an object. The second observation was that in a capitalist economy commodities exchanged at equivalent value, meaning that on average commodities could only exchange if they had the same quantity of labour embodied in them. How then can any surplus value can be created? No-one in a market economy can systematically get away with exchanging commodities at anything less than their prevalent exchange value, and these are equivalents. And yet there is such a thing as surplus value, according to Marx, in the form of capitalist profit.

The answer that Marx (1867, p. 270) gives is that the capitalist wage contract enables the capitalist to command a use value that is itself the source of exchange value, namely labour power. The quantity of labour embodied in a worker, considered as a commodity on the labour market, is the amount of labour necessary to reproduce the worker for future production. This is the exchange value that workers can command in the labour market. But the use to which workers can be put is that of producing exchange values, and in a typical working day the labourers will produce greater exchange value than they receive in wages. They will produce enough in exchange value to meet their subsistence needs in, say, five hours, but the labour contract will specify that they work for eight hours and the exchange value created in the extra three hours is appropriated by the capitalist. The appropriation of this surplus is the essence of exploitation, according to Marx, and the rate at which it occurs yields the rate of exploitation.

The classical marxist view contains a number of in-built problems, the most serious of which relate to variations of skill; that is, variations in the quality of labour. Marx was aware of variations in skill and recognized that not all workers were equally efficient. He inferred from this that exchange value was determined by the 'socially necessary' labour power embodied in a commodity, but it is difficult to identify the value of socially necessary labour power without resorting, in a circular way, to prices in the economy. Even if this problem can be solved, there is the problem of accounting for variations in the quality of labour (Elster, 1985, pp 129–31). Marx was tempted to think that such variations could be explained as a mixture of unskilled labour plus education, but this ignores variations in skill that are not produced through the educational system.

The most plausible alternative accounts of exploitation have an explicitly normative principle of distribution built into them. This applies, for example, to Roemer's (1982) game-theoretic treatment of the subject. This is built around the notion of a game which players may or may not find it advantageous to play. Exploitation exists if players are required to play a game, under specified conditions, although they would be better off not participating. Thus, feudal exploitation exists if workers would be better off in a system in which they controlled their own labour power rather than had it controlled by feudal relations of production, and capitalist exploitation exists if workers would be better off in an economy in which they had control of their *per capita* share of productive capital.

This definition of exploitation within a capitalist economy raises two noteworthy points. First, although clearly written in a marxist tradition, it comes close to Ackerman's (1980) explicitly liberal treatment of the subject, in which there is a significant burden of proof upon anyone who wishes to justify an unequal allocation of economic resources, and in which exploitation is therefore the product of the exercise of power to maintain a discursively unjustifiable allocation. Second, the appeal to a per capita share raises unavoidably normative questions. Why should an equal share be taken as the bench mark? This clearly raises questions of SOCIAL JUSTICE (18). Interpreters of Marx have disputed whether Marx thought exploitation unjust (see Geras, 1986, pp. 3–57), but it should be clear that any theory of exploitation which avoids the fallacies contained in the labour theory of value must appeal at some point to a theory of justice.

APW

Extended Sympathy

Putting yourself in the shoes of another is a common piece of moral phenomenology. It is sometimes claimed, however, that it can form an important element in the theory of social choice by means of the idea of extended sympathy, defined by Arrow (1963a, p. 114) as a willingness to make comparisons of the form 'state *x* is better (or worse) for me than state *y* is for you'. This approach might be especially attractive for someone sceptical of the idea of **interpersonal comparisons of utility** (⊞), but who nevertheless wished to go beyond the Pareto principle in matters of social choice in order to make judgements on the relative merits of social alternatives based upon the distribution of income. Judgements of extended sympathy would supposedly enable the affluent to say that it is better for the poor to have an increase in marginal income than themselves, without dependence upon putatively meaningless propositions about interpersonal comparisons of utility.

Despite the appeal of the idea, there are considerable problems in its use, all of which are connected with the question of how a judgement of extended sympathy might be justified. How could an individual validly claim that state *x* was better (or worse) for herself than state *y* for another? One crucial issue here is whether the description of the alternative social states includes an account of the personal characteristics of the individuals, or whether it merely includes a specification of role situations. If the latter, it is clear that extended sympathy judgements are limited in scope: they simply mean that you find *x* better for you, with your personal characteristics, than you would find state *y* with the same personal characteristics. This is clearly a meaningful comparison, but it has nothing to say about social choices in which the relative advantages of two separate individuals is to be determined. If, however, in making an extended sympathy judgement you are supposed to imagine yourself taking on the personal characteristics of another, then it is difficult to see how it differs from an interpersonal comparison of utility, or from the fantasies of those who imagine that they are Napoleon or the King of China (compare Williams, 1973, pp. 42–3).

To highlight the nature of these epistemological difficulties, let us imagine that sympathy functions in the way **Hume** (⊞) thought it did, namely as the reproduction in our experience of the pleasures that we recognize are felt by others. Such an account of sympathy, as Rawls (1971, pp. 185–92) points out, could provide an account of how choices would be made in a Rawlsian original position. Persons in the original position (see SOCIAL JUSTICE (18)) would imagine themselves leading each life in turn and, since sympathetically imagined pains cancel out sympathetically imagined pleasures, the best choice would be that which maximized the net balance of pain over pleasure; and all parties in the original position would endorse the principles of classical utilitarianism. The logic of extended sympathy seems to have a close affinity with the logic of utilitarianism.

The problem here is that of imagining the thought-experiment that is being supposed by considering sympathetic persons in the original position. If such persons are to compare pains and pleasures across different individuals, they must preserve an identity in difference: that is, they must accurately reproduce in themselves the pleasures and pains experienced by others, while at the same time retaining their own distinctive viewpoint providing the focus of commensurability and summation. Such identity in difference seems flatly self-contradictory.

The problem is that comparisons based on extended sympathy seem to provide an ethical framework for judgements about social choice while holding fast to a moral epistemology in which ethical judgements can be little more than expressions of personal preference or attitude, even if of a refined variety. This is to reverse the normal logic of evaluation in which attitudes, such as sympathy, are consequent upon a judgement of moral significance. As Bishop Butler (1726, pp. 125–6) pointed out, sentiments of fellow feeling depend upon the identification of injustice, and therefore have at their base a range of moral principles and evaluations. Extended sympathy therefore depends in part upon an account of social justice and it cannot provide the basis for such an account.

APW

Externalities

An externality occurs when, in a market economy, an activity carried out by one or more people affects the welfare of other people, and when this effect is not transmitted through market prices. (In other words, there is some mechanism, *external* to the market, by which some people's activities impinge on other people's welfare.) The externality is *negative* if the other people suffer a loss of welfare. For example, the burning of coal in the power stations of eastern England increases the acidity of lakes and rivers in Norway. This is a negative externality: Norwegian fishermen are harmed as an unintended by-product of a set of market transactions (between electricity consumers, electricity-generating companies and coal-producers) to which they are not parties. The externality is *positive* if the other people enjoy an increase in welfare. For example, rich landowners in northern England conserve heather moorland for grouse-shooting: as an unintended by-product, hill-walkers can enjoy a distinctive form of landscape. Externalities can be created both by activities of production (as in the case of the power stations) and by activities of consumption (as when coal is burned in people's homes).

In economic theory, there is no significant distinction between positive externalities and **public goods** (⌷). (A grouse moor may be thought of as a public good, consumed in a largely non-rival way by both grouse-shooters and walkers, but supplied as a result of the private interests of the grouse-shooters.) Negative externalities, too, can be re-described in the language of public goods. (An unpolluted atmosphere is a public good.) If the supply of public goods is left to private initiative, they tend to be supplied in less than Pareto-optimal (see **Pareto optimality** (⌷)) quantities. Similarly, in a market economy, activities that give rise to negative externalities tend to occur to a greater degree than is consistent with Pareto optimality, while the opposite is true for those that give rise to positive externalities. The classic economic solution to this is to impose taxes on activities which generate negative externalities and to subsidize those that generate positive ones.

Even in a perfectly competitive market, each person's private choices can affect the welfare of others. Suppose, for example, that wealthy people from towns start to buy holiday homes in country areas. This will force up the price of houses in these areas, benefiting the existing owners of such houses while harming local people who are trying to buy their first homes. These effects are *not* externalities in the standard sense (they are sometimes called *pecuniary* externalities). The difference is that these effects are transmitted through market prices. It can be proved that the outcome of trade in a perfectly competitive market is always Pareto-optimal (see ANARCHIC ORDER (12)). Thus, although pecuniary externalities affect the distribution of welfare in a competitive economy, they are no barrier to the achievement of Pareto optimality.

RS

Fact/Value Distinction

Statements of fact typically inform us that something is now, was, will be or is always the case. But, since our knowledge of the world is grounded in observation, such statements cannot tell us what should or should not be the case – for instance, as **Hume** (⌷) pointed out, that murder is wrong (see □). Nor can moral statements be established *a priori*, as Hume added, since any proof would need a moral statement as a premise, thus shifting the problem further back. His general conclusion, often summed up informally as 'You cannot get an "ought" from an "is"', is known as Hume's Law.

One effect of the scientific revolution of the sixteenth and seventeenth centuries was to divorce the causal order in nature from the moral order, which had previously been discerned there by men of learning. As modern scientific method became the model of rational enquiry, it became harder to offer rational grounds for believing in any external meaning or moral

> Take any action allowed to be vicious, wilful murder for instance.
> Examine it in all lights, and see if you can find the matter of fact or
> real existence, which you call *vice*. In whichever way you take it, you
> will find only certain passions, motives, volitions and thoughts.

> (Hume, 1740, book III, part 1, sec. iii)

purpose in the fabric of Heaven and Earth. Reason yielded to faith in such
matters, and the modern fact/value distinction became a familiar shibboleth
of science. That set a major problem for any rationally grounded ethics, since
moral statements threatened to reduce to, for instance, mere reports of the
speaker's attitude or commitments or misleading ways of describing the
norms prevalent in a particular society at a particular time.

Hume's own line was to ground a scientific ethics in the 'passions, motives,
volitions and thoughts' which an examination of human actions can reveal.
Human nature is the same everywhere, he held, and is moved by the same
natural sentiments, although in varying proportions. Some of these sentiments, such as sympathy for others, make for better, more comfortable
living, and a science of mind can identify and show how to encourage them.
This 'naturalistic' way of tackling the fact/value distinction is most fully
exemplified by **utilitarianism** (▣) with its scientific approach to the maximizing of human happiness. The main rival strategy, which also dispenses
with values external to human life for purposes of rational ethics, is that of
Kant (▣), which tries to show that it is rational to take a universal, moral
point of view, when deciding what one has most reason to do.

Neither attempt has saved social scientists from being caught in two minds
by the fact/value distinction. On the one hand, the cannon of *positive*
science seems to rule out all prospect of a *normative* science. On the other
hand, one main aim of social science, as for example with welfare economics, has always been to improve human conduct: witness Helvetius' remark
in the spirit of the Enlightenment that 'Ethics is the agriculture of the mind'.
Besides, it is not obvious that social research could ever be 'value-free', even
if one wished, since it may be impossible to eliminate values from the choice
not only of topics but also of methods. More disconcertingly for the present
volume, rationality threatens to be a concept in which positive and normative fuse, if the chapters on RATIONALITY (1), AUTONOMY (6) and
CULTURAL EXCHANGE (11) are right to suggest that there are 'expressive'
elements in the ideal-type case, and hence that the applications and practical
advice which derive from it cross the divide between fact and value.

MH

Fairness

The concept of fairness overlaps with that of justice (see SOCIAL JUSTICE (18)). The distinction between fairness and justice is a fine one, but it seems to be recognized in ordinary speech. An unbiased coin is 'fair' but not 'just'. If the players of a game have to decide which of them will have first move, they may agree that it is a fair solution to toss a coin: such a solution would not normally be called 'just'. An accused person has a fair trial if he has proper legal representation, the judge and jury are unbiased, and so on; but we may still ask whether, as a result of the trial, he receives his just deserts. Damaging criticism of a public figure is 'fair comment' if it is made without malice and in the context of free debate; it may still be unjust. Fairness is associated with the ideas of equal treatment and of absence of bias. It tends to be associated with procedures (tossing a coin, a trial, a debate) rather than with outcomes.

Rawls (1971) plays on this distinction when he calls his own theory of justice, 'justice as fairness'. Rawls asks us to imagine an 'original position' in which we have to agree the basic institutions of our society without knowing our own positions in it. This imaginary procedure of choice is fair because it allows no room for bias and treats everyone equally. Rawls then argues that the institutions that would be chosen by this fair procedure should also be regarded as just: justice should be construed in terms of fairness. But, for Rawls, 'justice as fairness' is only one 'conception' of justice (that is, one way in which we might conceive of justice): the *concept* of justice (that is, the core idea to which we all refer when we speak of justice) is not to be equated with fairness.

A notion of fairness similar to Rawls's can be found in a familiar procedure for cutting a cake: the person who cuts the cake has the last choice of slice. The cake-cutter has to determine the slices without knowing which slice will be hers. Suppose that the cake has to be divided between just two people: A cuts and B chooses. Then, it seems, neither person has any room for complaint about the size of his or her slice. B cannot claim that A's slice is bigger than his, since he was free to choose either slice. A cannot claim that B's slice is bigger than hers without admitting that she did not cut the cake fairly.

This cake-cutting conception of fairness has been developed in a strand of literature in economics, which has asked how goods should be allocated between people if the allocation is to be fair. To dramatize this problem, think of a country in the midst of a desperate war. Many goods are scarce. How are they to be rationed? A simple solution is to allocate every good equally between individuals, so that teetotallers receive an equal share of alcohol, and non-smokers of cigarettes. This certainly seems to be a *fair* solution: everyone is treated equally. But because it takes no account of tastes, it is also very inefficient. Is it possible to find a solution that is both fair and Pareto-optimal (see **Pareto optimality** (🖙))?

In the economics literature, fairness is interpreted in terms of the absence of **envy** (🖙), where 'envy' is understood in the benign sense of 'preferring another person's bundle of goods to one's own'. This way of thinking about fairness is due to Foley (1967). It was taken up by Varian (1974, 1975) and later by Baumol (1986). Sugden (1984) gives a more critical view of the enterprise. In the cake-cutting case, B has no reason to envy A's slice, since he was free to choose it for himself, while A has no reason to envy B's slice unless she cut the cake unequally. The problem is then defined as that of finding some distribution of goods between people that is both *envy-free* (no-one prefers another person's bundle to his own) and Pareto-optimal. It is easy to find such a solution for an exchange economy (that is, an economy without production, in which the only problem is to allocate given stocks of goods between individuals). All we need to do is to allocate all goods equally between individuals and then allow trade in a competitive market. This market will establish a price for each good; and since all individuals have the same endowments and face the same prices, they all have the same set of opportunities. If one person can afford a particular bundle of goods, so can anyone else. Thus no-one has any reason to envy anyone else's bundle, and the outcome of a competitive market is always Pareto-optimal (see ANARCHIC ORDER (12)).

This particular solution is an attractive one, which would probably strike most people as fair. An approximation to it can be found in rationing schemes in which people are allocated equal numbers of 'ration points' to be used as they choose, and in which each good has a price measured in ration points. (This system was used in the UK for some non-essential goods during the Second World War.) However, it is not clear that this solution is fair merely because it does not give rise to envy. The solution is also fair in the sense of being unbiased: everyone has exactly the same endowments, and everyone has exactly the same opportunities for trade. This is not true of all envy-free and Pareto-optimal solutions.

Consider the cake-cutting example again. The 'A cuts, B chooses' solution derives much of its appeal from an implicit assumption that the cake is homogeneous, so that all that matters is the *size* of each slice. But think of a case in which this assumption does not hold. Imagine that A and B have received a parcel containing a box of cigarettes, a bottle of whisky and a box of chocolates. A smokes, likes chocolate but does not drink, and would prefer the cigarettes to the chocolates. B drinks, likes chocolates but does not smoke, and would prefer the whisky to the chocolates. Would it be fair for A to divide the contents of the parcel into two bundles, and then for B to choose one of the bundles? If this procedure were followed, A could put the cigarettes and the chocolates into one bundle and the whisky into the other, confident that B would choose the second bundle. Neither person would envy the other's bundle. Nevertheless, A has been able to acquire the chocolates because she made up the bundles: in this sense, the procedure is biased in her favour. The point of this example is that when individuals' tastes differ, envy-freeness may not correspond with ordinary ideas of fairness.

It is perhaps more satisfactory to think of envy-freeness as a necessary rather than as a sufficient condition for fairness. If in an exchange economy, one person envies another's bundle of goods, then there is a clear implication that the two people have not faced the same opportunities. According to this interpretation, a demonstration that envy-freeness and Pareto-optimality were *in*compatible would have some significance. And if we move from an exchange economy to one with production, this turns out to be the case.

In an economy with production, we have the additional problem of determining how much labour each person should perform. The usual way of modelling this case is to treat leisure as an additional good which enters into each person's 'bundle'. Thus A envies B if A would prefer to have B's bundle of goods and leisure rather than her own. The difficulty here is that peoples' productivities may differ, so that we cannot transfer hours of leisure between individuals in the way that we can transfer physical goods. (To 'transfer' an hour of leisure from B to A, we must require B to work an extra hour while A works an hour less. But if A is more productive than B, this transfer will reduce the quantities of other goods that are available for allocation.) It is quite possible for A to envy B at the same time as B envies A, without there being any way in which they could eliminate this mutual envy by changing places.

It is, of course, perfectly possible to ensure that everyone faces the same opportunities as everyone else. We can ensure this by giving people equal endowments of physical goods and then allowing them access to a market in which each good has a market-clearing price and in which labour is bought at a given wage rate, independent of the worker's productivity. This might be thought of as a form of socialism. On most accounts of fairness, this would be fair. But if workers' productivities differed, it would not be Pareto-optimal. Conversely, we might give everyone equal endowments of physical goods and then establish a competitive market in goods and labour. The more productive workers would then command higher wages: the result would be Pareto-optimal, but the less productive workers would have fewer opportunities than the more productive.

If an economy contains many individuals who differ both in productivity and in tastes, it is generally impossible to find any allocation of goods and leisure that is both envy-free and Pareto-optimal. Notice that this is not a problem of incentives: envy-free and Pareto-optimal allocations simply do not exist. The problem of arriving at such an allocation could not be solved, even if there were an omniscient central planner, and even if all individuals were willing to follow the planner's instructions. Thus if it is correct to treat envy-freeness as a necessary condition for fairness, there seems to be a deep conflict between fairness and efficiency.

RS

Feasible Set

Choice only becomes an interesting problem when it is constrained. Important constraints include wealth, time, supplies of raw materials, minimum nutritional requirements, and the necessity to meet contractual obligations. The feasible set is a complete list of actions which do not contravene any of these constraints. For example, on a day trip to the seaside, the feasible set of actions (such as swimming, sunbathing, playing, eating and drinking) is dictated by time, money and the availability of attractions.

BRL

Felicific Calculus

The utilitarian approach to social choice requires a balancing of the pleasurable consequences of an action against its painful consequences. Bentham provided a model of how this might be achieved in his discussion of how pains and pleasures could be measured (see **Bentham** (▣) **utilitarianism** (▣); see also □ p. 262)), and the idea that actions are right or wrong in proportion as they tend to promote the net balance of pleasure over pain has been a central feature of utilitarianism ever since.

APW

General Equilibrium

General equilibrium can be contrasted with partial equilibrium. Some variables, which are held constant in partial equilibrium analysis, are allowed to vary in general equilibrium. Thus, for instance, a partial equilibrium analysis of the determination of price in one market takes the price of inputs and other commodities as fixed, whereas a general equilibrium analysis is concerned with the determination of all prices in the economy.

The attraction of partial equilibrium analysis is one of simplicity and tractability. It is relatively easy in our example to study a single market in isolation. By comparison, general equilibrium must take account of the interdependencies between markets. The price in one market affects the equilibrium in another and so on throughout the economy; and when everything depends on everything else in this way, it is frequently difficult to say anything at all.

However, the attraction of tractability should not mask the dangers of partial equilibrium analysis. What happens in isolation can be misleading when the whole is more than the sum of its parts; and there are some celebrated examples of this non-reducibility in general equilibrium analysis.

The deduction that competitive markets can produce Pareto-efficient allocations of resources is one example. No individual in these markets intends, through his or her action in any particular market, to produce an efficient allocation of resources, but Pareto-efficiency results. It is as if the individuals had been guided by an invisible hand to produce an outcome that no one intended. The behaviour of markets as a whole in this case is not a simple summation of what happens in isolated individual markets. Likewise, in Marx, it appears to make perfect sense for an isolated individual capitalist to cut his or her workers' wages, but this action can generate contrary results when generalized across all capitalists, yielding lower sales and profits. As a final illustration, it would plainly be foolish to be guided by the partial equilibrium insight that standing up is a solution to poor visibility in a sports stadium. In these cases, the whole cannot be studied by building on a series of partial equilibrium insights into the functioning of its parts. Instead, general equilibrium analysis is required.

The term 'general equilibrium' is often used to describe a particular kind of general equilibrium analysis, neoclassical general equilibrium theory. Indeed, it is sometimes used in an even more restricted sense to apply to the Arrow–Debreu models in neoclassical economics. Like the following of partial equilibrium insights, this usage can be misleading. There are other types of neoclassical general equilibrium theory which offer a contrasting perspective on the operation of markets (for instance, the overlapping generations model) and, as the above example from Marx suggests, there are models of general equilibrium which lie outside the neoclassical tradition.

SHH

Hayek, Friedrich August (1899–)

Friedrich Hayek spent the first three decades of his life in Austria. In 1931 he moved to the UK, teaching at the London School of Economics and becoming a British citizen. Between 1950 and 1962 he worked at the University of Chicago. Now in his nineties, he lives in Germany and continues to write.

In the 1930s and 1940s, he wrote a series of papers (collected in Hayek, 1948) on the role of knowledge in economics and on the economics of socialism. The central problem of economics, he argued, is that of coordinating the plans of many independent individuals, each of whom is using knowledge that is private to him or her. The market system provides a solution to this problem: each agent, acting in his own interests, responds to price signals which in turn reflect the information held by all agents. The market should be seen as a process which discovers and transmits previously unknown information, and not in terms of the static equilibrium models of neoclassical economics. Hayek challenged the view, common among economists of the time, that an economy could be organized efficiently through central planning or 'market socialism'.

In 1944 Hayek published a polemical work, *The Road to Serfdom*, in which he argued that central planning, however well-intentioned, would be incompatible with individual freedom and would ultimately lead to totalitarianism. Although praised by Keynes, this book had a hostile reception in the UK, where Hayek's scholarly comparisons between contemporary socialism and Hitler's national socialism offended popular sentiments. In his subsequent work, particularly *The Constitution of Liberty* (1960) and the three volumes of *Law, Legislation and Liberty* (1973, 1976, 1979), Hayek develops the themes of *The Road to Serfdom* in a more philosophical way. The concept of spontaneous order is applied not only to the economic system, but also to the legal system and to morality. Hayek argues the importance for liberty of the 'rule of law': laws should not represent *ad hoc* commands by government, but should express general principles which apply to a wide range of cases. In a more conservative vein, he argues that human civilization depends on our willingness to abide by laws and moral codes which have evolved spontaneously, and whose workings we cannot fully understand.

RS

Hegel, Georg Wilhelm Friedrich (1770–1831)

According to Hegel, in modern commercial society and its accompanying political order, individuals can express their freedom on three levels. As subjects of law, they can do what they want, provided that they respect the rights of others. As moral subjects, they can exercise an autonomous moral will (compare with **Kant** (▤)) by acting as they should. As members of their particular community, they can direct their lives in accord with its particular ethical norms. This third level (*Sittlichkeit*) is exemplified in the family, in the economic and social life of civil society and in the political realm of the state. In an ideally rational political system, as analysed in *Philosophy of Right* (1821), all of these modes of expression can coexist.

Rational choice theorists will find Hegel deeply instructive on the relation of rationality to individual freedom, conceived first instrumentally, then in

noral terms and finally in communitarian spirit. They will also be interested
oy his version of the idea that individually rational choices sum to outcomes
which, although intended by no-one, advance the progress of human history.
Thanks to 'the cunning of Reason', history advances in dialectically related
stages until the society just described becomes historically possible. (See the
posthumous *Lectures on World History* (1822–1830) in Hegel (1837). See
also C. Taylor (1975, 1979).)

MH

Hobbes, Thomas (1588–1679)

Leviathan (1651), written in the aftermath of the English Civil War, is
inspired by a conviction that traditional accounts of political authority no
longer suffice. Hobbes offers a radically new analysis, which takes men as

WAR AND PEACE

Hereby it is manifest, that during the time men live without a common
power to keep them all in awe, they are in that condition which is
called war; and such a war, as is of every man, against every man.
For WAR, consisteth not in battle only, or the act of fighting; but in
a tract of time, wherein the will to contend by battle is sufficiently
known: and therefore the notion of *time*, is to be considered in the
nature of war; as it is in the nature of weather. For as the nature of
foul weather lieth not in a shower or two of rain; but in an inclination
thereto of many days together: so the nature of war, consisteth not in
actual fighting; but in the known disposition thereto, during all the time
there is no assurance to the contrary. All other time is PEACE.

Whatsoever therefore is consequent to a time of war, where every man
is enemy to every man; the same is consequent to the time, wherein men
live without other security, than what their own strength, and their own
invention shall furnish them withal. In such condition, there is no place
for industry; because the fruit thereof is uncertain: and consequently no
culture of the earth; no navigation, nor use of the commodities that may
be imported by sea; no commodious building; no instruments of moving, and removing, such things as require much force; no knowledge of
the face of the earth; no account of time; no arts; no letters; no society;
and which is worst of all, continual fear, and danger of violent death;
and the life of man, solitary, poor, nasty, brutish and short.

(Hobbes, 1651, ch. 13)

self-interested mechanical creatures bent on their own preservation and advantage. He envisions an original state of nature, marked by 'a war of all against all', where there is 'continual fear, and danger of violent death; and the life of man is solitary, poor, nasty, brutish and short' (see □). To escape this natural condition of mankind, men make a contract with each other to create 'a common power to keep them all in awe' and thus allow the pursuit of the 'commodious living' which all seek. But they are so quarrelsome and so keen to steal a march on one another that 'covenants without the sword are but words'. Hence political authority must be armed and absolute, even though its proper purposes are limited.

Hobbes thus rests a case for social and political organization on 'natural laws' and individual self-interest. His sharply reasoned and splendidly written text remains crucial for rational choice and game theory, whether or not one accepts his dour view of human nature. There are also other major works, including *The Elements of Law* (1640) and *De Cive* (1642, second edition 1647), usefully anthologized in Peters (1962). John Plamenatz's edition of *Leviathan* (1962) has a very helpful introduction.

MH

Hume, David (1711–1776)

David Hume, like his younger friend **Adam Smith** (⧉), was a leading figure of the Scottish Enlightenment – a remarkable outburst of work in philosophy and the social sciences in eighteenth-century Scotland. Hume's main philosophical work was *A Treatise of Human Nature* (1740). Disappointed at the reception of the *Treatise*, Hume adopted a more polished (but less direct and engaging) style of writing and reworked his arguments into two books, *An Enquiry Concerning Human Understanding* (1748) and *An Enquiry Concerning the Principles of Morals* (1751).

Hume approaches the classic philosophical question 'What can we know?' by enquiring into the workings of the human mind; in modern terms, his work is as much about psychology as it is about philosophy. Hume argues that many of the properties that we attribute to the external world are in fact to be explained in terms of properties of our minds. One important instance of this concerns causation. We use the concept of causation to explain the relationships between events, but this concept has no rational foundation. All we can observe is that certain kinds of events are associated with certain other kinds. The human mind is constituted to recognize such associations and to classify them in the scheme we call 'causation'.

Hume uses a similar argument in relation to our moral beliefs. We use concepts such as 'good' and 'bad' as though they described properties of the external world, independent of ourselves. But, in fact, these concepts merely describe the sensations created in our minds by the things we call 'good' or 'bad'. One implication of this argument is that propositions concerning what *ought* to be the case cannot be deduced from propositions about what *is* the case (see **fact/value distinction** (📖)). According to Hume's account, actions are regarded as good or bad according to the sensations of approval or disapproval that they would produce in a spectator who felt impartial sympathy for everyone affected by those actions. This leads to a moral and political theory that is similar in some ways to utilitarianism.

RS

Interpersonal Comparisons of Utility

Consider the utility numbers in a pay-off matrix for a typical one-shot two-person game such as Battle of the Sexes:

		Jill	
		Bullfight	Concert
Jack	Bullfight	3, 2	1, 1
	Concert	0, 0	2, 3

The utility information seems curiously precise: Jack receives three utiles (microwatts of inner glow?) if he and Jill both choose the bullfight, this being one more than she receives, and also two more than he would receive were she to choose the concert. How seriously are we to take such figures?

In part, they are simply a graphic device to aid thought. Cardinal numbers could (usually) be replaced with ordinal rankings (showing, for instance, that Jack prefers the top left cell to the bottom right). There is (usually) no need to suppose that a *level* of utility is being identified (for example, by 0,0) or that definite comparisons are involved, for instance in assigning Jack the same pay-off in the top left cell as Jill has in the bottom right. Therefore an incipient puzzle can apparently be avoided by allowing *intra*personal comparisons of utility in ordinal form and waving away *inter*personal ones.

Economists often take this avoiding action, because they are nervous about unobservables. Irving Fisher defined utility as 'a psychic flow of inner satisfaction'. This seems to make it impossible even for Jack to measure his own utility in any objective way, let alone for him (or any observer) to measure Jill's. Hence it is thought properly scientific to dispense with such measuring, or even to work with revealed preferences (see CONSUMER

THEORY (2)) or some other behavioural indicator. Indeed, there has been a recent tendency to regard an agent's utility schedule not as an explanation of his preferences but merely as a mathematically neat way of stating his preferences. This nervousness can perhaps be traced to alarm at what philosophers term the problem of 'other minds', that of how one person can know what is in the mind of another. If a mind is thought of as a logically sealed box to which only the owner can have access, then the problem is acute.

For philosophers who do not accept this view of the mind, however, alarm is misplaced. Is there really any good reason for doubting that Jill would receive more utility from a free holiday in Venice than Jack would receive from being boiled in oil? After all, one can always ask them. Common sense here lends suspicion to a widespread philosophical opinion that the problem must have been misconceived, if behaviourism, with its narrowness of vision, is its solution. Meanwhile, economists can hardly avoid pronouncing on matters of distribution. Would it increase overall welfare if higher taxes on the rich were devoted to higher incomes for the poor? What are the effects of redistributing the budget of the National Health Service between primary and secondary care? Such questions are no more philosophically peculiar than asking how a benevolent uncle can best bequeath his possessions among nephews and nieces with different tastes. Indeed, the simplest questions of supply and demand can be discussed 'objectively', in terms of people's willingness to pay, only if one can compare the satisfactions which money makes possible. The study of economics could hardly get off the ground without making interpersonal comparisons of utility.

MH

Kant, Immanuel (1724–1804)

A moral agent acts from 'a good will', one obedient to the 'categorical imperative', which bids us do whatever would be the duty of anyone in the same position. A good will is not swayed by self-interest, by inclination or even by utilitarian calculation of consequences. It always treats other agents as ends in themselves, never as means to the agent's ends. Someone possessed of a good will is fully rational and autonomous. A group of such agents form 'a kingdom of ends' or, in political terms, a *Rechstsstaat* of autonomous persons with equal rights under the impersonal aegis of law. This is the core of Kant's ethics and theory of practical reason as expressed especially in Kant (1785, 1788). It is relevant to the theory of choice partly because of its 'two-tier' moral psychology, in which reasons can trump preferences based on inclination, partly because of the tempting thought that rational agents can escape the Prisoner's Dilemma by doing what is impartially best for both, and partly as a source of the rights and duties crucial for 'deontological liberalism', as in Rawls' theory of justice (see SOCIAL JUSTICE (18)).

MH

Keynes, John Maynard (1883–1946)

Keynes's influence has extended far and wide in this century. He was a government adviser, a prolific political writer, an international negotiator, joint architect of the postwar international economic order, the first chairman of the Arts Council, a financial wizard, and he wrote a celebrated book on economics, *The General Theory of Employment, Interest and Money*. At crucial stages in the argument of this book, Keynes relies on ideas concerning decision-making under uncertainty which he had developed in his earlier work, *A Treatise on Probability* (1921).

The General Theory argues that a *laissez-faire* market system will not automatically generate full employment; and that serious unemployment can only be avoided by government intervention which is designed to manage the level of aggregate demand. This view has been extremely influential, spawning the so-called 'Keynesian economics' and 'Keynesianism' of the postwar period. The argument turns, in part, on an

GOODBYE TO ALL THAT

When the accumulation of wealth is no longer of high social importance, there will be great changes in the code of morals. We shall be able to rid ourselves of many of the pseudo-moral principles which have hag-ridden us for two hundred years, by which we have exalted some of the most distasteful of human qualities into the position of the highest virtues. We shall be able to afford to dare to assess the money motive at its true value. The love of money as possession – as distinguished from the love of money as a means to the enjoyments and realities of life – will be recognized for what it is, a somewhat disgusting morbidity, one of those semi-criminal, semi-pathological propensities which we hand over with a shudder to the specialists in mental disease. All kinds of social customs and economic practices, affecting the distribution of wealth and economic rewards and penalties which we now maintain at all costs however distasteful and unjust they may be in themselves, because they are tremendously useful in promoting accumulation of capital, we shall be free, at last, to discard.

(Keynes, 1931, pp. 369–70)

analysis of how individuals rely on conventions when making decisions under uncertainty. In advancing this suggestion Keynes draws on the distinction between **risk and uncertainty** (▢), arguing that probability calculations are not the only consideration in situations of genuine uncertainty (▢ p. 60, ▢ p. 350).

Decision-making under uncertainty had been Keynes's central concern in *A Treatise on Probability*. There he argued that individuals, when faced by genuine uncertainty, rely on rational intuitions and conventions. By the time of *The General Theory*, the early emphasis on the role of rational intuitions had given way to that of conventions.

Keynes also promoted a particular vision of the 'good life'. He was an idealist, believing that the progress of ideas would increasingly enable individuals to pursue the true 'goods' of life, love, friendship and beauty. This version of the 'goods' in life is derived from G.E. Moore's *Principia Ethica* (1903) and it led Keynes to reflect that many of the motives, such as the pursuit of profit, which we take to be honourable and central to human activity today, will be revealed later for what they are. They have no intrinsic worth: they are simply means which help hasten the day when love, friendship and beauty will hold the stage (see ▢).

SHH

Lexicographics

During the Olympic Games, 'medal tables' are published showing the relative standing of each country. In these tables, countries are ranked by the number of gold medals that their athletes have won. Countries whose athletes have won equal numbers of gold medals are ranked in terms of the number of silver medals won and, similarly, countries whose athletes have won equal numbers of both golds and silvers are ranked by the number of bronzes won. This is a *lexicographical ordering*. The term 'lexicographical' is derived from the analogy with word ordering in dictionaries (the order of words is determined by the alphabetical order of their first letters; two words with the same first letter are ordered in terms of their second letters; and so on).

The entities being ranked (countries, in the above example) may be thought of as having numerical *scores* on each of a number of *dimensions* (gold, silver and bronze). If we are to produce a single ordering of the entities, we have to combine these scores in some way. A lexicographical ordering starts from an ordering of the dimensions in terms of *significance* (gold is more significant than silver, silver is more significant than bronze) and then, when scores are combined, any difference – however small – on a more significant dimension outweighs any difference – however large – on a less significant one. If France has one gold and 50 silvers, while Italy has two golds and no silvers, Italy ranks above France – just as 'azygous' comes before 'baba' in a dictionary.

Lexicographical preference orderings give rise to theoretical problems because such preferences cannot be represented by utility functions. Imagine a consumer whose preferences are defined over bundles containing gold and silver, and that these two goods are infinitely divisible. Suppose that her preferences over bundles are lexicographical in the same way in which Olympic medal tables are. Then each bundle can be represented by a point in a two-dimensional space of the kind in which indifference curves are normally drawn. But if the consumer's preferences are lexicographical, she must have a *strict* preference between each pair of non-identical bundles (that is, she cannot be indifferent between them). Thus there can be no indifference curves. If we try to assign utility numbers to bundles, we must assign a different number to every bundle. This would require us to use as many numbers as there are points in a two-dimensional space. To put an abstruse mathematical theorem very crudely, there are not enough numbers to go round.

Economists have generally regarded lexicographical preference as no more than a mathematical curiosity which can be assumed away by invoking suitable axioms of 'continuity' (see RATIONALITY (1)). It is part of the folk wisdom of economics that everything can be traded-off against everything else; the idea that one good might be regarded as infinitely more valuable than another is thought rather perverse.

From a more theoretical viewpoint, however, lexicographical orderings are of some interest. Suppose that you are trying to assess the ranking of Ireland in relation to Denmark in the Olympic medals table. All you know is the (ordinal) ranking of the two countries in terms of golds, silvers and bronzes (say, the two countries have equal numbers of golds, Denmark has more silvers than Ireland, but Ireland has more bronzes than Denmark). This information is sufficient to give you the answer you need (Denmark is ranked above Ireland). Conversely, suppose that you are given the job of designing a rule for determining the overall ranking of various countries' Olympic performances. You are told that the rule must generate an ordering of countries in all possible circumstances; that it must give some positive weight to all medals; and that it should have the property that the ranking of each pair of countries depends only on the ranking of those countries on the three dimensions of gold, silver and bronze. The only rules that satisfy these requirements are lexicographical ones. The point of this example is that if we impose certain kinds of restrictions on the properties of overall rankings, we end up with lexicographical rules.

The *difference principle* proposed by John Rawls (see SOCIAL JUSTICE (18)) has some similarities with lexicographical rules. Rawls considers the problem of ranking different *social states*; that is, different ways in which a society might be organized. We know the welfare of each individual in each society, measured on a single numerical scale (which Rawls calls the quantity of 'primary goods' possessed by the individual). Rawls's proposal is that any two social states should be ranked according to the relative welfares of the least well-off individuals in those states; if the comparison yields a tie, we should consider the welfares of the next-least well-off individuals, and so on. Suppose, for example, that there are three individuals, 1, 2 and 3. In social state A, their respective welfare levels are 10, 12 and 13. In social state B, their welfare levels are 200, 10 and 11. Then the difference principle ranks A above B. Intuitively, the idea is that a unit of welfare enjoyed by a relatively poor person is infinitely more valuable than a unit of welfare enjoyed by a relatively rich person.

Lexicographics enter into Rawls's theory of justice at other points. In particular, Rawls (1971, p. 250) argues that his principle of liberty has lexicographical priority over the difference principle, so that 'liberty can be restricted only for the sake of liberty'. Isaac Levi (1986) is another philosopher to have made extensive use of lexicographical principles of choice. Levi presents a theory of rational individual choice in which preferences can be incomplete; thus a person may face a choice problem in which two or more options are 'admissible', but there are no rational grounds for preferring one admissible option to another. He then suggests that the maximin principle (see **risk aversion** (⚲)) may be used as a kind of tie-breaker.

RS

Market Socialism

The term 'socialism' is variously used, but it would standardly be taken to imply abolition of private ownership of the means of production and control of productive assets by representatives of the community. But what is the relationship between socialism in this sense and markets? This debate was inaugurated by **Von Mises** (⚲) (1935) in his discussion of the problem of economic calculation under socialism. Von Mises argued that, with the abolition of private ownership of the means of production, a socialist commonwealth would have no way of rationally calculating the alternative uses of scarce resources. Socialists were reduced, according von Mises (1935, p. 88), to explaining 'how, in the cloud-cuckoo lands of their fancy, roast pigeons will in some way fly into the mouths of the comrades'. **Hayek** (⚲) pressed the argument further by asserting that, even if it were in principle possible for a planning board running collectively owned assets to allocate resources rationally, the practical tasks of assembling the information necessary would render the attempt at rational planning beyond human capacity (Hayek, 1935, pp. 207–14).

One response to this line of criticism was advocated by Lange and Taylor (1938). In this version of market socialism there is freedom for workers to enter alternative occupations and freedom for consumers to choose alternative bundles of goods given their tastes and income. Managers of enterprises are expected to control production by mixing factor inputs according to rules specified by a central planning board, and in line with the principle that the marginal cost of factor inputs should equal prices. For consumer goods and the services of labour, prices are determined by the market: in all other cases they are fixed by a central planning board. The expectation is that by the appropriate fixing of prices the economy will achieve an economically efficient and stable allocation of prices.

This solved the problem posed by von Mises, but did it solve the problem posed by Hayek? Lange believed that it did, because he held that the pricing of goods in a capitalist market was achieved by a process of trial and error, and a central planning board would require a shorter series of trials than capitalist owners, since the board would have a much wider knowledge of what was going on in the whole economic system than any private entrepreneur could (Lange and Taylor, 1938, p. 89). This assertion clearly raises a number of issues (discussed in RISK, IGNORANCE AND IMAGINATION (4) and ANARCHIC ORDER (12)). It is certainly not self-evident, and the experience of centrally planned economies, in so far as it is relevant to the theoretical debate, is not encouraging. This experience has led to a search for alternative forms of market socialism in which workers' management and control plays a central role.

Under this form of market socialism, workers hire capital rather than capital hiring workers. Cooperatives of producers join together to produce goods and services, but their productive activity is subject to the discipline of the market. Each cooperative must pay the going rate for the factors of production that it employs, and it can only clear its stocks if customers are willing to pay the prices asked. In such a system, the role of the government is positive, but limited. The government may assure the supply of public goods, bring about the redistribution of income from factor returns by means of taxes and transfers, and regulate the supply of money and effective demand to ensure economic growth. However, government management of productive assets is generally to be discouraged.

As an arrangement of political economy, market socialism is favoured by those who are simultaneously impressed by the liberal's demand for freedom and the socialist's demand for economic and social equality. **John Stuart Mill** (⊞) favoured something like market socialism in his discussion of the 'Probable futurity of the working classes' in the *Principles of Political Economy* (Mill, 1848, Vol. 2, pp. 758–96), and a group of active Fabians have recently advocated a variety of market socialism (Le Grand and Estrin, 1989).

Capitalist-inclined critics of market socialism assert that, despite appearances, market socialism presupposes an authoritarian state. Under market socialism there would presumably be no, or only highly restricted, contracts of employment, just as under capitalism there are no contracts of slavery or feudal vassalage. Critics allege that this implies an authoritarian restriction (Nozick, 1974, pp. 250–3). Under capitalism, it is said, both workers' cooperatives and conventional capitalist firms are permitted, and there are no legal restrictions on workers forming cooperatives. Under market socialism, only cooperatives are permitted and the conventional capitalist firm is forbidden, thus violating the neutrality displayed by the capitalist state. This argument requires the assumption that merely permitting both cooperatives and capitalist forms yields neutrality in the forms of economic organization, encouraged by the legal system. David Miller (1989) contests this assumption, claiming that the simultaneous tolerance of cooperatives and capitalist forms yields a bias in favour of the latter, since workers under capitalism have to pay a special moral price to enjoy rights of cooperative ownership.

Although the argument derived from moral neutrality is not very powerful, there are other, and more significant problems with market socialism. Thus, it is alleged that workers' cooperatives tend to favour members over non-members, since their maximand is average member income and not profit as given by the point of production at which marginal income equals marginal cost. The observable consequence of this tendency would be underemployment or less satisfactory conditions for new members in comparison to established members. There is also the problem of risk-spreading. In the absence of a market in shares, workers have their savings tied up in the same firms as their employment, thus leaving them no opportunity to spread their economic risks. If workers begin to lend to one another, the system begins to resemble people's capitalism or a property-owning democracy, whereas if they save with the state, its officials will come to acquire substantial economic power by virtue or their control of deposited assets, contrary to the libertarian impulse.

Further difficulties arise over ordinary income returns, which present a problem of social justice, in the form of rent, even under market socialism. Rental income is defined as the difference between a worker's income and the income that would be just sufficient to induce the worker to perform the same job: it follows that *all* intramarginal workers enjoy rent (Bergson, 1967, pp. 662–3), and it can be argued that it is the rental component of income that should be eliminated on grounds of justice.

Market socialists continue to be ingenious in devising institutional solutions to these problems. The main obstacle to the implementation of such a programme is likely to remain political, rather than economic, however, since instead of appealing to the union of the sets of libertarians and egalitarians, it typically appeals to the small minority of the population in the intersection of the sets.

APW

Marshall, Alfred (1842–1924)

In company with Stanley Jevons, Carl Menger, Léon Walras and **Francis Edgeworth** (🖹), Alfred Marshall was a founding father of what is now called neoclassical economics. As an undergraduate he studied mathematics and hoped to become an evangelical priest; he turned to economics in his mid-twenties. Most of his working life was spent at the University of Cambridge, where he became Professor of Political Economy in 1885.

His main work was *Principles of Economics* (1890). He had worked out many of his main ideas in the 1870s, and these had become widely known long before the *Principles* were published – to great critical acclaim – in 1890. In marked contrast to both Walras and Edgeworth, Marshall distrusted theoretical abstractions, insisting that theory should be subordinate to application and mathematics to plain English (see □). He rejected the model of rational 'economic man' as an unhelpful caricature, appealing instead to commonsense ideas about the actions and motives of ordinary people. The main object of economics, he thought, was to show how the human condition could be bettered. To modern readers, Marshall can sometimes seem prosy and moralizing. But despite his studied avoidance of abstraction, he made major theoretical innovations. The core ideas of microeconomics – the determination of price by the intersection of supply and demand curves, the theory of the firm and of the industry, the distinction

---

MATHEMATICS AND ECONOMICS

I had a growing feeling in the later years of my work at the subject that a good mathematical theorem dealing with economic hypotheses was very unlikely to be good economics: and I went more and more on the rules – (1) Use mathematics as a shorthand language, rather than as an engine of enquiry. (2) Keep to them till you have done. (3) Translate into English. (4) Then illustrate by examples that are important in real life. (5) Burn the mathematics. (6) If you can't succeed in (4), burn (3). This last I did often.

(Alfred Marshall; in Recktenwald, 1973, p. 279)

between short-run and long-run equilibrium, elasticity and consumer's surplus – are in large part due to Marshall.

RS

Marx, Karl Heinrich (1818–1883)

Marx's 'historical materialism' offers a view of history as the progressive advance of human needs and capabilities. Capitalism constitutes a particular epoch in this history and it will be superseded by communism, wherein the fullest realization of human potentials will be achieved.

While, according to Marx's account, history delivers an ever richer and expanding form of individual self-realization, the process of history has surprisingly little to do with the individual *qua* individual. The early Marx of the *The Economic and Philosophical Manuscripts of 1844* (1932) may have shown a particular concern with the alienated condition of individual workers under capitalism (see □). However, the later Marx was increasingly concerned with exposing how the things that go on behind the backs of individuals are responsible for this alienation under capitalism.

The idea that there is something other than individual wills at work is famously set out in the Preface to *A Contribution to the Critique of Political Economy* (1858) (□ p. 304). Here, we find that there is always an irreducible social component to individual action, and this frustrates any analysis of history which runs through individuals alone. The crucial irreducible

---

ALIENATION

What, then, constitutes the alienation of labour? First, the fact that labour is external to the worker, i.e. it does not belong to his essential being; that in his work, therefore, he does not affirm himself but denies himself, does not feel content but unhappy, does not develop freely his physical and mental energy but mortifies his body and ruins his mind. The worker therefore only feels himself outside his work and in his work he feels outside himself. He feels at home when he is not working, and when he is working he does not feel at home. . . . Lastly, the external character of labour for the worker appears in the fact that it is not his own, but someone else's that it does not belong to him, that in it he belongs not to himself, but to another.

(Marx, 1932, pp. 110–11)

components are the economic relations that structure individual action and, according to Marx, they change to facilitate the advance of the material forces in society. This alternative account of history, with its emphasis on a changing structure which is independent of individual intentions, is sometimes referred to as a type of 'structural-functionalism' (see **structuralism** (☞) and Cohen, 1978).

Marx spent much of his later life attempting to unravel the inner workings of capitalism. For this purpose, he developed a distinctive labour theory of value. This was designed to go below what seems to be happening on the surface, in markets and the like, by revealing the workings of capitalism's deeper economic structure. For instance, it enabled him to argue that the origin of profit was the exploitation of workers, and that accumulation under capitalism would become increasingly prone to crisis. These insights into political economy buttressed his historical materialism, supporting, in particular, the contention that it would be the working class who would overthrow capitalism to lay the foundations for communism. The primary work in this field is *Capital*. It was never completed: volume 1 was published in 1867; Marx continued to work on volumes 2 and 3 until his death and they were published posthumously (1885, 1894). In addition, we have the rough draft of his ideas from *the Grundrisse* (1939) and the three volumes, *Theories of Surplus Value* (1905–10), in which he discusses other theories in political economy.

Of course, Marx recognized that workers often fail to appreciate their exploitation. One explanation of this failure, which he advances, revolves around the role of 'ideology' in belief formation. An 'ideology' represents the world in a systematically distorted fashion: for instance, in the idea that religion makes man rather than the other way round. As Elster (1985) has noted, Marx's famous observations on how individuals come to hold this particular inverted belief are similar to that of the theory of **cognitive dissonance** (☞):

> Man makes religion, religion does not make man. Religion is the self consciousness and self esteem of man who has either not yet found himself or has already lost himself again. . . . [Religion] is the fantastic realisation of human essence because the human essence has no true reality. . . . Religion is the sigh of the oppressed creature, the heart of a heartless world. . . . It is the opium of the people.
>
> (Marx, 1843, p. 175)

Marx was also a political activist, who wrote prolifically on contemporary events. These writings provide many rich insights into the difficulties of taking collective action and the complex interactions between the state and the economic structure. The best known of them is, perhaps, *The Manifesto of the Communist Party* which he wrote with Engels (Engels and Marx,

1848). After the recent events in the USSR and Eastern Europe, it may be tempting to discount his political legacy. However, this would be a mistake. Marx's ideas have been – and remain – extremely influential in social democratic politics. Indeed, there is probably no better way of appreciating how Marx's ideas have affected the politics of the twentieth century than by consulting the concrete proposals in *The Manifesto of the Communist Party*. For the most part, it is doubtful that they will appear to new readers as surprisingly controversial, because they have largely become an accepted part of the way in which society is organized in most rich (capitalist) countries!

SHH

Maslow's Hierarchy of Human Needs

Maslow (1970) argues that there is a hierarchy of human needs. At the lowest level, the individual has simple physiological needs, the bread-and-butter biological requirements, and these must be satisfied before all others. Once this has been done the individual becomes concerned with higher material needs, those associated with safety and security. Thereafter, the individual switches attention to social needs, those associated with a sense of recognition and affection which comes from belonging to a group. Finally, there is the highest need of self-actualization that comes from the creative search for truth and meaning in life. The material conditions of a society will crucially determine the potential for progress up this hierarchy of needs: but it is perfectly possible, when there is material abundance, for particular individuals to become fixated with lower-level needs and thus fail to ascend the hierarchy.

SHH

Mill, John Stuart (1806–1873)

John Stuart Mill, the eldest of James and Harriet Mill's six children, grew up to be one of the leading British intellectuals of his day. His work on logic (Mill, 1843) and his exposition of political economy (Mill, 1848) became the standard works on their subjects in the nineteenth century.

Mill carried on his father's and **Jeremy Bentham's** (⊡) commitment to **utilitarianism** (⊡), but, after a youthful crisis in which he sensed the futility of a mechanistic view of humanity, he sought to extend the concept of utility by giving it a broader interpretation as 'the permanent interests of man viewed as a progressive being' (Mill, 1859, p. 74). Like all utilitarians, he employed a strategy of argument in which conventional or commonsense morality was interpreted as being grounded in utilitarian considerations, and in *Utilitarianism*, for example, he argued that justice and utility coincided because the idea of a right, derived from the concept of justice, meant no more than something 'which society ought to defend me in the possession of' (Mill, 1863, p. 309), and society would only make this defence on grounds of general utility. *On Liberty* pressed home the progressive concept of utility, showing how a utilitarian concern for long-term happiness ought to favour the development of unpopular opinions and experiments in living. It also advanced the famous 'harm principle', by which individuals ought to be left free to do that which is harmless to the public at large, even if it harms the agent or other consenting adults. Despite Mill's attempt to show the affinity between the principle of liberty and the principle of utility, many commentators have sensed an unresolved conflict between them. Thus Devlin (1965) advances utilitarian arguments for the restriction of personal liberty, while Hart (1963, pp. 32–4) notes a gap between a utilitarian concern for a person's well-being and Mill's libertarian fear of **paternalism** ([?]).

Mill possessed a strong sense of the importance of education, and this emerges clearly in his account of representative government, which he justifies on the grounds that participation in public affairs enlarges human understanding and the identification of interests (Mill, 1861). Active local government and widespread public discussion, as well as universal franchise, were the instruments with which to achieve these ends. Although Mill's educational justification of democracy has struck some as elitist, it is as well to remember his remark that there is absolutely no reason why the objects of cultivated human interest 'should not be the inheritance of everyone born in a civilized country' (Mill, 1861, p. 265).

APW

von Mises, Ludwig Elder (1881–1973)

A central figure in the Austrian school of economics, the early work of von Mises was concerned with money and business cycles. However, he is probably best known for his contribution to the socialist calculation debate of the 1920s and 1930s, and as an exponent of an *a priori* methodology in economics (see □).

He was one of the early doubters of the practicalities of socialism, and a strong advocate of a *laissez-faire* market system. In particular, writing in 1920 (and 1922), he argued that a socialist government could not calculate economically, and thus organize an economy, without prices. At first, the problem of prices and calculation was linked to the absence of markets, particularly of capital markets. Later, however, it was expressed as a problem of information: a central planner could not collect and process the

FROM THE ARMCHAIR

Without theory, the general a prioristic science of human action, there is no comprehension of the reality of human action . . . experience concerning human action is conditioned through praxeological categories. . . . If we had not in our minds the schemes provided by praxeological reasoning, we should never be in a position to discern and grasp any action.

(von Mises, 1949, pp. 39–40)

What assigns economics its peculiar and unique position . . . is the fact that its particular theorems are not open to verification or falsification on the ground of experience. . . . The ultimate yardstick of an economic theorem's correctness or incorrectness is solely reason unaided by experience.

(von Mises, 1949, p. 858)

As a method of economic analysis econometrics is a childish play with figures that does not contribute anything to the elucidation of the problems of economic reality.

(von Mises, 1962, p. 63)

information which would be necessary to replicate the operation of markets mathematically (see Hayek, 1935).

Methodologically, von Mises was opposed to the logical positivism that cast social science in the same mould as natural science and tested theories empirically. Instead, he argued that economic laws could be discovered by logical deduction from the self-evident proposition that humans are purposive – an approach which he referred to as 'praxeology'. This approach is sustained throughout his major later work, *Human Action: a Treatise on Economics* (1949), and it leads him to, among other things, a pure time-preference theory of interest.

SHH

Newcomb's Problem

Imagine that you are shown two boxes. One is transparent, and contains $1000. The other is opaque: it contains either $1 million or nothing – you do not know which. You do know, however, that the contents of the box have already been determined. You must choose one of two options: either you take only the contents of the opaque box (the *one-box act*), or you take the contents of both boxes (the *two-box act*). But there is a catch. The contents of the opaque box have been chosen by a super-intelligent being called the Predictor, which has shown itself to be extraordinarily successful in predicting the choices that people will make in this particular experiment. It observes the subject of each experiment before choosing what to put in the opaque box; and it has, of course, observed you before deciding what to put in your opaque box. If it predicts that the subject will take only one box, it puts in $1 million; if it predicts that the subject will take both boxes, it puts in nothing. You know that several hundred people have already been through the experiment. Many of these people chose to open only the opaque box, and all of them found it contained $1 million. Many others chose to open both boxes, and all of these people found nothing in the opaque box. On the basis of this evidence, you believe it to be extremely probable that the Predictor will correctly predict your choice. What should you do?

This is Newcomb's Problem, constructed by William Newcomb and introduced to the literature of decision theory by Nozick (1969). The problem is interesting because we are tempted by two different lines of thought, and both of them cannot be right.

Some people are convinced by the *two-box argument*, which runs as follows. There are two relevant events: that the opaque box contains $1 million, and that it contains nothing. Whichever of these events obtains, the two-box act has a better consequence than the one-box act. So, by a dominance argument, you should open both boxes. Other people are convinced by the following *one-box argument*. You believe it to be extremely probable that the Predictor will correctly predict your choice. So, for you, the subjective probability that there is $1 million in the opaque box, conditional on your choosing the one-box act, is close to one. Using this probability, you can see that the one-box act gives you $1 million with probability close to one. By the same argument, the subjective probability that there is $1 million in the opaque box, conditional on your choosing the two-box act, is close to zero. So the two-box act gives you $1000 with probability close to one. Comparing these two probability distributions of consequences, the one-box distribution is clearly preferable. So you should open only one box.

A few commentators, such as Horgan (1981), have endorsed the one-box argument. But there is something close to a consensus that the two-box argument is correct, and that the one-box argument is fallacious. This position is taken by Nozick (1969) himself and, for example, by Gibbard and Harper (1978), Lewis (1979) and Eells (1985). There is a common core to these arguments, which can be presented roughly as follows.

It is correct to regard the propositions 'The opaque box contains $1 million' and 'The opaque box contains nothing' as events in the relevant sense, and the dominance principle is indeed a principle of rationality. Thus the two-box argument is correct. If you, the subject of the experiment, are sufficiently rational to see this, then you will choose the two-box act. We must infer that the Predictor is very skilled at identifying how rational a subject is before the experiment begins. If it concludes that the subject is rational enough to recognize the validity of the two-box argument, it puts nothing in the opaque box. So if you can recognize the validity of the argument, you can be virtually certain that the Predictor knows that you can, and thus that there is nothing in the opaque box. This means that you are virtually certain that, were you to choose the one-box act, you would win nothing. This is a counterfactual proposition, since you will not in fact choose this act; it describes a 'possible world' in which the contents of the box and your powers of reasoning are exactly as in the actual world, but you choose the one-box act. This is the counterfactual you should use when deciding what to do: by using it, you can see that you should choose the two-box act. It is, then, not true that were *you* to choose the one-box act, *you* would win $1 million; and so the one-box argument is invalid.

Even if this argument is correct, we are left with the suggestion that rational choice theory may be in some sense self-defeating. Imagine two people, irrational Irene and rational Rachael, who go through the experiment. Irene is convinced by the one-box argument. She opens only one box, and wins $1 million. Rachael is convinced by the two-box argument. She opens both boxes and wins $1000. Rachael then asks Irene why she did not open both boxes: surely Irene can see that she has just thrown away $1000. Irene has an obvious reply: 'If you're so smart, why ain't you rich?'

This reply deserves to be taken seriously. Both one-box and two-box arguments are based on an instrumental conception of rationality. It is taken as given that more money is more desirable than less, and that rationality is about choosing the best means for reaching the most desired outcomes. The relevant difference between Irene and Rachael is that they reason in different ways. As a result of this difference, Irene finishes up with $1 million and Rachael with $1000. Irene's mode of reasoning has been more successful, measured against their common criterion of success. So are we entitled to conclude that, nevertheless, it is Rachael who is rational?

RS

Pareto Optimality

Pareto optimality, named after Vilfredo Pareto (1848–1923), is a central concept in welfare economics, and represents an attempt to avoid the problem of **interpersonal comparisons of utility** (⬚).

Conventional (or *Paretian*) welfare economics starts from three value judgements. First, each person's preferences are taken as indicators of that person's welfare. This rules out **paternalism** (⊠). Second, the welfare of a society depends only on the welfare of the persons who comprise it. This rules out any conceptions of social welfare which transcend individuals. (A Welsh nationalist, for example, might want to say that the survival of the Welsh language is vitally important for Wales as a nation, quite independently of whether it is good for the individuals who live inside the boundaries of Wales.) Third, if one person's welfare increases while no-one's decreases, then social welfare increases. As the cases of paternalism and nationalism suggest, these value judgements are not entirely uncontroversial. Any theoretical analysis, however, requires simplifications. For most economic purposes, these judgements are probably fairly acceptable.

Suppose that we compare two states of affairs, x and y, and find that every individual in the relevant society either prefers x to y or is indifferent between them, with at least one person having a strict preference for x. Then, according to the value judgements presented in the previous paragraph, social welfare is greater in x than in y. In this case, x is said to be *Pareto-preferred* to y. Equivalently, a move from y to x is a *Pareto improvement*. If everyone is indifferent between x and y, then x and y are *Pareto-indifferent* or *Pareto-equivalent*. If some people prefer x to y but others prefer y to x, then x and y are *Pareto-non-comparable*. In this case, Paretian welfare economics simply has nothing to say about the ranking of x and y. It does *not* say (as critics sometimes claim) that if x and y are Pareto-non-comparable, then they are equally good.

A state of affairs w is *Pareto-efficient* or *Pareto-optimal* if there exists no other feasible state of affairs v such that v is Pareto-preferred to w. In other words, w is Pareto-optimal if there is no way of making any person better off than he is in w which does not make someone else worse off. Given the value judgements of Paretian welfare economics, there is a clear sense in which a Pareto-sub-optimal state of affairs is undesirable: for every such state of affairs, there exists a feasible alternative which is clearly better (that is, Pareto-preferred). Notice, however, that this does not imply that all Pareto-optimal states of affairs are better than all Pareto-sub-optimal ones.

For example, imagine an economy in which the only economic problem is to divide 100 units of consumption between two individuals, A and B; it is also possible to throw units of consumption away. Assume that each individual cares only about his own consumption. Then the set of Pareto-optimal outcomes contains all those outcomes in which A's and B's consumption sums to 100. The outcome $(100, 0)$ in which A consumes 100 units and B consumes nothing, is Pareto-optimal, just as $(50, 50)$ is. The outcome $(49, 49)$ is Pareto-sub-optimal. Paretian welfare economics tells us that $(49, 49)$ is undesirable, but only because it is clearly inferior to other feasible outcomes such as (50, 50). It does *not* tell us that (49, 49) is inferior to (100, 0), even though the latter is Pareto-optimal and the former is not.

There have been many proposals to extend Paretian welfare economics so that Pareto-non-comparable states of affairs can be ranked. The most widely accepted of these proposals is the *compensation test* or *potential Pareto improvement test*. Suppose that *x* is the *status quo*, that *y* is some alternative state of affairs, and that *x* and *y* are Pareto-non-comparable. The compensation test asks whether those individuals who would gain from a move from *x* to *y* could fully compensate those who lose from the move, and still remain net gainers. In other words, the test is whether the move from *x* to *y* offers a *potential* Pareto improvement – a potential that could be realized by some system of compensation payments. Suppose, for example, that *y* is the policy of installing street lighting in a residential area, at some given cost which is to be borne by taxpayers in general. There will be some maximum sum of money that each beneficiary of the lighting scheme would be willing to pay in order to have the benefits of the lighting. If the total of all these sums of money is greater than the cost of the scheme, then the scheme satisfies the compensation test. Economists have been much concerned with some problem cases in which the compensation test's ranking of two states of affairs depends on which of them is the *status quo*, but in practice these problems are probably not very significant. Compensation tests are widely used in cost–benefit analysis (see PLANNING (10)), although the normative arguments for using them remain controversial.

RS

Paternalism

Paternalism is best defined by contrast with a strict liberalism. Strict liberalism insists that each person is the best judge of his or her own welfare. Paternalism asserts that sometimes people may not be the best judges of their own welfare, and that some other agency needs to substitute its judgement for their choice. The metaphor is obviously drawn from the relationship between parents and children, but it is typically applied to public policy or legislation, where the compulsory wearing of car seat belts or requirements to contribute to social insurance schemes provide examples of practices that are often labelled paternalistic.

Arguments abound over the justification and implications of paternalism. The assumption that persons are the best judges of their own welfare underlies the proof in general equilibrium theory that a competitive equilibrium produces a Pareto optimum (see **Pareto optimality** (⑨)), so to question the assumption is to cast a long shadow over an otherwise impressive edifice. From Aristotle (*Nicomachean Ethics*, book 7) onwards, philosophers have been concerned with the problem of weakness of will, and many have drawn attention to the difficulty that people have of seeing the long-term consequences of their actions, aptly summarized in Pigou's reference to a 'defective telescopic' capacity. Even J. S. Mill, who was so enamoured of liberal legislation, thought that contracts of slavery should not be permitted for the reason that it is not freedom to alienate freedom (Mill, 1859, p. 236). It would seem that the impulse to save people from themselves is difficult to resist. Against these tendencies libertarians have urged the rights of individuals to live their own lives and make their own mistakes, and have highlighted the counterproductive effects of paternalist legislation which, by creating victimless crimes, encourages the abuse of public authority and an increase in fraud and blackmail. They also draw attention to the fact that the liberal principle states that persons are the *best*, not the *perfect*, judges of their own welfare.

Clearly, many political and philosophical puzzles lurk in the concept of paternalism. On the political side much rests upon whether one focuses on the practice or the rationale of public policy. Many apparently paternalistic practices, for example compulsory health insurance, may be given nonpaternalistic rationales; for example, a desire to constrain the effects of professional self-regulation (Weale, 1978). In philosophical terms, the most interesting questions prompted by paternalism concern the identity of the self. How far can the choices of the earlier self bind the actions of the later self (Parfit, 1984)? Can you coherently place an obligation on yourself in the role of worker or motorist when you vote in your role as citizen? Suppose that you come to assent to a justification of paternalist legislation that you previously resisted. Why not simply count this as brainwashing? So far, these philosophical problems have proved highly intractable, and so political arguments to which they are attached will remain unresolved for some time.

APW

Path Independence

Path independence is the requirement that, for a given set of feasible alternatives, the final choice from the alternatives should remain independent of the path, or stages, by which the choice was made. To illustrate this requirement, consider how it is common on committees to vote on alternatives in subsets; for example, the amendment versus the motion and *then* the motion versus the *status quo*. The requirement of path independence says that the final choice should not depend on whether this procedure is followed or another procedure in which all the alternatives are voted on simultaneously (Plott, 1973). Thus, if x is chosen from $\{x, y\}$ and from $\{x, z\}$, it should also be chosen from $\{x, y, z\}$. This requirement cannot be assumed to hold generally, and it is violated in standard committee procedures every time there is a preference profile leading to a Condorcet cycle (see **Condorcet winner** (▦)) under majority rule.

Path independence is important because it shows that Arrow's Impossibility Theorem does not depend upon anthropomorphising society. Arrow (1963, p. 120) justified his condition of transitivity by saying that it made the choice of final outcome independent of the path to it. The conditions of path independence show how this intuition can be validated, and that Arrowian impossibilities are not problems merely for a 'group mind' but for the operation of social choice procedures.

APW

Preference Ordering

A preference ordering is a ranking of all possible outcomes in accordance with one's preferences. To obtain such an ordering, an individual must be able to compare any two outcomes, x and y, and judge whether one is 'preferred to' ($>$) or is 'at least as good as' ($\geqslant$) the other, or alternatively, that it is a matter of 'indifference' ($\sim$) between them. Repeated pairwise comparisons of the possible outcomes then generate an ordering, provided that an outcome can always be compared with itself (reflexivity), that these comparisons cover all possible outcomes (completeness), and that when $x \geqslant y$ and $y \geqslant z$ then $x \geqslant z$ (transitivity).

SHH

Probability Distribution

Suppose that we conduct a controlled experiment, the outcome of which is nevertheless uncertain. For example, two coins are tossed and we are interested in the total number of heads. Although we cannot predict the exact number with certainty, we can say that some events (in particular, 1 head) are more likely than others (0 or 2 heads). Since it is equally likely that the two coins fall {H, H} or {H, T} or {T, H} or {T, T}, the probability of the event 2 heads is 1/4, the probability of 1 head is 1/2, and that of 0 heads is 1/4. A probability distribution is a complete list of the theoretical probabilities attached to each mutually exclusive event. If the coins are unbiased, this is an objective probability distribution. However, in non-experimental situations our probability assessments must be based on partial information, judgement and intuition, as well as objective criteria, and this results in a subjective probability distribution.

BRL

Public Goods

Economists often distinguish public goods from private goods by two characteristics, *non-rivalness* and *non-excludability*.

A good is non-rival in consumption if one person's enjoying more of the good does not reduce the ability of others to enjoy it. A classic example of a non-rival good is a television transmission: your ability to receive a transmission is unaffected by whether or not I am receiving it at the same time. In contrast, an ordinary consumer good such as coffee has the property of rivalness: if I consume a cup of coffee, you cannot consume that cup too.

A good is non-excludable to the extent that it is difficult or costly to operate a system of charges, denying access to the good to people who do not pay the charge. Coastal protection against floods is a good example of a non-excludable (as well as non-rival) good: if the Thames Barrage is to protect some Londoners against the danger of flooding, it must protect them all. For many non-rival goods, however, it is not particularly difficult to exclude non-payers. An uncongested swimming pool or bridge, for example, is a non-rival good; but it is easy to charge people for using it. Satellite television companies have designed ways of excluding non-payers from enjoying their non-rival good. Conversely, a bicycle is a rival good, but it is all too easy to steal a parked bicycle. Excludability is a matter of degree. It also depends on prevailing moral standards: the more honest people are, the easier it is to exclude non-payers.

The modern theory of public goods derives largely from a paper of Paul Samuelson (1954), although the idea of public goods is very much older. Samuelson takes the case of a pure public good, which is non-rival and non-excludable. (More accurately: no exclusion is practised.) He asks what conditions must be satisfied for the quantity of such a public good to be **Pareto-optimal** (⧉). To simplify Samuelson's model, consider an economy in which there are many individuals and two goods. One good is a public good, and the other a private (that is, rival and excludable) one. The utility enjoyed by any individual will depend on two things: the quantity of the private good that *he* consumes, and the *total* quantity of the public good (which he enjoys along with everyone else).

Now suppose that the public good can be produced by some process which uses the private good as its only input. This allows us to define the *marginal cost* of the public good in terms of the private one (in other words, the amount of the private good that must be forgone in order to produce an additional unit of the public one, a 'unit' being taken to be very small). For any individual, we can also define the *marginal valuation* of the public good in terms of the private one (that is, the amount of the private good that the individual would just be willing to forgo in order to increase the supply of the public good by one unit). Pareto-optimality requires that the marginal cost of the public good is equal to the *sum* of all individuals' marginal valuations. (If the sum of the marginal valuations is greater than the marginal cost, it is possible to make everyone better off by increasing the supply of the public good and dividing the extra cost between individuals in proportion to their marginal valuations. Conversely, if the sum of the marginal valuations is less than the marginal cost, it is possible to make everyone better off by reducing the supply of the public good.)

Suppose that the supply of the public good is financed by voluntary contributions. If each individual maximizes utility, taking the others' contributions as given, no-one will have any reason to increase his contribution beyond the point at which the marginal cost of the public good is equal to *his own* marginal valuation. Thus, if there are many individuals, voluntary contributions will normally fall far short of the amount required to produce Pareto optimality. Typically, only a few individuals (those who value the public good most highly) will make any contributions at all: the rest will take 'free rides'.

These conclusions are the implications of a particular theory of rational choice. It is arguable that in some real-life cases, public goods are supplied much more successfully through voluntary contributions than would be the case if people behaved according to the theory. (In the UK, for example, the lifeboat service – a non-rival good for which exclusion, although technically feasible, is not practised – is financed by voluntary contributions.) Nevertheless, economists from Adam Smith on have generally agreed that pure public goods are unlikely to be provided efficiently by private initiative, and that their supply should be a government responsibility.

Disagreement tends to focus on questions about how far particular goods have the properties of publicness. How far, for example, do the benefits of hospital care accrue to the patients, and how far to the wider population? Are theatres primarily providing a service to their customers, or does everyone benefit in some less direct way from the preservation of a theatrical tradition? Does the survival of blue whales in the Southern Ocean enter into the utility functions of people who will never see them? Questions such as these are difficult to answer. (It may be that they do not have clear answers, even in principle: their answers may depend on how the concept of preference is interpreted.) Economists often regard an individual's private choices as the only reliable evidence about his preferences. It is of the nature of a non-excludable good that individuals are never confronted with choices between consuming and not consuming the good; thus preferences for such goods are never revealed in individuals' choices. When public goods are supplied by government, the problem of discovering people's preferences remains. Democratic voting is at best a highly imperfect mechanism for revealing individuals' preferences (see SOCIAL CHOICE (13)).

RS

Risk and Uncertainty

Any situation in which the events and outcomes associated with actions are not known can be broadly characterized by uncertainty . However, the term 'uncertainty' is also often used more narrowly to refer to a particularly radical type of 'not knowing', and it is distinguished from a weaker sense of 'not knowing' which is associated with 'risk'.

In 'risky' situations, the individual does not know the outcomes with certainty but he or she can attach probabilities to each of the possible outcomes. The **probability distribution** (⌘) may be objective in the sense that it corresponds to the actual distribution of these outcomes, or it may be subjective in the sense that it merely reflects the individual's beliefs about the distribution of these outcomes. As is suggested in RATIONALITY (1), the process of decision-making need not be qualitatively affected by the presence of uncertainty in this sense of 'risk'. Utility maximization simply becomes expected utility maximization.

In contrast, when there is radical 'uncertainty', individuals cannot attach numerical probabilities: or, to put this slightly differently, even if they can suggest a probability number when pressed, they have very little confidence in that figure rather than another, and this qualitatively alters their behaviour.

The distinction is commonly attributed to both Keynes (1921, 1936) and Knight (1921), and it is central to their work. Indeed, they would argue, respectively, that without this distinction it is impossible to understand the origin of unemployment and profit. Both saw the presence of 'uncertainty' as the cause of a departure from the conventional model of decision-making by allowing a role for rational intuitions, and Keynes further emphasized the part played by social conventions as guides to decision-making under these conditions (see □). While the work of these two economists is a testament to the fertility of the distinction between 'risk' and 'uncertainty', it remains a controversial topic, particularly for those who maintain a subjective interpretation of probability, and who argue that in cases in which there is no good reason to attach one probability rather than another, then equal probabilities should be assigned. (Savage (1954) is the major reference for the subjective approach: according to his account probability assessments are encoded within individual preference orderings, and so subjective probabilities are revealed by the individual's choices.)

One difficulty with the use of the equal assignment rule to transform cases of 'uncertainty' into 'risk' is that it presumes we know the full range of possible outcomes, even though we do not have any good reason for attaching particular probabilities to each of them; whereas part of the problem for those who suffer from 'uncertainty' is that they do not know the full range of possible outcomes. Indeed, how could anyone know the

PRECARIOUS CONVENTIONS

The state of long-term – expectation . . . does not solely depend on the most probable forecast we can make. It also depends on the confidence with which we make the this forecast. . . . The outstanding fact is the extreme precariousness of the basis of knowledge on which our estimates of prospective yield (on investments) have to be made. . . . If we speak frankly, we have to admit that our basis of knowledge for estimating the yield ten years hence of a railway, a copper mine . . . the goodwill of a patent medicine . . . a building in the City of London amounts to little and sometimes nothing. . . .

In practice, we have tacitly agreed, as a rule to fall back on what is, in truth, a convention'

(Keynes, 1936, pp. 149–52; see also □ p. 60)

full range unless he or she can predict the future growth of knowledge, and how this will affect the world? One must allow for the growth of knowledge and one's own ignorance, and this means conceding that some events, which are unimaginable now, will transpire in the future. To know in this way that what we know is limited is to undercut the general applicability of the equal probabilities assignment rule, because it means that we know that we cannot know the complete range of possible outcomes.

Even when the full range of possible outcomes is known, it seems from the Ellsberg (1961) paradox (see HOW PEOPLE CHOOSE (3)) that risk is not treated in the same way as uncertainty. Apparently, people do not use the equal assignment rule in these circumstances, thus marking a practical distinction between 'risk' and 'uncertainty'.

SHH

Risk Aversion

Suppose that someone is offered a gamble with a monetary **expected value** (🔢) of zero (for example, the gamble might offer a 1 in 10 chance of winning £10 000 in return for the certain payment of £1000). Such a gamble is said to be *actuarially fair*. A person who refuses actuarially fair gambles is *risk-averse*. One who is indifferent between taking on and not taking on such gambles is *risk-neutral*, while one who has a positive preference for actuarially fair gambles is *risk-loving*. In expected utility theory, these different attitudes to risk correspond to different properties of the utility-of-wealth function. Risk aversion corresponds to diminishing marginal utility of wealth, risk neutrality to constant marginal utility, and love of risk to increasing marginal utility.

Economists usually assume that the utility-of-wealth function is smooth, with diminishing marginal utility. This implies that individuals are generally risk-averse, but are approximately risk-neutral in relation to gambles involving very small changes in wealth. This leads to an important conclusion about *risk-spreading*. The risk of a gamble is 'spread' when it is shared between individuals. (For example, the gamble described in the previous paragraph might be shared between 1000 people, each being offered a 1 in 10 chance of winning £10 in return for a certain payment of £1.) Gambles with positive expected money values but which no one individual would take on can be made acceptable by being spread among many individuals. Insurance markets and the institution of shareholding can be interpreted as risk-spreading devices.

The extreme case of risk aversion is represented by the *maximin* principle. A person who follows this principle chooses the course of action for which the worst outcome that could occur is least bad. Thus, for example, he would refuse to pay £1 for a 99 in 100 chance of winning £10 000: the worst outcome from accepting this gamble is the loss of £1, while if he rejects the gamble, he is certain not to lose anything. According to the maximin principle, then, you should choose as though Murphy's Law were true: the worst possible event will always occur. There are good grounds for following the maximin principle in zero-sum games, where the worst outcome for you is the best for your rational opponent (see GAME THEORY (7)), but in other cases the principle seems unreasonably cautious. The assumption that this principle would be followed behind the 'veil of ignorance' is crucial to Rawls's derivation of his 'difference principle' (see SOCIAL JUSTICE (18)), also **lexicographics** (🔯)).

RS

Rousseau, Jean-Jacques (1712–1778)

Rousseau's theory of the social contract subordinates citizens wholly to the 'General Will' of the sovereign body which they have created, and yet insists that, even when forced to obey, they 'remain as free as before'. (Rousseau, 1762, book I). The key idea is that 'the passage from the state of nature to civil society produces a remarkable change in man', transforming him from 'a narrow and stupid animal' into 'a creature of intelligence and a man' with 'moral freedom, which alone makes him master of himself' (see □). In contrast to Hobbes, Locke and Hume, Rousseau works with a 'positive' notion of freedom (see AUTONOMY (6)) and fashions a collectivist

A REMARKABLE CHANGE IN MAN

The passing from the state of nature to the civil society produces a remarkable change in man; it puts justice as a rule of conduct in the place of instinct, and gives his actions the moral quality they previously lacked. It is only then, when the voice of duty has taken the place of physical impulse, and right that of desire, that man, who has hitherto thought only of himself, finds himself compelled to act on other principles, and to consult his reason rather than study his inclinations. And although in civil society man surrenders some of the advantages that belong to the state of nature, he gains in return far greater ones; his faculties are so exercised and developed, his mind is so enlarged, his sentiments so ennobled, and his whole spirit so elevated that, if the abuse of his new condition did not in many cases lower him to something worse than what he had left, he should constantly bless the happy hour that lifted him for ever from the state of nature and from a narrow, stupid animal and made a creature of intelligence and a man.

Suppose we draw up a balance sheet, so that the losses and gains may be readily compared. What man loses by the social contract is his natural liberty and the absolute right to anything that tempts him and that he can take; what he gains by the social contract is civil liberty and the legal right of property in what he possesses. If we are to avoid mistakes in weighing the one side against the other, we must clearly distinguish between *natural* liberty, which has no limit but the physical power of the individual concerned, and *civil* liberty, which is limited by the general will; and we must distinguish also between *possession*, which is based only on force or 'the right of the first occupant', and *property*, which must rest on a legal title.

We might also add that man acquires with civil society, moral freedom, which alone makes man the master of himself; for to be governed by appetite alone is slavery, while obedience to a law one prescribes to oneself is freedom.

(Rousseau, 1762, book I, ch. 8)

approach to social choice (see SOCIAL CHOICE (13)). In relation to this, his *Discourses* develop ideas about human nature, about corrupt and uncorrupt society and about power and inequality, in the spirit of the opening sentence of chapter 1 of *The Social Contract* that 'man was born free and everywhere he is in chains'. G.D.H. Cole's English edition of these works, cited in the bibliography, is notably well-introduced.

MH

Schumpeter, Joseph (1883–1950)

Joseph Schumpeter was born into the Austro-Hungarian Empire in 1883, and became Professor of Economics at the University of Graz in 1911. In the 1930s he was a refugee from Nazism and he became Professor of Economics at Harvard University in 1932.

In the field of social choice Schumpeter is most widely read today for his elitist theory of democracy, set out in *Capitalism, Socialism and Democracy*, first published in 1942 in the US and 1943 in the UK (Schumpeter, 1943). The centrepiece of this theory is that the role of the people in a democracy is not to govern but to choose those who are to govern them. In advancing this claim, Schumpeter is mindful both of the possibility of majority tyranny and of the difficulty of defining a clear notion of the public good, once we allow that different individuals can have irreducibly distinct moral evaluations. In passing he quotes a successful politician to the effect that just as businessmen deal in oil so politicians deal in votes, a remark that underlies subsequent developments in the spatial theory of electoral competition (Schumpeter, 1943, p. 285).

Schumpeter's theory of democracy forms part of a larger argument in which he anticipates the transition from capitalism to socialism. Unlike Marx, Schumpeter saw capitalism as doomed by its success, its achievements in creating economic growth leading to the cultural contradictions of an anti-capitalist mentality in the population, particularly among intellectuals. His acute insights into the cultural consequences of capitalism prefigured more recent theories of the rise of post-materialism (for example, Inglehart, 1977). In his economic theory Schumpeter stands as a maverick between the neoclassical and Austrian schools (see RISK, IGNORANCE AND IMAGINATION (4)) – unbranded, yet claimed by both.

APW

Search Theory

In the models of markets found in old-fashioned introductory textbooks, firms and consumers are assumed to be 'perfectly informed'. The concept of perfect information is still widely (and legitimately) used by economic theorists as a simplifying device, but it is not an essential part of the standard theory of rational choice. Search theory represents an attempt to model the workings of markets on the assumption that all agents are rational (in the conventional sense) but not perfectly informed. McKenna (1987a,b) provides a good survey of this area of economic theory.

Consider a very simple case. Suppose that a consumer has decided to buy one unit of some good. She knows a large number of shops which sell this good, and that the quality of the good is the same at all the shops. (Think of a branded durable good, such as a particular model of freezer.) However, she does not know what price is charged by each shop. She can find out the price charged by any shop, but only by incurring some cost (perhaps the cost of travelling to the shop, or the cost of a telephone call). One possible strategy open to her is to collect price quotes from every shop. This will ensure that she buys at the cheapest possible price, but will involve high 'search costs' (the cost of collecting quotes). At the other extreme, she might choose a shop at random and pay whatever price that shop charges, thus minimizing search costs at the risk of paying a high price for the good. There are many other possible strategies, lying between these two extremes. For search theory, the problem is to find the optimal search strategy – the one that maximizes expected utility.

In order to bring this problem within the domain of conventional rational choice theory, we have to make some assumptions about the consumer's *beliefs* about the range of prices she might encounter. A typical assumption is that the consumer knows the probability distribution of prices in the market (for example, she knows that at any given shop, there is a probability of 0.1 that the price is £450, a probability of 0.2 that the price is £425, and so on). Given an assumption of this kind, and given assumptions about the consumer's attitude to risk, the problem of choosing an optimal search strategy has a straightforward mathematical solution. Many interesting theories of market behaviour have been constructed from foundations of this kind. For example, Salop and Stiglitz (1971) present a theory of 'Bargains and Ripoffs' in which otherwise identical, profit-maximizing firms choose to sell the same good at different prices as a rational response to a world in which search costs are higher for some consumers than for others.

However, it is not clear that real people, faced with search problems, behave according to these theories. The results of experimental investigations suggest that people may instead use rules of thumb which are suboptimal. For example, a consumer who has collected price quotations of £450, £430 and £400 in that order is more likely to seek a fourth quotation than one who has collected the same quotations in the opposite order. (It is as if people are unconsciously looking for time trends in their experience, even in cases in which there are no rational grounds for expecting to find them.) Hey (1987) reports a good example of this kind of experiment.

Although the consumers of search theory are not perfectly informed, they know exactly what they are looking for (a low price for a given good) and where to look (the given set of shops); and they know all the relevant probabilities. Because so much is assumed to be known, the problem of search can be reduced to one of calculation. This rather sanitized conception of market uncertainty contrasts strongly with the 'Austrian' conception, in which alert agents continually discover possibilities which they could not have foreseen, even in a probabilistic sense (see RISK, IGNORANCE AND IMAGINATION (4)).

RS

Shapley–Shubik Index

The Shapley–Shubik index is a proposal for measuring the distribution of power in committees or other situations in which social choice outcomes depend upon voting rules. The assumption behind the index is that power is a zero-sum phenomenon, so that those who win by a vote gain something, the value of which equals the losses to losers. Voting games are therefore characterized by losing and winning coalitions, and the intuition driving the Shapley–Shubik index is that an individual's power is given by the probability of his or her being decisive or pivotal in forming a winning coalition.

To see the logic of this approach, consider a simple three-person voting game, in which a majority win something of value and the minority achieve nothing. Imagine that coalitions are formed by individuals combining together in random order. Then there are six possible ways in which coalitions can form, and on two of these six occasions any particular individual, say individual 1, ought to be pivotal in forming a winning coalition. This is illustrated in table 1.

Table 1 The formation of a majority coalition in a three-person game: the figures denote the order in which individuals form possible coalitions. Those set in bold type denote the occasions on which individual 1 is decisive or pivotal in forming a winning coalition.

Majority winning		Minority losing
1	2	3
1	3	2
2	**1**	3
2	3	1
3	1	2
2	3	1

Now consider the value to an individual of being in a winning coalition as distinct from being in a losing coalition. Since we are assuming that power is zero-sum, we may as well assign a value of 1 to the winning coalition and the value of zero to the losing coalition.

The so-called Shapley–Shubik index brings these two aspects of coalition formation together in a general formula (see Luce and Raiffa, 1957, pp. 245–50). For coalitions of any size and for any number of players the formula provides the power index for any individual. Corresponding to the two elements of probability and the value of winning, the Shapley–Shubik, index has two parts: a coefficient measuring the relative frequency with which an individual is pivotal; and the sum of all the values to an individual of the coalitions in which he or she participates. The formula is as follows (see Luce and Raiffa, 1957, p. 249):

$$\phi_i(v) = \Sigma\gamma_n(s)[V(S) - v(S - (i))] \qquad S \text{ a subset of } I_n$$

where s is the number of elements in S, I_n is the set of all individuals and

$$\gamma_n(s) = \frac{(s-1)!(n-s)!}{n!}$$

In this formula, the idea is to make an individual's power depend on the value of participating in that game to the individual. Thus ϕ_i is the power of an individual and V is the characteristic function of being in a particular coalition; that is, the value to a player of being in a coalition.

The way in which the formula works can be seen by considering a numerical example for a simple three-person majority voting game. For the individual 1, the Shapley–Shubik index is:

$$\phi_i = \frac{2!\,0!}{3!}[v(\{1,2,3\}) - v(\{2,3\})] + \frac{1!\,1!}{3!}[v(\{1,2\}) - v(\{2\})]$$

$$+ \frac{1!\,1!}{3!}[v(\{1,3\}) - v\{3\}] + \frac{0!\,2!}{3!}[v(\{1\}) - v(\emptyset)]$$

The difference between what everyone $\{1, 2, 3\}$ and what a majority coalition $\{2, 3\}$ will receive is zero, and the difference between what 1 will receive in a solitary coalition, and what nobody ($\emptyset$) will receive is also zero. Hence the only relevant coalition values are those in which 1 is pivotal: and 1 is pivotal on two occasions, once in relation to individual 2 and once in relation to individual 3. With random coalition formation, individual 1 is likely to be pivotal on two out of every six occasions on which a majority coalition is formed. Hence, in sum, 1 is pivotal 1/3 of the time and this is the power index. This result accords with intuition.

The power index is trivial in this case, but this is not always the case. Consider a three-person majority voting game in which there are weighted votes: two players have two votes each and one player has one. Common sense suggests that the player with one vote has less power than the other two, but this is not the result given by the Shapley–Shubik index. Since the player with one vote is pivotal to the formation of a majority coalition on just as many occasions as the other two players, the index of power for each player is identical, despite the difference in voting weights.

How useful is the Shapley–Shubik index likely to be? Barry (1989a, pp. 272–84) has argued that such an index is vitiated by the assumption that power is a zero-sum phenomenon. If we think of power as the ability to obtain that we want despite the opposition of others, then being in a majority makes us powerful, no matter how large the majority is, so long as the outcome for which the majority is voting has the quality of a **public good** (⟨?⟩) for members of that majority. On the other hand, there are forms of majoritarian behaviour, for example the formation of governments in which there are only a limited number of cabinet portfolios, to be selected from legislatures in which no one party has overall control, in which the zero-sum aspect of power is uppermost. Those in the governmental coalition gain a prize to the exclusion of those left outside. In these circumstances, Riker's (1962) use of the Shapley–Shubik index to show that winning coalitions will be only of minimum winning size has great fecundity.

APW

Sidgwick, Henry (1838–1900)

Henry Sidgwick held the Knightbridge Chair of moral philosophy at the University of Cambridge, and is the author of major works in the theory of ethics and politics (Sidgwick, 1891, 1901).

Sidgwick wrote in the utilitarian tradition. In *The Methods of Ethics* (1901) he aimed to show the coincidence of what he termed intuitional or commonsense morality and the method of utilitarianism. His approach is well illustrated in his discussion of justice, where he argues that utilitarianism provides a method for balancing conflicting commonsense intuitions about, on the one hand, the duty to obey existing laws and, on the other, the duty to overturn bad laws: 'Utilitarianism at once supports the different reasons commonly put forward as absolute, and also brings them theoretically to a common measure, so that in any particular case we have a principle of decision between conflicting political arguments' (Sidgwick, 1901, p. 441).

For Sidgwick, the coincidence between commonsense morality and utilitarianism was necessarily incomplete. Unless this were so utilitarianism would lose its critical function in relation to positive morality. Moreover, there were some moral intuitions; for example, the Benthamite 'everybody to count for one and nobody for more than one', for which Sidgwick could not provide a utilitarian rationale (Sidgwick, 1901, p. 417). In his approach, Sidgwick has good claim to be regarded as the founder of Rawlsian 'reflective equilibrium' and, although never an exciting writer, his work always repays careful scrutiny.

APW

Smith, Adam (1723–1790)

Surprisingly few people would disagree with the assessment that Smith's *The Wealth of Nations* is a singularly important book on economics. Across a wide spectrum, from Marx to contemporary conservatives, it has been hailed as a masterpiece.

It is probably best known for its arguments in favour of a market system; in particular, the argument that the force of competition will act as an invisible hand guiding the individual pursuit of self-interest in markets so as to promote the public good (see □ p. 180). This argument is an embryonic version of what is sometimes regarded as the pinnacle achievement of modern neoclassical economics: the demonstration that, under certain conditions, competitive equilibria are Pareto-optimal (see **Pareto Optimality** (⊞)) (see ANARCHIC ORDER (12)). In a similar fashion, Smith's remarks on the problems and dangers of restraints on trade have notable contemporary resonance. For instance, the first comment in the adjacent box could represent the views of any government department concerned with anti-trust regulation. Likewise, the second comment in that box on the delusions of sovereigns could apply with equal force to the modern central planner (□ and see PLANNING (16)).

However, this is neither the central argument for markets in *The Wealth of Nations*, nor is it really a part of the central theme of the book. Pareto-efficiency is a static attribute of markets and, above all else, in *The Wealth of Nations* Smith focuses on dynamics. He is concerned with the historical emergence of the 'commercial' form of market organization and with the source of its dynamic vitality. The key to the growth of an economy, for

---

BEWARE THE VISIBLE HAND!

People of the same trade seldom meet together, even for merriment and diversion, but the conversation ends in a conspiracy against the public, or some contrivance to raise prices.

(Smith, 1776, p. 128)

The sovereign is completely discharged from the duty, in the attempting of which he must always be exposed to innumerable delusions, and for the proper performance of which no human wisdom or knowledge could ever be sufficient; the duty of superintending the industry of private people, and of directing it towards the employments most suitable to the interest of the society.

(Smith, 1776, p. 651)

him, is the division of labour; and the extent of the division of labour depends on the size of markets. Thus, the central argument for markets is that artificial regulations and constraints on economic freedom are to be abhorred because they diminish the size of the market, prevent the division of labour and thus halt the material progress of society.

This dynamic and historical perspective is crucial for the pathos of *The Wealth of Nations*. Smith reveals ambiguous feelings about the material progress which he analyses, and to understand this we must return to his earlier book, *The Theory of Moral Sentiments* (1759).

In *The Theory of Moral Sentiments*, Smith is concerned with the origin of morality, with how self-interested individuals manage to act in a non-self-interested, disinterested fashion. His explanation turns on the natural sympathy which we feel for others:

> How selfish soever man may be supposed, there are evidently some principles in his nature, which interest him in the fortune of others, and render their happiness necessary to him, though he derives nothing from it except the pleasure of seeing it.
>
> (Smith, 1759, p. 1)

MIXED BLESSINGS?

> The man whose whole life is spent in performing simple operations . . . has no occasion to exercise his understanding, or exercise his invention in finding out expedients for removing difficulties which never occur. He naturally loses, therefore, the habit of such exertion, and generally becomes as stupid and ignorant as it is possible for a human creature to become. The topour of his mind . . . [renders him incapable] of conceiving any generous, noble, or tender sentiment, and consequently of forming any just judgement concerning many even of the ordinary duties of private life.
>
> (Smith, 1776, p. 734)

Smith's pessimism later deepens (p. 747):

> A man of low condition, on the contrary, is far from being a distinguished member of any great society. While he remains in a country village his conduct may be attended to, and he may be obliged to attend to it himself . . . But as soon as he comes into a great city, he is sunk in obscurity and darkness. His conduct is observed and attended to by nobody, and he is therefore very likely to neglect himself, and to abandon himself to every sort of low profligacy and vice.

The sympathy that we feel for others and the sympathy that they feel for us entails that we are motivated, in part, by the sympathy which others have for us: that is to say, the assessment which others make of our actions influences the value which we place on them. How do we know what others feel, particularly about things that we do? In part, this involves an imaginative leap. However, it also depends on a stable and shared set of public evaluations, encoded in laws and other informal moral rules that are found in the community.

The Theory of Moral Sentiments contains many further insights into human motivation, and Smith's later notion of an invisible hand is foreshadowed when he argues that it is a rather different invisible hand which deceives us into the belief that riches are associated with individual happiness. However, in *The Wealth of Nations* it is the requirements of imagination and a shared community of values for the exercise of morality which pose the problems for Smith. For it is the advance of the division of labour which saps the creative and imaginative spirit and establishes the anonymous and fractured conditions of urban life (see □).

Unfortunately, it seems that material advance is achieved at the expense of moral health; but here, as elsewhere, Smith finds that – his enthusiasm for the market notwithstanding – there remains a legitimate role for government. In this instance, it is public education which is supposed to help to keep our moral sentiments alive!

SHH

Social Welfare Function

The idea of a social welfare function was introduced to economics by Abram Bergson (1938) and developed by Paul Samuelson (1947). It was originally seen as a way of avoiding the problem of **interpersonal comparisons of utility** (🖙). Let a *social state* be understood as a complete description of society. Then we may think of political choices being made among social states, just as individuals choose among consumption bundles. Imagine someone who has full responsibility to make choices on behalf of society – the *social decision-maker*. It is characteristic of the Bergson–Samuelson approach that social choices are viewed in this way, as issuing from a single mind. (Critics sometimes complain that this view of social choice corresponds with the politics of benevolent despotism, and that is inappropriate for democratic societies: see, for example, Buchanan (1954).) Just as a rational individual is assumed to have a preference ordering over consumption bundles, so we might expect a rational social decision-maker to have an ordering over all social states, and that her choices would be derived from this ordering. This *social ordering* represents the decision-maker's subjective judgements about the social good – her *social welfare* judgements. Given certain technical assumptions, preferences can be accorded a numerical representation by use of a utility function. In exactly the same way, social welfare judgements can be accorded a numerical representation by use of a *social welfare function*.

It is conventional to impose some structure on social welfare functions by introducing some substantive principles. Three principles are usually invoked: that social welfare depends only on the welfare of individuals; that social welfare increases whenever the welfare of any individual increases; and that each individual's preferences are an indicator of that person's welfare. These *Paretian value judgements* (compare with **Pareto optimality** (🕮)) are often regarded by economists as uncontroversial.

Now let x represent any social state. Let society be made up of persons 1, . . . , n. Each person i will have preferences over social states, which may be represented by a utility function u_i, so that $u_i(x)$ represents the utility that person i derives from state x. Let $w(x)$ represent the level of social welfare in state x. Then, if we accept the Paretian value judgements, we may write:

$$w(x) = f(u_1(x), \ldots, u_n(x))$$

where f is an increasing function (that is, whenever the value of any $u_i(x)$ term increases, everything else remaining unchanged, the value of $w(x)$ increases). Here f is a *Bergson–Samuelson social welfare function*.

This approach leaves us with considerable freedom to choose between alternative specifications of the social welfare function: different specifications will correspond to different views about social welfare. One particularly simple specification is:

$$w(x) = u_1(x) + \ldots + u_n(x)$$

In terms of mathematical structure, this corresponds to the classical utilitarian view that the welfare of society is the sum of the utilities of all individuals (see SOCIAL JUSTICE (18)). The interpretation, however, is different. For the utilitarian, the utility functions $u_1(x), \ldots, u_n(x)$ measure the pleasures and pains of the n individuals on a single *objective* scale. In the Bergson–Samuelson approach, there is still a sense in which a single scale is being used, since without a single scale, the operation of addition would make no sense. But the scale is now a *subjective* one; a $u_i(x)$ term is to be understood as a measure of how much, in the judgement of some particular social decision-maker, person i's position in state x contributes to social welfare. The Bergson–Samuelson approach does not do away with the need for interpersonal comparisons, but it makes them subjective.

Bergson and Samuelson take individuals' preferences as given. However, as Arrow (1963a) first noticed, their approach assumes that a social decision-maker, when given full information about individuals' preferences, will be able to come up with a Bergson–Samuelson social welfare function – no matter what those preferences might be. This amounts to assuming that the decision-maker has some procedure for generating a Bergson–Samuelson social welfare function from information about preferences. Can such a procedure exist? Arrow posed this problem in the following way. Suppose that the decision-maker has to generate a social ordering of all social states. Let this ordering be R. Each individual i has a preference ordering R_i over social states. Given knowledge of the *profile* $(R_1, \ldots, R_n)$ of individuals' preferences, the decision-maker must come up with a particular social ordering R. Thus the procedure she is using must be capable of being described as a function F, where

$$R = F(R_1, \ldots, R_n)$$

That is, the function must assign a social ordering to every profile of preferences. Such a function is an *Arrow social welfare function*. Arrow presents a set of conditions which we might expect such a function to satisfy and then, in his Impossibility Theorem, shows that no function can satisfy them all (see **Arrow's Theorem** (📖) SOCIAL CHOICE (13)).

RS

Strategic Manipulation and Insincere Voting

Voters behave insincerely when they do not cast their votes in accordance with their true preference. Insincere voting is rational when it leads to a better outcome than would be achieved by sincere voting. The existence of majority rule cycling (see **Condorcet winner** (📖)) and provides one context within which insincere voting becomes rational.

To see how insincere voting arises, consider a particular example. Suppose that there are three equal-sized blocs of voters, A, B and C, with the following preference profile:

> A: $x > y > z$
> B: $z > x > y$
> C: $y > z > x$

Suppose that x is a proposal for policy, y is an amendment to that proposal and z is the *status quo*. Under conventional committee procedure, y will first be pitted against x as the amendment versus the proposal, and the winner of that contest will be pitted against the *status quo*. If all voters vote sincerely z will win, and under normal committee procedure it will not be pitted against y.

Voters in bloc A prefer x to y, but they may strongly dislike z, while having only a mild preference for x over y. In these circumstances, it will pay them to vote insincerely. If, in the contest between x and y, they vote for y against x, contrary to their true preferences, they will ensure that y is pitted against z in the final round of voting, so that the *status quo* will be overturned.

Insincere voting of this sort is one example of strategic manipulation, but other forms of strategic manipulation are available to those who control AGENDAS (17). These other forms include determining the order of business, splitting or amalgamating notions, and introducing new business on to the agenda.

How susceptible are voting schemes to manipulation of this sort? Gibbard (1973) and Satterthwaite (1975) have shown that strategic voting and manipulation are inherent in all voting processes. In effect, this is an application of **Arrow's Theorem** (☝). There are aggregation schemes that are proof against insincere voting, but they violate one or more of the Arrow conditions. An example is provided by the so-called 'responsive lottery' in which all first preference votes are put into a bag and one is drawn out at random and declared the winner. This is proof against insincere voting, since no voter has an incentive to declare anything less than his or her first preference, but it will clearly violate Arrow's condition of the independence of irrelevant alternatives since, with the same preference profile over x and y, x will sometimes be preferred by the responsive lottery, while y will be preferred at other times.

APW

Structuralism

Rational choice theorists and game theorists are usually individualists, who regard structures and systems as an outcome (intended or unintended) of sums of individual decisions. They also tend to be empiricists (or positivists in some senses of the term), who hold that scientific explanations stand or fall by the test of experience. Structuralists object on both counts. They believe in unobservable structures which shape preferences, beliefs and choices, in wholes which are more than the sum of their parts and in scientific knowledge where experience is not the (only) criterion. These are broad commitments, however, which leave room for dispute about, for instance, whether the determining structures are natural or cultural, social or psychological, political or economic, and whether the methodological aim of science is explanation (as with materialists) or understanding (as with idealists). Thus structuralists will all contend that this book, despite the inclusion of a chapter on POWER (15), has too little to say about the nature of power, especially of institutional power, and so has tended to overlook structural constraints on seemingly free choices and to treat agents as consenting equals, when they are not. But, whereas old-style marxian economists explain power by reference to the forces and relations of production, recent critical theorists are more inclined to see power relations as structural elements in the discourses which shape individual thinking. In either case, the result is a battery of objections to the suggestion aired in ANARCHIC ORDER (12) that the conventions needed for cooperative games can emerge from interaction in reiterated non-cooperative games.

MH

Time Inconsistency/Subgame Perfection

According to Greek mythology, Ulysses wanted to hear the exquisite voices of the Sirens. He was passing close by and, in principle, there was nothing to prevent him from listening to them while continuing his journey. However, he recognized that the power of these voices was such that he would steer the ship ever closer to the rocks where the Sirens were located. The ship would be wrecked and he would be unable to continue his journey.

Formally, Ulysses faced a problem of time inconsistency in his optimal plan. His optimal plan was to listen to the Sirens and then continue his journey. But this was time inconsistent, because once he had embarked on the plan by listening to the Sirens he would not have been able to implement the later part of the plan, the rest of his journey. By contrast, a time consistent optimal plan is one that specifies a sequence of actions $(a_t, a_{t+1}, a_{t+2}$ and so on), one for each moment in time $(t, t+1, t+2$ and so on), which enjoys the property that the individual will actually choose in each time period the action specified by the plan. Thus, when $t+1$ occurs, having undertaken a_t in t, the individual will still choose a_{t+1} as the best action rather than some other, and so on.

The time inconsistency arises because the Sirens affect Ulysses's preferences. His perception of the best action changes in the middle of the plan and this leads him to deviate from the original version. There are many examples of time inconsistency which are derived from similar variations in preferences across time (see Schelling, 1984), and they pose interesting problems for the individual optimizer. For instance, Ulysses implemented his optimal plan by denying himself freedom at the later stage of the plan. Having instructed his men to tie him to the mast and to ignore any orders to do anything other than sail past the rocks, he told them to plug their ears and row! This is a kind of 'one step back in order to advance two steps forward' approach, which is discussed in Elster (1979); it is also sometimes called exercising 'self-command'.

Time inconsistency in optimal plans also arises, in a manner which raises similar questions about freedom, when the structure of interaction between individuals has a particular form. For instance, a government which implements its inflationary policy after the private sector has formed its inflationary expectations may be unable to persuade the private sector to expect no inflation, even though the government prefers this to inflation. The difficulty is that a government may like an unanticipated inflation most of all, because this produces reductions in unemployment. In these circumstances, governments cannot persuade the private sector to expect non-inflation. It cannot claim to have a plan of non-inflation because the private sector realizes that such a plan is not time consistent. In so far as the non-inflation plan was believed by the private sector, they would appreciate that there would be an incentive for the government to deviate from the plan by inflating, because this would produce an unanticipated inflation. Rather like the case of Ulysses, it has been argued that this problem of time inconsistency in optimal plans can be avoided through a restriction on the macroeconomic freedom of governments (see Kydland and Prescott, 1977).

When such interactions are treated formally in GAME THEORY (7), the requirement of time consistency is entailed by the concept of subgame perfect equilibrium. This concept applies to games with a dynamic structure, and requires that an equilibrium strategy specify moves at each stage in the game which are also the equilibrium moves for the subgame which is formed by starting at that stage of the game. Thus, for instance, the moves at the last stage of the game which are specified in a perfect equilibrium must be equilibrium moves in a game which is defined by the last stage (see GAME THEORY (7)). The problem of time inconsistency in optimal plans then surfaces when perfect equilibria are Pareto-dominated by other possible strategy pairs in the game.

SHH

Time Preference and Discounting

Faced with a given amount of wealth to be consumed either this year or next, most people would prefer to consume rather more than half in the current year. This is what is meant by time preference. Part of the reason behind this psychology is the risk that death or disability may deprive the person of her enjoyment in the later period. Other risks relate to the possible loss or confiscation of wealth between periods. It may also be that consumers suffer from myopia and underestimate their potential future pleasure – a misjudgement that Pigou eloquently described as 'defective telescopic faculty'. A quite separate and important source of time preference is expected economic growth, combined with diminishing marginal utility of consumption. The faster expected growth is, and the more rapidly marginal utility declines as consumption increases, then the greater is the value of present versus future consumption. These sources of time preference for the individual need not be given equal weight by the social planner; for instance, in conducting a cost–benefit analysis (see PLANNING (16)). Individuals may undervalue the preferences of future generations (for example, the birth of new citizens should be set against time preference due to the chance of death), and society may well not wish explicitly to build myopia into its decision-making.

An important application of time preference is known as discounting, which is a way of coverting future benefits (or costs) into equivalent present values. If time preference is such that £1 now is valued equally to £1.05 next year, then the rate of time preference (or discount rate) is 5 per cent. More generally, if the decision-maker values £$(1 + r)$ next year equally to £1 now, the annual discount rate is r. Benefits received in t years time, b_t, are converted to the present value, b_0, using the formula $b_0 = b_t/(1 + r)^t$. A particular application of discounting is in the valuation of a constant stream of benefits, b, which are expected to be received *ad infinitum* (such as an annuity). The present value is simply b/r. For example, suppose that a field that can only be used for agriculture generates an annual income of £400; then, with a discount rate of 5 per cent, it has a capitalized value of £8000.

BRL

Utilitarianism

Broadly speaking, utilitarianism is the doctrine that actions are to be judged by their consequences. **Jeremy Bentham** (1748–1832) (▣), its founder as a systematic philosophical and social theory, made the test one of whether the consequences promote 'the greatest happiness of the greatest number'. He introduced the theory in the famous passage cited below (see □).

Here Bentham mixes a psychological theory that everyone is governed by his own pain and pleasure with an ethical theory that each should aim for the greatest happiness of the greatest number. The former does nothing to prove the latter. Indeed, it sets an obvious problem of how someone wholly governed by his own pleasures can even aim for the general happiness. Bentham's idea was that, with suitable legal penalties for antisocial behaviour, reason will guide self-interest to promote the general good. But that needs to be proved, and the proof of utilitarianism also remains a problem.

Later utilitarians have broadened the idea of happiness. J.S. Mill distinguished 'higher' from 'lower' pleasures, remarking famously, 'It is better to be a human being dissatisfied than a pig satisfied; better to be Socrates

NATURE'S GOVERNANCE

Nature has placed mankind under the governance of two sovereign masters, *pain* and *pleasure*. It is for them alone to point out what we ought to do, as well as to determine what we shall do. On the one hand the standard of right and wrong, on the other the chain of causes and effects, are fastened to their throne. They govern us in all we do, in all we say, in all we think: every effort we can make to throw off our subjection, will serve but to demonstrate and confirm it. In words a man may pretend to abjure their empire: but in reality he will remain subject to it all the while. The *principle of utility* recognises this subjection, and assumes it for the foundation of that system, the object of which is to rear the fabric of felicity by the hands of reason and of law.

(Bentham, 1789, ch. 1)

dissatisfied than a fool satisfied' (1861, chapter 2; see also □ p. 265). The higher pleasures, conveniently, were those of 'a being who is *of course* concerned for others' (1861, chapter 3; his italics). Then G.E. Moore, calling himself an 'ideal utilitarian', widened the category of what is good-in-itself to include personal affection, aesthetic enjoyment and other refined states of mind in 'the greatest good of the greatest number' (Moore, 1903). More recently, others – especially economists – have restated the aim, with deliberate vagueness, as the satisfying of as many preferences of as many people as possible.

Bentham was an 'act-utilitarian', as distinct from later 'rule-utilitarians', who hold that an action is right only if it conforms to rules the general observance of which would have the best consequences. Whereas an act-utilitarian would presumably break a promise whenever greater utility resulted, a rule-utilitarian keeps promises, because that is the most useful rule. This distinction does not remain simple for long, however, since act-utilitarians recognize that a broken promise damages a useful practice of promise-keeping, whereas a rule-utilitarian recognizes that rules can have exceptions. With the former willing to countenance rules of thumb (to cut down uncertainty and excessive calculation), and the latter willing to build in exceptions (to avoid a charge of 'rule worship'), the two strands tend to come together (Lyons, 1965). But each retains characteristic problems. Act-utilitarianism has been claimed to be self-defeating, in that a world in which everyone knew everyone to be an act-utilitarian would fall demonstrably short of the greatest happiness of the greatest number. Rule-utilitarianism avoids this snag, but is claimed to produce inferior outcomes in a world in which not everyone is a rule-utilitarian.

A common objection to all versions of utilitarianism is that they warrant the exploitation of the few for the sake of the many. This problem of majorities and minorities has led critics to reject utilitarian approaches to SOCIAL JUSTICE (18), unless individual rights can somehow be built in (despite Bentham's saying that 'talk of natural rights is nonsense, and talk of natural and imprescriptible rights is rhetorical nonsense, nonsense on stilts'). Nonetheless, both intellectually and historically, supporters of utilitarianism have been leading champions of the welfare state and of the spread of democracy, in accordance with Bentham's dictum 'everybody to count for one, nobody for more than one'. In short, utilitarianism still has plenty of life in it.

MH

Utility Function

At its most basic, a utility function is a numerical representation of a preference ordering. Thus, it attaches a number to each possible bundle of goods such that a higher number represents a higher rank of preference. Suppose that we label a bundle of five apples and three eggs as x, and a bundle of two apples and one pizza as y. Then, $u(\cdot)$ is a utility function as long as $u(x) > u(y)$ whenever the person prefers x to y, $u(x) < u(y)$ whenever the person prefers y to x, and $u(x) = u(y)$ whenever she is indifferent between x and y. It is only the rank order of preferences that matters, and no psychological significance should be attached to the absolute size of the number $u(\cdot)$. For example, if $u(x) < u(y)$ then exactly the same information is given by either $u(x) = 76.1$ and $u(y) = 76.5$ or $v(x) = 0$ and $v(y) = 1000$. Because the utility function depends only on ordinal preference, any function which preserves that ranking is equally valid. More formally, $v(\cdot) = t[u(\cdot)]$ represents the same preference order as $u(\cdot)$ as long as the transformation $t[\ ]$ is monotonic.

The conditions for the existence of an ordinal utility function are set out in (1) RATIONALITY which also describes the extra requirements, originally provided by von Neumann and Morgenstern, that are necessary to construct a cardinal expected utility function. Suppose that p is the probability of receiving x and that $[1 - p]$ is the probability of receiving y; then the central theorem of expected utility is that $u(px + [1 - p]y) = pu(x) + [1 - p]u(y)$. In words, the utility of a lottery is equal to the **expected value** (⚥) of the utilities of each possible outcome. Expected utility functions are cardinal in that they do measure the extent to which one bundle is preferred to another for an individual (although they do *not* provide an index that is interpersonally comparable). For instance, if we add a third bundle, z, to the above example, and expect $u(z) = 76.4$, then it must be true that $v(z) = 750$. More precisely, $t[.]$ is restricted to being positive and linear so that $t[u(x)] = a + b[u(x)]$, where a and b are constants and $b > 0$ (for example, $a = -76.1$ and $b = 2500$).

This modern treatment of utility functions contrasts with traditional utilitarianism, which assumed the existence of some absolute, cardinal measure of pleasure that could be compared across individuals (see **felicific calculus** (🔢)).

BRL

Value of Life

In 1984, The *New York Times* reported that life was valued at $3.5 million by the Occupational Safety and Health Administration, while the Federal Aviation Administration valued life at $650 000 and the Environmental Protection Agency apparently used figures that ranged between $400 000 and $7 million. Such considerable differences may seem surprising and indeed slightly worrying. But how should we put an economic value on life?

A traditional response is to calculate the present discounted value of the earnings which are forgone by death. This is an easy calculation to perform but, since it only provides a figure for the loss of GNP which follows from death, it is not obvious that it measures the true value of a person's life. Indeed, to rely on such a method would produce the perverse result that the value of someone's life, once he or she retires, is zero.

Instead, economists working within the cost–benefit analysis framework have preferred a willingness-to-pay criterion (see also CONSUMER THEORY (2)). Just as we attribute a value to noise pollution or road congestion by asking how much people are willing to pay to avoid it, or how much they would have to be paid to compensate for it, so we should ask people how much they would accept in compensation for death, or how much they would be willing to pay to avoid it. As promising as this might seem in the case of problems such as noise pollution, it does not seem at first sight to offer much help with the valuation of life. After all, how could one be compensated for one's own death? It seems that life would have to receive an infinite valuation; and, consequently, any project which involved the risk of life would be rejected since the benefits could never exceed the costs.

However, economists have escaped this conclusion by arguing that for the most part we are not concerned with valuing life as opposed to death. Rather, we are interested in valuing small changes in the probability of death; and this does not pose the same sort of difficulty. Indeed, we routinely make decisions which involve exposure to more or less risk of this sort:

as, for instance, when we decide not to use the pedestrian crossing which is located 50 m away because it would be less convenient than crossing the road here. Granted that we do value such small changes in the risk of death, it becomes possible to generate an estimate of the implied valuation of life. As this is an inference based on probabilities, it is sometimes referred to as the valuation of a statistical life. The calculation works like this.

Suppose that someone is willing to do something which exposes them to an additional risk of death of 1 in 1000 when paid an additional $2000. Then, in a community of 1000 similar such people, the death of one person is valued at $2 million, because this is the sum they are collectively willing to receive in compensation for the extra risk posed by the additional death within their group.

There are two ways in which such calculations have been performed by economists. One utilizes the evidence on the willingness to trade risk for income which is revealed by the premiums paid to those in risky occupations. Thus, for instance, the additional risk of being a steeplejack can be compared with extra earnings of steeplejacks, as compared with other individuals with similar qualifications in jobs with normal risks. In the UK, this has generated figures of between $170 000 and $6 million (in 1983 constant $s) for the estimated value of statistical life (see Jones-Lee, 1985). The alternative approach involves questionnaires. People are asked, for example, how much extra they would be willing to pay in order to fly with an airline which has some particular smaller number of fatalities per passenger mile. Again, this has produced widely varying estimates, ranging from $170 000 to $2.4 million, for the value of life (see Jones-Lee, 1985).

Both approaches have their critics. People who become steeplejacks may not appreciate the risks entailed, and their attitudes to risk may change as a result of experience on the job, especially if they suffer **cognitive dissonance** (⌸). In particular, they may become more risk-loving and hence require smaller risk premiums than others. Likewise, there is the traditional suspicion that when faced with a questionnaire people do not respond in the same way to hypothetical questions as they do to real-life decisions. These difficulties may help to explain why both methods have produced such widely varying estimates of the value of life. However, it should also be recognized that the differences could reflect genuine differences in the way in which we value life and assess risks in different settings. There are well-documented biases in risk perception (see Tversky and Kahneman, 1981) which might explain some of the variety; and it is also well known that we value life more highly when it is exposed to dangers which are beyond an individual's control than when some of the dangers are perceived as controllable. Thus, it is often noted that people are willing to pay more to save life in connection with air and rail transport than in connection with road transportation.

This may help to explain the differences in valuation, but it raises a problem for the policy-maker. Should life be valued differently in different contexts? This is a tricky issue because anxieties generated by false probability assessments are as real for those who experience them as those which follow from accurate probabilities. Likewise, if people feel that motorists contribute to their accidents in ways in which airline passengers do not, then it may make sense to devote less to public safety measures on the roads than in the skies so as to discourage motorists from contributing to accidents. On the other hand, there is something which smells decidedly fishy from an ethical point of view in the practice of valuing some lives more highly than others.

In addition, there is a deeper and more vexatious problem with respect to the statistical life approach which should be addressed. Broome (1978) has observed that cost–benefit analysis is usually justified by appealing to the potential Pareto-improvement criteria (see **Pareto optimality** (🔲)) and this entails that it should be possible to compensate those who are disadvantaged by some proposal. He argues further that, if a particular proposal increases the chances of death (among some group) and it is known that eventually someone will die, then compensation is impossible since there is no way that you can compensate someone who is dead for their own death. Thus, according to cost–benefit criteria, the proposal must be rejected. The construction of the statistical life concept to cover this problem is, he suggests, a dubious and unfair use of people's ignorance. The argument runs like this:

> Consider any project in which an unknown person will die. Because whoever it is does not know it will be him, because of his ignorance, he is prepared to accept ridiculously low compensation for letting the project go forward. The government does not know who will be killed either, but it knows it will be someone, and it knows that, whoever it is, no finite amount of compensation would be adequate for him. The cost of the project must therefore be infinite and it is only the ignorance of the person destined to die that prevents his demanding infinite compensation. It may be true that sometimes we are forced to make decisions based on imperfect knowledge if nothing better can be done. But this is one case where the problems of imperfect knowledge can be easily eliminated. If there is to be a death, we know at once that the cost, defined as the compensation required for the loss, is infinite. Any other conclusion is a deliberate and unfair use of people's ignorance. (Broome, 1978, p. 95)

Broome gives several illustrations of how the statistical life approach can produce strange results. For instance, suppose that one project will cause the death of a single person and it is known who it will be, while another project will cause the death of 1000 people but their identities are not known. In a sufficiently large population, it is conceivable that the people would demand a finite sum in compensation for the extra risk entailed with the second project, whereas in the case of the first project the person who is to die would demand an infinite sum. Hence, the second project will be preferred.

Some may doubt the impossibility of compensating someone with a finite sum for his or her death but, nevertheless, these are troubling thoughts for anyone who wishes to employ the statistical approach to the valuation of life. Unsurprisingly, they have sparked a lively debate, which can be followed in the 1979 volume of the *Journal of Public Economics*. For now, it suffices to note that Broome regards his arguments as telling against the use of cost–benefit analysis in these matters: other criteria and arguments must be employed when life is at stake, because life cannot be given a meaningful monetary valuation.

SHH

Walrasian Auctioneer

Léon Walras (1834–1910) was a French-born economist who spent much of his working life at the Academy of Lausanne in Switzerland. He was one of three economists, working independently of one another in the early 1870s, who originated the concept of marginal utility. (The two others were Stanley Jevons and Carl Menger; none of them were aware of the earlier work of H. H. Gossen on the same subject.) Walras's most significant contribution to economics, however, was general equilibrium theory. His approach to economics, characterized by theoretical abstraction and the use of mathematics, prefigures twentieth-century developments in the subject.

In his main work, the *Éléments d'économie politique pure* (1874), Walras presents a mathematical model of the determination of prices in what he calls a perfectly competitive market. He justifies his strategy of modelling an ideal form of competition by appeals to principles of scientific method, asking: 'What physicist would deliberately pick cloudy weather for astronomical observations instead of taking advantage of a cloudless night?' (p. 86). For any pair of commodities in Walras's market there is a ratio of exchange. In equilibrium, these ratios of exchange must be such that no profits can be made by arbitrage. This allows Walras to express equilibrium ratios of exchange in terms of a single commodity: if there are m goods, there are $m - 1$ ratios of exchange or prices. For each commodity he defines an 'effective demand' and an 'effective offer' (or supply). These depend on the prices of all commodities and are derived on the assumption that each individual maximizes utility, taking prices as given. General equilibrium exists when prices are such that, for each commodity, demand and offer are in balance. Walras formulates this as the solution of a set of simultaneous equations.

Walras then has to show that this 'theoretical solution' has some relevance to real markets. He does this by arguing that, in a real market, the price of any commodity will rise if the quantity demanded is greater than the quantity offered, and will fall if the opposite is true. He goes on to say:

> What must we do in order to prove that the theoretical solution is identically the solution worked out by the market? Our task is very simple: we need show only that the upward and downward movements of prices solve the system of equations of offer and demand by a process of groping [*tâtonnement*].
> (p. 170)

What follows is a mathematical argument (which by modern standards is more of a conjecture than a proof). Walras claims that it is possible to solve his system of simultaneous equations by an iterative procedure. Start from any arbitrary list of prices for goods $1, \ldots, n$. Suppose that at these prices, good 1 is in excess demand. Then raise the price of good 1 relative to all other goods, keeping the ratios of exchange between these other goods constant, until demand and supply for good 1 are in balance. (If initially good 1 is in excess supply, reduce its price until demand and supply are in balance.) Now repeat this procedure for each of goods $2, \ldots, n$; and then start again with good 1, and so on. Eventually, Walras argues, we shall arrive at an equilibrium list of prices.

Walras seems to be claiming that real markets – or at least, highly organized markets such as stock exchanges – adjust to equilibrium by means of a process that is similar to the *tâtonnement* process that he has outlined. Interestingly, he makes no reference to an auctioneer, and what he seems to have in mind is a market in which prices are determined by the interactions of many independent brokers. But the connection between the actions of the brokers and the *tâtonnement* process is never made clear. Subsequent theorists have found it simplest to interpret the *tâtonnement* process as a rule to be followed by an auctioneer, and to interpret Walras as claiming that real markets work *as if* presided over by an auctioneer who adjusts prices in response to excess supplies and demands. We are left with a powerful analysis of equilibrium, but with only a sketch of how it might come about. Walras's difficulty in providing a convincing account of how general equilibrium is reached is one that economic theorists continue to wrestle with.

RS

Bibliography

Abreu, D. 1986: Extremal equilibria of oligopolistic supergames. *Journal of Economic Theory*, 39, 191–225.

Ackerman, B. A. 1980: *Social Justice in the Liberal State*. New Haven and London: Yale University Press.

Akerlof, G. A. 1970: The market for 'lemons': quality uncertainty and the market mechanism. *Quarterly Journal of Economics*, 84, 488–500.

—— 1980: A theory of social custom, of which unemployment may be one consequence. *Quarterly Journal of Economics*, 94, 749–75.

—— 1982: Labor contracts as partial gift exchange. *Quarterly Journal of Economics*, 97, 543–69.

—— 1987: Loyalty filters. *American Economic Review*, 73, 54–62.

Akerlof, G. and Dickens, W. 1982: The economic consequences of cognitive dissonance. *American Economic Review*, 72, 307–20.

Allais, M. 1953: Le comportement de l'homme rationnel devant le risque: critique des postulats et axiomes de l'école americaine. *Econometrica*, 21, 503–56.

—— 1979: The foundations of a positive theory of choice involving risk and a criticism of the postulates and axioms of the American school. In M. Allais and O. Hagen (eds), *Expected Utility Hypotheses and the Allais Paradox*. Dordrecht: Reidel.

Allison, G. 1972: *Essence of Decision*. Boston: Little, Brown.

Appleby, L. and Starmer, C. 1987: Theories of choice under uncertainty: the experimental evidence past and present. In J. Hey and P. Lambert (eds), *Surveys in the Economics of Uncertainty*. Oxford: Blackwell.

Aristotle: *Nicomachean Ethics*. Harmondsworth: Penguin, 1955 edition.

Aronson, E. 1988: *The Social Animal*. New York: W. H. Freeman.

Arrow, K. J. 1963a: *Social Choice and Individual Values*, 2nd edn. New Haven: Yale University Press (1st edn 1951).

—— 1963b: Uncertainty and the welfare economics of medical care. *American Economic Review*, 53, 941–71.

—— 1970: Exposition of the theory of choice under uncertainty. In K. J. Arrow (ed.), *Essays in the Theory of Risk Bearing*. Amsterdam: North Holland.

—— 1974: *The Limits of Organization*. New York: Norton.

Arrow, K. J. and Debreu, G. 1954: Existence of an equilibrium for a competitive economy. *Econometrica*, 22, 265–90.

Austen-Smith, D. 1983: The spatial theory of electoral competition: instability, institutions and information. *Environment and Planning C: Government and Policy*, 1, 439–59.

Austin, J. 1832: *The Province of Jurisprudence Determined*. London: Weidenfeld and Nicolson, 1954.

Austin, J.L. 1961: Ifs and cans. In J.L. Austin, *Philosophical Papers*. Oxford: Clarendon Press.

Axelrod, R. 1984: *The Evolution of Cooperation*. New York: Basic Books.

Ayer, A.J. 1936: *Language, Truth and Logic*. Harmondsworth: Penguin, 1971.

—— 1954: Freedom and necessity. In A.J. Ayer, *Philosophical Essays*. London: Macmillan.

Azariadis, C. 1981: Self-fulfilling prophecies. *Journal of Economic Theory*, 25, 380–96.

Bacharach, M. 1976: *Economics and the Theory of Games*. London: Macmillan.

Bagehot, W. 1867: *The English Constitution*. London: Fontana, 1963.

Ball, L., Mankiw, N. and Romer, D. 1988: The new Keynesian economics and the output–inflation trade-off. *Brookings Papers on Economic Activity*, I, 1–60.

Barry, B. 1978: *Sociologists, Economists and Democracy*. Chicago: University of Chicago Press.

Barry, B.M. 1989a: *Democracy, Power and Justice*. Oxford: Clarendon Press.

—— 1989b: *Theories of Justice*. London: Harvester.

Baumol, W. 1986: *Superfairness: Applications and Theory*. Cambridge, Mass.: MIT Press.

Becker, G. 1962: Irrational behaviour and economic theory, *Journal of Political Economy*, 22, 1–13.

—— 1976: *The Economic Approach to Human Behaviour*. Chicago: University of Chicago Press.

Becker, G. and Stigler, G. 1977: De gustibus non est disputandum. *American Economic Review*, 67, 76–90.

Bell, D.E. 1982: Regret in decision making under uncertainty. *Operations Research*, 30, 961–81.

Benn, S.I. 1976: Rationality and political behaviour. In S.I. Benn and G.W. Mortimore (eds), *Rationality and the Social Sciences*. London: Routledge and Kegan Paul.

Benoit, J.-P. and Krishna, V. 1985: Finitely repeated games. *Econometrica*, 17, 317–20.

Bentham, J. 1789: *An Introduction to the Principles of Morals and Legislation*, J. Burns and L. Hart (eds). London: Athlone Press, 1970.

Berlin, I. 1969: *Four Essays on Liberty*. Oxford: Clarendon Press.

Berger, P.L. 1966: *Invitation to Sociology*. Harmondsworth: Penguin.

Bergson, A. 1938: A reformulation of certain aspects of welfare economics. *Quarterly Journal of Economics*, 66, 366–84.

—— 1967: Market socialism revisited. *Journal of Political Economy*, 75, 655–73.

Bernheim, B.D. 1984: Rationalizable strategic behavior. *Econometrica*, 42, 1007–28.

Bernstein, E. 1899: *Evolutionary Socialism*. New York: Schocken, 1961.

Bernstein, R.J. 1983: *Beyond Objectivism and Relativism*. Oxford: Basil Blackwell.

Binmore, K.G. and Dasgupta, P. (eds) 1986: *Economic Organizations as Games*. Oxford: Basil Blackwell.

—— 1987: *The Economics of Bargaining*. Oxford: Basil Blackwell.

Binmore, K.G., Rubinstein, A. and Wolinsky, A. 1986: The Nash bargaining solution in economic modelling. *Rand Journal of Economics*, 17, 176–88.

Binmore, K.G., Shaked, A. and Sutton, J. 1985: Testing non-cooperative bargaining theory: a preliminary study. *American Economic Review*, 75, 1178–80.

Bispham, J. and Boltho, A. 1982: Demand Management. In A. Boltho (ed.), *The European Economy: Growth and Crisis*. Oxford: Oxford University Press.

Black, D. 1958: *The Theory of Committees and Elections*. Cambridge: Cambridge University Press.

Blau, P.M. 1964: *Exchange and Power in Social Life*. New York: John Wiley.

—— 1968: Interaction: social exchange. In D.L. Sills (ed.), *The International Encyclopedia of the Social Sciences*. New York: Macmillan and Free Press, vol. 7.

Boadway, R.W. and Bruce, N. 1984: *Welfare Economics*. Oxford: Basil Blackwell.

Boudon, R. 1986: The logic of relative frustration. In J. Elster (ed.), *Rational Choice*. Oxford: Basil Blackwell.

Bowles, S. 1985: The production process in a competitive economy: Walrasian, neo-Hobbesian, and Marxian models. *American Economic Review*, 75, 16–36.

Bradley, F.H. 1886: My station and its duties. In *Ethical Studies*. Oxford: Oxford University Press.

—— 1927: *Ethical Studies*. Oxford: Clarendon Press, 1962.

Brittan, S. 1989: The case for the consumer market. In C. Veljanovski (ed.), *Freedom in Broadcasting*. London: Institute of Economic Affairs.

Broome, J. 1978: Trying to value a life. *Journal of Public Economics*, 9, 91–100.

Brown, J.A.C. 1954: *The Social Psychology of Industry*. Harmondsworth: Penguin.

Buchanan, A. 1985: *Ethics, Efficiency, and the Market*. Oxford: Clarendon Press.

Buchanan, J.M. 1954: Individual choice in voting and the market. *Journal of Political Economy*, 62, 334–43.

—— 1975: *The Limits of Liberty*. Chicago: University of Chicago Press.

Buchanan, J. and Tullock, G. 1965: *The Calculus of Consent*. Michigan: University of Michigan Press.

Butler, J. 1726: *Fifteen Sermons*, W.R. Matthews (ed.). London: Bell, 1969.

Campbell, R. and Sowden, L. (eds) 1985: *Paradoxes of Rationality and Cooperation*. Vancouver: University of British Columbia Press.

Chew, S.H. 1983: A generalization of the quasilinear mean with applications to the measurement of income inequality and decision theory resolving the Allais paradox. *Econometrica*, 51, 1065–92.

Coase, R. H. 1937: The nature of the firm. *Economica*, 4, 386–405.

Cohen, G. A. 1978: *Karl Marx's Theory of History: a Defence*. Oxford: Oxford University Press.

Cornford, F. M. 1908: *Microcosmographia Academica*. London: Bowes and Bowes, 1964.

Coser, L. 1956: *The Functions of Social Conflict*. London: Routledge and Kegan Paul.

Crawford, V. P. and Varian, H. R. 1979: Distortion of preferences and the Nash theory of bargaining. *Economic Letters*, 3, 203–6.

Crosland, C. A. R. 1956: *The Future of Socialism*. London: Jonathan Cape.

Cross, J. 1969: *The Economics of Bargaining*. New York: Basic Books.

Dahl, R. A. 1956: *A Preface to Democratic Theory*. Chicago: University of Chicago Press.

—— 1957: The concept of power. *Behavioral Science*, 2, 201–15.

—— 1961: *Who Governs?* New Haven: Yale University Press.

Dasgupta, P. 1988: Trust as a commodity. D. Gambetta (ed.), *Trust*. Oxford: Basil Blackwell.

Dawes, R. and Thaler, R. 1988: Anomalies: cooperation. *Journal of Economic Perspectives*, 2, 187–9.

Dawkins, R. 1976: *The Selfish Gene*. Oxford: Oxford University Press.

Deaton, A. and Muellbauer, J. 1980: *Economics and Consumer Behaviour*. Cambridge: Cambridge University Press.

Debreu, G. and Scarf, H. 1963: A limit theorem on the core of an economy. *International Economic Review*, 4, 235–46.

Devlin, P. 1965: *The Enforcement of Morals*. Oxford: Oxford University Press.

Dodgson, C. L. 1884: *The Principles of Parliamentary Representation*. London: Harrison.

Douglas, M. and Isherwood, B. 1979: *The World of Goods*. New York: Basic Books.

Downs, A. 1957: *An Economic Theory of Democracy*. New York: Harper and Row.

Dworkin, G. 1988: *The Theory and Practice of Autonomy*. Cambridge: Cambridge University Press.

Dworkin, R. 1977: *Taking Rights Seriously*. London: Duckworth.

—— 1986: *Law's Empire*. London: Fontana.

Earl, P. 1986: *Lifestyle Economics*. Brighton: Wheatsheaf.

Edgeworth, F. Y. 1881: *Mathematical Psychics*. London: Kegan Paul.

Eells, E. 1985: Causality, decision, and Newcomb's paradox. In Campbell and Sowden (1985), op. cit.

Ellman, M. 1979: *Socialist Planning*. Cambridge: Cambridge University Press.

Ellsberg, D. 1961: Risk, ambiguity, and the savage axioms. *Quarterly Journal of Economics*, 75, 643–69.

Elster, J. 1979: *Ulysses and the Sirens*. Cambridge: Cambridge University Press.

—— 1983: *Sour Grapes: Studies in the Subversion of Rationality*. Cambridge: Cambridge University Press.

—— 1985: *Making Sense of Marx*. Cambridge: Cambridge University Press.

—— (ed.) 1986: *The Multiple Self*. Cambridge: Cambridge University Press.

Emmet, D. M. 1958: *Function, Purpose and Powers*. London: Macmillan.

—— 1966: *Rules, Roles and Relations*. London: Macmillan.

Engels, F. and Marx, K. 1848: *The Manifesto of the Communist Party*. Harmondsworth: Penguin, 1973.

Esping-Andersen, G. and Korpi, W. 1984: Social policy as class politics in post-war capitalism: Scandinavia, Austria, and Germany. In J. H. Goldthorpe (ed.), *Order and Conflict in Contemporary Capitalism*. Oxford: Clarendon Press.

Farquharson, R. 1969: *Theory of Voting*. New Haven: Yale University Press.

Festinger, L. 1957: *A Theory of Cognitive Dissonance*. Stanford: Stanford University Press.

Fishbein, M. A. and Ajzen, I. 1975: *Belief, Attitude, Intention and Behaviour: An Introduction to Theory and Research*. Reading, Mass.: Addison-Wesley.

Foley, D. 1967: Resource allocation and the public sector. *Yale Economic Essays*, 7, 45–98.

Frankfurt, H. 1971: Freedom of the will and the concept of a person. *Journal of Philosophy*, 68, 5–20.

Freeman, R. B. and Medoff, J. L. 1979: The two faces of unionism. *The Public Interest*, 57, 69–93.

Freud, S. 1916–17: *Introductory Lectures on Psychoanalysis*. In J. Strachey and A. Freud (eds), *The Standard Edition of the Complete Psychological Works of Sigmund Freud*, Volume 16. London: Hogarth Press.

Friedman, M. 1953: On the methodology of positive economics. In *Essays on Positive Economics*. Chicago: Chicago University Press.

—— 1962: *Capitalism and Freedom*. Chicago: University of Chicago Press.

Frolich, N. and Oppenheimer, J. A. 1978: *Modern Political Economy*. Englewood Cliffs, New Jersey: Prentice-Hall.

Frydman, R. and Phelps, E. (eds) 1983: *Individual Forecasting and Aggregate Outcomes*. Cambridge: Cambridge University Press.

Fudenberg, D. and Tirole, J. 1987: Understanding rent dissipation: on the use of game theory in industrial organization. *American Economic Review: Papers and Proceedings*, 77, 176–83.

—— 1989: Noncooperative game theory for industrial organization: an introduction and overview. In R. Schmalensee and R. Willig, *Handbook of Industrial Organization*, Volume 1. Amsterdam: North-Holland.

Garfinkel, H. 1967: *Studies in Ethnomethodology*. Englewood Cliffs, New Jersey: Prentice-Hall.

Gauthier, D. 1966: *The Logic of Leviathan*. Oxford: Clarendon Press.

—— 1986: *Morals by Agreement*. Oxford: Clarendon Press.

Geras, N. 1986: *Literature of Revolution*. London: Verso.

Gibbard, A. 1973: Manipulation of voting schemes: a general result. *Econometrica*, 41, 587–601.

Gibbard, A. and Harper, W. L. 1978: Counterfactuals and two kinds of expected utility. In C. A. Hooker, J. J. Leach and E. F. McClennen (eds), *Foundations and Applications of Decision Theory*. Dordrecht: Reidel; abridged version reprinted in Campbell and Sowden (1985), op. cit.

Giddens, A. 1979: *Central Problems in Social Theory*. London: Macmillan.

—— 1989: *Sociology*. Cambridge: Polity Press.

Goffman, E. 1968: *Asylums*. Harmondsworth: Penguin.

—— 1969: *The Presentation of Self in Everyday Life*. Harmondsworth: Penguin.

—— 1975: *Frame Analysis*. Harmondsworth: Penguin.

Gouldner, A.W. 1960: The norm of reciprocity. *American Sociological Review*, 25, 161–78.

Green, H. 1971: *Consumer Theory*. Harmondsworth: Penguin.

Grether, D. and Plott, C. 1979: Economic theory and the preference reversal phenomenon. *American Economic Review*, 69, 623–38.

Habermas, J. 1979: *Communication and the Evolution of Society* (transl. T. McCarthy). Boston, Mass.: Beacon Press.

—— 1985–6: *The Theory of Communicative Action*. Cambridge: Polity Press.

Hahn, F. 1980: *Money and Inflation*. Oxford: Basil Blackwell.

Hahn, F. and Hollis, M. (eds) 1979: *Philosophy and Economic Theory*. Oxford: Oxford University Press.

Halévy, E. 1972: *The Growth of Philosophic Radicalism*. London: Faber and Faber.

Halsey, A.H., Heath, A.F. and Ridge, J.M. 1980: *Origins and Destinations*. Oxford: Clarendon Press.

Hamlin, A.P. 1986: *Ethics, Economics and the State*. Brighton: Wheatsheaf.

Hardin, R. 1982: *Collective Action*. Baltimore: Johns Hopkins University Press.

Hargreaves Heap, S.P. 1988: Unemployment. In J. Eatwell, M. Milgate and P. Newman (eds), *The New Palgrave*, volume 4, 745–9. London: Macmillan.

—— 1989: *Rationality in Economics*. Oxford: Basil Blackwell.

Harrod, R.F. 1951: *The Life of John Maynard Keynes*. New York: Harcourt Brace.

Harsanyi, J.C. 1955: Cardinal welfare, individualistic ethics, and interpersonal comparisons of utility. *Journal of Political Economy*, 63, 309–21.

—— 1967: Games with incomplete information played by 'Bayesian' players, I: The basic model. *Management Science*, 14, 159–82.

—— 1968: Games with incomplete information played by 'Bayesian' players, II: Bayesian equilibrium points. *Management Science*, 14, 320–34.

—— 1973: Games with randomly disturbed payoffs: a new rationale for mixed strategy equilibrium points. *International Journal of Game Theory*, 2, 1–23.

—— 1977: *Rational Behaviour and Bargaining Equilibrium in Games and Social Situations*. Cambridge: Cambridge University Press.

Hart, H.L.A. 1963: *Law, Liberty and Morality*. Oxford: Oxford University Press.

Hayek, F.A. 1935: The present state of the debate. In F.A. Hayek (ed.), *Collectivist Economic Planning*. London: Routledge and Kegan Paul.

—— 1944: *The Road to Serfdom*. London: Routledge and Kegan Paul.

—— 1948: *Individualism and Economic Order*. Chicago: University of Chicago Press.

—— 1960: *The Constitution of Liberty*. London: Routledge and Kegan Paul.

—— 1973: *Law, Legislation and Liberty*, volume 1. *Rules and Order*. Chicago: University of Chicago Press.

—— 1976: *Law, Legislation and Liberty*, volume 2. *The Mirage of Social Justice*. Chicago: University of Chicago Press.

—— 1978: *New Studies in Philosophy, Politics, Economics, and the History of Ideas*. Chicago: University of Chicago Press.

—— 1979: *Law, Legislation and Liberty*, volume 3. *The Political Order of a Free People*. Chicago: University of Chicago Press.

Heath, A. 1976: *Rational Choice and Social Exchange*. Cambridge: Cambridge University Press.

Hegel, G. W. F. 1821: *Philosophy of Right* (transl. T. M. Knox). Oxford: Clarendon Press, 1942.

—— 1837: *Philosophy of History* (transl. J. Sibtree). New York: Dover, 1956.

Held, D. 1987: *Models of Democracy*. Cambridge: Polity Press.

Hey, J. D. 1979: *Uncertainty in Microeconomics*. Oxford: Martin Robertson.

—— 1987: Still searching. *Journal of Economic Behavior and Organization*, 8, 137–44.

Hicks, J. R. 1932: *The Theory of Wages*. London: Macmillan, 1966.

Hirschman, A. O. 1970: *Exit, Voice, and Loyalty*. Cambridge, Mass.: Harvard University Press.

Hobbes, T. 1651: *Leviathan*. There are many editions, including: M. Oakeshott (ed.), Oxford: Basil Blackwell, n.d.; J. Plamenatz (ed.), London: Fontana, 1962; R. Tuck (ed.), Cambridge: Cambridge University Press, 1991.

Hodgson, G. 1984: *The Democratic Economy*. Harmondsworth: Penguin.

—— 1988: *Economics and Institutions*. Cambridge: Polity Press.

Hollis, M. 1988: *The Cunning of Reason*. Cambridge: Cambridge University Press.

Horgan, T. 1981: Counterfactuals and Newcomb's problem. *Journal of Philosophy*, 78, 331–56; reprinted in Campbell and Sowden (1985), op. cit.

Horton, J. (1992): *Political Obligation*. London: Macmillan.

Hospers, J. 1961: *Human Conduct*. London: Rupert Hart-Davis, 1969.

Hume, D. 1740: *A Treatise of Human Nature*, L. A. Selby-Bigge (ed.). Oxford: Clarendon Press, 1978.

—— 1742: *Essays, Moral, Political and Literary*, T. H. Green and T. H. Grose (eds). London: Longman, 1889.

—— 1748: *An Enquiry Concerning Human Understanding*, L. A. Selby-Bigge (ed.). Oxford: Clarendon Press, 1975.

—— 1751: *An Enquiry Concerning the Principles of Morals*, L. A. Selby-Bigge (ed.). Oxford: Clarendon Press, 1902.

Inglehart, R. 1977: *The Silent Revolution*. Princeton: Princeton University Press.

Jones, S. 1984: *The Economics of Conformism*. Oxford: Basil Blackwell.

Jones-Lee, M. 1985: The value of life and safety: a survey of recent developments. *The Geneva Papers on Risk and Insurance*, 10, 141–73.

Kagel, J. H., Battalio, R. C., Rachlin, H. and Green, L. 1981: Demand curves for animal consumers. *Quarterly Journal of Economics*, 96, 1–15.

Kahneman, D. and Tversky, A. 1979: Prospect theory: an analysis of decision under risk. *Econometrica*, 47, 263–91.

Kalai, E. and Smorodinsky, M. 1975: Other solutions to Nash's bargaining problem. *Econometrica*, 43, 513–18.

Kant, I. 1785: *Groundwork of the Metaphysic of Morals* (transl. H. J. Paton under the title *The Moral Law*). London: Hutchinson, 1953.

—— 1788: *Critique of Practical Reason*. Translated and edited by L W. Beck, *Critique of Practical Reason and Other Writings in Moral Philosophy*. Cambridge: Cambridge University Press, 1949.

Kelly, G. A. 1955: *The Psychology of Personal Constructs*. New York: Norton.

Kelly, J. S. 1978: *Arrow Impossibility Theorems*. New York: Academic Press.

Keynes, J.M. 1921: *A Treatise on Probability*. London: Macmillan.
—— 1931: *Essays in Persuasion*. London: Macmillan.
—— 1936: *The General Theory of Employment, Interest and Money*. London: Macmillan.
Kirzner, I.M. 1973: *Competition and Entrepreneurship*. Chicago: University of Chicago Press.
—— 1979: *Perception, Opportunity and Profit*. Chicago: University of Chicago Press.
Klein, B., Crawford, R. and Alchian, A. 1978: Vertical integration, appropriable rents, and the competitive process. *Journal of Law and Economics*, 21, 297–326.
Knight, F. 1921: *Risk, Uncertainty and Profit*. Boston: Houghton Mifflin.
Kreps, D.M. 1990: *A Course in Microeconomic Theory*. Brighton: Harvester Wheatsheaf.
Kreps, D.M. and Wilson, R. 1982a: Reputation and imperfect information. *Journal of Economic Theory*, 27, 253–79.
—— 1982b: Sequential equilibria, *Econometrica*, 50, 863–94.
Kreps, D.M., Milgrom, P., Roberts, J. and Wilson, R. 1982: Rational cooperation in the finitely repeated Prisoner's Dilemma. *Journal of Economic Theory*, 27, 245–52.
Kuhn, T.S. 1970: *The Structure of Scientific Revolutions*, 2nd edn. Chicago: University of Chicago Press.
Kydland, F. and Prescott, E. 1977: Rules rather than discretion: the inconsistency of optimal plans. *Journal of Political Economy*, 85, 473–92.
Lange, O. and Taylor, F. 1938: *On the Economic Theory of Socialism*, B.E. Lippincott (ed.). Minneapolis: University of Minnesota Press.
Le Grand, J. and Estrin, S. (eds) 1989: *Market Socialism*. Oxford: Oxford University Press.
Leijonhufvud, A. 1968: *On Keynesian Economics and the Economics of Keynes*. London: Oxford University Press.
Lerner, A. 1934: Economic theory and socialist economy. *Review of Economic Studies*, 2, 51–61.
—— 1937: Statics and dynamics in a socialist economy. *Economic Journal*, 47, 253–70.
Levi, I. 1986: *Hard Choices*. Cambridge: Cambridge University Press.
Levitt, B. and March, J.G. 1988: Organizational learning. *Annual Review of Sociology*, 14, 319–40.
Lewis, D.K. 1969: *Convention: a Philosophical Study*. Cambridge, Mass.: Harvard University Press.
—— 1979: Prisoner's dilemma is a Newcomb problem. *Philosophy and Public Affairs*, 8, 235–40; reprinted in Campbell and Sowden (1985), op. cit.
Lichtenstein, S. and Slovic, P. 1971: Reversals of preference between bids and choices in gambling decisions. *Journal of Experimental Psychology*, 89, 46–55.
Lichtheim, G. 1964: *Marxism*. London: Routledge and Kegan Paul.
Lijphart, A. 1984: *Democracies*. New Haven: Yale University Press.
Lindley, R. 1986: *Autonomy*. London: Macmillan.
Lindman, H. 1971: Inconsistent preferences among gambles. *Journal of Experimental Psychology*, 89, 390–7.

Littlechild, S.C. 1986: Three types of market process. In R. M. Langlois (ed.), *Economics as a Process*. Cambridge: Cambridge University Press.

Lively, J. 1975: *Democracy*. Oxford: Basil Blackwell.

Locke, J. 1690: *Two Treatises of Government*, P. Laslett (ed.). Cambridge: Cambridge University Press, 1960.

Loomes, G. and Sugden, R. 1982: Regret theory: an alternative theory of rational choice under uncertainty. *Economic Journal*, 92, 805–24.

Loomes, G., Starmer, C. and Sugden, R. 1989: Preference reversal: information-processing effect or rational non-transitive choice? *Economic Journal*, 99, Supplement, 140–51.

Lucas, R.E. 1972: Expectations and the neutrality of money. *Journal of Economic Theory*, 4, 103–24.

Luce, R.D. and Raiffa, H. 1957: *Games and Decisions*. New York: John Wiley.

Lukes, S. 1974: *Power: a Radical View*. London: Macmillan.

Lyons, B.R. and Varoufakis, Y. 1990: Game theory, oligopoly and bargaining. In J. Hey (ed.), *Current Issues in Microeconomics*. London: Macmillan.

Lyons, D. 1965: *Forms and Limits of Utilitarianism*. Oxford: Clarendon Press.

Macfarlane, A. 1978: *The Origins of English Individualism*. Oxford: Blackwell.

Macpherson, C.B. 1962: *The Political Theory of Possessive Individualism*. Oxford: Oxford University Press.

McKenna, C.J. 1987a: Theories of individual search behaviour. In J.D. Hey and P.J. Lambert (eds), *Surveys in the Economics of Uncertainty*. Oxford: Basil Blackwell.

—— 1987b: Models of search market equilibrium. In J.D. Hey and P.J. Lambert (eds), *Surveys in the Economics of Uncertainty*. Oxford: Basil Blackwell.

McLean, I. 1982: *Dealing in Votes*. Oxford: Martin Robertson.

—— 1987: *Public Choice*. Oxford: Basil Blackwell.

McLellan, D. 1974: *Karl Marx: His Life and Thought*. London: Macmillan.

McNeil, B.J., Pauker, S.G., Sox, H.C. and Tversky, A. 1982: On the elicitation of preferences for alternative therapies. *New England Journal of Medicine*, 306, 1259–62.

Machina, M. 1982: 'Expected utility' theory without the independence axiom. *Econometrica*, 50, 277–323.

—— 1987: Choice under uncertainty: problems solved and unsolved. *Journal of Economic Perspectives*, 1, 121–54.

Maine, Sir H.S. 1880: *Ancient Law*. London: John Murray.

Malinowski, B. 1920: Kula. *Man*, 51, 97–105.

—— 1922: *Argonauts of the Western Pacific*. London: Routledge and Kegan Paul.

Marglin, S.A. 1967: *Public Investment Criteria*. London: Allen and Unwin.

—— 1974: What do bosses do? The origins and functions of hierarchy in capitalist production. *Review of Radical Political Economics*, 6, 60–112.

Marin, A. 1983: Your money or your life. *Three Banks Review*, 138, 20–38.

Marquand, D. 1988: *The Unprincipled Society: New Demands and Old Positions*. London: Jonathan Cape.

Marshall, A. 1890: *Principles of Economics*. London: Macmillan, 1949.

Marx, K. 1843: Preface to a contribution to the critique of Hegel's Philosophy of Law. In *Selected Works*, Volume 1. London: Lawrence and Wishart, 1975.

—— 1852: *The Eighteenth Brumaire of Louis Bonaparte*, In K. Marx and F. Engels, *Collected Works*, Volume 11. London: Lawrence and Wishart, 1979.

—— 1859: *A Contribution to the Critique of Political Economy*. Moscow: Progress Publishers, 1970.

—— 1867/1885/1894: *Capital*, Volumes 1, 2 and 3 (transl. B. Fowkes). Harmondsworth: Penguin, 1976, 1978, 1981.

—— 1905–10: *Theories of Surplus Value*. Moscow: Progress Publishers, 1963.

—— 1932: *Economic and Philosophical Manuscripts of 1844*, D. Struik (ed.). New York: International Publishers, 1971.

—— 1939: *Grundrisse*. Harmondsworth: Penguin, 1972.

Maslow, A. 1970: *Motivation and Personality*. New York: Harper and Row.

Mauss, M. 1925: *The Gift*. London: Routledge, 1988.

—— 1938: *A Category of the Human Mind: the Notion of Person: the Notion of Self*. In M. Carrithers, S. Collins and S. Lukes (eds), *The Category of the Person*. Cambridge: Cambridge University Press, 1985.

May, K.O. 1952: A set of independent, necessary and sufficient conditions for simple majority decision. *Econometrica*, 20, 680–84.

Maynard Smith, J. 1978: The evolution of behaviour. *American Scientist*, 37, 136–45.

—— 1982: *Evolution and the Theory of Games*. Cambridge: Cambridge University Press.

Mead, G.H. 1934: *Mind, Self, and Society*. Chicago: University of Chicago Press.

Mill, J.S. 1843: *A System of Logic*. London: J.W. Parker.

—— 1848: *Principles of Political Economy*, J.M. Robson (ed.). Toronto: University of Toronto Press, 1965.

—— 1859: *On Liberty*, M. Warnock (ed.). London: Fontana, 1962.

—— 1861: *Representative Government*, H.B. Acton (ed.). London: Dent, 1972.

—— 1863: *Utilitarianism*, M. Warnock (ed.). London: Fontana, 1962.

Miller, D. 1989: *Market, State and Community*. Oxford: Clarendon Press.

von Mises, L. 1912: *The Theory of Money and Credit*. London: Jonathan Cape, 1934.

—— 1922: *Socialism: an Economic and Sociological Analysis*. London: Jonathan Cape, 1936.

—— 1935: Economic calculation in the socialist commonwealth. In F.A. Hayek (ed.), *Collectivist Economic Planning*. London: Routledge and Kegan Paul.

—— 1949: *Human Action: a Treatise on Economics*. London: Hodge.

—— 1962: *The Ultimate Foundation of Economic Science*. Princeton, New Jersey: Van Nostrand.

Moore, G.E. 1903: *Principia Ethica*. Cambridge: Cambridge University Press.

Morriss, P. 1987: *Power: a Philosophical Analysis*. Manchester: Manchester University Press.

Muth, J. 1961: Rational expectations and the theory of price movements. *Econometrica*, 29, 315–35.

Nagel, T. 1973: Rawls on justice. *Philosophical Review*, 82, 226–34.

Nash, J.F. 1950: The bargaining problem. *Econometrica*, 18, 155–62.

—— 1953: Two-person cooperative games, *Econometrica*. 21, 128–40.

Nelson, R.R. and Winter, S.G. 1982: *An Evolutionary Theory of Economic Change*. Cambridge, Mass.: Harvard University Press.

von Neumann, J. and Morgenstern, O. 1947: *Theory of Games and Economic Behavior*, 2nd edn. Princeton: Princeton University Press.

Nietzsche, F. 1882: *The Joyful Wisdom*.

Nove, A. 1983: *Feasible Socialism*. London: Allen and Unwin.

Nozick, R. 1969: Newcomb's problem and two principles of choice. In N. Rescher et al. (eds), *Essays in Honor of Carl G. Hempel*. Dordrecht: Reidel.

—— 1974: *Anarchy, State and Utopia*. New York: Basic Books.

Olson, M. 1965: *The Logic of Collective Action*. Cambridge, Mass.: Harvard University Press.

Owen, R. 1813: *A New View of Society*. Harmondsworth: Penguin, 1970.

Parfit, D. 1984: *Reasons and Persons*. Oxford: Clarendon Press.

Pateman, C. 1988: The patriarchal welfare state. In A. Gutman (ed.), *Democracy and the Welfare State*. Princeton: Princeton University Press, 231–60.

Pearce, D. 1984: Rationalizable strategic behavior and the problem of perfection. *Econometrica*, 52, 1029–50.

Perrow, C. 1986: *Complex Organizations: a Critical Essay*, 3rd edn. New York: Random House.

Peters, R.S. (ed.) 1962: *Body, Man and Citizen*. London: Collier Macmillan.

Peters, T. and Waterman, R. 1982: *In Search of Excellence*. London: Routledge and Kegan Paul.

Pigou, A.C. 1920: *The Economics of Welfare*. London: Macmillan.

Pliny, n.d.: *The Letters of Pliny the Younger*, translated and introduced by B. Radice. Harmondsworth: Penguin, 1963.

Plott, C. 1973: Path independence, rationality and social choice. *Econometrica*, 41, 1075–91.

Popper, K. 1945: *The Open Society and its Enemies*. London: Routledge and Kegan Paul.

Pugh, D.S. (ed.) 1984: *Organization Theory*. Harmondsworth: Penguin.

Putterman, L. (ed.) 1986: *The Economic Nature of the Firm: a Reader*. Cambridge: Cambridge University Press.

Quiggin, J. 1982: A theory of anticipated utility. *Journal of Economic Behavior and Organization*, 3, 323–43.

Radner, R. 1980: Collusive behaviour in non-cooperative epsilon equilibria of oligopolies with long but finite lives. *Journal of Economic Theory*, 22, 136–54.

Rasmusen, E. 1989: *Games and Information*. Oxford: Basil Blackwell.

Rawls, J. 1971: *A Theory of Justice*. Cambridge, Mass.: Harvard University Press.

Recktenwald, H.C. (ed.) 1973: *Political Economy: a Historical Perspective*. London: Collier Macmillan.

Riker, W.H. 1962: *The Theory of Political Coalitions*. New Haven: Yale University Press.

—— 1980: Implications from the disequilibrium of majority rule for the study of institutions. *American Political Science Review*, 74, 432–46.

—— 1982: *Liberalism Against Populism*. New York: W.H. Freeman.

—— 1986: *The Art of Political Manipulation*. New Haven: Yale University Press.

Riker, W.H. and Ordeshook, P. 1973: *Positive Political Theory*. Englewood Cliffs, New Jersey: Prentice-Hall.

Robertson, D.H. 1930: *Control of Industry*. London: Nisbet.

Robbins, L. 1935: *An Essay on the Nature and Significance of Economic Science*, 2nd edn. London: Macmillan.

Roemer, J. 1982: *A General Theory of Exploitation and Class*. Cambridge, Mass.: Harvard University Press.

—— 1988: *Free to Lose*. London: Radius.

Roth, A.E. 1988: Laboratory experimentation in economics: a methodological overview. *Economic Journal*, 98, 974–1031.

Rothbard, M. 1983: *The Essential von Mises*. Washington. D.C.: Ludwig von Mises Institute.

Rousseau, J.-J. 1762: *The Social Contract*, edited together with the *Discourses* by G.D.H. Cole. London: Dent, 1973.

Rubinstein, A. 1982: Perfect equilibrium in a bargaining model. *Econometrica*, 53, 85–108.

Runciman, W.G. 1966: *Relative Deprivation and Social Justice*. Berkeley: University of California Press.

Salop, S. 1987: Evaluating uncertain evidence with Sir Thomas Bayes: a note for teachers. *Journal of Economic Perspectives*, 1, 155–60.

Salop, S. and Stiglitz, J.E. 1971: Bargains and ripoffs: a model of monopolistically competitive price dispersion. *Review of Economic Studies*, 44, 493–510.

Samuelson, P.A. 1947: *Foundations of Economic Analysis*. Cambridge, Mass.: Harvard University Press.

—— 1954: The pure theory of public expenditure. *Review of Economics and Statistics*, 36, 387–9.

Sargent, T. and Wallace, N. 1975: Rational expectations, the optimal monetary instrument, and the optimal money supply rule. *Journal of Political Economy*, 83, 241–54.

Satterthwaite, M. 1975: Strategy proofness and Arrow's conditions. *Journal of Economic Theory*, 10, 187–217.

Savage, L.J. 1954: *The Foundations of Statistics*. New York: John Wiley.

Schattschneider, E.E. 1960: *The semi-sovereign People*. New York: Holt, Rinehart and Winston.

Schelling, T.C. 1956: An essay on bargaining. *American Economic Review*, 46, 281–306; reprinted in Schelling (1960), op. cit.

—— 1960: *The Strategy of Conflict*. Cambridge, Mass.: Harvard University Press.

—— 1978: *Micromotives and Macrobehavior*. New York: Norton.

—— 1984: Self-command in practice, in policy and in a theory of rational choice. *American Economic Review*, 74, 1–11.

—— 1988: The value of life. In J. Eatwell, M. Milgate and P. Newman (eds), *The New Palgrave: a Dictionary Economics*, volume 4, 793–96. London: Macmillan.

Schmalensee, R. and Willig, R. (eds) 1989: *Handbook of Industrial Organization*, volume 1. Amsterdam: North-Holland.

Schoemaker, P. 1982: The expected utility model: its variants, purposes, evidence and limitations. *Journal of Economic Literature*, 20, 529–63.

Schopenhauer, A. 1851: *Parerga and Paralipomena*, transl. E.F.J. Payne. Oxford: Clarendon Press, 1974.

Schotter, A. 1981: *The Economic Theory of Social Institutions*. Cambridge: Cambridge University Press.

Schumpeter, J. 1954: *Capitalism, Socialism and Democracy*, 3rd edn. London: Allen and Unwin.

Schutz, A. 1973: *Collected Papers*, volume 1. The Hague: Martinus Nijhoff.

Scott, A. 1990: *Ideology and the New Social Movements*. London: Unwin Hyman.

Selten, R. 1965: Spieltheoretische behandlung eines oligopolmodells mit nachfragetragheit. *Zeitschrift für die gesamte Staatswissenschaft*, 121, 301–24, 667–89.

—— 1978a: Re-examination of the perfectness concept for equilibrium points in extensive games. *International Journal of Game Theory*, 4, 25–55.

—— 1978b: The Chain Store paradox. *Theory and Decision*, 2, 127–59.

Sen, A. K. 1970: *Collective Choice and Social Welfare*. San Francisco: Holden-Day.

—— 1977: Rational fools. *Philosophy and Public Affairs*, 6, 317-44, reprinted in Hahn and Hollis (1979) and in Sen (1982), op.cit.

—— 1979: Personal utilities and public judgements: or what's wrong with welfare economics? *Economic Journal*, 89, 537–58.

—— 1982: *Choice, Welfare and Measurement*. Oxford: Basil Blackwell.

—— 1985: *Commodities and Capabilities*. Amsterdam: North-Holland.

Sen, A. K. and Williams, B. 1982: *Utilitarianism and Beyond*. Cambridge: Cambridge University Press.

Shackle, G. L. S. 1949: Probability and uncertainty. *Metroeconomica*, 1, 73–80.

—— 1955: *Uncertainty in Economics*. Cambridge: University Press.

—— 1958: *Time in Economics*. Amsterdam: North-Holland.

—— 1961: *Decision, Order and Time in Human Affairs*. Cambridge: Cambridge University Press.

—— 1966: *The Nature of Economic Thought*. Cambridge: Cambridge University Press.

Shaked, A. and Sutton, J. 1984: Involuntary unemployment as a perfect equilibrium in a bargaining model. *Econometrica*, 52, 1351–64.

Shawcross, W. 1979: *Sideshow*. London: André Deutsch.

Shubik, M. 1982: *Game Theory in the Social Sciences: Concepts and Solutions*. Cambridge, Mass.: MIT Press.

—— 1984: *A Game Theoretic Approach to Political Economy*. London: MIT Press.

Sidgwick, H. 1891: *The Elements of Politics*. London: Macmillan.

—— 1901: *The Methods of Ethics*, 6th edn. London: Macmillan.

Simmel, G. 1908: *The Sociology of Georg Simmel*, translated and edited by K.H. Wolff. New York: Free Press, 1950.

Simon, H. A. 1945: *Administrative Behavior*. New York: Free Press (2nd edn 1976).

—— 1978: Rationality as process and as product of thought. *American Economic Review*, 68, 1-16.

Slovic, P. and Lichtenstein, S. 1983: Preference reversals: Q broader Perspective. *American Economic Review*, 73, 596–605.

Smart, J. J. C. and Williams, B. 1973: *Utilitarianism: For and Against*. Cambridge: Cambridge University Press.

Smith, A. 1759: *The Theory of Moral Sentiments*, D.D. Raphael and A.L. Macfie (eds). Oxford: Clarendon Press, 1976.

—— 1776: *The Wealth of Nations*. Oxford: Clarendon Press, 1976.

Spence, M. 1974: *Market Signalling*. Cambridge, Mass.: Harvard University Press.

Steedman, I. and Krause, U. 1986: Goethe's Faust, Arrow's Impossibility Theorem, and the individual decision taker. In J. Elster (ed.), *The Multiple Self*. Cambridge: Cambridge University Press.

Sugden, R. 1981: *The Political Economy of Public Choice*. Oxford: Martin Robertson.

—— 1983: Free association and the theory of proportional representation. *American Political Science Review*, 78, 31–43.

—— 1984: Is fairness good? A critique of Varian's theory of fairness. *Nôus* 18, 505–11.

—— 1986a: New developments in the theory of choice under uncertainty. *Bulletin of Economic Research*, 38, 1–24.

—— 1986b: *The Economics of Rights, Co-operation and Welfare*, Oxford: Basil Blackwell.

—— 1991: Rational choice: a survey of contributions from economics and philosophy. *Economic Journal*, 101, 751–85.

Sugden, R. and Williams, A. 1978: *The Principles of Practical Cost–Benefit Analysis*. Oxford: Oxford University Press.

Sutton, J. 1986: Non-cooperative bargaining theory: an introduction. *Review of Economic Studies*, 53, 709–24.

Tawney, R.H. 1964: *Equality*. London: Allen and Unwin.

Taylor, C. 1975: *Hegel*. Cambridge: Cambridge University Press.

Taylor, C. 1979: *Hegel and Modern Society*. Cambridge: Cambridge University Press.

Taylor, M. 1976: *Anarchy and Cooperation*. Chichester: John Wiley.

—— 1987: *The Possibility of Cooperation*. Cambridge: Cambridge University Press.

Thaler, R.H. and Ziemba, W.T. 1988: Anomalies: parimutuel betting markets: racetracks and lotteries, *Journal of Economic Perspectives*, 2, 161–74.

Thompson, D.F. 1988: Representatives in the welfare state. In A. Gutman (ed.), *Democracy and the Welfare State*. Princeton: Princeton University Press.

Tirole, J. 1988: *The Theory of Industrial Organization*. Cambridge, Mass.: MIT Press.

Titmuss, R.M. 1970: *The Gift Relationship*. London: Allen and Unwin.

Townsend, P. 1979: *Poverty in the United Kingdom*. Harmondsworth: Penguin.

Trevithick, J. 1977: *Inflation*. Harmondsworth: Penguin.

Tullock, G. 1974: Does punishment deter crime? *Public Interest*, 36, 103–11.

Tversky, A. and Kahneman, D. 1974: Judgement under uncertainty: heuristics and biases. *Science*, 185, 1124–31.

—— 1981: The framing of decisions and the psychology of choice. *Science*, 211, 453–8.

Varian, H.R. 1974: Equity, envy and efficiency. *Journal of Economic Theory*, 9, 63–91.

—— 1975: Distributive justice, welfare economics and the theory of fairness. *Philosophy and Public Affairs*, 4, 223–47.

—— 1978: *Microeconomic Analysis*. New York: Norton.

Varoutakis, Y. 1991: *Rational Conflict*. Oxford: Blackwell.

Walras, L. 1874: *Éléments d'économie politique pure* (transl. W. Jaffé as *Elements of Economics*.) London: Allen and Unwin, 1954.

Walzer, M. 1983: *Spheres of Justice*. Oxford: Martin Robertson.

Weale, A. 1976: Power inequalities. *Theory and Decision*, 7, 297–313.

—— 1978: Paternalism and social policy. *Journal of Social Policy*, 7, 157–72.

—— 1983: *Political Theory and Social Policy*. London: Macmillan.

Weber, M. 1910: *The Theory of Social and Economic Organisation*, (trans. 1947 by A.M. Henderson and T. Persons). New York: Free Press.

—— 1922: *Economy and Society*, G. Roth and C. Wittich (eds). New York: Bedminster Press, 1968.

—— and Camerer, C. 1987: Recent developments in modelling preferences under risk. *OR Spektrum*, 9, 129–51.

Williams, B. 1973: *Problems of the Self*. Cambridge: Cambridge University Press.

Williamson, O.E. 1975: *Markets and Hierarchies: Analysis and Anti-trust Implications*. New York: Free Press.

—— 1985: *The Economic Institutions of Capitalism: Firms, Markets and Relational Contracting*. New York: Free Press.

Willig, R. 1976: Consumer's surplus without apology. *American Economic Review*, 66, 589–97.

Winch, P. 1958: *The Idea of a Social Science*, London: Routledge and Kegan Paul.

Wittgenstein, L. 1953: *Philosophical Investigations*. Oxford: Blackwell.

Young, R. 1986: *Personal Autonomy: Beyond Negative and Positive Liberty*. London: Croom Helm.

Zeuthen, F. 1930: *Problems of Monopoly and Economic Warfare*. London: Routledge and Kegan Paul.

Index

Abreu, D., 116
accountability, 256
adverse selection, 159
advertising, 56, 58
agency problem, 157–9, 162
agendas, xiii, 363, 248–58
aggregation of demands, 26–7
Ajzan, I., 12
Akerlof, G., 140, 153, 160, 292–3, 298
Alchian, A., 165, 169
alienation, 336
Allais, M., 37, 40–1
Allais paradox, 37–42, 48–9
Allison, G., 232
altruism, 175
ambiguity, 46
anarchic order, xiii, 63, 178–95, 201, 333
anarchy, 200–5
anchor and adjustment process, 44
animal spirits, 60
anonymity, 206–9
appropriation, 279–80
Aristotle, 334
arms reduction game, 96
Aronson, E., 258

Arrow, K., ix, 10–11, 59, 61, 160, 186, 209–15, 216, 236, 289–91, 362
Arrow's Theorem, 209–15, 226–27, 255, 289–91, 346, 362–3
Austen-Smith, D., 227
Austin, J., 200
Austin, J.L., 305
Austrian school of economics, 54–6, 189, 233, 236, 308, 354–5
autonomy, xiii, 73–89, 232–3, 236
Axelrod, R., 125, 205
axioms of rational choice, 5–11
Ayer, A.J., 305
Azariadis, C., 312

Bacharach, M., 302–3
Bagehot, W., 70
bandwagons, 292–4
bargaining, xii, 191–2, 130–43, 157
   experimental evidence, 140–3
Barry, B.M., 72, 227, 230–1, 236–7, 356
battle of the sexes game, 107, 109, 112, 182, 256
Baumol, W., 320
Bayes's rule, 15, 53, 122, 150–3

Becker, G.,   viii, x, 16, 65, 83
Bell, D.,   41
Benn, S.,   227
Bentham, J.,   viii, 261–2, 296, 367, 338, 357
Berger, P.,   63, 71
Bergson, A.,   334, 360–2
Berlin, I.,   89
Bernheim, B.,   103
Bernstein, R.,   23
Binmore, K.,   129, 141, 143
Black, D.,   ix, 300
Blau, P.,   173
bootstrap equilibria,   293
Borda, J.-C. de,   ix, 297
Boudon, R.,   13
Bowles, S.,   169
Bradley, F.H.,   63
Brittan, S.,   223
Broome, J.,   371
Brown, J.A.C.,   167
Buchanan, J.,   277, 360
budget line,   28
Butler, Bishop,   306, 316
Butskellism,   221

capabilities,   272–4
Carroll L.,   297
Caser, L.,   64
chain store game,   xii, 117, 124, 149–53
Chew, S.H.,   41
chicken game,   106, 127, 184–5
coalition,   95
Coase, R.,   161
cognitive dissonance,   57, 88, 297–300
Cohen, J.,   337
collective goods,   66–7;
  see also public goods
commitment,   115
common knowledge,   97
compatibilism,   305
compensating variation,   30, 33–4
compensation test,   32–3, 344
competitive equilibrium,   186–8, 192–5

Condorcet, Marquis de,   ix, 300–1
Condorcet paradox,   207, 221, 223, 346, 362
Condorcet winner,   251
conflict,   138–140
consequences, interpretation of,   47–8
consumer surplus,   228–9
consumer theory,   xii, 26–35
contingent markets,   59
continuity,   331
contracts,   157, 160–1, 234
convention,   183–4;
  see also norms
convexity,   27
coordination game,   107–10
core,   140, 191–2, 214, 302–4
Cornford, F.M.,   252, 258
corporate culture,   168
cost–benefit analysis,   32, 240–2, 344, 369, 372
Crawford, R.,   165, 169
creative choice,   21–4
Cross, J.,   135
crossroads game,   181–2
Cuban missile crisis,   232
cultural exchange,   xii, 170–178
customs *see also* norms

Dahl, R.A.,   227, 231, 237
Darwin, C.,   125
Dasgupta, P.,   129, 143, 153
Dawes, P.,   129
de Tocqueville, A.,   13
Deaton, A.,   27
Debreu, G.,   59, 186, 192
demand function,   28
  law of,   29–32
demand management,   239, 242–5
democracy,   xii, 212–27, 254, 353
determinism,   304
Devlin, P.,   339
dialogue,   215
Dickens, C.,   296
difference principle,   272, 307, 331–2, 351
disappointment,   41–2
discounting,   365–6

distribution of income, 267–74, 278, 280–2
division of labour, 63, 66
Dodgson, C.L., 297
dominant strategy, 98–100
Douglas, M., 71–2
Downs, A., 66, 219, 225, 227
dung flies, 128
Dworkin, R., 20, 89, 306

Earl, P., 24
economic freedom, 359
economics of democracy, 11, 218–27
Edgeworth, F.Y., 191–2, 261, 303, 305–6, 335
Eells, E., 341
egalitarianism, 306–7
Eisenhower, D.D., 221
Ellsberg, D., 44–6
Ellsberg paradox, 44–6, 48, 350
Elster, J., 14, 22, 364
Emmet, D.M., 63–4
entrepreneurship, 53–5, 58, 60, 190–1
envy, 306, 320–2
equality, political, 207–8
equilibrium, 98, 307–8
  competitive, 186–8, 192–5
  general, 307, 322–3
  multiple, 107
  political, 219–22
  rational expectations, 307
  sequential, 122
  trembling hand (perfect), 111
  see also Nash equilibrium; 'dominant strategy'; core; Walrasian auctioneer
Esping-Andersen, G., 233
Estrin, S., 333
ethical preferences, 308
evolution, 205
evolutionarily stable strategy, 126, 182
evolutionary games, 125–7, 147
expectatations, 17, 244, 291–4
  see also trust; imperfect information
expected utility theory, 8–11, 36–49,

225, 267, 350–1
expected value, 313
expensive tastes, 269–70, 272–4
experimental method, 36, 48–9
extended sympathy, 271, 315–16
externalities, 193, 238–40, 316–17

fact–value distinction, 83, 317, 327
fairness, 141–3, 307, 319–22
Farquharson, R., 258
feasible set, 322
felicific calculus, 296, 322
Festinger, L., 24, 298
first-mover advantage, 115
Fishbein, M., 12
focal point, 108
Foley, D., 320
folk theorem, 116
framing effects, 39–40
Frankfurt, H., 89
free rider, 100, 175, 309, 348
free will, 304
freedom, 364–5
  negative, 73–4, 84
  positive, 74, 85–7, 351
Freeman, R., 165
Freud, C., 55
Freud, S., 24
Friedman, M., 199
Frydman, R., 312
Fudenberg, D., 129
future generations, obligations to, 278

gambling, 38–9
games, cooperative and non-cooperative, x, 95, 171, 203
  definition, 94
  extensive form, 112
  normal form, 96
  one-shot, 95
  repeated, 115–20
  rules of the, 95–7
  zero-sum, 102
game theory, ix, xi, 12, 93–129, 202, 226, 311 12

games *see* arms reduction; battle of the sexes; chicken; coordination; crossroads; evolutionary; hawk and dove; matching pennies; Prisoner's Dilemma; sharing a shilling
Garfinkel, H.,   19
Gauthier, D.,   65, 68, 72, 138, 203, 216, 277–8
general equilibrium,   307, 322–3, 372–4
   see also competitive equilibrium; Walrasian auctioneer
General Will,   251, 254, 256, 351
generalized expected utility theory,   41
Gibbard, A.,   341, 363
Giddens, A.,   18, 71
Giffen good,   30
Goffman, E.,   19, 64
Gossen, H.H.,   372
Gouldner, A.,   119
government intervention,   59–61
Grether, D.,   43

Habermans, J.,   22, 216
Hahn, F.,   312
Halévy, E.,   296
Halsey, A.H.,   65
Hardin, R.,   67
Hargreaves Heap, S.,   15
harm principle,   339
Harper, W.,   341
Harsanyi, J.,   120, 121, 135, 266–7, 271, 272, 274
Harsanyi doctrine,   53
Hart, H.L.A.,   339
hawk and dove game,   127
Hayek, F.,   54, 61, 189, 282–5, 323–4, 332, 333
Heath, A.,   65, 178
Hegel, G.W.F.,   324
Held, D.,   227
Hey, J.,   354
Hicks, J.,   140
Hicksian demand curve,   33–5
hierarchy of human needs,   11, 338

higher pleasures,   264–5
Hirschman, A.,   66
Hobbes, T.,   viii, 11, 65, 155, 181, 201–5, 276–7, 284
Hollis, M.,   14, 23, 76
Homer,   172, 175
homo economicus,   xii, 62–73, 169, 171, 174, 226
homo sociologicus,   62–72, 167, 226
homogeneity,   28, 32
Horgan, T.,   341
Horton, J.,   216
Hospers, J.,   89
Hume, D.,   68, 69, 184–5, 231–2, 263–4, 267, 270, 274–5, 277, 304, 315, 317–18, 326–7

ideology,   82, 337
ignorance,   54
imagination,   56–8
impartial spectator,   263–4, 267, 270, 274, 277, 284, 327
imperfect information,   15–17, 149–53, 241, 242–5
   see also trust; expectations
incentives,   268–9, 272, 321
income effect,   30
independence axiom,   41, 48, 137
indifference curve,   7, 27, 331
individuality,   80–1, 84, 88
inferior good,   30
information,   52, 97
   decentralization of,   188, 282
   see also imperfect information
institutions,   ix, 19
invisible hand,   179, 180
irrationality,   24, 150
iterated dominance,   100

Jevons, S.,   335, 372
Johnson, L.B.,   228
Jones, S.,   293
Jones-Lee, M.,   370
judgement,   23–4

Kagel, J.,   31
Kahneman, D.,   37, 39–40, 370

Kalai, E.,   138
Kant, I.,   21, 85–6, 89, 175, 318,
   324, 328
Kelly, J.S.,   213, 216
Kelly, G.,   24
Kennedy, J.F.,   232
Keynes, J.M.,   24, 60, 321–3, 349
King, Martin Luther,   230
Kirzner, I.,   54, 61. 189
Klein, B.,   161, 164–5, 169
Knight, F.,   349
Korpi, W.,   233
Krause, U.,   16
Kreps, D.,   61, 122–4, 150–1
Kuhn, T.S.,   66, 83
kula rings,   172
Kydland, F.,   365

Larige, O.,   189, 333
LeGrand, J.,   333
Levi, I.,   332
Leviathan,   viii, 325
   see also Hobbes
Levitt, B.,   169
Lewis, D.,   341
lexicographics,   6, 272, 330–2, 351
Lichtenstein, S.,   43–4
life cycle,   194–5
limited government,   214
Lindley, R.,   89
Lindman, H.,   43
Littlechild, S.,   58, 61
Lively, J.,   227
Locke, J.,   65, 278–80
Loomes, G.,   41, 44
Luce, R.D.,   129, 203, 355
Lukes, S.,   230, 233, 237, 258
Lyons, B.,   129, 143

McKenna, C.,   353
McLean, I.,   216, 227
McNeil, B.,   40
Macfarlane, A.,   65
Machiavelli, N.,   158
Machina, M.,   41
Macpherson, C.B.,   65
Main, H.,   65

majority decision,   206–9
Malinowski, B.,   172, 174
March, J.,   169
Marglin, S.,   169
market socialism,   189, 324, 332–5
market economy,   185–95, 282–5
   equilibrium,   218–19
   failure,   238–47
Marshall, A.,   335–6
Marshallian demand curve,   33, 35
Marx, K.,   20, 62, 246, 304, 323,
   336–8
Marxist theory of
   organizations,   164–6
Maslow, A.,   1, 338
matching pennies game,   104–5
Mauss, M.,   172
maximin,   103, 271, 332, 351
May, K.O.,   207
Maynard Smith, J.,   126–8, 185
Mayo, E.,   167
Mead, G.H.,   63, 69
median voter theorem,   219–22
Medoff, J.,   165
Menger, C.,   335, 372
Mill, J.S.,   74, 80–1, 84–5, 89, 108,
   145, 238, 261, 264–5, 305, 333,
   338–9, 366
Miller, D.,   334
Mises, L. von,   54, 332–3, 339–40
mixed strategies,   105–7, 226
monetarism,   243
monopoly,   228–9
Moore, G.E.,   330, 367
moral hazard,   159
Morgenstern, O.,   ix, 8, 214
Morriss, P.,   230, 237
Muellbauer, J.,   27
multiple equilibria,   17, 107, 292,
   308
multiple selves,   16
Muth, J.,   311
mutual aid,   144–8
   see also reciprocity
mutual advantage,   271–2, 274–8,
   282, 284
mutually assured destruction,   148 50

Nagel, T., 307
Nash equilibrium, 98, 101
Nash, J., 132–3, 137
natural rights, 278–82, 284–5
nature, law of, 276, 279–80;
　see also natural rights
needs, 272–4
Nelson, R., 169
neoclassical view, 51–4
Neumann, J. von, ix, 8, 214
neutrality, 206–9
new classical macroeconomics, 243
Newcomb's problem, 46, 340–2
Nietzsche, F., 158–9
norms, xi, 4, 17–21, 63, 67–9, 292,
　330, 360
Nozick, R., 148, 280–2, 306, 332,
　341
nuclear deterrence, 148–50

obligation, 175–8
　political, 201–5
oligarchies, 213
Olson, M., 66, 148
opportunism, 157, 159, 161
opportunity cost, 225
Ordeshook, P., 66–7, 226
organizations, xii, 155–69
original position, ix, 271–2, 315,
　319
Owen, R., 156

Pareto improvement, 241–2
Pareto optimality, 59, 108, 137,
　186–7, 268, 302, 317, 320–2,
　342–4, 347–8, 361
Pareto principle, 315, 344
Parfit, D., 345
Pateman, C., 65
paternalism, 339, 344–5
path independence, 213, 345–6
pay-off, 96
Pearce, D., 103
Perrow, C., 166, 169
Peters, R., 24, 299, 300
Phelps, E., 312
Pigou, A. C., 261

planning, xiii, 238–48, 284
players, 95
Pliny the Younger, 250, 254, 257
Plott, C., 43, 345
political equilibrium, 219–22
politics as collective action, 199
Popper, K., 82
positional goods, 234
positive responsiveness, 206–9
possessive individualism, 65
post-materialism, 353
potlach, 172
power, xiii, 82, 133–4, 137, 164–6,
　228–37, 252, 293–4, 334, 355–7,
　364
power index, 235
preference aggregation, 205–15, 217
　ordering, 5–7
　reversal, 43–4, 48
　single-peaked, 212
Prescott, E., 365
primary goods, 271, 332
Prisoner's Dilemma, xii, 98, 99, 116,
　119, 123, 125, 144–8, 177, 193,
　202–5, 244, 274, 302, 328
probability, 52–3, 58, 97
　distribution, 346
　subjective, 44, 46
property, evolution of, 184–5, 277
prospects, 8–11
public choice theory, viii
public goods, 144–8, 193, 240, 278,
　280, 317, 347–8, 357
　see also collective goods
Pugh, D., 169
Putterman, L., 169

Quiggin, J., 41

Radner, R., 18, 119
Raiffa, H., 129, 203, 355
Ramsey, F., ix
Rapoport, A., 126
Rasmusen, E., 129
rational beliefs, 15–7
rational choice theory, ix, 3, 4–17,
　225, 228–9, 237, 299

rational expectations equilibrium, 307

rational reconstruction, 68

rationality, ix, 62, 87, 214
  bounded, 17–21, 39–40, 44, 48, 124–9, 161
  expressive, 215
  instrumental, 3–17, 22–3, 311–12
  procedural, 4, 17–21
  see also rational choice; axioms of rational choice

rationalizability, 103–4

rationalization, 299–300

Rawls, J., viii, 270–2, 273, 276, 284, 306, 315, 319, 331–2, 351

Rechtsstaat, 86

reciprocity, 119

reflective equilibrium, 357

regret, 41–4, 47

relative deprivation, 71

relative frustration, 13

rent, 334

reputation, 123, 139, 150–3

returns to scale, 192–3

revealed preference, 31–2, 327

Ridge, J.M., 65

rights *see* natural rights

Riker, W.H., 66–7, 212–14, 216, 223, 226–7, 251, 257, 303, 357

risk *see* uncertainty

risk aversion, 271, 350–1

risk-spreading, 351

Robbins, L., viii

Robertson, D.H., 155

Robinson Crusoe, 62

roles, 63–4

Roth, A., 125, 142, 143

Rousseau, J.-J., 85, 251, 254, 256, 261, 351

Rubinstein, A., 132, 136, 143

rules of thumb, 4, 17–21

Runciman, W., 12

Salop, S., 354

Samuelson, P., ix, 31–2, 347, 360–2

satisficing, 18

Satterthwaite, M., 363

Savage, L., ix, 8, 45, 46, 47–8, 349

saving, 54

Scarf, H., 192

Schattschneider, E.E., 212

Schelling, T., 108, 134, 143, 364

Schmalensee, R., 169

Schopenhauer, A., 163

Schotter, A., 148

Schumpeter, J., 218, 353

Schutz, A., 64, 71

Scott, A., 72

search, 54

search theory, 15, 353–5

self
  command, 12, 364
  concept of, 345
  deception, 300
  love, 179–80
  respect, 22–3

Selten, R., 118, 128

Sen, A.K., 14, 89, 214, 216, 266, 274, 289

Shackle, G., 24, 56–8, 61

Shaked, A., 140, 141

Shapley–Shubik index, 235, 236, 355–7

sharing a shilling game, 303

Sidgwick, H., 261, 357

signalling, 160

Simmel, G., 170–1

Simon, H., 169

Slovic, P., 43–4

Smith, A., viii, 179–80, 221, 263–4, 267, 270, 274, 326, 348, 358–60

Smorodinsky, M., 138

social choice, xii, 63, 199–216, 226, 236, 301

social contract, viii, 276–8

social exchange theory, 170

social justice, xiii, 227, 259–85, 306–7, 315, 334

social welfare function, 187, 266–7, 360–2

socialism, 321, 324
  see also market socialism

socialization, 63, 65

solution concept, 98

sovereignty,   200–5
specific assets,   157, 161
Spence, M.,   160
Starmer, C.,   44
state of nature,   52
  in choice under uncertainty,   52
  in political philosophy,   276–9
Steedman, I.,   16
Stigler, J.,   16
Stiglitz, J.,   354
strategic behaviour,   114
strategic manipulation,   362–3
strategy,   95
structuralism,   19, 337, 363
subgame perfect Nash
    equilibrium,   113, 364–5
substitution effect,   30
Sugden, R.,   41, 44, 108, 127, 129,
    146–8, 320
Sutton, J.,   133, 140–3
symmetry of cross-substitution
    effects,   30, 32
sympathy,   263–4, 359–60
  see also extended sympathy

tâtonnement see Walrasian auctioneer
Tawney, R.H.,   229, 231
Taylor, F.,   189, 333
Taylor, F.W.,   166
Taylor, M.,   204, 216
Thaler, R.H.,   38, 129
Thatcher, M.,   222, 230
Thompson, D.,   215
time,   193–5
time inconsistency,   12, 364–5
time preference,   365–6
tit-for-tat,   123
Titmuss R.,   174
Townsend, P.,   71
transaction cost,   161–4
transitivity,   41–4, 47, 209
trigger strategy,   115
trust,   153, 160, 239, 244, 247
Tullock, G.,   299
Tversky, A.,   37, 39–40, 370

uncertainty and risk,   18, 52–3, 296,
    310–12, 329–30, 349–50

unemployment,   242–6, 292
utilitarianism,   5, 7, 48, 176, 261–5,
    267–70, 272, 274, 275, 276, 282,
    284–5, 315–16, 318, 338, 357,
    366–8
utility
  anticipated,   141
  expected *see* separate entry
  function,   6–11, 214
  interpersonal comparisons of,   315
  maximisation,   62
  weighted,   41

value of life,   369–72
Varian, H.,   320
Varoufakis, Y.,   129, 143
veil of ignorance,   271, 284, 351
virtues,   68–9
voting,   63, 66–7
  insincere,   362–3
  spatial theory of,   353

Walras, L.,   186–8, 335, 372–3
Walrasian auctioneer,   187–90, 372–3
Walrasian equilibrium *see* competitive
    equilibrium
Walzer, M.,   72
Waterman, R.,   24, 299, 300
weakness of will,   345
Weale, A.,   237, 306, 345
Weber, M.,   21, 98, 155, 231
welfare economics, fundamental
    theorems of   186–8
Welfare State,   244–5
welfarism,   265–7, 272, 284
Williams, B.,   315
Williamson, O.,   157, 161, 164, 165,
    169
Willig, R.,   35, 169
Wilson, R.,   122, 124, 150–1
Winch, P.,   305
Winter, S.,   169
Wittgenstein, L.,   305
Wolinsky, A.,   143

Young, R.,   89

Zeuthen, F.,   132, 134
Ziemba, W.,   38